Dutch Harbor

ISLANDS

CANADA

UNITED
STATES

Pacific Ocean

HAWAIIAN ISLANDS

Honolulu ꞏ OAHU
Pearl Harbor ꞏ MAUI
ꞏ HAWAII

JOHNSTON
ISLAND

PALMYRA ISLAND

CHRISTMAS ISLAND

Equator

0 STATUTE 500 MILES 1000

PHŒNIX

ISLANDS

LINE ISLANDS

MARQUESAS

ISLANDS

SAMOA
ISLANDS

Yamamoto

山本五十六

YAMAMOTO

The Man Who Menaced America

by John Deane Potter

NEW YORK · THE VIKING PRESS

Published in 1965 by The Viking Press, Inc.
625 Madison Avenue, New York, N.Y. 10022

Library of Congress catalog card number: 65-12974
Printed in the U.S.A.

First published in Great Britain as
Admiral of the Pacific: The Life of Yamamoto.

For

SEAMUS

in the hope that he will never participate
in anything like this

Contents

Illustrations

(The photographs without credit lines are reproduced by courtesy of Admiral Isoroku Yamamoto's son.)

Endpaper maps show the whole Northern Pacific area.

The Japanese characters facing the title page read *Yamamoto Isoroku*.

Acknowledgments

In the preparation of this book I owe much to a great many people for their help, especially:

Admiral Mitsumi Shimizu, Yamamoto's boyhood friend, and submarine C.-in-C. at the Pearl Harbor operation.

Rear-Admiral Kamahito Kuroshima, his Senior Staff Officer at Midway.

Captain Yasuji Watanabe, his Planning Officer, who brought his body back to Japan.

And other officers of the Imperial Japanese Navy, including Vice-Admiral Torao Kuwabara, Captain Sumitaka Nangai, Masataki Chihaya and Hitoshi Tsunoda.

Also Pearl Harbor Zero pilot, Iyozo Fujita, now a DC8 captain for Japan Air Lines.

Pearl Harbor torpedo pilot, Jinichi Goto.

Hiryu pilot, Hirosi Isiwata.

General Minoru Genda, former Chief of Staff of Japan's Self Defence Force.

Colonel Toshio Hashimoto.

General Susumu Nishura and his staff at Japan's Military History Section in Tokyo, who were their usual helpful selves.

Yamamoto's Japanese biographer, Eiichi Soramachi, for his help, particularly in showing me over the relics in the Yamamoto Museum in Nagaoka, his home town in Niigata prefecture.

And my two old friends, S. Chang of *Time-Life* and Koichi Obata, for their customary enthusiasm, encouragement and organization during my researches in Japan.

Thomas G. Lanphier, Jr, the pilot who shot down Yamamoto, Vice-President, Planning, the Raytheon Corporation, Lexington, Mass.

The Aerospace Studies Institute of the U.S. Air Force, Maxwell Air Force Base, Alabama.

The Navy History Division, Office of the Chief of Naval Operations, Washington, D.C.

The Office of Naval Intelligence, U.S. Navy.

And many former officers and men of both Japanese and American navies who fought in the Pacific.

Also Mrs Marjorie Perry for her indefatigable typing.

The material on pp. 104-5 from *Zero* by Martin Caidin (published in the United Kingdom by Cassell & Co. Ltd) is reprinted by permission of the proprietors, E. P. Dutton and Co. Inc.

In the Pacific and in the Indian Ocean we remember the multitudes of resentful sleeping warriors—in our ears we hear the whisper of their voices from the bottom of the sea.

COMMANDER HASHIMOTO,
IMPERIAL JAPANESE NAVY

Introduction

THAT Thursday evening the rush hour at Yokohama Central station was as crowded as ever. The swarthy muscular man, wearing a blue suit with the awkwardness of an officer out of uniform, fought his way through the jostling home-going crowds.

In his hand he carried a large *furoshiki*—a square of coloured cloth tied at the corners. This is the normal way Japanese carry parcels. Nearly all his fellow passengers carried one.

Few of them looked twice at the unassuming little man although one or two may have had a vague idea that they had seen him before. Peeping out of one corner of his parcel was a glint of gold braid. For folded inside the cloth was his uniform as a full admiral of the Imperial Japanese Navy.

The unobtrusive traveller was Admiral Isoroku Yamamoto, Commander-in-Chief of the Japanese Combined Fleet. He was on his way to Hiroshima on the Inland Sea, where his flagship *Nagato* lay at anchor surrounded by seven of the world's largest battleships.

But the spearhead of his gigantic fleet, the six big aircraft carriers, was not there. They were pitching and rolling in the stormy waters of the North Pacific bound for the American naval base at Pearl Harbor. Stealthily, in complete radio silence, they were approaching the unsuspecting American fleet berthed there to make the most historic surprise attack since the Trojan horse.

As the train steamed southwards towards the Inland Sea Admiral Yamamoto gazed through the steamy windows at the brown, frost-dusted winter fields. He glanced at the placid, half-dozing faces of his fellow first-class passengers. He was a sensitive man of needle-sharp intelligence and he must have speculated what they would have thought if they knew they had only a few short days of peace left to them.

He was one of the few men in the world who knew that. As the most important man in the Japanese navy he normally flew from

Tokyo to the military airfield nearest his flagship. That evening he chose the train because he might never have another opportunity.

The day before he had had the unexpected honour of being received by the Emperor Hirohito—a privilege normally only granted to Cabinet ministers. In the remote silence of the Imperial Palace in central Tokyo, hidden behind the high grey-stone walls, he had given the Emperor full details of his Pearl Harbor attack plan.

After he left the Palace he spent the afternoon with his wife and four children in the Tokyo suburb of Aoyama. He told his family he would not be home again for a long time and gave his children a little fatherly admonition, saying 'I want you to be good. Help your mother all you can and study hard while I am away.'

Then he took a taxi to an expensive geisha district, Tsukiji, near the port of Tokyo, to say goodbye to a geisha called Kikuji—Chrysan-themum Way—with whom he had been in love for six years. He sat on the straw-matting floor playing *hana fuda*—flower cards—with her for a small wager as if he had not a care in the world. The geisha house proprietress arrived and suggested they have dinner together, This was Yamamoto's usual procedure when he met Kikuji. This evening, however, he refused, saying he had an urgent appointment, He smilingly told the geisha house owner that he had already won seven yen from Kikuji at cards, 'enough to buy some sweets for my orderlies'. She grinned and said, 'Let me make it an even ten yen.' Yamamoto, also laughing, gave her a handful of small change and pocketed a new ten-yen note, saying, 'I never knew gambling could be so lucrative!' Waving cheerfully to Kikuji he left. It was a long time before she saw him again.

He went on to a secret party at Naval Headquarters where toasts were drunk by the senior Japanese admirals. The *sake*—the hot rice wine—and the plain, delicate cups were both gifts from the Em-peror. There was only one toast constantly repeated: 'Success at Pearl Harbor!'

Yamamoto, who was a teetotaller, took only a tiny sip for each toast. The admirals, becoming a little red-faced with the wine, were now excited about the plan. But only a few weeks before they had all bitterly opposed it.

The plan was his—and his alone. It was eighteen months since he had first thought of it. He had supervised the smallest detail, per-fected it, fought it single-handed past the opposition of every senior admiral, offered to lead it personally from the bridge of the leading carrier—and finally threatened to resign if it were not approved. Only then had they agreed to let him carry it out.

Now his masterpiece of naval planning was about to be tested. Within a few days the future of his country would be flung savagely into the balance. If negotiations with the United States broke down in Washington, as everyone expected them to, his carriers had orders to launch their planes.

For although Yamamoto had been bitterly opposed to war against England and America, he knew if it came Japan's only chance of survival was to destroy as quickly as possible her greatest threat—the United States Pacific Fleet.

After the party he drove to Yokohama Central. This would be the last peacetime train ride he would take. On Sunday morning the U.S. fleet would be lying in the mud at the bottom of Pearl Harbor and Japan would be at war.

Whatever happened, his whole destiny was bound up with the Pearl Harbor attack. He was gambling his country's own future upon it. He was also gambling with his own life.

For, sixteen months later, over a jungle-covered island in the South Pacific, the Americans were to shoot down and kill this little Japanese admiral as an act of revenge for Pearl Harbor.

Even if he had known this, it would not have made the slightest difference to him. Japan was on the brink of an international adventure which was going to change the face of the world. What importance had the death of one Japanese sailor—even if he was an admiral—in such a situation?

A Morning in December

1

A Schoolmaster's Son

THE schoolmaster in the small Japanese village of Kushigun Son-shomura—the village among the ancient pines—was enjoying the April sunshine. That year the cherry had blossomed early and the snow-filled winter blizzards were already fading from people's memory.

The schoolmaster Sadakichi Takano was playing his favourite game of *go*—a form of Japanese checkers or draughts—when one of his children came to interrupt him. His wife Mineko was in labour and she wanted a midwife. He sent the child for the nurse and continued with his game.

It was not that Sadakichi was a callous man, but he was no longer young. He was in his mid-fifties and this child which was about to be born was his seventh. Mineko was his second wife. He had married her when her elder sister, his first wife, died. Now he had five sons and a daughter, by both of them.

It was in the year 1884 that his seventh child—another son—was born. His father remained indifferent to him. He was a diligent diary-keeper but he did not mention his new son's birth on 4 April until three weeks later. He also had no idea what to call him. Eventually, when his wife told him he must think of a name for his youngest son, he said: 'I was fifty-six years old when he was born. Call him Fifty-Six.' And Fifty-Six he was duly named—Isoroku in Japanese characters.

This son, whose arrival was greeted so casually by his elderly father, soon became his greatest joy. He used to tell him tales of the old days a generation or so before when the tough warriors of the Echigo clan to which their family belonged—it means the men from over the mountains—had resisted the unification of Japan under the Emperor Meiji. The clan chieftains fighting for their local shogun were defeated in a series of fierce battles.

At the end of this civil war many of the leading *samurai* families

—noble followers of the shogun—were impoverished. This included schoolmaster Takano's family who lived in a very small wooden house in the village, not much bigger than a large rabbit hutch. There was little room in it for a family of nine.

The schoolmaster's family was one of the poorest in the town and his wife used to spin, weave and dye all the cloth for her children's clothes. Even in the depth of winter Isoroku wore only a blue-striped cotton kimono and straw sandals.

Fifty-Six's father was not only an expert on local military history, but was also famous for his delicate brush strokes in the old Chinese-style calligraphy which he taught to his youngest son. These were two things his son Fifty-Six never forgot—the Chinese writing and the war stories of long ago.

Soon after his birth, his father became headmaster of the primary school in the near-by market town of Nagaoka. It was 200 miles, across the Kiso mountains, to the east-coast ports of Yokohama and Kobe where foreign ships called. No strange ships sailed into the tiny fishing ports along Japan's bleak western coast. The west country was as isolated as it had been in the feudal days his father still talked about.

The great Emperor Meiji might be making great changes in far-away Tokyo but in that forgotten north-western corner nothing altered. The winters are fiercely cold there because icy winds blow straight from Russia across the few hundred miles of the Sea of Japan. When October came and snow fell heavily they were completely cut off from the rest of the world.

Snow usually fell to the depth of twelve or fourteen feet and the thatch-roofed houses disappeared until spring arrived. Each outside wall was sheltered by planks on poles under the eaves, making a dim corridor through the snow. Even in the worst blizzards people could still move along these passages with their snow walls. But their houses were in almost perpetual darkness. Only a grey uncertain daylight filtered through the oiled-paper windows.

At street corners tunnels were dug and the local inhabitants crossed many feet below the icy carpet. One of Isoroku's first jobs was to help his brothers shovel snow off the roof lest the weight of it cause their little wooden house to collapse. When it was soft they were marooned. But when it was frozen hard he and his brothers could go walking, wearing plate-shaped straw hats and straw cloaks.

As Isoroku walked to school in the dim light of the tunnels he tried to learn the characters of the Japanese language. He could not afford textbooks. He borrowed them and copied them out laboriously by hand.

The frozen catacombs protected the women and children but the men had to climb continuously through apertures into the strong light to work. Wearing home-made straw snowshoes, they collected wood, carried goods from one village to another, or went fishing in the icy waters of the near-by Shinano river.

In this remote place no one doubted the divinity of the Emperor Meiji, who was a direct descendant of the Sun Goddess. For was there not something unique about the people of Japan? Had not the gods Izanigi and Izanimi given birth to the four islands of Japan and the people who lived there?

For thousands of years this had been the belief. No one in that faraway province ever doubted it in spite of the rumours of strange, red-faced hairy foreigners wearing cloth tubes on their legs who walked freely about Tokyo, caring nothing for the ancient Japanese legends.

When the snow melted there were many exciting things for a small boy to do. There were Shinto festivals with dancers and musicians playing the *samisen*, the Japanese guitar. When he was six years old Isoroku attended one spring festival he never forgot. Some men performed a local dance, jigging and twirling, while balancing trays or plates.

Completely entranced, the little boy in the blue kimono stayed late watching them, and all that summer he practised this dance. When the next spring festival came he could do it as well as they could. His father was very amused and constantly asked him to dance it to entertain friends.

But relaxation was rare and schooling was hard. During the coldest mid-winter months the lessons became longer and more difficult. The classroom was heated only by a *hibachi*, a small glimmering charcoal burner. On the ninth day of December, traditionally supposed to be the coldest day of the year, even this tiny fire was extinguished.

Then the schoolchildren were given a hundred ideographs to write. They had to remain in the classroom until they were finished although their fingers became numb, purple and frozen. When their lessons were over they tried to thaw out their hands by rubbing them in the snow.

One of the great unfounded rumours about the little boy who grew up to be Japan's greatest admiral was that his schoolmaster father was fanatically anti-West. Stories have been circulated that he had a burning hatred of the Americans which he instilled into his son. It has been reported that his father told him tales of the barbarians 'who came in their black ships, broke down the doors of Japan, threatened the Son of Heaven, trampled upon ancient customs, demanded indemnities and blew their long noses on cloths which they put in their pockets instead of throwing away'.

It was said that from his earliest years Isoroku had a deep hatred of America and his one desire was to 'return the visit of Commodore Perry', the man who opened up Japan to the West.

Like most glib propaganda stories, it was far from the truth. The only foreigner in this district was an American missionary named Newall, who taught English at the Middle School. Isoroku's father allowed him and his brothers to call on the American at his home. He risked unpopularity by doing so because in those days Japanese villagers were exceedingly insular and suspicious.

It was from the American missionary that the little boy Isoroku first heard about Christianity. When he grew older he evinced a great interest in it and used to study the Bible with unfailing curiosity. When Newall moved away it was the schoolmaster's sons who called on him with farewell presents of handkerchiefs and other small gifts.

When Isoroku was twelve he left the primary school to go to Nagaoka Middle School, and life became more interesting. At the great New Year festival he would write the traditional messages in his best calligraphy as his father had taught him. He would also help his family to bake the ceremonial rice cakes. These were a big treat for children whose normal food was a small bowl of rice with an occasional cucumber, radish or eggplant. They drank green tea made from the shrubs in their own little garden.

On Sundays the family would go mushroom picking or fishing for salmon, which were plentiful in the rushing mountain streams in the neighbourhood. As he grew older, Isoroku also learned to fish in the sea for sole, mackerel, octopus and swordfish. It was there he first learned the ways of the wind and the waves. He also discovered their dangerous uncertainty. High winds were normal on that stormy coast. Once when his fishing boat capsized he swam in the cold sea to a cave in a cliff. He was marooned there for two days until the sea became calm enough for him to swim to the beach. But this was not a great ordeal for a boy who had been brought up as he had been.

The training of boys was based on the old Japanese proverb, 'The lioness pushes her cub over the cliff and leaves it to climb back alone'. His school went for long, military-style marches in the snow or rain—the worse the weather the longer the march.

The greatest adventure of the year was the annual military manœuvres. Ten thousand boys from schools all over the western provinces were divided into two armies. Half took position behind strong entrenchments and, an hour before dawn, the others attacked them. They had rifles, machine-guns and field-guns—all firing blanks —and were commanded by regular officers.

With this background it was not surprising that when he was fourteen the teacher's son suddenly became enthusiastic about athletics. He ran to school before breakfast, practised gymnastics there, ran back to breakfast and then ran back to school again for lessons. In the evening he did the same thing, practising for hours. He also played baseball as often as he could. As a result of this sudden devotion to athletics he dropped down from near the top of his class to sixteenth. But he did become the best sportsman at the school and wrote about sport, particularly baseball, for his school magazine.

It was during his athletic period, at the age of fifteen, that he decided to put his name down for the Naval Academy. He chose a good moment. The twentieth century had just begun and the re- formist Emperor Meiji was trying to build up a Western-style navy.

2

A Navy Is Born

MEIJI'S task was not easy because for more than two centuries the edict of the Shogun Hideoshi had been law in Japan. As a result of a catastrophic defeat at sea he had forbidden the construction of ships large enough to leave the shelter of the coasts. This had placed Japan in unique man-made isolation, completely cut off from the rest of the world. In a curious way the events that led to this edict had a great bearing on the Japanese plan for a surprise attack on Pearl Harbor. Far from being a bold novelty, it was in the classic Japanese tradition.

Japan's first experience of sea warfare came in the late thirteenth century when the Mongol Emperor Kublai Khan attempted to invade Japan. Fortunately for the unprepared Japanese a storm wrecked his fleet. This became known as the *kamikaze*, the divine wind. Centuries later, when their homeland was again under invasion threat from the Americans, the Japanese tried to make an artificial divine wind by recruiting *kamikaze* suicide pilots.

In the sixteenth century the Shogun Hideoshi attempted to return Kublai's attack by invading Korea and China. His army overran Korea but a squadron of primitive iron-clad Korean warships under Yi Sun-sin sank the Japanese ships, cut off their armies and forced their withdrawal.

This made Hideoshi realize the necessity of controlling the sea. When he tried a second time to invade Korea his plan was almost exactly the same as Yamamoto's at Pearl Harbor three and a half centuries later. In 1596, while peace negotiations were under way in Seoul, he made a surprise attack without warning. The defending ships were destroyed and the Japanese troops landed. But with the help of the Chinese, Yi Sun-sin had built a fleet. Again he annihilated the conquering army when it tried to sail back to Japan. The defeated Hideoshi issued his famous edict of isolation—and the Japanese were cut off from the rest of the world for over two hundred years.

It was not until the American Commodore Perry arrived just

over a century ago and forced them to open up their country that the Japanese saw the need for guns and ships. The ban on big-ship building was removed and Japan began to take her first steps towards the modern world.

Even without Perry's intervention it would probably have happened anyway. For in 1853—a year before Perry sailed his black ships into Tokyo Bay—Japanese were studying the principles of the steam-engine from the Dutch traders who were allowed to carry on restricted commerce with the Hermit Kingdom. Three years later, the Dutch gave Japan two steam-propelled cargo vessels in exchange for copper, lacquer, camphor and gold.

The big powers took an avuncular interest in Japan's budding navy. When the Japanese began to build warships it never occurred to the Western nations that the Japanese fleet could ever threaten them. The Imperial Navy began its career with two gifts—a six-gun paddle-wheeled steamer from the Dutch and a four-gun yacht from Queen Victoria.

The Americans sold them their first ironclad, the *Stonewall Jackson*. At the same time they also admitted a small number of Japanese to the Annapolis Naval Academy.

French engineers set up a dockyard for the Imperial Navy at Yokosuka, twenty miles from Yokohama. They spent ten years teaching the Japanese everything they knew about the construction of Western warships.

But it was Britain which made the most significant contribution. In 1873 she set up a naval college in Tokyo, where Admiral Douglas and thirty-three specially selected British officers and sailors helped to build up a modern Japanese navy. The Naval Academy was later transferred to the island of Etajima, near Hiroshima, where the main cadet dormitory was built of bricks brought specially from England.

By 1897 the Japanese were ordering warships faster than anyone except the British. Battleships were built in England, cruisers in France, Germany and America. They were also beginning to build their own ships in their French-founded main dockyard at Yokosuka. Soon Japan had a navy as big as many Western powers. She had seventy-six warships, including a fleet of large battleships. Many officers were needed to man them and the cream of Japanese youth was encouraged to apply for naval training. It was at this time that the schoolmaster's son from Nagaoka applied to join the Naval Academy at Etajima.

Isoroku was sixteen when he sat for the examination for the Naval Academy. He was not optimistic about his chances because he was competing against 300 others. He had already decided if he failed he would be a schoolmaster like his father. He came out second in the entrance examination.

The Naval Academy course lasted for four years. Cadets were not permitted to drink, smoke, eat sweets or go out with girls. Punishments did not exist—simply because disobedience did not. The lives of these dedicated, monastic youths would be devoted until death to the glory of the sacred Emperor and their homeland of Nippon.

The cadets marched everywhere, even from locker-rooms to playing fields. Saluting was so rigidly enforced that they stopped playing tennis to salute a passing officer although he too was wearing tennis clothes.

During the summer all cadets had to swim for three hours every day. In mid-summer they all went to Miyajima Island, ten miles away. There they lived in tents on the beach, wearing swimsuits all the time.

At the end of the course there was a mass swim back to Etajima. They swam back by '*buntai*'—group formation—in regimental lines and at equal intervals. Onlookers followed in small boats throwing them food and shouting encouragement.

They went into the water at 7 a.m. and emerged at Etajima, blue with cold and covered with jellyfish stings, at 8 p.m., thirteen hours later. Some were lifted bodily from the water, utterly exhausted, more dead than alive. After this mass swim ten per cent of the students were forced to withdraw from the Academy because of ill health.

After three years spent like this there came the final year's training on a windjammer. Aboard this ship the day began at 5 a.m. when the cadets scrubbed the decks with sand and coconuts. The philosophy of the newly born Japanese navy was that a sailor's duty was to learn first about the sea, not the ship. On these square-rigged ships the cadets were always close to currents, winds and storms.

It was a hard life but it made them into sailors. The ship carried twenty-seven sails, and boys perched high up on the yards furling the canvas soon learned where the wind was coming from. Barefoot cadets, who one day would be Japanese admirals, curled their toes round the ropes as they struggled with heavy wet sails slapping in the wind. When a storm came up they were in danger of being blown into the sea. Oddly enough this spartan training was not an idea of the austere Japanese. It was taught them by the Royal Navy.

When Isoroku graduated seventh from the Academy, Japan was about to test her strength as a full-scale naval power for the first time. Almost exactly three centuries after Hideoshi's defeat she once again attempted mainland conquest. Throughout the nineteenth century the Western nations had set an example of territory grabbing. Now, like a bumptious confident lightweight, Japan chose as her adversary the sleepy colossus, Russia.

This war also began with two acts which held ominous portents of Pearl Harbor forty years later. The Russian ship *Variag* lay safe in the neutral Korean port of Chemulpo when the Japanese Admiral Uriu challenged it. *Variag*'s commander pleaded with other foreign warships in the harbour to put up a joint resistance, as this was a flagrant violation of neutral waters. Some were willing to do so.

But, most significantly, the commander of the U.S. cruiser *Vicksburg* was not. He was all for allowing the newly fledged Japanese navy to have a go at the Russians. His attitude was not isolated. It reflected the pro-Japanese feeling in the United States at the time.

Admiral Uriu sank the *Variag* and landed troops in Korea. The American commander's attitude not only opened Korea to the Japanese but helped them to take their first step towards the conquest of Asia.

Russia now understood the Japanese threat to her own Asiatic expansion in Manchuria. Port Arthur and Vladivostok became the major Russian Far Eastern naval bases.

Negotiations began with Japan for Russian withdrawal from Manchuria. When they failed, war began in February 1904. How? With a minor Pearl Harbor. A surprise night destroyer attack was made on the Russian fleet at Port Arthur. This severely damaged three of the Russian battleships and sank a cruiser. Then Japan's most famous admiral, Togo, blockaded the port for months trying to tempt the Russian fleet out to fight. Any ship that did venture out was sunk.

Isoroku was overjoyed when he was posted as an ensign to the cruiser *Nisshin*, part of the protective screen for *Mikasa*, the flagship of the great Togo. This gave the eager young officer the perfect opportunity to observe at close quarters the tactics of one of the greatest modern admirals.

The main Russian fleet of twenty-seven ships sailed from Europe to raise the blockade of Port Arthur. It took seven months to come from the Baltic. On 27 May 1904 it was wiped out in one day in the Straits of Tsushima in a battle which was described by naval historian Hector C. Bywater as 'one of the most decisive naval actions in history'.

Why did Togo choose this spot to bring the Russians to action? For a peculiarly illogical, mystical Japanese reason. Seven centuries before, the attempted invasion of Japan by Kublai Khan had been turned back in those straits. Togo believed the souls of Japan's defenders who had died in that engagement would fight beside him in this one and thus ensure victory. On the other hand, he insured against ancestor absence by using the most brilliant up-to-date tactics.

His battleships and cruisers steamed into the straits ahead of the dog-tired Russian fleet while Admiral Uriu's fleet closed in behind them. Ensign Fifty-Six stood rigidly to attention on the deck of his ship when Togo's flagship raised the famous battle signal, 'The fate of the Empire depends upon this battle. Let every man do his utmost!' Even in this the Japanese navy copied the British. This was an adaptation of Nelson's famous signal before Trafalgar, 'England expects every man to do his duty'.

Within three-quarters of an hour the battle was over. In the first ten minutes the turret of the flagship *Suvorov* was blown away and other Russian warships burst into flames. With the flagship sunk, the Russian fleet was flung into complete confusion. At nightfall Togo withdrew his warships and sent his torpedo boats in to destroy the rest of the demoralized Russian fleet. By morning there were only four Russian ships left. They immediately struck their flags.

While the battle raged, Ensign Isoroku carried a silk handkerchief with good luck patriotic messages painted upon it which his mother had sent him. Later he wrote to his family about what had happened to him in the battle:

When the shells began to fly above me I found I was not afraid. The ship was damaged by shells and many were killed. At 6.15 in the evening a shell hit the *Nisshin* and knocked me unconscious. When I recovered I found I was wounded in the right leg and two fingers of my left hand were missing. But the Russian ships were completely defeated and many wounded and dead were floating on the sea. But when victory was announced at 2 a.m. even the wounded cheered.

He wrapped his mother's special handkerchief round his wounded hand. Later he sent it back to his family, still covered with dried blood, with the letter containing his account of the battle.

The young ensign came out of this historic battle minus two fingers but with the knowledge that he had taken part in the first great naval victory of Asia over the West.

3

Marriage, America and 5-5-3

AFTER the battle of Tsushima, Isoroku spent two months in hospital before going home as a conquering hero to stay with his family. It was summer and he went swimming in the Shinano river. The river contained a notorious whirlpool where many people had been drowned. But he swam straight into it deliberately to test his strength and courage.

But apart from a dare-devil streak he was a serious youth, who did not drink like the other officers. Often he was seen puzzling out sentences in the Bible. When other more frivolous junior officers attacked him for this he would reply very seriously that the Bible and other Western books had a great deal to teach Japan. This interest was obviously based on his early talks with the American missionary in his home town. After a time no one argued further with this beetle-browed earnest little student. His demeanour, even for a Japanese, was so solemn and intense that they left him alone.

He lived the uneventful life of any young naval officer of any nationality in peacetime. He went on training cruises to Korea and China. When he was twenty-six his squadron sailed across the Pacific to the west coast of America. The following year he went on a six-month voyage calling at every major Australian port. The years between 1904 and the outbreak of the First World War in Europe were spent like this. The year before the European war broke out his father died at the age of eighty-five and his mother followed him shortly afterwards.

The following year, at the age of thirty, in accordance with Japanese custom, he was adopted by the locally prominent family of Yamamoto. Unlike his schoolmaster father, they were rich and had the most elaborate private Buddhist shrine of the whole town in their house. They could proudly trace their ancestors back to the local clan chieftains, one of whom was a famous general in the shogun wars. In Japan it is often considered a disgrace to be adopted while your parents are still alive, unless by a close relation such as a childless aunt or uncle. But now both his parents were dead Isoroku felt he could respond to the Yamamoto invitation.

From every point of view it was a very satisfactory arrangement. He was one of the most prominent and promising young men in the province of Echigo—now included in the prefecture of Niigata —a lieutenant-commander with a brilliant future before him. Even in those days many people predicted he would become an admiral.

He formally renounced the name of Takano in a ceremony in a Buddhist temple and took the name of Yamamoto, which means 'Base of the Mountain'. Just after his adoption, the newly named commander was posted to Naval Headquarters, where he began to work for the first time on what was to become his main interest in life—naval aircraft and foreign communications.

He was still unmarried, which was unusual for a Japanese in his thirties. There were several reasons for this. One was his total immersion in his naval career, which gave him little time for romance. The second was that he had wanted to give as much money as he could to support his parents while they lived. The third was his mutilated hand, which he always kept out of sight because he feared it might give offence to a sensitive girl.

He was thirty-three before he began to look around seriously for a suitable bride. As a rising young naval officer in the expanding Imperial Navy he was a very good prospect and many 'go-betweens' approached him. These are marriage-brokers who try to bring together young couples whose families are in the same financial and social sphere. Through these third parties approaches came from several admirals' daughters eager to marry an officer who would one day possibly be an admiral himself.

The young Commander Yamamoto rejected them all and looked for a girl from his own home province. One day a friend introduced him to the daughter of a local dairy farmer. She was called Reiko Mihashi and because she was 5 feet 4 inches in height she was considered too tall and therefore difficult to marry off. Japanese men, who are short themselves, dislike tall girls because they give them an inferiority complex. This did not worry young Commander Yamamoto. History was to witness he was the last man on earth to suffer from an inferiority complex.

Although Reiko came of an old northern clan family like the

Yamamotos, she had led an unconventional life. Instead of sitting at home ceremoniously pouring green tea and arranging flowers like most middle-class Japanese girls of her time, she helped on her father's farm. Ever since she left school she had milked the cows and delivered the milk.

She was the type to appeal strongly to Yamamoto, who wrote her a long letter proposing marriage and telling her about himself. Most of his letter contained a list of his personal faults and the drawbacks of being married to a career naval officer. He did not want her to contemplate marriage under any romantic illusions.

After this letter, the traditional interview was arranged in her home. This meant the young people could be alone for the first time and size each other up. The girl was quite at liberty to reject her suitor but this seldom happened because not only was great family pressure generally put upon her but she was trained in unquestioning obedience. As Reiko was too tall and not especially beautiful her mother afterwards confessed she chose a dimly lit room for the first heart-to-heart talk between the young couple.

Her mother need not have been so anxious. When Reiko came in shyly, knelt and bowed low to the young naval officer who wanted to marry her, they talked together for the first time and decided they liked each other. Western-style love of course did not enter into the transaction. Shortly afterwards they were married in a Buddhist temple.

While they looked for a new house they went to live in Yamamoto's bachelor home in Tokyo. When the bride's mother came to visit her newly married daughter she was horrified at the way she was living. Most of the furniture consisted of beer crates bequeathed to her· husband by his drinking friends. These were used as tables or as holders for charcoal burners. His mother-in-law was really offended when her daughter offered her a cup of tea from a chipped rice bowl. She explained timidly that there were no cups in the house—and she did not like to bother her busy important husband with such trifles. Her mother, much more used to handling Japanese men, soon put an end to this happy-go-lucky ménage. She insisted Yamamoto and his bride move into their new, properly furnished home right away.

No sooner had they settled in than Yamamoto was ordered to go on a two-year course at Harvard University. Wives did not enter into the Imperial Navy scheme of things, so he sailed alone from

Yokohama to San Francisco in a mail steamer. Half the passengers were Japanese and the rest foreigners, mostly Americans. After a few days Yamamoto decided the Japanese were too shy and stuffy. Few of them had left Japan before and they were very withdrawn and stiff with their fellow voyagers. He decided to change all that.

Suddenly one night after dinner he stood on his head in the lounge. Then, seizing two plates from a table, he went into his traditional dance. At the end of it everyone, although startled, applauded him. As a result of his rather crazy intervention the passengers mixed much more freely for the rest of the trip.

After four days' sightseeing in Washington—the city where one day, it was to be alleged, he wanted to receive the surrender of the U.S.A.—he went on to Boston. The prices in America surprised him and he wrote home complaining that they were three times higher than in Japan.

But he liked the country and got on well with Americans, often performing his folk dance at the request of other students. His other amusements were *go, shogi* (Japanese chess) and baseball. He also learned a new card game called poker which was to become one of the passions of his life. The bluff, luck and anticipation the game demanded were ideally suited to his temperament.

He still kept his liking for *shogi*, but one Japanese fellow student kept beating him. This led him to devise a typical stratagem. He suggested they should play a non-stop series of games until one or the other was exhausted. They began one Saturday evening, and played all night and the next day, not even leaving the table for meals. Twenty-six hours later, just before midnight on Sunday, Yamamoto staggered from the table, the winner, leaving his worn-out opponent snoring among the scattered chessmen.

His two years at Harvard were not all play. He was one of the most serious hardworking students who ever attended the university. The main object of his economic studies was oil—the life blood of the modern navy. He sat up late at night absorbing every aspect of the American oil industry.

On one vacation he decided to explore the situation at first hand. He had very little money but he hitch-hiked to Mexico. Kindly Americans who gave this shaggy-browed, earnest Japanese student lifts in their early motor-cars or horse-and-buggies little knew that one day he was to give them the greatest shock in their whole history.

In Mexico Yamamoto toured the oil fields, staying in the cheapest hotels. Soon this mysterious young oriental attracted the attention of the authorities. They demanded his papers, assuming he was either a spy or a political refugee. A report went to the Japanese Embassy in Washington telling them that one of their nationals was nearly destitute in Mexico, living on bread, bananas and water, The Embassy was able to assure the astonished Mexicans that this tramp was one of their most promising naval officers who was on a post-graduate course at Harvard.

Before he left Harvard he became such an expert on oil and so well known to many American oil firms through his researches that several of them offered him a job. He refused because he had no wish to leave the Imperial Navy. But their attitude impressed him. He contrasted the imaginative approach of the Americans, who would give a job to anyone they found useful, to the rigid and unbending Japanese attitude.

While he was at Harvard, World War One was drawing to a close. And an incalculable new war weapon—the aeroplane—was growing up. Yamamoto studied every report on planes in action on the Western Front and toured American aircraft factories. He had already decided that the key to future wars lay in air power.

Although he had seen battleships turn the tide of history in Togo's great battle, he was already dreaming of a future warship which would not fire guns but launch aeroplanes. He had begun to plan ahead in terms of planes rather than the traditional battleships, a view which never changed.

It was a surprising piece of constructive imagination at a time when aeroplanes were still clumsy and primitive. The aircraft carrier had not been invented but there had been significant experiments. Even before that war a plane had taken off from a temporary plat- form on the forward part of the U.S.S. *Birmingham*. The pilot, Eugene Ely, twelve months later made the first ship landing when he put his plane down on the stern of the U.S.S. *Pennsylvania*. These feats were regarded merely as stunts. While he was at Harvard Yamamoto read details of these experiments and did not regard them as stunts. His brain was already fermenting with the role of planes in a future naval war.

When, at the end of the war in 1918, the Royal Navy completed the world's first carrier, Yamamoto was enormously interested. The Americans were slow to follow. They did not commission *Langley* until 1922. *Lexington* and *Saratoga* were commissioned ten years after the first British carrier.

The 'twenties were an oasis of peace in the world. The armies and navies of most nations stagnated through lack of funds. During that period Americans just did not think about war. Only in Japan were powerful groups already looking towards China, and promising young officers obtained promotion with unusual rapidity.

In 1923, at the age of thirty-nine, Yamamoto became a captain with his first big command, executive officer of the new air-training centre at Kasumigaura. This fledgling flying school was copied from the R.A.F. training school at Cranwell in Lincolnshire.

Yamamoto, although a leading theorist about aircraft, could not fly. To remedy this he took flying lessons in the morning and caught up with his executive work in the afternoon or late at night after a couple of games of *shogi*.

The naval air corps, then in its infancy, badly needed a strong leader and champion. Yamamoto was the ideal person to be cast for this role. His strong, confident personality had an immediate effect.

In those days, because of the large number of fatal accidents, a flying career was not particularly attractive. Many of the high-ranking Japanese naval officers would not fly. A class-mate of Yamamoto's, Admiral Zengo Yoshida, who was a predecessor of his as Commander-in-Chief Combined Fleet, refused in any circumstances to set foot in an aeroplane. Other high-ranking officers tried not to be so timidly old-fashioned. They paid lip service to the importance of naval aviation and urged young naval officers to become pilots. Their enthusiasm faded rapidly, however, if one of their sons wanted to become a flying officer. And they actively discouraged their daughters from marrying flyers.

As a result of this feeling in the service the pilots who paraded before Yamamoto for the first time were an untidy, undisciplined Cinderella group. He took one long look at them and abruptly ordered them to get their hair cut. This was a great shock to the long-haired young flyers who regarded themselves as eccentric individualists far beyond the reach of ordinary naval discipline. When they protested, their new chief mollified them with the joking remark, 'I don't want any thickheads here. If you get your hair cut it will help to keep a cool head!'

Although he was nearly forty—twenty years older than most of his officers—he took part in all their sports. He even ran in their marathon race and came in second. The boy who had run to school before breakfast was still fit although he was now a middle-aged man.

It was this behaviour which led the pilots, a hard-drinking lot, to respect their new boss although he was neither a drinker nor a career flyer. He did not mind their drinking. He used to attend all their parties, sending out for *sake* for them but drinking cold tea himself. He was quite candid about his teetotalism, saying, 'I have not drunk since I was commissioned. I found I was not strong in the head and made a fool of myself so I stopped.'

When he ran the flying school his main preoccupation was night flying. Although this was extremely hazardous in those early days, he insisted on every pilot having the maximum night-flying training. In spite of the high casualties among both pilots and aircraft, he persisted because he was convinced a plane attack at night would always have the advantage of surprise.

Such tough leadership was an exception among Japanese naval officers. Influenced by British naval traditions, the Japanese insisted that a naval officer should be a gentleman. They failed to assimilate the whole lesson. They confused an easygoing affability for gentlemanliness and did not grasp that firm discipline lay behind the polite British mask. The result was that the Imperial Navy bred many amiable and intelligent Flag Officers, but few of them were real fighting commanders.

After his eighteen months spent training naval pilots, Yamamoto was sent back to America. From 1925 to 1927 he was naval attaché in the Japanese Embassy in Washington. His duty was to learn everything he could about the power policies, ship building and defence programmes of the United States. American naval officers liked him mainly because he was a first-class card player who was willing to sit up any night playing poker. Occasionally when the cards became dull he would do his plate dance to the great amusement of his American hosts.

Just as the students at Harvard had taught him poker, the American officers introduced him to a more complicated game, bridge. He quickly became outstanding at it. He explained his brilliance as a bridge player like this: 'Our language has no alphabet and each single word or syllable is represented by a character. A Japanese has to keep five thousand ideographs in his head. After that it is child's play to remember only fifty-two cards.'

He never lost his love of baseball, which he had learned as a teenager at school. Whenever work was slack he sneaked out of his office to watch a ball game and hardly ever missed a Washington Senators' match.

Many younger Japanese naval officers began to arrive in America to attend American universities as Yamamoto had done. He always insisted on seeing them and gave them all the same advice: Mix with American students as much as possible. Do not speak Japanese for the first six months. When you go to New York travel by subway or bus; no one ever found out much about any city by riding in taxis. Buy a second-hand car so you can tour and learn about the United States in the vacations.

His own painstaking attitude was revealed when he took a young naval officer to an official reception given by President Calvin Coolidge. Afterwards Yamamoto asked him what was the colour of the President's necktie. When the astonished lieutenant replied he did not know, Yamamoto said very seriously: 'It is important on every occasion to remember every detail.'

When Captain Yamamoto returned from America the peaceful 'twenties were giving way to the turbulent 'thirties. Most of the turmoil in the 'thirties was due to the Japanese who had already decided upon the conquest of Asia.

Only one great obstacle was in the way. Japan had emerged from World War One the victorious ally of Britain and America. As a reward for her help in that war she had been given all the German possessions in the Pacific north of the Equator—the Marianas and the Carolines—which became known as the Japanese Mandates. The possession of these islands placed her in a position to challenge the U.S.A. for control of the Pacific. But throughout the 'twenties Japan's naval power was governed by the 5-5-3 agreement. This meant that for every five ships Britain and America built Japan could only build three. Japan had faithfully followed the treaty and reduced her navy to the smallest of the big powers. When her leaders began to have more and more vainglorious dreams about the conquest of Asia this agreement stood in the way. As the older admirals raised in the tradition of the Royal Navy retired or died, younger, tougher voices were increasingly heard demanding that Japan be allowed to build a bigger navy. The United States had been alarmed when Japan pushed for a fleet ratio of seven to ten at the Washington naval conference in 1921. For naval experts agreed that in fleet warfare the defending force must be fifty per cent stronger than the attackers.

If the Japanese seven-to-ten ratio had been agreed, America would have had only a forty-three per cent margin of superiority; and that missing seven per cent could mean all the difference between victory and defeat if Japan attacked. The conference, dominated by the United States and Britain, finally adopted a three-to-five ratio for capital ships. Aircraft carriers, which were to settle the mastery of the Pacific twenty years later, were not even mentioned because they were practically non-existent. But the agreed battleship ratio gave America a comfortable sixty-seven per cent margin of superiority over Japan.

Japan began to expand her navy, building as near to the limitations as she could. The post-war Japanese navy centred on battleships which included the flagship *Nagato*. Eight new battle cruisers under construction, including *Akagi* and *Amagi*, were much larger than any foreign ship planned. The Japanese also planned to construct a giant battleship of 48,000 tons.

Japan had one light carrier, *Hosho*, and in March 1923 Lieutenant Sunishi Kira, later to become a vice-admiral, was the first Japanese pilot to land on a carrier deck.

Although naval air power was still considered to be a small experimental auxiliary, it was decided to build two small aircraft carriers of 12,500 tons each. The maximum tonnage of Japan's battleships was still restricted by international agreement so they took an important step. They decided to convert the battle cruisers *Akagi* and *Amagi* into large aircraft carriers. They changed the name of *Amagi* to *Kaga*. In 1927 a new light carrier *Ryujo* brought the Japanese total up to four fleet carriers.

Japan was beginning to lead the world in naval design and armaments. The destroyers she built at the end of the 'twenties were fifteen years ahead of their time. They were faster than any destroyers built in England or America and had twin-mounted five-inch guns. Similar armament was not introduced into the U.S. Navy until the middle of World War Two.

At a naval conference in London in 1930, Yamamoto, with his fluent English and detailed knowledge of the American navy, was a delegate. He was instrumental in getting agreement to a plan that Japan could have equality in submarines and light cruisers.

When he returned after the conference, he became a commander of the First Air Fleet and at once fiercely stepped up training. Again a large number of pilots died, mostly through trying to land on the new aircraft carriers. When the pilots protested to him that the training was too tough, he replied, 'The Japanese fleet lags a long way behind the West. . . There is very little time to attain their level. That is why I regard death in training the same as a hero's death in action. The Japanese spirit should not fear death.'

Shaken by this mixture of common sense, patriotism and the usual injection of Japanese fanaticism, pilots returned obediently to their risky training. Before they took off, just to remind them that he regarded their flights as near-war, Yamamoto made them salute a list of pilots already killed in training.

In 1931 came the Manchurian Incident. Yamamoto, now a rear-admiral, became head of the technical arm of the navy. From this key position he was even more determined to make aircraft the main striking force of the fleet. In those days the Japanese aircraft industry was as shoddy as many of the other goods the country produced. Japanese military planes were mostly bought from Britain and America.

Although he received no support from the senior Japanese admirals, the outbreak of the Manchurian trouble gave him the opportunity to insist on more aircraft production.

Yamamoto wanted torpedo planes and long-range bombers but most of all he wanted a fast fighter that could fly off the deck of an aircraft carrier. He gave orders to the Japanese aircraft factories to produce their own planes experimentally. Mitsubishi, the big industrial combine, submitted plans for a navy fighter. It was designed by an Englishman named Smith who had been a designer at the British aircraft pioneer firm of Sopwith's. It became one of the most famous planes in the world—the Zero.

At the same time, with the militarists gaining increasing control of the Japanese Government, the naval hold-down was more and more actively criticized in Japan. The outcry became so great that it was decided in 1934 to hold another naval conference in London.

The obvious Japanese representative was Vice-Admiral Yama-moto, who had already publicly attacked the Japanese naval ratio as 'this national degradation'. He was named chief delegate with full powers. He sailed from Yokohama for Seattle, spending most of his time in his cabin playing poker. When he arrived in the United

States he refused all newspaper interviews. He also refused to read the American papers in case any cunning Western arguments might sway him before he could put Japan's case at the conference.

The American Press, however, took a great interest in him. As he travelled across America to New York in a locked compartment they gave him great publicity. Someone else who was holding the headlines was General William Mitchell, leading a big campaign for greater American air strength. His view was that American military planes must be designed specifically to fight Japan in the Pacific. Newspapers daily gave prominence to his dramatic statements that war with Japan was inevitable.

Yamamoto broke his silence once to comment on Mitchell's views. He said blandly, 'I do not look upon the relations between the United States and Japan from the same angle as General Mitchell. I have never thought of America as a potential enemy and the naval plans of Japan have never included the possibility of an American–Japanese war.' Most Americans thought General Mitchell was a crazy alarmist and that it was the little Japanese admiral who was talking horse-sense.

In New York Yamamoto again refused to see the reporters. Japanese interpreters brushed them off, saying, 'The admiral is so sorry but he does not speak English'. The Press never questioned this untrue explanation. As he was still unknown in the West few people knew about his two years at Harvard and a further two years as naval attaché in Washington.

He sailed on the *Berengaria* for England, still refusing to leave his cabin. When he landed at Southampton in the early morning of 16 October 1934, he immediately called a Press conference on the dockside and in fluent English announced, 'Japan can no longer submit to the ratio system. There is no possibility of compromise by my Government on that point.'

The London Conference of 1934, the last attempt to limit naval forces by treaty, was immediately doomed to failure by this dockside statement. On behalf of Japan, Yamamoto firmly rejected any further extension of the 5–5–3 ratio. He demanded national self-determination of armaments as a sovereign right. In other words, a dangerous free-for-all armaments race.

Talks dragged on for over two months into 1935 but the situation remained exactly as it was when he had stepped onto the Southampton docks. He compared the endless exhausting talks to the twenty-six-hour game of *shogi* he had played while a student at Harvard. In the same way he wore out his opponents and won.

He was smiling, polite, and obstinately adamant. Prime Minister Ramsay MacDonald asked him, 'If the other powers agree to paper parity will Japan promise not to build to it?' It was a typical silly MacDonald attempt at meaningless compromise and Yamamoto would have none of it. He replied, 'Very sorry, but no. If we have parity—we build.'

On the other hand, during his long stay in London at Grosvenor House, he became personally very popular with his British and American opponents. He was invited to visit Lloyd George, the war-time ex-premier, at Churt. He became very friendly with Ramsay MacDonald himself and one evening the Chief of Naval Staff, Lord Chatfield, lost twenty pounds to him at bridge.

He attended many society and Government dinners and, although he always refused to talk about the conference, he would animatedly discuss bridge or poker. Only once was he forced into making a comment. That was when a genial British fellow guest at dinner one night asked him, 'Tell me why you don't agree with the naval ratio?' Yamamoto put his knife and fork down and said with a grin, 'I am smaller than you but you don't insist I eat three-fifths of the food on my plate. You allow me to eat as much as I need.'

Yamamoto also stole the headlines by a revolutionary proposal he made for the abolition of all capital ships and aircraft carriers. In view of his own personal obsession with aircraft carriers this was a remarkable suggestion. He said that if Japan were given a free hand in Asia she might agree to a world programme of disarmament.

No one realized how completely frank he was being when he said, 'We consider the aircraft carrier the most offensive of all weapons. If we are concerned with reducing the menace of one country to another, the logical thing is to get rid of this most menacing weapon first.'

When asked if this abolition took place how the United States and Great Britain could defend their possessions in the Far East, Yamamoto made a typical Japanese reply, 'They would need only one defence—justice and international friendship.'

Was this offer genuine? No one will ever know. Certainly Yamamoto showed no sign of regret that the first successful world attempt to limit armaments, begun in Washington in 1921, was smashed by him in London thirteen years later.

It was suggested that if the ratio were abandoned the three powers should agree to exchange information on one another's naval building programmes. Yamamoto had the last word. 'Such an arrangement would be of no advantage to Japan,' he stated bluntly. 'Japan can find out at all times what the other powers are building. But you can't find out what we are doing.' Again he was being completely frank, as the performance, design and size of Japanese warships were later to reveal.

Before he left London Yamamoto was careful not to blame the other powers for the collapse of the conference. The Americans and British were not so tactful. They blamed him and the Japanese squarely for its failure.

Yamamoto could never have returned home if he had agreed to the ratio remaining. It was an open secret in Japan that if he did not succeed in getting the ban removed the supernationalist societies like the Black Dragon had vowed to assassinate him and his whole delegation.

A parade of admirals accompanied by 2,000 members of patriotic societies, including members of the sinister Black Dragon, greeted him with enthusiastic 'banzais' on his return to Japan. Instead of being assassinated he went to the Palace to be congratulated by Emperor Hirohito.

The way the war clouds were darkening was revealed in a Japanese Navy Ministry handout: 'A naval construction programme must be regarded as a stage in the rapid expansion of our international strength. We therefore must be firmly resolved to overcome any difficulties that may arise so the victorious position in which the Empire now finds itself may increase in glory.'

While the international scene became more gloomy as Japan initiated the naval armaments race, a dramatic episode occurred in Yamamoto's personal life. He fell in love.

After the 1934 conference there was a series of welcome home celebrations for him. One of them was a geisha party in the expensive district of Tsukiji, near the port of Tokyo. The prettiest and most popular geisha there, called Kikuji, noticed a high-ranking naval officer with two fingers missing trying to prise open the lacquer lid of a soup bowl which the heat had caused to stick. She bowed and leaned forward to help him but Yamamoto, always excessively sensitive about his maimed hand, told her brusquely to go away and mind her own business. No one ever speaks to a top geisha

like that. Shocked and furious, Kikuji in her turn did an unheard of
thing. She abruptly left the party while it was still in progress.

A few days later, at another party given as part of the Japanese
navy celebrations, Yamamoto again met Kikuji, who had been
brought along to sing and play the *samisen*. This time she was
formally introduced to him by another naval officer, who said, 'This
man is going to be Japan's greatest admiral. Be nice to him.'

Kikuji glanced at him coldly and replied, 'Really? He looks more
like a country yokel to me.'

This retort, far from annoying Yamamoto, delighted him. For this
was the way he was fond of referring to himself. He was constantly
describing himself as 'a country boy' or 'just a common sailor'. He
laughed so loudly at her reply that soon Kikuji found herself giggling
behind her fan.

That was the start of their relationship. Two evenings later he
arrived alone at the Tsukiji geisha house where she lived and asked
her to join him for dinner. Very soon he was recognized among the
geisha and the restaurant proprietors of Tokyo as Kikuji's lover. In
pre-war Japan to be the lover of a beautiful and sought-after geisha
was a complicated and costly procedure. There were two ways to
become her *danna*—or patron. One way was for a rich man to buy
a geisha out of her house and install her in her own home as his
mistress. This usually cost a fortune. The only other way was to
'allow' her to remain in the geisha house but have first call upon
her. The difference between these two types of *danna* was simple—
money. The first arrangement cost very much more than the second.

Yamamoto could afford neither. He had an admiral's pay but he
also now had four children. Admittedly he was allowed lavish ex-
penses for entertainment by the navy but he was far too honourable
a man to spend that money on a geisha.

In fact he landed himself in a unique position. He was now such a
famous man that his patronage gave prestige to the geisha houses
and restaurants he frequented. It was sound business for the geisha
house to let him see as much of Kikuji as he wished as his presence
attracted many other naval officers as customers.

Whenever he was working late hours at the Navy Ministry, she
would sneak out of the geisha house for an hour or so to bring
him some raw fish and rice in a little bowl which she placed on his
desk. She sat happily with him while he ate his supper.

Sometimes the navy put on lavish parties with as many as forty geisha to entertain their guests. When Kikuji was present Yamamoto used to do his special turn. He stripped off his trousers to perform his 'African king dance'. With the lower part of his body wrapped in a bath-towel, but still with his admiral's jacket on, he would do his famous plate dance. These performances generally came to an end with Yamamoto standing on his head.

But life with Kikuji was not all jolly parties. She was not only devoted to him but jealous. She noticed he always kept a small black notebook carefully hidden in the inside pocket of his admiral's jacket. As he was a sailor, she suspected it contained the names of girls in every port he called at. Slyly one evening while he was taking a bath she pulled it out and read it. It did not contain any girls' names, only those of the men under his command who had been killed undergoing the tough training he had sent them on.

On his side Yamamoto was equally devoted to Kikuji. He began seeing her so much that another admiral visited her secretly to ask her to stop seeing him, 'For the sake of the Imperial Navy'. When Yamamoto telephoned her after this she refused to see him. Worried and jealous in case she had found another *danna*, he took a taxi to ask her what was the matter. Did she no longer love him? In tears she confessed that she was only behaving like this in obedience to the admiral's request. Yamamoto told her that she was to ignore his fussy interfering advice. She was only too glad to do so and their love affair continued until his death.

4

The Ocean Monsters

AFTER Yamamoto's stonewalling victorious stand at the London conference the Japanese rushed into a frenzy of battleship building. That autumn Japan notified London and Washington that she was withdrawing from the naval treaty. Even as the notice of the withdrawal reached them, the keel of the giant battleship *Yamato*—to be Yamamoto's flagship in the most disastrous naval battle in Japan's history—was laid down in the Kure naval yard. Soon afterwards a start was made on two other great battleships, the *Musashi* at Nagasaki and the *Shinano* at Yokohama.

Japan had not built a battleship for fifteen years. The biggest battle cruiser in the world was still H.M.S. *Hood*, 42,000 tons, built by the British before the post-war naval treaty. Japan planned to build battleships nearly twice her size. *Yamato* and her sister ship *Musashi*, 863 feet long and 73,700 tons, were to be the largest battleships ever built. The main gun turrets weighed as much as a large destroyer and the ships' side armour was 16 inches thick. They had nine 18-inch guns firing a 3,200-lb. projectile—fifty per cent heavier than a 16-inch shell.

Four of these giant battleships were planned. The *Yamato* was completed in December 1941 and the *Musashi* eight months later. The third vessel, the *Shinano*, laid down at Yokosuka early in 1940, was later converted into the world's biggest aircraft carrier. Construction on the fourth ship was abandoned.

The object behind these monsters was to give Japan a decisive tonnage lead because the naval planners banked on the fact that the United States was unlikely to build a ship which was too big to go through the Panama Canal.

At this time too the Japanese began to disguise their naval plans. Twenty-foot fences shielded all this frenzied shipbuilding activity from view and the strictest security was enforced.

Navy Minister Admiral Mitsumasa Yonai announced in the Diet

in 1937, 'The Imperial Navy has no force to match the combined strength of Great Britain and the United States. It has no intention of building to such a level.'

While he spoke, *Yamato* was already laid down and *Musashi* and *Shinano* were completed blueprints. They were to be splendid reinforcements to Japan's ten existing battleships: *Nagato, Mutsu, Fuso, Yamashiro, Ise, Hyuga, Kongo, Hiei, Haruna* and *Kirishima*.

The only Japanese admiral who was unenthusiastic about the building of these great ships was Yamamoto. After his triumph in London he had been appointed Vice-Minister of the navy. From that powerful position he soon made his views known loudly and ceaselessly, insisting that these giants were obsolete even before their keels were laid. He maintained the view he had first formed at Harvard in World War One—the answer to supremacy in modern sea battles, especially in the Pacific, was the aircraft carrier.

In his position as Vice-Minister, Yamamoto's opinionated character began publicly to emerge. Although the admirals disagreed with him, the younger officers, especially those from the Kasumi-gaura flying school who were now beginning to climb the ladder of seniority, were on his side.

Among his intimates he was eloquent in his condemnation of battleship building, saying, 'These ships are like elaborate religious scrolls which old people hang up in their homes. They are of no proved worth. They are purely a matter of faith—not reality.'

On another occasion he remarked furiously, 'Military people always carry history around with them in the shape of old campaigns. They carry obsolete weapons like swords and it is a long time before they realize they have become purely ornamental. These battleships will be as useful to Japan in modern warfare as a *samurai* sword.'

These outbursts gradually did nudge the Japanese navy into becoming more air-minded. At Yamamoto's insistence two new carriers were built. They were the 30,000-ton 34-knot *Shokaku* and *Zuikaku*, both much more modern and faster than Japan's other big carriers *Akagi* and *Kaga*.

In spite of this the Japanese navy still did not agree with the view which Yamamoto had given at the London Conference, that the carrier was one of the most 'effective of armaments'. In 1937 the Japanese held the same conception concerning the role of aircraft carriers as the Americans. This was to use carriers as an air umbrella, secondary to a striking force of battleships.

Yamamoto began to be criticized in Japan for his declared policy for the development of aircraft carriers at the expense of battleships. Many people thought his neglect of battleships was dangerous. He insisted that the aerial torpedo delivered from a carrier was the most effective attack weapon against big ships. 'How can you destroy a battleship except with another battleship?' he was asked.

'Torpedo planes can do it,' he replied, and quoted the old Japanese proverb: 'The fiercest serpent may be overcome by a swarm of ants.' Pearl Harbor and the sinking of the *Prince of Wales* and the *Repulse* were one day to make his meaning clear.

While these eve-of-war wrangles were going on behind the scenes in Japan, Yamamoto made another brief appearance in the American Press. This was when he poured oil on troubled waters after the American gunboat *Panay* had been bombed by Japanese aircraft in China. In December 1937, as Vice-Minister of the navy, he issued a statement thanking the U.S. Government for its acceptance of Japanese apologies and pledging the navy to be much more careful in its future conduct.

Gradually Yamamoto's imaginative air policy began to be accepted. For years he had demanded long-range flying boats because he said that if the Japanese navy were to control the Pacific they would be needed to take off on long flights from the Japanese Mandated Islands. By the late 'thirties he had them. They could fly 800 miles with a 2,000-lb. bomb or torpedo.

The first the world knew about them was in 1938. The China War was still on when twenty of them took off from Japan's southern island of Kyushu to bomb Shanghai. They returned without re-fuelling. Western navies were astonished as they were still under the impression that all Japanese aircraft were shoddy and of no danger to the West. But this feat seems to have made no lasting impression on American or British intelligence services.

While the long-range flying boats were coming off the production line another of Yamamoto's babies, the Zero, was put into production. Japan's limited industrial capacity turned out as many as it could. This plane was to be one of the best fighters in World War Two, dominating the Pacific for two years.

In the late 'thirties Japan has an unusual advantage which even she did not fully appreciate. The same ignorant super-optimists who had confidently told Britain before Dunkirk that Hitler had only cardboard tanks were happily handing out similar speculative nonsense about Japan. Both the United States and Britain were sadly misinformed about the performance of Japanese aircraft. American aviation magazines constantly belittled the Japanese air force, assuring their readers that it could never effectively fight the Americans and the British. The American magazine *Aviation* reported that Japanese pilots suffered from the world's highest accident rate and were definitely inferior to the Chinese pilots. It added that the Japanese trained less than 1,000 pilots a year and that the Japanese air force would never develop enough air power for large-scale operations.

It added that Japan's aviation engineering depended entirely upon old-fashioned copies of planes made in the United States, Great Britain, Germany, Italy and the Soviet Union. It concluded, 'America's aviation experts can say without hesitation that the chief military airplanes of Japan are either outdated already or are becoming outdated. . . .' The only place where the article stumbled on the truth was where it said that Japanese industry could not possibly meet the requirements of a war. Another magazine assured its readers, 'The Japanese navy air force consists of four aircraft carriers with 200 planes.' These magazine articles appear to be ludicrous by hindsight. But they accurately reflected the international evaluation of Japanese military air power.

Yamamoto, who had read all these American military magazines ever since he was a naval attaché in Washington, must have been delighted at the ignorance they revealed. They proved how successful was the Japanese campaign to conceal their increasing strength from foreign observers. This secrecy was so successful that before Pearl Harbor the very existence of the Zero was unknown. It was several months before the Americans were able to form an accurate impression of this new fighter.

The American and British attitude was best illustrated by the reliance they placed upon the antiquated Brewster Buffalo. American aviation experts boasted, 'It is the most powerful fighter in the orient, far superior to anything the Japanese air force has.' After the first Zero appeared every Buffalo flew on a suicide mission.

The Japanese navy, building up its armaments rapidly, had no doubt who the ultimate enemy would be if war came. Ever since the end of their war with Russia Japan's main enemy had been the United States. With two great powers facing each other from opposite shores of the Pacific this was inevitable.

At the end of World War One the Imperial Defence Policy designated the United States as potential Enemy Number One, with Russia Number Two. The navy, however, had no doubt that 'the potential enemy is always America'.

Japanese admirals, always in favour of an advance towards Singapore, knew this must inevitably lead to a clash with the United States. In the two decades between the wars, Yamamoto was only one of many high-ranking officers of the Japanese navy who served in America. They were well equipped to make an accurate assessment of the U.S. fleet. Among the Japanese admirals who served in Washington was Osami Nagano, Chief of the Naval General Staff.

On the other hand, the rise of Soviet power in the post-war years became an obstacle to Japan's aggression in China. The army accepted the fact that if they continued their policy of conquest to the north sooner or later friction must come with Russia. For the same reason as the navy sent its officers to Washington, the top graduates of the army staff college were assigned to duty in Moscow. This two-standard preparedness policy prevailed until the eve of the Pacific war.

A Pacific war must be a sea war, and the navies on both sides of the ocean knew if it came they would gain important successes and suffer equally great defeats. Neither Admiral Harold R. Stark, Chief of U.S. Naval Operations, nor the Japanese admirals including Yamamoto desired war. They tried everything to avoid it. But this joint American–Japanese navy view was not shared by the Japanese army.

For the Japanese army had created a revolutionary political movement similar to the Nazis in Germany. In 1936, a year after the abrogation of the naval treaty in London, they gained effective control of the Government. Bloated from their Chinese conquests and feeling all-powerful, they looked upon the rest of the Eastern world as just another piece of booty ready to fall into their acquisitive hands.

The navy, on the other hand, continued to observe the Emperor Meiji's order to remain loyal to the civil power. While the army meddled, overthrew and finally ruled, the navy found itself manœuvred into a position where it could not help itself. Despite feeble gestures of resistance it was finally forced to go along, although dragging its feet, with the army's feverish plans for Asiatic conquest.

One man was determined not to be misled by the military fanatics who he was convinced were going to involve his country in disaster. This was Yamamoto, who was as determined as they were. His often-expressed unchanging view was that war with Britain and America could not possibly end in victory. From his position as Navy Vice-Minister he became deeply involved in what he described as 'trying to dam the mainstream'.

Then in this immediate pre-war period three events took place which were to have significant implications for the future of the world.

The first was when President Roosevelt, in the hope of deterring Japan from further aggression, ordered the American fleet to concentrate on Pearl Harbor instead of the west coast. This convinced many Japanese admirals that the United States was making positive preparations for armed intervention against them. They began talking about 'a dagger pointed at the heart of Japan'. An attack on Pearl Harbor was always under naval study but it was considered extraordinarily difficult. When Roosevelt moved the fleet it was taken out of the naval files, dusted off—and returned as being still too difficult.

At the same time both Hitler and Mussolini were urging Japan to join them in a defensive three-power pact. The army command, now firmly in control of the Government, was very much in favour of this. The navy was not. Both Yamamoto and his chief, Mitsumasa Yonai the Navy Minister, were strenuously opposed to strengthening any ties with Germany and Italy. Despite tremendous army pressure, Yamamoto was especially adamant on this point. His argument was that any pact with the Axis was certain to bring Japan into conflict with England, America—and possibly Russia. Like everything else he undertook there were no half measures in his attitude. A compromise plan which the army tried to put through was killed by him. He repeated his firm opinion, 'Japan would be extremely foolish to do this and make enemies of Great Britain and the United States.'

His outspokenness made him many enemies, particularly among the extreme nationalists. They called him pro-American and a traitor to his country and threatened to assassinate him. But he remained unperturbed and when Yonai urged him to have a secret police bodyguard he refused.

Soon he became the chief source of opposition to war with the West. This was not because he was a traitor and pro-American as his bloodthirsty enemies alleged. He was as patriotic as they were but no one knew more than he did about the Japanese navy. In spite of the might of its great capital ships and increasing number of aircraft carriers, he knew it was too weak to challenge the combined naval strength of Britain and America.

He unceasingly expressed the view that if war came eighty per cent of the burden would fall on the navy, which was not up to the task. This realistic attitude was like a lit fuse to the fanatical, conquest-drunk army.

When asked outright, 'Don't you think our gallant navy will win?' he replied just as forthrightly: 'No, I do not.' This reply not only infuriated the militarists but puzzled other more reasonable Japanese. How could the father of Japan's splendid new navy, the man who practically singlehanded was responsible for the creation of the air arm, say a thing like that?

When the accusations of being a traitor increased as a result of this remark he replied, 'I am serving my country just as if I were commanding in action. I am fighting a battle to bring my countrymen round to a sensible way of thinking. They can kill me—but they can't kill that.'

As his would-be assassins became more menacing his Japanese fatalism rose to the surface. Although his face was very well known, he went for long strolls in Tokyo and rode on tramcars alone in civilian clothes. He went walking alone from the Navy Ministry to the bookshop district of Tokyo, browsing along the stalls, the perfect target for any assassin.

He was now so famous—or notorious—that journalists called on him constantly and he kept on the most cordial terms with them. When they visited him at 2 a.m. he would open the door himself—he was still up working—although they might have been nationalist killers knocking at his door.

By the middle of 1939 the international situation became much worse. The Cabinet was in practically continuous session, trying to make up its mind to agree to the Axis's more urgent offers of a pact. At this time Yamamoto decided that his anti-war stand could only end in his assassination. He wrote a note which he placed in a box to be opened after his death in which he said, 'I regard it as a great honour to die for what I consider to be right.'

At the same time Admiral Yonai overruled Yamamoto's objections and ordered him to have a special police guard both at his office and his official residence. Wherever he went he was surrounded by a squad of armed plain-clothes police.

Eventually Yonai decided even this precaution was not enough. The only way to remove him from the daily peril to which his outspoken anti-war stand had brought him was to remove him from the political sphere altogether. In mid-August he was appointed Commander-in-Chief of the Combined Fleet—the *rengo kantai*—with the rank of full admiral. Yonai confessed afterwards, 'It was the only way to save his life—to send him off to sea.'

This was the highest honour the Japanese navy could bestow, and even Yamamoto could not decline it. It came as a complete surprise to him. When he was told the news the teetotal admiral drank a whole glass of beer at one gulp. The transfer from the dangerous political position as Navy Vice-Minister to sea duty meant strict obedience to the Imperial Rescript, 'Men of the services should not participate in politics.'

Two weeks after his appointment came the third event which was to alter the course of history. The Germans invaded Poland and World War Two began. Yamamoto then knew he had not much time left. He flung himself into the job of preparing the navy for any emergency with his usual ruthless, enthusiastic drive. His impact was felt at once. Almost as soon as he stepped onto the bridge of the flagship *Nagato* he laid down his fleet policy:

1. Priority must be given to air training.
2. If war breaks out the American fleet in Hawaii must be brought to decisive battle at the earliest opportunity.

The earliest opportunity? When would that be? His mind began constantly to revolve round the problem.

5

Yamamoto Commands the Fleet

As the Commander-in-Chief of Japan's gigantic fleet, Yamamoto's duty was to protect his homeland. Others might make the decision for war but he had to be ready for it.

First, as his fleet directive laid down, all training must be stepped up. Pilots worked ceaselessly. But always standing on the bridge of his flagship as the last plane came into land on the carrier decks was their C.-in-C., Admiral Yamamoto.

When Yamamoto took over the Combined Fleet the first exercise under his command revealed how incredibly poor was the accuracy of Japanese bombers. Four groups of nine planes released their dummy bombs from only 1,000 feet in the open sea against a weaving battleship. Not one bomb hit her.

Yet when three dive bombers attacked the same target they registered one successful hit. She was also hit with an airborne torpedo. In view of the success of dive bombing and torpedoing, many high-ranking naval officers thought level bombing should be eliminated.

Yamamoto disagreed. He gave a glimpse of the way his mind was working when he said, 'As long as I am Commander-in-Chief I will not do away with level bombing. True, our level bombing accuracy at sea has been poor. The reason for the poor ratio of bomb hits lies in the free evasive movement of the target vessel. There is no reason for us to select only these difficult targets. I hope that much further study and practice will be conducted.'

This was two and a half years before Pearl Harbor. It was the first glimpse of an idea for attacking stationary targets such as anchored warships. It brought him back to his old hobby-horse — continued tough training. Without it no bombing attack could be successful. As a result, by the time of the Pearl Harbor attack, Japanese naval planes had undoubtedly attained the world's highest rate of accuracy in level bombing attacks. They were equally skilful in launching aerial torpedoes.

He also changed the rather lackadaisical behaviour of the fleet staff officers. When officers assembled after manœuvres or battle exercises for a critique, the senior officer who presided seldom guided the discussions. Nor did he offer any incisive comments. At the end of it, all he said was, 'Thank you, gentlemen,' in what he conceived to be the best Royal Naval tradition. The officers were constantly left wondering whether they were on the right track or not.

Admiral Yamamoto quickly altered all that. In conferences after the fleet manœuvres he took a leading part in the discussions. If some movement had been carried out wrongly he was quick to point it out. He also explained clearly how he wanted it done in the future. He did not want his staff officers to act as a brains trust. He made it evident that he alone was going to decide the policy and make the tactical decisions.

Although this seemed novel to many of his officers, he knew that in battle there is no time to debate moves as there is round a conference table. Nor can decisions be made by a majority vote. Battles are won by a commander who swiftly makes up his mind and backs his own judgment. For each move, once made, is irrevocable. Few men can make such decisions with certainty. Certainly no other Japanese admiral could. They require special courage and self-confidence—which Yamamoto had.

His monastic daily routine also impressed his officers. His work generally finished at five o'clock in the evening, when he played a game of Japanese chess. He went to bed at nine o'clock but lay in his bunk studying papers until well past midnight. He awoke at four o'clock and stayed in bed reading more papers until 6.30 a.m. because he did not want to disturb the other officers.

His short sleeping hours were partly due to insomnia, from which he suffered after he was appointed Commander-in-Chief. He admitted as much in a speech to the pupils of his old school, the Nagaoka Middle School, a few months after his appointment, when he said, 'I have never slept well since my appointment because whether Japan goes ahead or ends in ruin depends a great deal upon how I discharge my duties.'

Yamamoto had other problems, particularly the one he had studied so earnestly in America. In one leap his country had jumped from rickshaws to machines. And no machine could work without oil.

He was particularly conscious of the situation because his home town, Nagaoka, was the only place in Japan with oil wells. Oil had been known to exist there for 200 years, but it was not until 1876, when the Japanese Government engaged an American geologist to survey the area, that wells were dug. They were not very rich.

When Yamamoto was a boy his native province of Echigo supplied most of the oil for Japan. His rickshaw homeland used very little in the days before warships and automobiles. Now his home province could provide only the equivalent of a few spoonfuls for Japan's growing needs. Certainly Japan did not have enough oil to fuel Yamamoto's fleet. Where was the nearest place from which it could be obtained? Java in the Dutch East Indies. If war came that would have to be one of the first objectives. It would be a primary invasion task for the army.

In the meantime he continued to make his fleet ready for any emergency. That winter they left to carry out extensive manœuvres in the stormy North Pacific. This fleet training in the remote Pacific was the beginning of a plan which was soon to surprise the world. The ships anchored in out-of-the-way uninhabited arctic bays. One of these was Tankan Bay, a large secret harbour in the Kurile Islands. This is where Yamamoto's carriers were to rendezvous two years later on their fateful voyage to Pearl Harbor.

During its rigorous training programme the fleet anchored for only two or three days every month. After the tough winter voyages they were allowed to relax for two months by going for short cruises along the China coast. A Japanese training pamphlet said, 'With tenacious and tireless spirit we are striving to reach a superhuman degree of skill and perfect fighting efficiency.'

Apart from trying to bring the fleet up to the peak of efficiency, Yamamoto also remained constantly interested in the welfare and private life of his young officers. He often gave a lecture to them which went like this, 'I don't drink but that is my nature. It may not be yours. If you do drink freely, please remember never to discuss naval business at banquets or in restaurants. Nor can you become a great man if you are thrown into ecstasies by praise from a woman. Don't rush to get married. Stay single until you are thirty. Your job has special claims which makes an early marriage not a good idea. I married at thirty-five but I have never regarded it as a late marriage.'

After six months in command, with the training going well, he felt much more confident about his officers and men. In February

1940 came a big Japanese national festival—the 2,600th anniversary of Japan's first Emperor Jimmu, the son of Amaterasu the Sun Goddess, from whom the Japanese Emperors claim to be descended. There was a big naval review and a great celebration in the open space before the Imperial Palace in Tokyo which the Emperor and Empress attended.

Yamamoto stayed with his fleet, excusing himself to Naval Head-quarters by saying, 'I am very much involved with the movements of ships in the war with China. I must be on guard to see our country is not attacked while we are celebrating.' It seems like a typical Japanese excuse. Probably he so highly disapproved of the dangerous patriotic fervour this festival aroused that, although he would lead his fleet in review in his position as its admiral, he did not want to be involved in any open warmongering with the army and politicians in Tokyo. The Chief of Naval Staff, Nagano, knowing the views he held and how forcefully he might express them, was just as happy to let him remain at sea.

In the political arena events were moving headlong. After no less than seventy Cabinet meetings, the Japanese decided to take the plunge and join forces with the Axis powers in Europe. The signing of the Tripartite Pact between Germany, Italy and Japan in September 1940 was not very binding. Japan only agreed to enter the European war on the Axis side should the United States join Britain against them. Even this limited commitment was regretted by many cautious people in Japan. They included the Emperor and the Prime Minister, Prince Konoye. Admiral Yonai, Yamamoto, and most of the navy were also vigorously against it. All of them were overridden by the all-powerful army.

Yamamoto was deeply perturbed. He now began to wish bitterly that he had not taken on the non-political job of Commander-in-Chief. There is no doubt if he had remained in Tokyo he would once again have risked his life by opposing the German–Italian alliance with its inevitable war against Britain and the United States.

Unfortunately for Japan and the world Yamamoto remained semi-exiled aboard his flagship *Nagato*. He still retained one small optimistic hope. Perhaps when it came to the point of no return the majority of the admirals, instead of a handful led by him, would see the folly of it all. Without the navy, no matter how threateningly the army rattled their sabres, Japan could not start a war.

If the navy stood firm the situation might yet be saved. Yamamoto

said hopefully of Zengo Yoshida, his successor as Vice-Minister—
the man who refused to fly—'He is a good Navy Minister and will
be able to take care of the position without my support. He is every
bit as stubborn as I am. We can sleep easily while he is in charge.'

Yamamoto's optimistic faith proved unjustified. Yoshida was not
made of his timbre and the job proved too much for him. He became
ill and had to resign. His place was taken by a much weaker man,
Koshiro Oikawa, who became the reluctant tool of the army. When
the Tripartite Pact was signed he tagged along, slightly protesting.

The Prime Minister, Prince Fumimaro Konoye, was a cultivated
Westernized man but he was weak and vacillating. Even he became
alarmed at the way the country seemed to be tumbling helter-skelter
into war—and perhaps ruin. He invited Yamamoto to come and
see him at Takigaiso, the Prime Minister's official residence. Konoye
asked him what chance there was of victory if war broke out with
Britain and the United States.

Yamamoto did not hesitate. He replied bluntly, 'I can raise havoc
with them for one year or at most eighteen months. After that I can
give no one any guarantees.'

It was a most prophetic utterance. It made it plain that, if Japan
had to fight a long war, her leading admiral saw only defeat at the
end of it. Konoye knew the British and Americans well enough to
realize his statement made sense.

After his talk with Yamamoto, Konoye made a feeble last-minute
attempt to create a better understanding with the United States. But
the situation had gone too far and his policy only angered the army.
General Tojo, who had begun to take much more direct control of
State affairs, attacked Konoye for practising 'soft diplomacy'.

If war came with Britain and the United States, could Japan be
protected from attack? Again only the navy had the answer.

Unfortunately when Tojo became premier the following year, the
Naval High Command did not advise him in the same direct way as
Yamamoto had spoken to Konoye. They were afraid to tell him
that in a long conflict defeat and invasion were certain. Instead the
navy drifted along with his war plans.

One admiral put it like this:

The primary responsibility for Japan's going to war rests on the
navy. We cannot blame the ignorant and reckless army. Neither
public opinion nor the Emperor could have halted the plunge

towards war—but the navy could have. The navy alone was in a position to stand against Tojo. If it had done so Japan could not have gone to war. The navy, with its broad outlook on the world, gave way to the insular army. The navy is to blame.

Yet nearly all the other navy leaders lacked Yamamoto's courage and conviction. Wrote Vice-Admiral Tomiji Koyanagi: 'Reluctantly the navy was dragged to war. There was much vacillating and capitulating in the navy high command.'

As Yamamoto fully realized, the navy in spite of its big ship-building programme was not well prepared for a long war. It was woefully weak in flying crews. In January 1940 Japan had 3,500 naval pilots—although they had a greater number on active service than the American navy,

As the instructor at the Kasumigaura Flying Training School said, 'The greatest weakness lay in the steady replacement of qualified flying crews. And the difference between the veteran flier and the novice is as great as a man to a child.'

One of the instructors at Kasumigaura, Lieutenant Takekatsu Tanaka, a far-sighted and capable officer, prepared and submitted 'a proposed plan for training 15,000 pilots'. The navy command dismissed Tanaka's proposal as the wild dream of a young air force officer.

It never reached Yamamoto. Yet twenty months later in August 1941 the navy called for the annual training of 15,000 pilots. The decision came too late. By that time war was just round the corner and it was impossible to train tens of thousands of pilots in the short space of time left.

Naval officers knew the United States and Britain were formidable adversaries in the air. But they had great and justified confidence in the ability of Zero fighters to gain air control over any battle area. The navy Zero fighter was the equal of between two and five enemy fighters, depending on the type.

During that fateful simmering summer of 1941, army and navy staff officers frequently discussed the possibility of war against the United States and England. The majority of them agreed that eventual war with America was inevitable. Yet when the navy's leaders found themselves having to choose between war and peace —the majority wanted peace.

In particular the senior admirals cautioned against blind belief in

Japanese invincibility. Retired admirals Keisuke, Okada, Mitsumasa Yonai, and Soemu Toyoda spoke up strongly against war. They pointed out the unpalatable fact that most of their wars, including the one of 1904, far from being 'overwhelming Japanese triumphs', as described by jingoistic historians, had in reality been barely won. As this by inference denigrated Togo's great victory over the Russians no one took the slightest notice. It was like trying to convince Americans that George Washington was an inveterate liar.

Yamamoto sided with the senior admirals for more recondite reasons. No one knew Japan's naval strength and national resources better than he did. That is why he again repeated the clear-cut warning he had given to Konoye that the fleet could not be counted upon to fight successfully for more than a year. He said:

> If it is necessary to fight, in the first six months to a year of war against the United States and England I will run wild. I will show you an uninterrupted succession of victories. But I must also tell you that if the war be prolonged for two or three years I have no confidence in our ultimate victory.

The much younger, war-mad military group could always brush off the arguments of the older men as old-fashioned and out-of-touch. But those of Japan's most brilliant admiral were a different matter. The only way to deal with him was to cold-shoulder him and become deaf to his treasonable ravings. He became a lone voice crying in the wilderness.

A year after his appointment as Commander-in-Chief in November 1940, Yamamoto thought constantly of retirement. He confided to his friends that he wanted to grow flowers and catch fish in the Shinano river near his home, and even named Admiral Mineichi Koga as his successor. Koga was in fact to succeed him, but in the most tragic circumstances.

There is no doubt Tojo and the army clique would have been glad to see the back of him. But they had no control over the fleet and as war loomed the Imperial Navy was not going to lose their greatest admiral since Togo. The dichotomy of Yamamoto's position was now at its zenith. As a level-headed patriotic Japanese, he had no wish to see his country rush into a war which he was certain could only end in her defeat, and the knowledge that he was the only Japanese who could lose the war in a day made him very sensitive to the dangers involved.

At the same time, in his capacity as Commander-in-Chief, he was working furiously to perfect a plan which, if it succeeded, would give Japan at least a chance. He realized that, whatever his personal feelings, he could not retire until he had prepared the fleet for any emergency. The navy must try and destroy the American warships as quickly as possible. If he could strike a blow hard enough to cripple the Pacific fleet there might be a chance of negotiated peace before Japan was beaten to her knees.

He even quarrelled with Prince Konoye over the situation. The dispute revealed the differences deep in their characters. Konoye was an aesthetic liberal politician who read English poetry as a relaxation. Yamamoto was an athletic, hearty, painstaking naval officer who liked poker and bridge and seldom read anything except training manuals.

Yet it was he, not the seemingly pacific Konoye, who risked his life and fought to the very end to keep Japan out of a world war. In the end the aristocratic Konoye became irritated with the Jeremiah-like tirades of the schoolmaster's son. Instead of still fighting for peace, he felt the situation was now so tense that Yamamoto ought to be devoting all his time to preparing the navy.

At this time Yamamoto made a surprising speech to his old Middle School in Nagaoka. In it Japan's most famous admiral gave his view of America for the last time. He said:

> Most people think Americans love luxury and that their culture is shallow and meaningless. It is a mistake to regard the Americans as luxury-loving and weak. I can tell you Americans are full of the spirit of justice, fight and adventure. Also their thinking is very advanced and scientific. Lindbergh's solo crossing of the Atlantic is the sort of valiant act which is normal for them. That is a typically American adventure based on science.
>
> Do not forget American industry is much more developed than ours—and unlike us they have all the oil they want. Japan cannot beat America. Therefore she should not fight America.

This speech stood out like an unmoving boulder in the rushing torrent of inaccurate hate propaganda poured out by the militarists. It caused a sensation among service chiefs and politicians. The army, glowing from their successful semi-colonial war in China, regarded Yamamoto's point of view as plain cowardice. It was also too much for Konoye, who was in his last days of premiership, soon to be replaced by General Tojo. He now said the army was right and Yamamoto was irresponsible and too Americanized. He no longer had any doubt that the admiral was on the side of the West.

Konoye did not care to say anything like this to Yamamoto's face, and his views were conveyed to Yamamoto by tittle-tattle. Apparently this was the one time he was ever known to lose his temper. When he heard about Konoye's remarks he shouted furiously, 'I am a Japanese. I only do what is best for my country. It is Konoye and his friends who are irresponsible. They are behaving like delinquent children.'

Distrusting Japan's intentions, America began to make fleet dispositions. In February 1941 the fleet at Pearl Harbor became the Pacific Fleet, commanded by Admiral Husband E. Kimmel. The small American force in the Far East, commanded by Admiral Thomas C. Hart, was for prestige purposes designated the United States Asiatic Fleet.

Although America was not yet at war in Europe, in the spring of 1941 Admiral Stark, Chief of Naval Operations, transferred the carrier *Yorktown* and three battleships from the Pacific to the Atlantic, where the greater part of the British navy was concentrated against the comparatively small German fleet. The Axis powers had no operational carriers.

At the time of Pearl Harbor there were nine battleships in the Pacific, and eight in the Atlantic keeping watch on the Axis. There were also four carriers in the Atlantic and only three in the Pacific. These three Pacific carriers faced ten Japanese.

Meanwhile the Japanese army's advance in Asia still continued blatantly. Combined with the worsening situation in Europe, this was bound to lead to war. In July 1941 the Japanese announced that the French Vichy Government had agreed 'to a joint protectorate of Indo-China' and Japanese troops marched in. The Americans regarded this Japanese advance as the last straw. They countered by freezing all Japanese assets in the United States. This meant shutting off their supply of oil. If Japan did not have oil her military machine would stop.

The United States, acting jointly with Great Britain and Holland, also applied the most drastic economic sanctions to Japan.

In many ways the embargo came too late. Up to then, in spite of the tense international situation, American manufacturers had been free to sell to Japan the latest planes, range-finders, fire-control apparatus and many other items of military and naval equipment. The Japanese, with their usual frugality, bought a few samples of each and copied them. Japan had also managed to stock-pile large supplies of scrap-steel, mostly bought from America.

But the oil embargo was a different matter. The Japanese navy depended entirely upon imported fuel oil. Yamamoto called for the figures. The fleet had a reserve of 6,450,000 tons of oil, enough for eighteen months' supply. Even if used with the greatest economy, it would be exhausted in three years. After that, as he had predicted, they could not fight.

Therefore the oil ban amounted to an ultimatum. Japan must come to terms with the United States or fight. But how? Obviously the army plan to seize the oilfields in the Dutch East Indies must have priority. But while the Japanese invaded Java what would the formidable American fleet anchored in Pearl Harbor do?

The Chief of Naval General Staff, Admiral Osami Nagano, wanted the whole might of the navy to be used in a crushing attack to capture the East Indies oil-producing islands before the U.S. Pacific Fleet could sail out of Pearl Harbor to prevent it.

The Japanese navy were convinced that, in the event of war, the American fleet would carry the offensive into the western Pacific. The Imperial Navy would then attack and destroy the American fleet in Japanese home waters. This was the orthodox defence plan.

Japanese warships were designed to this end. Crew accommodation was ruthlessly sacrificed to build ships superior to the enemy —if only by one gun or torpedo tube or a single knot of speed.

The light cruiser *Yubari* was the prototype of these ships. With their motto, 'We rely upon our readiness to meet the enemy when he comes', they were specially designed to operate in the rough seas surrounding Japan.

In those days the idea of sending ships to attack distant Hawaii hardly entered the minds of the navy leaders. Only Yamamoto was haunted by the possibility that the United States might attack while most of Japan's fleet was in the Indies. If they did, he would not be able to stop them. His plans were already well advanced to prevent this.

Yet if Yamamoto had been aware of the U.S. fleet's war plans for the Pacific he might have considered the Pearl Harbor plan unnecessary. The United States navy was going to play the game by the same rules as its opponents, the Imperial Navy. In the event of war with Japan the U.S. navy was to operate Plan Rainbow Five.

This called for the abandonment of the Philippines and other vulnerable outposts in the western Pacific. After allowing a time for consolidation, American navy strategists visualized a decisive battle with the Japanese fleet in the vicinity of the Marshall Islands or the Carolines. Ironically enough, this Rainbow Plan for a battle area in the western Pacific dovetailed exactly with the strategy which the Japanese fleet had been planning for thirty years—and which was about to be overturned by Yamamoto. In other words, admirals on both sides agreed that Pearl Harbor was out of reach of the Japanese fleet.

The basis of Plan Rainbow Five was the acceptance that Japan could conquer everything she wanted in the Philippines and Malaya —if she left Pearl Harbor alone. The Japanese naval view was that from captured forward bases their submarines and aircraft would deal piecemeal with the Pacific Fleet.

Under the Rainbow Plan the American fleet aimed to capture Japanese positions in the Marshalls and the Carolines, including their main base at Truk. It was estimated that the Pacific Fleet could accomplish this in six to nine months. Then it would proceed to the relief of the Philippines and other Japanese-held territory. Further big sea battles would take place in these areas.

American navy planners credited the Japanese admirals with enough strategic sense to appreciate this situation and abide by the rules. The State Department also assumed that even the military-mad Japanese Government had sufficient political wisdom to avoid an act of unqualified aggression which would bring an angry America united into the war.

They reckoned without Yamamoto. One of the least orthodox admirals on either side of the Pacific, he was convinced that the United States would move immediately into the Pacific to threaten Japan's southern operations. Not only to prevent this threat, but because he did not wish to leave the initiative in American hands, he planned to deliver a crushing blow at the heart of the United States fleet in far-off Hawaii at the outbreak of war.

For a fleet in Hawaii, as Roosevelt had intended, was a much greater threat to Japan than one based on the west coast. It could easily advance into the western Pacific, menacing Japan itself.

Another reason for his attack plan was that Yamamoto gloomily appreciated that the balance of naval strength must gradually favour America. Every day the war lasted the chance of Japan gaining a victory steadily diminished.

He had also learned the lesson of the long-drawn-out war Japan had fought in China for years. If she fought another like that, miserable defeat was certain. His idea was a quick paralysing knockout. If a knockout were not possible, the only answer was to rock the giant America before he came out of his corner fighting. Perhaps this might cause him eventually to throw in the sponge or accept a points decision.

Yet even today many American naval authorities remain deeply pained concerning Japan's attack on Pearl Harbor. This is mainly because Yamamoto did not obey the rules as laid down in Rainbow Five. The naval historian S. E. Morison demonstrates this point of view:

> This surprise attack on Pearl Harbor, far from being 'a strategic necessity' as the Japanese claimed even after the war, was a strategic imbecility. One can search military history in vain for an operation more fatal to the aggressor. On a tactical level Pearl Harbor was wrongly concentrated on ships rather than permanent installations and oil tanks. On a strategic level it was idiotic, on the high political level it was disastrous.

Many pre-war American admirals were also convinced that Pearl Harbor was invulnerable to Japanese attack. So the place was wrapped in a lotus-like peace.

This was in spite of several warnings from the Americans themselves. In January 1932 the U.S. Naval Planning Board ordered 200 warships to test the defences of Pearl Harbor. When the fleet gathered in Californian waters it was the greatest naval concentration seen in the Pacific up to that time.

The newly built carriers, *Saratoga* and *Lexington*, sailed across the Pacific accompanied by four destroyers. The commander, Admiral Yarnell, flew his flag in *Saratoga* instead of a battleship. He also called his group by a name one day to become well known in the Pacific War—a task force.

Twenty-four hours away from Oahu, Yarnell ran into thick weather, which made his force less likely to be spotted. At dusk on Saturday, 6 February, he knew he could reach Oahu by dawn on

Sunday morning. He reckoned, rightly, that the defences would be less alert than usual.

When his fleet was sixty miles north-east of Oahu, 150 planes took off in the pre-dawn dark from the two carriers, which were pitching in heavy seas—just as the Japanese were to do nine years later.

When the American planes emerged from the clouds they found the greatest naval base in the world spread before them. No defending plane came up to intercept them as they dived in mock attacks. They 'sank' all the heavy naval vessels in the harbour.

At Admiral Yarnell's study group afterwards, many officers demanded a new type of navy, still organized round battleships but with maximum air power to support them. For this amazingly successful attack had upset all naval concepts. Naval planes had got through undetected and unmolested. Yet no one listened— except perhaps in Tokyo. There is little doubt Yamamoto studied intelligence reports of this advanced manœuvre. He certainly followed Yarnell's attack almost exactly on the morning of 7 December 1941.

Not every American naval officer shared the general complacent view that Pearl Harbor was inviolate. On 16 January 1941, almost a year before Pearl Harbor, Rear-Admiral—later Vice-Admiral— Patrick L. N. Bellinger, commander of Patrol Wing Two, wrote a warning letter to the Chief of Naval Operations:

I arrived here on October 30th 1940, with a point of view that the international situation was critical especially in the Pacific. I was impressed by the need to be ready today rather than to-morrow. After taking over command of Patrol Wing Two, I was surprised to find the Hawaiian Islands, an important naval advance outpost, was operating on a shoestring. The more I looked at it the thinner the shoestring appeared to be.

His letter went on to complain that Patrol Wing Two lacked modern planes, spare parts, engines, properly trained personnel— in fact, everything.

His letter did have some effect. Some months later Patrol Wing One, normally based on San Diego, was ordered to reinforce Wing Two in Hawaii. But Admiral Bellinger still remained unhappy about the general situation. Three months after he wrote that letter he was Air Defence Officer of the Pearl Harbor naval base. In collaboration with Major-General Frederick L. Martin, commanding general of the Army Air Forces in Hawaii, he completed a joint defence plan which correctly forecast the direction, the size of the force, and the strategy by which the Japanese would attack. It was correct even to the hour.

On 31 March 1941 he and General Martin drew up an army and navy air plan in the event of a sudden hostile action against Oahu or the fleet in Hawaii. Analysing probable Japanese strategy, both officers foresaw that the Japanese would approach via 'the vacant sea where no trade routes exist'—which they did.

They said the Japanese would strike at dawn, having launched their planes 350 miles north of Pearl Harbor. They came nearer —200 miles away.

Like Yamamoto, Bellinger and Martin also closely studied Japanese naval history, and they made these statements:

> In the past Japan has never preceded hostile action by a declaration of war.
>
> Japanese submarines and a fast raiding force may arrive in Hawaiian waters with no prior warning from the U.S. intelligence service.
>
> A sudden successful raid against American ships and naval installations in Oahu might prevent effective action by their forces in the West Pacific for a long period.

The Martin–Bellinger estimate contained many astonishingly accurate prophecies. They predicted:

1. A declaration of war preceded by a surprise submarine attack on American ships in the Hawaii area.
2. A surprise attack on Oahu including ships and installations at Pearl Harbor.
3. A combination of the two.

They concluded that the most likely form of attack on Oahu would be by planes launched from carriers within 300 miles. On the other hand, if there was a submarine attack, this might indicate the presence of a large undiscovered surface force. This would probably be composed of fast ships accompanied by at least one carrier.

When was the best time to attack? A surprise attack at dawn might find the U.S. forces in a poor condition of readiness and pursuit would be slow to start. The major disadvantage of a daybreak attack was that the American ships would have all day to find and attack the fleeing carriers.

If the carriers attacked at dusk they would have all night to escape. The disadvantage of this plan would be that the hostile ships would have to spend the day of the attack approaching the island. They might easily be observed.

Yet, as the Martin–Bellinger report pointed out, under existing conditions that might not be a serious disadvantage. For until an act of war had been committed, the United States would probably take no offensive action. The only thing lost would be complete surprise.

If hostilities had already commenced, a night attack would offer certain advantages. But for an initial crippling blow a dawn or dusk attack would have a better chance of a big success, especially if submarine attacks were co-ordinated with any air attack.

The day after Martin and Bellinger had completed their report, out of the blue came a signal from the Chief of Naval Operations to commandants of all naval districts, which said:

Personnel of your naval intelligence service should be advised that past experience shows Axis powers often begin activities in a particular field on Saturdays and Sundays or on national holidays of the country concerned. They should take steps on such days to see the proper watches and precautions are in effect.

When the Martin–Bellinger plan reached Washington on 20 August 1941 it was accompanied by a most prophetic letter from General Martin to the Army Air Forces. This said:

Our most local enemy Orange [Japan] can probably bring a maximum of six carriers against Oahu. The early morning attack is therefore the best plan of action open to the enemy. They must also appreciate to avoid detection by friendly surface vessels the most probable avenue of approach is from due north.

That could have been written by Yamamoto, who at that time was completing exactly the same plan aboard his flagship *Nagato* in the Inland Sea.

6

An Unpopular Plan

HOW was the Pearl Harbor idea born? It began as a glimmer in Yamamoto's mind nineteen months before.

In late April and early May 1940, eight months after he took over command, the Combined Fleet held manœuvres paying special attention to mock air attacks. As a result of his stepped-up training, these attacks were remarkably successful. Warships, dodging skilfully, seemed to have eluded both the first and second assault waves of torpedo bombers. But when the referees gave their verdict, they said that, in spite of its twisting and elusive actions, the fleet had sustained heavy damage. In their view aerial torpedoes had halved its strength.

At the end of the exercise, while walking along the quarter-deck of the flagship *Nagato*, his chief-of-staff, Admiral Shigeru Fukudome, said to Yamamoto, 'It is beginning to look as if there is no way a surface fleet can elude aerial torpedoes. Is the time ripe for a decisive fleet engagement using aerial torpedo attacks as the main striking power?'

Yamamoto paused and gazed across the deck for a long time before he replied, 'An even more crushing blow could be struck against an *unsuspecting* enemy force by mass torpedo attack.'

It was May 1940, but there is no doubt that Yamamoto was already thinking of the powerful U.S. fleet in Pearl Harbor. But they all agreed it must remain an impossible dream. Now Yamamoto, 'the father of Japanese aviation', who had believed ever since he was at Harvard that future naval wars would be decided by air power, was beginning to evolve a specific scheme for a surprise full-scale air attack which might make the impossible possible.

Admiral Shigeru Fukudome, the last survivor of the high-ranking officers who planned Pearl Harbor, had been with Yamamoto since the start of the European war. In November 1939 he was transferred from command of the flagship *Nagato*, promoted to rear-admiral, and placed on special duty with Yamamoto. Shortly afterwards he became his chief of staff.

As Yamamoto did not mention the matter again, Fukudome took the view that it was just a passing thought. Obviously the scheme was too wild-cat and inoperable to consider further.

Then, six months later, something happened in the European war which made Yamamoto's interest flare up again. In November 1940 the Royal Navy made an attack on the Italian fleet anchored at their base at Taranto. Twenty-one planes from carriers of the British Mediterranean Fleet sank three Italian battleships in a night attack. Their loss for these great prizes was only two planes.

Yamamoto called for urgent reports from the Japanese naval attachés in Rome and London. He closely studied details of the successful attack on the Italian battleships in the enclosed harbour of Taranto.

The reports revealed one vital fact. The depth of the water in Taranto harbour was forty-two feet or less. This had always been considered too shallow for aerial torpedoes. Now the British naval attacks on the Italian fleet disproved this. Aerial torpedoes could be rigged to run through in shallow water.

Yamamoto gazed at the reports for a long time. If the British could sink ships at such a depth, why not repeat this type of attack on a much bigger scale? For the depth of water in Pearl Harbor was—forty-five feet.

The reports from London and Rome revealed that in the successful Taranto attack the Royal Navy's Fleet Air Arm had used special torpedoes because conventional torpedoes were useless in shallow water. These special torpedoes had been fitted with wooden fins so they would run straight and not 'porpoise' in shallow waters.

The importance of the British attack was not lost on the U.S. navy either. Navy Secretary Frank Knox sent Army Secretary Henry L. Stimson a memorandum which said:

The success of the British aerial torpedo attack against ships at anchor suggests that precautionary measures be taken immediately to protect Pearl Harbor against a surprise attack in the event of war between the United States and Japan. The greatest danger will come from the aerial torpedo. The highest priority must be given to getting more interceptor planes, A.A. guns and additional radar equipment.

Stimson agreed and warned the Hawaiian command to strengthen itself against possible surprise air attack.

A month later, just before Christmas 1940, Admiral Husband E. Kimmel, commander of the U.S. fleet, replied, 'Anti-torpedo nets at Pearl Harbor would restrict boat traffic by narrowing the channel.' By this decision he doomed most of his big battleships.

In the same week that Kimmel rejected the safety precaution of torpedo nets Fukudome was pacing the deck of the flagship *Nagato* with Yamamoto discussing the British air attack. Yamamoto suddenly turned to him and said, 'An air attack on Pearl Harbor might be possible now, especially as our air training has turned out so successfully.' This was the first time Yamamoto had mentioned openly to anyone the specific idea of a surprise attack on the U.S. Pacific Fleet.

At that moment he decided to turn the idea into reality. Yamamoto said to Fukudome, 'Get me a senior flying officer whose past career had not influenced him in favour of conventional operations. I want him to study this fleet aerial torpedo problem in all its aspects. Keep this matter a secret from all the other fleet staff officers.'

Fukudome chose Rear-Admiral Takijuro Ohnishi, one of the navy's foremost flyers, who at the end of the war was to become the organizer of the first *kamikaze*—suicide units. As chief of staff of the 11th Air Fleet of shore-based bombers, he was frustrated because his own planes had not enough range to deliver an attack on Hawaii from Japanese bases in the Marshalls. It was a round trip of 4,000 miles.

Yamamoto knew Ohnishi well. He had only been a short time on the naval staff and when Yamamoto entrusted him with the first-stage planning of Operation Hawaii he was certain that his approach would not be hampered by conventional operational thinking.

He confidently outlined his plan to Ohnishi. He wanted to strike a crippling blow at the U.S. Pacific Fleet, simultaneous with the launching of the southern operations to capture the oil areas. Ohnishi listened, outwardly impassive, but inwardly astonished and excited.

At first only these three knew the secret. But as the planning became more detailed Ohnishi asked permission to consult Commander

Minoru Genda, an experienced air staff officer who shared Yamamoto's belief in the supremacy of naval air power. The more important fact was that he had just arrived back in Japan after serving
as assistant naval air attaché for two years in London. In this
capacity he had sent the reports on the Taranto operation. Being an
expert on this attack, he was at once in favour of the Pearl Harbor
plan.

Before he was posted to London he had been a fighter pilot whose
skill and daring in China had won his unit the nickname of the
'Genda Circus'. Then as air operations officer in the Shanghai area
in 1937 he had introduced new methods of mass long-range operations by fighter aircraft.

The secret planners, from Yamamoto to Genda, realized that
Japan was not short of carriers for such an operation. The carrier
flagship, the 36,000-ton twenty-eight-knot *Akagi*, was one of the
largest and most formidable carriers in the world. In fact it was this
spectacular carrier which had originally shown the Americans the
future potential of carrier warfare. She had been laid down in 1920
at Kure naval yard as a 42,000-ton battle cruiser. Three years later,
she was converted to a first-line carrier. Her only drawback was
that, although she was larger than the *Lexington* and *Saratoga*, she
carried only sixty planes.

Her sister ship, *Kaga*, displaced 35,000 tons but had a speed of
only twenty-three knots. When first built, she was one of the strangest
looking warships ever to sail the seas, with 300-foot-high funnels on
each side of her deck.

In the later thirties both *Akagi* and *Kaga* were modernized. *Kaga*
lost her tall funnels for more conventional aircraft carrier island
superstructures, and her speed was raised up to *Akagi*'s twenty-eight
to thirty knots.

There were also two smaller 17,500-ton carriers, *Hiryu* and *Soryu*.
The commissioning of the new 30,000-ton *Zuikaku* and *Shokaku* in
August 1941 would raise the number of Japanese fleet carriers from
four to six.

Genda's view was that all six must be used in this operation. He
also made two other points:

1. Special care must be taken to select only the most competent
commanders and the best-trained flyers.
2. Complete secrecy must be maintained before the attack.

That was the chief worry. Could they manage to keep it completely secret? If not, the Japanese fleet might meet a surprise counterattack. 'And there were many spies in Japan that year,' commented Admiral Fukudome cryptically.

But it was no use beginning preparation for this great gamble without information. Messages were sent to Japanese consuls on the west coast of America, and in the Philippines and Hawaii, asking for reports on the movements of American ships. This move was in itself dangerous. Widespread espionage always carried the risk of a breach of security. Such a breach nearly gave away Yamamoto's plan at the very beginning. Yet when it leaked out in a roundabout way the scheme seemed so incredible that it was either ignored or firmly disbelieved.

In January 1941, just after Yamamoto had ordered a full study plan of Pearl Harbor, a Japanese interpreter employed by the Peruvian Legation in Tokyo, in a moment of drunken patriotic indiscretion, exclaimed at a diplomatic party, 'The American fleet will disappear!'

Peru's alert Minister to Japan, Mr Ricardo Rivera-Schreiber, gently questioned him about where the attack would come. At San Diego? No. San Francisco? No. South Pacific? No. Then, pulling himself together, the Japanese interpreter became suddenly silent, bowed and left.

Schreiber pondered his remark and said, 'By a process of elimination I decided that Pearl Harbor must be the spot. On 27 January I called on the United States Ambassador in Japan, Joseph C. Grew, and told him my findings and conclusions.'

The same day Grew, also a diligent diplomat, sent this message to Washington:

> The Peruvian Minister has informed a member of my staff that he has heard from many sources, including a Japanese source, that in the event of trouble breaking out between the U.S. and Japan the Japanese intend to make a surprise attack against Pearl Harbor with all their strength and employing all their equipment. The Peruvian Minister considered the rumours fantastic but he considered them of sufficient importance to convey all this.

Grew's message was relayed to Admiral Kimmel with this comment: 'The Division of Naval Intelligence places no credence in these rumours. Furthermore based on known data regarding the present disposition and deployment of Japanese naval and army forces no move against Pearl Harbor appears imminent or planned for the foreseeable future.

In the same week Ohnishi and Genda's plans for the Pearl Harbor attack were beginning to take their first shape. But the great mystery still remains. How much did the Japanese interpreter know? Was it just an alcoholically inspired guess — or did he have any information? It is quite possible he knew just enough to be dangerous because all interpreters attached to foreign embassies were agents of the Japanese intelligence service.

Towards the end of April, Ohnishi called on Fukudome to discuss the detailed plan drawn up by him and Genda before it was submitted to Yamamoto. They again emphasized two points:

1. The technical problem — Pearl Harbor was so shallow that aerial torpedoes would strike the bottom if launched in the ordinary way.

2. The tactical problem — could a surprise attack be made successfully? Without the surprise element the operation could not be carried out.

After pointing out the difficulties, Ohnishi estimated Operation Hawaii had a sixty per cent chance of success. Fukudome was not so optimistic. Ever since Yamamato had put forward the idea months before on the quarter-deck of *Nagato*, he had thought it reckless. Now, having studied the detailed plan, his view was that it had only a forty per cent chance of success.

When massive opposition to the operation was put forward later by the Naval General Staff it was mainly based on Fukudome's views. He admitted freely later, 'Had I been entrusted with the study of the idea instead of Ohnishi I would certainly have recommended to Yamamoto that Operation Hawaii be abandoned.'

Although Ohnishi was not enthusiastic about the plan and Fuku-dome even less so, the report convinced Yamamoto that a carrier-borne air assault on Pearl Harbor was possible.

He was still opposed to war, but the more he realized it was coming the more he was determined to force through his Pearl Harbor plan. At the end of July he had a long talk with Vice-Admiral Mitsumi Shimizu, commander of the submarine fleet, who had been a cadet with him. Yamamoto said to him, 'The international situation is getting so bad it looks as though we can't avoid war. If we fight both Britain and America we will be defeated. I would like Britain to keep out of it and try to get them to act as a mediator but I know she cannot do it. If war comes, our only chance is to destroy the fleet in Pearl Harbor and send submarines to the west coast of America.'

But that was easier said than done. For instance, how was Yamamoto to obtain his information about the Pacific Fleet in Pearl Harbor before he made the attack? He did not have a great spy network, as some commentators have suggested. His network was practically non-existent, and as a result his information was scanty.

The American magazines, which contained so much totally false information about Japanese planes, supplied him and his staff with many useful facts about U.S. war preparations. These magazines and the American newspapers gave a fairly clear picture of the country's preparations, progress and expansion of military installations. Some of them were extremely detailed.

Following his orders, at the beginning of the year there was also a constant flood of reports from the naval attaché at the Japanese Embassy in Washington and other Japanese consular establishments along the west coast and the Philippines. Most interesting to him were those from the Honolulu consul, Nagao Kita.

It rapidly became evident that a full-time spy would be needed there to co-ordinate all this information and glean more. The navy soon provided Yamamoto with a man for the job. He was twenty-eight-year-old Ensign Takeo Yoshikawa, a policeman's son who had retired from active service in the Imperial Navy of 1936 because of ill-health. He had been transferred to Naval Intelligence in Tokyo and for four years had studied English. He was very alert and bright. While training he intercepted a shortwave radio broadcast in English from Australia regarding transport movements. He got a 'thank-you' letter from Hitler for this.

In 1940 he successfully took his English language examination and was appointed a junior Foreign Office official. This was his cover. After a year in the Foreign Office he was groomed for an intelligence assignment to Hawaii. He studied everything about the U.S. navy from *Jane's Fighting Ships* and *U.S. Naval Institute Proceedings* to the very informative American magazines.

Yoshikawa arrived in Honolulu in August 1941 under the cover name of Vice-Consul Morimura. His orders were to behave as a diplomat but report in code through the consul Kita on the day-to-day readiness of the American fleet in the base. Every week he sent an account of the movement of ships in Pearl Harbor.

In the same month—August—as Yoshikawa began to operate as a full-time spy in Honolulu, all the Japanese fleet commanders and senior staff officers went to Tokyo for war games. These were to perfect the final operational plans for a Pacific campaign. None of them knew they included Yamamoto's plan for a surprise attack on Pearl Harbor.

Two rooms were prepared instead of the usual one. In the big room the general strategy for naval war in the whole Pacific was played out for three days. In a smaller second room Yamamoto's plan for the Pearl Harbor attack was watched by a group of high-ranking staff officers. No one was very enthusiastic about it. The main worry was how many carriers they might lose. It was finally decided to 'sink' carriers by the roll of a dice. The dice showed two carriers lost. This may seem a strange procedure, but, the Japanese argue: Is there any definite way of deciding the changing, inexplicable fortunes that happen in battle?

Hardly anyone, and certainly no senior officer, came out in favour of the risky Pearl Harbor venture. The Naval General Staff had already completed a plan for the entire fleet to be employed in the southern invasions. When they heard of Yamamoto's scheme they were violently opposed to it.

After the war games, during the first two weeks in September, a war plans conference was held continuously at the Naval War College in Tokyo. All the admirals still remained convinced the proposal was far too risky.

The Chief of Naval Staff, Admiral Nagano, had wider doubts. 'Why stir up America?' he argued. He had spent a long time in the States and, like Yamamoto, had a healthy respect for the American fleet. He pleaded, 'Our principal teacher in respect of the necessity of emphasizing aircraft carriers has been the U.S. Navy. We had no other teacher in this respect. Let Japan concentrate on the old plan. Let us take the rich East Indian island of Java. Then when the U.S. Pacific Fleet approaches Japan to counter-attack it can be annihilated in home waters.' Unknown to him, of course, this dovetailed exactly into the American admirals' Plan Rainbow Five.

Yamamoto fully shared his respect for the U.S. Navy. That was why he was convinced his only chance was to smash it at once. He argued that if he waited for the Americans to sail out into the western Pacific their fleet might destroy him. Therefore he must destroy it first.

Japan had enough carriers to strike at Pearl Harbor at the same time as she made her southward advance towards Java. Why not bring off both operations before the Pacific Fleet could attack? If the United States were hit hard at Pearl Harbor she would not be able to recover herself before Japan occupied the Philippines, Malaya and the East Indies.

Nearly everyone was against him. The Naval General Staff said plainly that the plan was too much of a gamble. Its sole chance of success depended upon taking the American fleet by surprise. If this failed, the attack would be a major disaster. They also urged that the strength of the American, British and Dutch naval forces should not be underestimated.

Even Vice-Admiral Chuichi Nagumo, commander of the carriers which must spearhead any attack on Pearl Harbor, was opposed to the idea. He believed that his carriers should be used to help the conquest of the vital oil regions. He added a most prophetic warning that the largest carrier could be quickly and effectively disabled by a few bomb hits. Six months later at Midway he was proved to be right.

However, a younger carrier admiral, Rear-Admiral Tamon Yamaguchi, was an enthusiastic supporter of the Yamamoto plan. If the U.S. Pacific Fleet remained intact, he argued, how could Japan possibly exploit any success in the south?

Yamamoto himself undoubtedly would have called off the operation if he had known the real story of American counter-espionage. A year before Yoshikawa landed in Honolulu, America made a spectacular espionage break-through which was to prove to be her main instrument in winning the Pacific war.

In August 1940, Colonel William F. Friedman, after eighteen months' work, broke Japan's diplomatic code. From that date onwards American army and navy cryptographers began deciphering and translating Japan's most secret messages. The fact that the Americans could read the top-secret Japanese code was their greatest single asset in fighting the Pacific war. It was worth more to them than a fleet of carriers.

They knew the Japanese intentions and plans as soon as they were signalled to their own admirals. For instance, all Yoshikawa's messages which were signalled from the consulate in the diplomatic Purple code were read by the Americans.

There are various speculations about how the code was broken. Even today, more than twenty years after Pearl Harbor, the secret remains a secret. The Japanese still do not know how it was achieved and a handful of American officers who do know how it was done cannot—and will not—talk about it. One thing is certain. No Japanese officer ever revealed it.

This leaves several theories. One is that the British Admiralty made the first break-through. There is no confirmation of this but it must be remembered that they had had a long association with Japan and had been largely responsible for founding her navy. The nucleus of the Japanese naval code may easily have been given to them by the Royal Navy.

All secret codes used by the embassies of big powers are based on the ciphers used by their navies. If you can break the naval cipher you generally have the key to the secret diplomatic code. This means you can read the smallest secret message signalled from a Foreign Ministry to its ambassadors abroad.

Another legend behind the breaking of the code tells of a Japanese trawler which sank in the Bering Sea in May 1940. Aboard it was a Japanese naval officer who had been scouting the area between Russia and Alaska. His body was picked up by a Norwegian ship and in his pocket, wrapped in oilskin, was the key to the Japanese naval codes. This ship sailed to Alaska and handed the code book to the American authorities. Although the date fits in neatly with the time Colonel Friedman began his research, the story is undoubtedly untrue.

It is possible that the body of a Japanese naval officer was picked up. In those tense pre-war days there were many Japanese officers, disguised as fishermen, carrying out spying trips round the American coasts. But the code-book story must be untrue because the Japanese naval code book was specially designed to prevent this very situation. Even the lighter code books used in aircraft were made too big to fit in the widest pocket. They also had two-pound weights strung along them so that they would sink to the bottom of the sea if anything happened. They could only be captured if they sank with the ship. The Americans did obtain several code books in this way —but only after the war began.

There are two naval codes—soft and hard. The 'soft' code for inter-ship messages is largely a waste of time for any navy. Any trained cryptographer can read it. Before and after Pearl Harbor, at the Hashira anchorage in the Inland Sea, a staff of 120 Japanese navy cryptographers deciphered 200 American fleet messages every day. The 'hard' code, the one in which the top-secret messages were sent from the Navy Department to admirals, they could not read. Yet the Japanese should have had the advantage in code-breaking because there were at that time many more of them fluent in English than Americans who spoke Japanese.

The American navy unit for intercepting foreign radio signals, in the charge of Captain Laurence F. Safford, had a staff of 300. It had intercept stations at Washington, Florida, Maine, Maryland and Cavite in the Philippines. In order to decode Purple quickly a computer was needed, but there were only four in existence. The army and navy each had one in Washington. There was one in Cavite in the Philippines. The fourth was in Great Britain, given in return for the secrets of the German—or Japanese?—code at the outbreak of war. A fifth was being made for Pearl Harbor when Yamamoto attacked.

The Japanese themselves had only one decoding machine, and that was of crude design. It was made by an Imperial Navy technician named Tanabe and was used in Naval Headquarters in Tokyo.

The fact that Purple priority messages could be read was the best-kept secret of the war. The only people who saw them were the Secretary of War, the Chief of Staff, the Director of Military Intelligence, the Secretary of the Navy, the Chief of Naval Operations, the Chief of War Plans Divisions and the Director of Naval Intelligence, the Secretary of State—and, of course, the President. Each had a key to a locked pouch. They opened it and scanned the messages very quickly while a messenger stood by, waiting to take them away and destroy them.

It was this top-level secrecy that saved Yamamoto from disaster at Pearl Harbor. Only the smallest possible group of persons knew that the code was being read. If the secret had leaked out, the Japanese would at once have changed the cipher. Because of this, neither Admiral Kimmel nor any of the other senior officers in Pearl Harbor were given any of the information. They remained as unprepared as if the code had never been cracked.

Events now were beginning to move quickly. On 6 September

1941, while the naval staff was still arguing, a decision was made at the Imperial Conference to go to war with the United States when necessary. This meant war plans must immediately be shifted into top gear.

Throughout September there were intensive daily discussions between the Naval General Staff and Yamamoto's Combined Fleet staff officers about the overall operational plan in the coming war. The problem of the Hawaii operation was shelved as something about which no one could agree.

After seeing the result of the war games and hearing the naval staff objections, even the original planner, Admiral Ohnishi, backed out. He came to see Fukudome and said he now agreed with him that the Hawaii operation was too risky. He asked to see Yamamoto to suggest he gave up the whole idea.

Senior carrier commander Vice-Admiral Nagumo, another leading opponent of the Hawaii Plan, agreed with him. He sent his chief of staff, Rear-Admiral Ryunosuke Kusaka, along with Ohnishi when he called on Yamamoto aboard the flagship *Nagato*. There they both earnestly advised the admiral to give up the idea. Yamamoto refused to hear of it.

Not everyone was pessimistic. Some planning officers, fired by Yamamoto's enthusiasm, wanted an amphibious force to seize Pearl Harbor and occupy Oahu. This led to further arguments with the Naval General Staff. Deputy Chief Vice-Admiral Seiishi Ito pointed out that all Japan's tankers and transports were needed for the southern invasion. They could not be spared for such a risky double operation.

Yamamoto agreed with him. He decided no landing on the island of Oahu should be attempted, as it would be impossible to release the landing craft within less than a month after the southern operations. This would be too long an interval after the Pearl Harbor air attack. The Americans would have had time to recover and the slow speed of the convoy would make the initial landings very vulnerable to air and sea attack. Also, landings so far away in the Pacific would mean an insuperable supply problem.

This did not mean he was not pushing ahead with his preparations for the air attack, completely ignoring pessimistic opposition from the Naval General Staff. His final plan called for torpedo attacks against the ships anchored in Pearl Harbor. If successful, this would be the most effective way of putting the U.S. fleet out of action for a long period. Two great obstacles faced him when he considered this plan:

1. Pearl Harbor was narrow and shallow.
2. It was probably equipped with torpedo nets.

To overcome the first problem, stabilizers would have to be attached to the torpedoes and they must be launched from an extremely low altitude, which meant well-trained, brave pilots. These he knew he had. From the naval ordnance factories he ordered 1,000-lb. torpedoes on the British model, with specially constructed wooden fins, which would run straight when they hit the water.

But a torpedo attack could not be a guaranteed success unless he was sure that the ships had no torpedo nets. Yoshikawa was not able to establish this but he sent a message saying that the battleships were moored in pairs. This would make torpedo attacks against the inboard ships ineffective. As a result of this message from Honolulu, Yamamoto adapted bombs from 16-inch armour-piercing battleship shells. They could drop them on the decks of ships which torpedo bombers could not reach.

Another problem was the route the carriers were to take. There were three choices:

1. The northern route. The Japanese carriers had a short cruising range and would have to be refuelled on the way to Hawaii. Winter storms in the North Pacific would make this difficult, especially for smaller escort vessels like destroyers, which would have to refuel twice at sea on the way.
2. A central Pacific route passing south of Midway to Oahu.
3. The southern route through the Marshalls.

The last two courses would take the carriers through calm waters, and fuelling would be easier. On the other hand, the risk of detection by passing merchant ships would be much greater. These routes would also bring them within range of American patrol planes based on Wake, Midway, Palmyra and Johnston Islands.

Yamamoto finally decided to use the northern passage between the Aleutians and Midway. There were many cogent reasons for this:

In those icy unfriendly waters there was not much chance of encountering foreign merchantmen. Destroyers could be sent ahead and if they ran into any commercial vessels the carriers and escorting warships could quickly change course to avoid detection. If the seas proved too rough for refuelling the destroyers would have to be left behind.

On 13 September the staff study, still containing the possibility of two carriers being sunk, was issued by Yamamoto as Combined Fleet Secret Order No. 1. Two days later Field-Marshal Hajime Sugiyama, Chief of the Army General Staff, flew to Kure on the Inland Sea to meet Yamamoto, who assured him the Pearl Harbor victory over the Americans must help the army situation. As it was purely a naval operation which would not involve troops in any way, Sugiyama raised no objection to it.

On 24 September Tokyo requested Honolulu to divide Pearl Harbor into five areas. Future reports would make reference to these areas. Tokyo was especially interested in the location of battleships, carriers and destroyers. The Japanese consul in Honolulu was also ordered to report exactly where each ship in harbour was anchored or moored within these areas.

Even though Yoshikawa's frequent messages were read in Washington no one suspected the slightest danger to Pearl Harbor. The reason was that other Japanese consulates, in Vancouver, Portland, San Diego, San Francisco, Manila and Panama, supplied as much detailed information as Honolulu. No one read any particular danger to ships anchored in Pearl Harbor. This was part of Yamamoto's cover plan.

Yoshikawa was now working very hard collecting information. He went swimming to get information on beach gradients and the height of tides. He was not so ill advised as to take pictures or sketch. He memorized everything and wrote it down when he got home.

In the daytime he wandered through Pearl City. Most evenings he spent in a Japanese restaurant, the Shuncho-ro, which had an excellent view of the harbour. Often he stayed there until dawn watching which ships sailed out. He used to strike up conversations with American sailors in bars. He cautiously tried to obtain information from Nisei girls who entertained American sailors. His first great disappointment came when he made tentative attempts to sound out these girls and other Hawaiian-born Japanese. To his astonishment he discovered they were fanatically loyal to the United States.

Even when Yoshikawa was asked to report three times a week, instead of weekly, still no American suspicions were aroused. Because of the shortage of Japanese translators his messages in answer to the Tokyo requests were not translated until two weeks later. Although Purple had priority, there was always a backlog of messages.

There was also the high degree of complacency about the situation in both Pearl Harbor and Washington. When Commander Alwin P. Kramer, a naval expert in Purple, received some of Yoshikawa's messages he marked one with an asterisk remarking on the zeal and efficiency with which the Japanese collected detail. Nor did Admiral Stark think it necessary to forward the substance of Yoshikawa's messages to Admiral Kimmel.

Meanwhile Yamamoto was putting the finishing touches to his First War Plan. His most urgent problem was the training of skilled pilots for the operation. In September he selected Kagoshima Bay on the southernmost tip of Kyushu for the principal flying training ground, as it bore a very close relationship to the narrow confines of Pearl Harbor. Hundreds of planes dived low over the Shiro Mountains into the Iwasaki Valley. Then they skimmed the waters of the bay, releasing torpedoes. Four times a day they also had to practise carrier take-offs and landings. Another constant feature of their training was to make them fly out to sea and find their way back just above the waves. This exercise would help stray planes to return to the carriers by flying too low to be molested by American fighters.

Every pilot made more than fifty flights. And during the thousands of flights few accidents occurred. The local residents, completely unaware of their purpose, called these practice flights the 'Navy Circus'. The pilots had no more inkling than anyone else of what their final mission would be—if there were to be a mission. For although this intensive training was going on, the naval staff still doubted if Operation Hawaii would succeed—and how much would be lost if it failed!

The Naval General Staff gave Yamamoto five main objections to the plan:

1. Success depended solely upon surprise. It was a large-scale operation employing sixty ships. They would have to be dispatched a month before the outbreak of war and were likely to attract attention. The intelligence networks of Great Britain, the United

States and Russia were believed to have been greatly extended. The Naval General Staff doubted if secrecy could be maintained.

2. They did not agree that the Americans would make straight for Japan at the outbreak of war. They estimated that they would first establish advance bases in the Marshall Islands and then attempt island-hopping strategy. This meant Operation Hawaii was not so vital that it must be executed regardless of risk. If it were not carried out the Japanese would have time to concentrate all their strength in a decisive engagement for which they had long trained. It would be wiser to seek this battle in familiar waters.

3. Almost all naval vessels participating in the Hawaii operation would have to be refuelled at sea *en route*—the destroyers at least twice. Weather statistics showed that on only seven days of the month were conditions suitable for refuelling at sea in the North Pacific. If refuelling proved impossible, Hawaii would fail and all ships involved would have been uselessly diverted from other planned operations. One hitch could lead to another. If refuelling at sea met with difficulties the radio would have to be used, forfeiting secrecy. (This actually happened later, in the battle of Midway.)

4. The Radio Intelligence section of the Naval General Staff knew that the American daily air patrol had been extended to 600 miles from Oahu. This meant the task force would probably be spotted by American planes. Since the carriers would have to sail to within 200 miles of Pearl Harbor before launching their attacks there was a considerable risk of a counter-attack.

5. Any hint that this plan was in operation must at once wreck the negotiations then going on between the United States and Japan.

For the navy had not given up all hope of successful negotiations. Admiral Nagano, Chief of the Naval General Staff, had great faith in his close friend, Admiral Kichisaburo Nomura, who had been sent in January 1941 as joint ambassador to Washington to try and iron out the differences over oil and Indo-China. In the middle of October Nagano still had hopes that Nomura, who had an American wife, would be able to break the stalemate. He repeatedly told Yamamoto, 'Nomura is a great fellow. He will succeed.'

Of course not every naval officer was against war. The Japanese jingoistic attitude was well expressed by Captain Hideo Hiraide, Director of Naval Intelligence, who said on 17 October, the day Tojo became Prime Minister:

> America, feeling her insecurity, is carrying out naval expansion on a large scale. But at the moment America is unable to carry out naval operations in both the Atlantic and Pacific simultaneously. The Imperial navy is prepared for the worst and has completed all necessary preparations. In fact, the Imperial navy is itching for action when needed.

One action it did not seem to be itching for was Pearl Harbor. Opposition to this plan, apart from Admiral Yamaguchi, was almost total. Even Admiral Nagumo, the carrier commander, remained as half-hearted as ever.

At the end of October, when he received the naval staff's five detailed objections to his plan, Yamamoto lost patience with them. He sent his operations officer, Rear-Admiral Kamahito Kuroshima, to Tokyo with a letter which said:

> The presence of the U.S. fleet in Hawaii is a dagger pointed at our throats. Should war be declared, the length and breadth of our southern operations would immediately be exposed to a serious threat on its flank.
>
> The Hawaii operation is absolutely indispensable. Unless it is carried out Admiral Yamamoto has no confidence that he can fulfil his assigned responsibility. The numerous difficulties of this operation do not make it impossible. Weather conditions worry us most but as there are seven days in a month when refuelling at sea is possible the chance of success is by no means small. If good fortune is bestowed upon us we will be assured of success.
>
> Should the Hawaii operation by chance end in failure, that would merely imply that fortune is not on our side. That should also be the time for definitely halting all operations.

He concluded, 'If this plan fails it will mean defeat in war.' Although the senior admirals were disturbed by this last sentence it helped to bolster their faith in Yamamoto. They felt he would never take the risk if he were not completely confident of success.

Yamamoto had warned his messenger not to return without obtaining permission. When the Naval General Staff still wavered Kuroshima telephoned Yamamoto aboard his flagship to report.

He replied, 'Tell them I will step down as Commander-in-Chief and take over the carriers to direct the attack personally.'

When Kuroshima came back from the telephone and delivered this message the staff officers, although visibly shaken, still would not budge. After another hour's argument Kuroshima went into another room and once again telephoned the Commander-in-Chief. He told him the officers were adamant that the carriers must be used to reinforce the attack on Java.

The telephone conversation was very brief. White-faced, Kuroshima came back to the half-dozen admirals sitting round the table and said tersely, 'I have the authority of the Commander-in-Chief to tell you if you do not agree to his plan he must resign from his position and retire into civilian life.'

It was an emotional moment. It was also the showdown. Yamamoto had put both his own career and the Japanese navy in the balance. One admiral with tears in his eyes said, 'This situation must go before Nagano, the Chief of Staff, at once.'

Yamamoto's emissary was taken to the office of Vice-Admiral Ito, the Deputy Chief of Staff. When he heard what had happened, he immediately stepped into Nagano's office without making any comment. While Kuroshima and the other officers waited tensely outside they could hear the murmur of voices. Then Admiral Nagano came out and, putting his arm round Kuroshima, said, 'I fully understand how Yamamoto feels. If he has that much confidence he must be allowed to carry on. I will approve his plan.'

It was a reluctant capitulation but Yamamoto had won. Kuroshima flew at once to the flagship in the Inland Sea with the order from Nagano approving the plan.

It was 3 November 1941. Only thirty-five days remained before the attack.

7

Off to Tankan Bay

YAMAMOTO wasted no time because he had none to waste. Next day a large crate was delivered to the carrier *Akagi*. It contained a mock-up of Pearl Harbor and the surrounding terrain.

All pilots were summoned by Commander Genda, now supervising flight training, into the gunroom of *Akagi*. He told them without preliminaries that they were preparing a plan to attack Pearl Harbor. This gave the answer to a problem which had been puzzling flyers for some weeks. They had repeatedly been ordered to make mock attacks on stationary objects instead of moving targets, which would have been normal in a naval battle. Now they saw the reason for this—ships at anchor in harbour.

Genda unrolled a map of Oahu and a more detailed one of Pearl Harbor. Even the most fatalistic patriotic pilot confessed to 'feeling a cold chill' as Genda in a level voice outlined the plan for the first time.

Speaking in his cold incisive tones, he told them that, if surprise were to be achieved, torpedo bombers must go in first. If not, the dive bombers would attack. Half-elated and half-fearful, the pilots listened as the brisk expressionless little commander began to go into details of the plan he had been so long helping to prepare.

Next day Yamamoto issued Operation Order No. 1 as a Top Secret document. It contained the outline of the initial operations including a surprise attack on Pearl Harbor.

It was dated 5 November. On this day the Pearl Harbor attack ceased to be just a staff officer's dream and became a reality. Dealing with it, Order No. 1 stated, 'In the East the American fleet will be destroyed. The American lines of operation and supply lines to the orient will be cut. Enemy forces will be intercepted and annihilated. Victories will be exploited to break the enemy's will to fight.'

Under the heading 'Preparation for the Outbreak of War', Operation Order No. 1 provided that, 'when the decision is made to complete overall preparations for operations an order will be issued establishing the approximate day—Y-Day—for the commencement of operations.' The order further provided that 'the time for the outbreak of war—X-Day—will be given in an Imperial Headquarters Order'.

Yamamoto was in a hurry. Two days later he issued the following order: 'The task force, keeping its movements strictly secret, shall assemble in Tankan Bay by 22 November for refuelling.' Tankan Bay—also called Hitokappu Bay and Tankappu-Wan—is in the Kuriles, a thousand miles from Hokkaido, Japan's northern island.

The army, which had minimum interest in Pearl Harbor, were anxious to start the war. They originally intended operations to begin on 1 December with a series of co-ordinated attacks. At the beginning of November, Yamamoto came to Tokyo to meet General Terauchi who was in charge of the southern operations against Singapore, Java, Burma and the Philippines. Yamamoto asked him if he would agree to an attack on the second Sunday in December instead of the first to give his fleet a little time to prepare.

Terauchi and the Imperial G.N.Q. agreed. It was decided to raise the curtain on the Pacific war with an assault on Hawaii at 8.30 a.m. on 7 December, Hawaiian time.

Sunday was chosen as a result of a message from Honolulu. A few days before Lieutenant-Commander Suguru Suzuki of the Japanese Imperial Navy, disguised as a steward on a merchant ship, called on Hawaiian Consul-General, Nagao Kita. He slipped a tiny ball of rice paper into Kita's hand containing ninety-seven questions. The key question was, 'What day would most ships be in Pearl Harbor?'

When the question was passed to him, Yoshikawa replied without hesitation. 'Sunday—Kimmel brings his fleet into Pearl Harbor every weekend.'

When Yamamoto set 7 December as X-Day he formally appointed Vice-Admiral Chuichi Nagumo as commander of the Pearl Harbor striking force. He had a task force of twenty-three warships including six aircraft carriers, *Akagi*, *Kaga*, *Soryu*, *Hiryu*, *Zuikaku* and *Shokaku*. Protecting these carriers were the old but modernized battleships, the 31,000-ton *Hiei* and *Kirishima*, two 12,000-ton fast cruisers, *Tone* and *Chikuma*, one light cruiser and nine of the newest destroyers.

Aboard the six carriers scheduled for the operation were 423 planes. Thirty were for patrol over the fleet. Forty were held in reserve and 353 were to attack Oahu. This group consisted of 100 Kates, loaded with 16-inch shells for high-level bombing, 40 Kates for torpedo bombing, 131 Val dive bombers and 79 Zero fighters. Cruisers and battleships also provided a number of float planes for reconnaissance and to aid the combat air patrol.

On 10 November Admiral Nagumo issued his first orders from his carrier flagship *Akagi* anchored in the Inland Sea. On the same day the new Combined Fleet Chief of Staff, Admiral Matomi Ugaki, who had succeeded Fukudome, now posted to Naval Head-quarters, gave the flag officers a rousing patriotic do-or-die speech in which he said:

A gigantic fleet has massed at Pearl Harbor. This fleet will be utterly crushed at one blow at the very beginning of our hos-tilities. Should these plans fail at any stage our navy will suffer the wretched fate of never being able to rise again.

The success of our surprise attack on Pearl Harbor will prove to be the Waterloo of the war to follow. For this reason the Imperial navy is massing the cream of its strength in ships and planes to ensure success.

It is clear that America's enormous heavy industry is being im-mediately converted to the manufacture of ships, planes and other war material. It will take several months for her manpower to be mobilized against us. If we ensure strategic supremacy at the very outset by attacking and seizing all key points at one blow while America is still unprepared we can swing the scales of later operations in our favour. Heaven will bear witness to the righteous-ness of our struggle.

Pearl Harbor Day was still nearly a month away, but on that note the first of Yamamoto's ships began to sail to the secret harbour in the Kuriles.   *del*   Nov. 1

The attack on Pearl Harbor really commenced on 10 November when twenty-seven of Japan's big submarines, the best in the world in those days, set off across the Pacific. While the air attack was made on Pearl Harbor, most of them were to encircle Oahu Island. They would also intercept American reinforcements and supplies from the west coast of Africa.

The navy counted heavily on the submarine force. They believed that even if Nagumo's attack failed, the submarine operation would do great damage to the U.S. fleet.

They could see no hitch arising here. The I-class were the finest submarines in the world and had the best crews. These great under-water cruisers had a displacement of 1,955 tons. They were 320 feet long and had a cruising range of 12,000 miles at fourteen knots. This meant they were capable of sailing to California and back without refuelling—a performance only paralleled by the atomic submarines of today. Even the smaller R.O. class of 500–1,000 tons could cruise to Hawaii and return on a single fuelling.

Eleven of the I-class submarines had small planes abaft their conning towers. This formidable advance force of twenty-seven sub-marines was under orders 'to transmit information to Nagumo's carriers and torpedo any ships that escaped air attack'.

Blockading Hawaii should be an easy task for these highly trained Japanese submarines. Submarine attacks could also be continued over a longer period than the air attacks and in the end they would inflict more damage.

The submarines began to leave Kure and Yokosuka, the Japanese naval bases, a week before Nagumo's first carrier was due to sail. While Nagumo took the northern course the submarines sailed along the southern route. Both forces maintained strict radio silence.

For four days the big submarines left in groups of three. But five I-class boats stayed behind. They were to transport Pearl Harbor's most secret weapon, known by the code name of Target A.—midget submarines.

The midget submarine was not a weapon produced overnight. The idea was first suggested by Captain Noriyoshi Yokou who had served in the Imperial Navy in the Russo–Japanese war. In the late 'twenties he started to study a way to counteract the slow submerged speed of the submarine which often allowed her targets to escape. The limited range of her torpedoes was also unsatisfactory. The answer to both of these problems seemed to be contained in the one-man submarine which he called Target A. It was a typical Japanese suicide weapon which would 'assure a hit by releasing a torpedo piloted by one man from a mother submarine'.

Target A first came to the notice of the Japanese naval staff early in 1933. Fleet Admiral Prince Fushimi, then Chief of the Naval General Staff, was interested in the idea but said he would give his approval only if he were assured that 'this weapon is not used for body-crashing'.

As this guarantee could not be given, the blueprint was placed in a pigeon-hole. Three years later, in 1936, an officer of the naval staff watched a small one-man underwater craft being used for fishing in Kyushu, Japan's southernmost island. Would an adaptation of this meet Naval Headquarters' requirements? It was manœuvrable and a man might be able to fire a torpedo from it and escape.

Experimental work began on midget submarines which were still broadly based on Captain Yokou's plan for 'human torpedoes'. The shape of the midget submarine was an exact enlarged replica of a torpedo with a small conning tower attached. A year after work had begun on them one was successfully constructed.

When Yamamoto began planning Pearl Harbor, midget submarines had become a feasible weapon forty-one feet long with a displacement of fifty tons. Propelled by electric batteries, they could cruise for eight hours at a slow speed of five knots.

They were secured to the mother submarine by four heavy clamps. The midgets also had an access hatch to the big I-class mother submarine and were connected to her by telephone. Three tenders, *Chitose*, *Mizuho* and *Nisshin*, were built for them.

In the spring of 1941, *Chitose* made the first successful test launching of a midget submarine. Following this, twenty midget submarines were built and were given intensive trials. The navy saw them as perhaps an important weapon. But how were they to use them? The original intention was to release them close to the enemy during a naval battle so that they could attack his warships in the confusion. Was any other use possible?

That summer, while Yamamoto was preparing his plans for Pearl Harbor, naval lieutenants Manji Iwasa and Keiyu Matsuo suggested using these small submarines for a surprise attack upon the outbreak of war. Their plan was still based on Captain Yokou's suicidal blueprint and they admitted the crews could not be rescued after they had launched their torpedoes.

When the idea was put up to Yamamoto as a possible further attack on Pearl Harbor, he said, 'If they go inside the bay they can never return. Such an entry is unnecessary.' He rejected the idea because he would not tolerate its suicidal aspect.

When the two young lieutenants pleaded to go on, he insisted the midgets' range be improved and plans drawn up for their recovery by mother ships after they had attacked. Yamamoto's main objection was that once the midgets had completed their attacks inside Pearl Harbor they did not have sufficient cruising range to return to a safe point outside. This meant they could not be picked up by the big submarines.

Following his objections, the two officers spent months working out a method of recovering the little submarines. In the early autumn they petitioned Yamamoto to reconsider their scheme. The improved midgets now had a cruising range of up to 175 miles and could now do a fifty-minute underwater run of eighteen miles at twenty knots. This gave them a much better chance of being rescued by the bigger submarines. Yamamoto decided to include them in the Pearl Harbor attack.

These two-man submarines, now called the Special Naval Attack Unit, were manned by volunteers led by Lieutenant Iwasa who had helped to think up the idea. The nine other volunteers selected for the Pearl Harbor attack were Lieutenants Furuno and Yokoyama, Ensigns Hiro and Sakamaki, and Petty Officers Sasaki, Yokoyama, Ueda, Katayama and Inagaki.

This type of suicidal mission made a special appeal to the Japanese concept of courage. In spite of Yamamoto's preoccupation with their safety, none of the men who volunteered to man the midgets expected to return alive. They were determined to sink the American warships even if they had to ram them. Their spirit was the same as that of the later special attack—*kamikaze*—units.

On 13 November, a party given by the Japanese submarine fleet commander, Admiral Mitsumi Shimizu, was held aboard the mother ship *Katori*.

The plan of attack which had been agreed was that the midgets would slip into Pearl Harbor just before dawn and lie submerged all day while the planes attacked. They would then make a surprise attack after sunset when the Americans thought they were safe. They could then escape in the darkness.

Shimizu discovered the ten young volunteers were very excited when they came to the party. Their senior officer, now Commander Iwasa, explained to the admiral, 'None of us feel we will get back alive. Let us attack either during or just after the carrier attacks.'

At first Shimizu would not hear of it, but Iwasa persisted, saying, 'After such a long trying voyage we will be impatient to attack. It will be too hard a test to keep us waiting for twelve hours until nightfall. Some of us might become so excited we will give the game away.'

At last Shimizu agreed, saying that each midget commander, once inside the harbour, could attack according to his own judgment and local conditions. If he wanted to attack at the same time as the planes, he could.

This was the spirit when just before dusk on 18 November five large submarines, *I–16, I–18, I–20, I–22* and *I–24*, left Kure naval base under the maximum secrecy and headed for the Pacific. Each carried on board the secret weapon Target A stored in a large tube on deck. Commanding this Special Attack Unit was Captain Hanku Sasaki, Japan's leading torpedo expert.

As the last I-class submarines sailed, surface groups began to move out of the Inland Sea in small sections so as not to arouse any suspicion.

Although the special torpedoes had been rushed into production in mid-September they had not all been delivered when the carriers were ready to sail. Yamamoto ordered the carrier *Kaga* to stay behind until the last moment to load the remainder of the special wooden-fin torpedoes. When she sailed for Tankan Bay, aboard her were scores of naval technicians who worked day and night getting the last torpedoes ready for distribution to the other carriers.

The most unwarlike attribute of this grim grey fleet was their names. With typical Japanese unpredictability the four old carriers of the Pearl Harbor Attack Force had poetic names, like *Akagi* (Red Castle), *Kaga* (Increased Joy), *Soryu* (Green Dragon) and *Hiryu* (Flying Dragon).

The newest carriers, 826 feet long, were *Shokaku* (Soaring Crane) and *Zuikaku* (Happy Crane). The destroyers had even more romantic names like *Kasumi* (Mist of Flowers), *Shiranuhi* (Phosphorescent Foam) and *Tanikaze* (Valley Wind).

Although these prettily named ships were now sailing ready for their secret attack, Yamamoto was still short of one piece of basic information: Did the American warships have torpedo nets to protect them from torpedo-carrying planes? Yoshikawa still could not answer the torpedo-net question nor say if the big American carriers would be in port.

To disguise the movements of submarines and surface ships, the battleships in the Inland Sea stepped up their radio communications. The Inland Sea radio was crowded with fake messages which were picked up, as they were intended to be, by the American monitoring services. Commanders received false war plans for Chinese targets. These were changed at the last moment to bring them into the southeast invasions. This was the start of Yamamoto's deception plan. It worked well.

Working from the false traffic set up by Yamamoto, American intelligence advised Kimmel and Washington that traffic analysis for the past few days indicated that all known carriers were still in the Inland Sea. Radio intelligence monitoring which submitted a daily report to the Fleet Intelligence Officer, Commander Layton at Pearl Harbor, was reassuring, giving no hint of trouble.

In addition to the mass of fake naval radio messages, other deception plans were put into operation to give the impression that the fleet was still in Japanese waters. Large parties of sailors from Yokosuka Naval Barracks were sent every day to Tokyo on sightseeing tours.

Foreign observers, noting that the city was swarming with sailors, drew the obvious conclusion that the fleet was not only still in Japan, but half its crews were on leave in Tokyo. The Japanese liner *Tatsuta Maru* left Yokohama bound for Honolulu. She returned to Japan only when her captain received news of Pearl Harbor.

Although American listeners did not notice any slackening off in Japanese naval radio traffic because of Yamamoto's deception plan, Pacific Fleet intelligence officers at Pearl Harbor did notice that the call signs of two carrier divisions went off the air.

This established to their own satisfaction that the Japanese high seas fleet was on the move, for the absence of normal radio traffic indicated that radio silence had been imposed on Japanese warships. Commander Layton said, 'Never in the history of Japanese naval communications had there been such a complete absence of messages to and from carriers.' Even the unworried command at Pearl Harbor began to wonder a little about the mysterious radio silence. When Kimmel asked Layton where the Japanese carriers were he was told, 'I think they are in home waters—frankly I don't know where they are.'

Kimmel smiled as he said, 'Do you mean to say they could appear round Diamond Head and you wouldn't know it?' Layton replied demurely, 'I hope they would be sighted before that.'

While Kimmel and his officers held these bantering conversations, Admiral Nagumo's fleet ploughed on stealthily through the North

Pacific, maintaining strict radio silence, guarded by destroyers which steamed ahead to scan every yard of the turbulent ocean. By 22 November they were all in Tankan Bay in Etorofu, the biggest of the Kuriles.

The Kuriles—also called the Chrisima Islands—consist of sixteen islands. The southern islands, including Etorofu, are sparsely populated. Scores of walrus and seals were sprawling on the beaches when the carriers anchored in Tankan Bay.

When the pilots crowded the carrier decks for their first glimpse of land all they saw was a signal station, a tiny concrete pier and a group of fishermen's huts. There was also a small factory for canning the abundant salmon and salmon trout found there. The snow-covered hills protected the ships against both the howling winds from the North Pole and unwanted observation. It was the perfect secret hideout for the big fleet.

Stacked by the little concrete pier were thousands of oil drums that had been sent on ahead. Working parties began to take this extra oil aboard as a precaution in case the sea proved too rough for refuelling from tankers. Half-frozen Japanese sailors worked all daylight hours in lashing northern blizzards to haul the drums on to the carriers. Containers were even lashed onto the carriers' decks.

While sailors worked loading fuel, the carrier pilots studied the latest intelligence reports and debated the best method of attack. Someone asked what they should do if their fuel tanks were hit and they could not get back to the carriers. A fighter flight leader, Fusata Iida, said, 'There is only one course open to a Japanese warrior if that happens. He must pick the best American target and crash into it.' After a short silence, everyone agreed that was the only thing to do.

Towards the end of November, both sides knew the negotiations between the United States and Japan were doomed as neither government would retreat an inch. They were only bargaining for time. Through Purple, Washington knew that the Japanese Foreign Office had set the end of November as a deadline for the conclusion of the talks, after which 'things are automatically going to happen'.

Deciphered Japanese messages revealed that the Japanese now regarded the conversations as hopeless. The ambassadors, however, were ordered still to pretend to negotiate 'to prevent the United States from becoming unduly suspicious'.

Washington expected a Japanese attack on the Philippines, Malaya or Borneo. Why not Pearl Harbor? American officials were so hypnotized by Japan's obvious preparations to move southward they never dreamed she might strike elsewhere as well.

They agreed with the original Japanese naval staff plan that all carriers must sail to support the south-east Asian landings.

On 24 November, when Nagumo's ships were refuelling in Tankan Bay, Admiral Kimmel was advised that a favourable outcome of the negotiations with Japan was very doubtful and 'movements of the Japanese naval and military forces indicate in our opinion a surprise aggressive movement in any direction including an attack on the Philippines or Guam as a possibility'.

Next day, 25 November, Yamamoto issued his sailing orders:

1. The task force keeping its movements strictly secret will leave Tankan Bay on the morning of 26 November and advance to a standby position on the afternoon of 3 December speedily to complete refuelling.

2. The task force keeping its movements strictly secret and maintaining close guard against submarines and aircraft will advance into Hawaiian waters. Upon the very opening of hostilities it will attack the main force of the U.S. fleet in Hawaii and deal it a mortal blow. The first air raid is planned for the dawn of X-day—exact date to be given by later order.

3. Upon completion of the air raid the task force, keeping close co-ordination and guarding against the enemy's counter-attack, will speedily leave enemy waters and return to Japan.

4. Should negotiations with the United States prove successful, the task force shall hold itself in readiness forthwith to return and reassemble.

On 26 November, Admiral Kimmel received a despatch from the Navy Department which began: 'This despatch is to be considered a war warning.' The war message was based not so much on de-ciphered messages as on an American note demanding that Japan evacuate China and support the régime of Chiang Kai-shek. No one expected the Japanese to accept such demands. But as diplomatic talks were still going on Yamamoto, when he outlined his plan for attack, emphasized that it must only be launched should negotiations fail. Whether the attack went in at all was to be determined by the outcome of the diplomatic manœuvring going on in Washington.

It was 6 p.m. on 26 November when Nagumo's carriers sailed

from Tankan Bay in a dense fog. Even then the attack was not yet definite.

On the day they sailed from their secret hideout in the Kuriles in mist-shrouded darkness, the final decision for war was made at a conference between the cabinet and the military leaders. Not even Premier Tojo knew until that morning that Nagumo's ships had weighed anchor for Hawaii. The navy did not like to divulge its secret attack plan to the Prime Minister, who was an army man.

Even when Foreign Minister Shigenoru Togo asked when the war would start, because he said Japan must give notification of the commencement of hostilities through the usual procedure, Admiral Osami Nagano, Navy Chief of Staff, replied, 'We're going to make a surprise attack.'

Vice-Admiral Ito, Navy Vice Chief, added, 'We do not want to terminate negotiations until hostilities have begun—in order to achieve the maximum possible effect with the initial attack.' This remark so annoyed Shigenoru Togo he left the conference.

Although Nagano had approved Yamamoto's plan his was not the last word. As Chief of the Naval General Staff he was responsible to the throne for naval operations. Under the old Japanese constitution, the opening of hostilities was the prerogative of the Emperor alone.

So the two top naval and military leaders, Admiral Osami Nagano and Field Marshal Hajime Sugiyama, went to explain the plan to the Emperor. But the Emperor proved difficult. He would not give it the Imperial go-ahead by signing the rescript.

For months Emperor Hirohito had become very anxious about the way first Tojo and now the navy were behaving. He sent for Grand Chamberlain Marquis Kido and expressed his great concern. Ignoring Kido's own oft-stated view that war with the West was inevitable, he commanded him to arrange a gathering of the Jushin —the elder statesmen.

It was far too late. Nagumo was three days out from Tankan Bay when there gathered at the Palace Baron Wakatsuki, Prince Konoye, Admiral Okada, Baron Hiranuma, Admiral Yonai, and Generals Abe, Hayashi and Hirota.

They assembled at 9.30 a.m. to read an analysis of the international situation written by Tojo, Foreign Minister Togo, and other ministers. The Emperor entertained them to lunch and in the afternoon invited them to put forward their own views. Most of them elected for peace and advised moderation to the Emperor. The only ones who said war was the only course left open were two generals—Abe and Hayashi.

The senior elder statesman, Baron Wakatsuki, agreed with Yamamoto's views. He said he was not at all sure the country would be able to bear the burden of a long war. But these elder statesmen —unlike the revered Jushin of the Meiji era—had no more influence than the man in the street.

Even the Emperor's younger brother, Prince Takamatsu, could do nothing. Next day Takamatsu, himself a naval officer, requested an interview with the Emperor. He told the Mikado that resorting to force must at all costs be avoided. He was emphatic that the navy was not prepared for war.

This was perhaps the most ironic interview of all in that frantic fortnight before the curtain went up on war. Prince Takamatsu was also unaware that Nagumo's six carriers were already heading for Hawaii.

On 1 December the Imperial Conference finally decided on war with Britain, America and the Netherlands. At this meeting Admiral Ito climbed down a little from his previous position. He stated he had no objection to delivering in Washington the notification of the termination of the negotiations at 12.30 p.m., Washington time. He assured the worried Foreign Minister Togo this would leave a proper interval between the negotiation and the attack, which was due at 2 p.m. Washington time. This would in fact have given America one and a half hours' notice.

This was later altered after debate between senior admirals. Some said there must be complete surprise while obeying the civilized rules of warfare. Yamamoto belonged to that school of thought. Others looked to Togo's Port Arthur without-warning attack as a precedent. It was finally decided that an hour and a half was too long and dangerous an interval. It was agreed that at least half an hour should be allowed to elapse between the delivery of the declaration of war in Washington and the bombing of Pearl Harbor. This was mainly at Yamamoto's insistence.

The Emperor then signed the rescript. In spite of his personal misgivings there was nothing else he could do. The country was now irrevocably committed to war.

After signing the instrument of war the Emperor sent this message to Yamamoto: 'We, by ordering this despatch, delegate you to have

the responsibility of commanding the Combined Fleet. The respon-
sibilities of the Combined Fleet will be extremely heavy, and success
or failure in the matter involves the fate of the country. You have
made progress by urging the importance of fleet drill for many years
and you must be determined to meet our expectations by exalting
our force and authority throughout the world by annihilating the
enemy.'

Yamamoto replied: 'I was overwhelmingly impressed by the
gracious Imperial Rescript at the outbreak of the war and I shall
carry out the Emperor's great orders with reverence. The officers
and men of the Combined Fleet have sworn to do their utmost and
they will accomplish the aim of the despatch. They are determined
to accept and carry out the Emperor's commands.'

Absolute secrecy was of such utmost importance that only the
pilots and staff officers who had prepared the plan knew what was
ahead of them. It was not until the last provisions and oil had been
taken aboard and the fleet prepared to steam away from Tankan
Bay that their destination was known.

When they heard Yamamoto's battle order that the carriers were
'to advance into Hawaiian waters and upon the very opening of
hostilities attack the main force of the U.S. fleet in Hawaii', even
the normally impassive, well-disciplined Japanese sailors were
amazed—then exultant. One sailor called Kuramoto wrote in his
diary, 'Attack on Pearl Harbor—a dream come true! What will the
people at home think when they hear the news? Won't they be
excited? I see them clapping their hands and shouting with joy. We
will teach the Anglo-Saxon scoundrels a lesson!'

The Japanese ambassador in Washington, Kurusu, and his co-
ambassador, Admiral Nomura, were still continuing to negotiate
with the Americans and had no inkling of the Pearl Harbor attack.

After the decision had been made for war in Tokyo a message to
them in Washington said, 'Situation continues to be increasingly
critical. However, to prevent the United States becoming unduly
suspicious we have been advising the Press and others that though
there are wide differences between Japan and America the negotiations
are continuing.'

After that message both ambassadors knew something would
happen very soon. But when—and where? One of the Japanese
diplomats in Washington said to Ambassador Kurusu, 'The Government want to keep on negotiating. In the meantime we have a crisis

on hand and the army is champing at the bit—and you know the army!'

Kurusu laughed and replied, 'That's why I doubt if anything can be done.' Although he had not been officially informed he had strong suspicions he might be being used as a decoy.

He was right. Already the Japanese carriers were several days out from Tankan Bay. The man who did not even suspect their approach was Admiral Kimmel. The only way he could have learned about the approaching Japanese ships was by direct air reconnaissance. Yet even when he received the war warning on the day Nagumo left Tankan Bay, Admiral Kimmel did not institute long-range reconnaissance against possible air attacks on Pearl Harbor. It was not an oversight but a decision reached after lengthy consultation with his officers. This decision is all the more inexplicable as everyone knew war was coming.

Events still moved in the near-normal peacetime way at Pearl Harbor. On 28 November William F. Halsey sailed from there to deliver marine fighters to Guam and carry out continual searches up to 300 miles for signs of hostile ships. Before he left, Halsey in a lengthy conference with Admiral Kimmel asked him how he must behave if he met any Japanese forces. Kimmel replied, 'Use your common sense.'

Halsey, the most aggressive American admiral in the Pacific, said it was the best order he had ever received. If he found a single Japanese sampan he would sink it. But how was he going to find the sampans? He was sailing south-west for Guam in the wrong direction and had no hope of spotting Nagumo. In a way he was lucky. Although he would have alerted Pearl Harbor, the mighty fleet would have blown him out of the water.

On Friday, with less than forty-eight hours to go, Task Force Two, consisting of the carrier *Lexington*, three heavy cruisers and five destroyers, left Pearl Harbor to carry planes to Midway. Admiral J. H. Newton, who commanded this most valuable unit of the Pacific Fleet, was not shown the war warning.

That week Admiral William C. Hart, C.-in-C. U.S. Asiatic Fleet, sent a despatch to Naval Operations, with a copy to Admiral Kimmel, concerning the celebrated 'Winds code' to be employed in Tokyo news broadcasts. This was to advise when diplomatic relations were on the verge of being severed. '*Higashi no kaze ame*', 'East Wind Rain' meant war with the United States, Britain and the Netherlands.

If Japanese–Russian relations had been punctured, the message would be '*Kita no kaze kumori*', North Wind Cloudy. The American radio monitors in Hawaii listened twenty-four hours a day to monitor broadcasts employing this code.

They managed to pick one up. Captain Safford, the leading naval cryptographer, received a report that a naval radio operator had monitored an overseas news broadcast from station J.A.P. Tokyo. It said, '*Higashi no kaze ame*', East Wind Rain.

Captain Safford had no doubt this meant war. This was the tip-off which might have prevented the U.S. fleet being surprised at Pearl Harbor the way the Russians had been surprised at Port Arthur in 1904.

The wind message was correctly interpreted in Washington as meaning war. But war in Manila, Hong Kong, Singapore and Batavia —5,000 miles away from Pearl Harbor. It was passed to Admiral Harold R. Stark, Chief of Naval Operations, and nobody in the Navy Department saw fit to relay the news to Hawaii.

In Pearl Harbor no change was made in the state of readiness of naval aircraft. Half the Pacific Fleet aircraft were still on four hours' notice. No effort was made to keep warships at sea to intercept possible raiding forces approaching through the dangerous northern sector.

Yet a full-scale alert at Pearl Harbor twenty-four hours before Nagumo reached his launching position would have been picked up by his diligent radio interceptors aboard his flagship *Akagi*. It would have caused the Pearl Harbor carrier task force to turn back to Japan early on Saturday morning.

It did not happen because Yamamoto had imposed strict radio silence on his carriers and set up a spate of false signal traffic which entirely misled the unsuspecting Americans. His first bluff had succeeded.

8

Togo's Flag Flies Again

ON 1 December, when the Cabinet ratified Tojo's decision to start the war, Nagumo had been sailing towards Hawaii for five days. Next day, following the Emperor's reluctant agreement, the Imperial G.H.Q. issued a top-secret order that hostile action was to begin on 7 December, Hawaiian time.

Yamamoto aboard his flagship *Nagato* in the Inland Sea immediately broadcast the historic cryptic message, '*Nagata Yama nabore* —climb Mount Nagata'. This was a mountain in Formosa, the highest in Japanese territories.

When they received the message to 'climb the highest mountain' Nagumo's fleet darkened ship and went to standby stations. The war was about to begin.

American intelligence reports still insisted, 'Japanese major ship strength remains in home waters as well as the greatest proportion of the carriers.' A later report added, 'All Japanese surface radio calls of forces afloat change promptly at 0004 1 December. The last time they were changed was only a month ago. Previously calls were changed after six months or more.'

The summary stated: 'The fact that service calls lasted only one month indicates an additional progressive step in preparation for operations on a large scale.' But not at Pearl Harbor, of course.

The Japanese luck was holding. The Americans were taken in by the false radio messages and they did not meet a single ship or plane in the lonely, dangerous North Pacific. Japanese destroyers steamed several miles ahead with orders to sink at sight any American ships and board neutrals to prevent radio transmissions.

Also, as zero hour approached, Vice-Consul Morimura was busy picking up urgent last-minute information. He reported *Lexington*'s departure. Also on the day the *Lexington* sailed, American intelligence intercepted a radio telephone call between a person in Honolulu called Mori and someone in Japan. The Japanese was interested in the daily flights of aeroplanes, particularly large planes from Honolulu. He also wanted to know whether searchlights were being used —and how many ships were in Pearl Harbor.

Mysterious references were then made to various types of flowers. This was presumed to be a code to give information to an approaching Japanese attack force. Navy Intelligence did not regard the message itself as urgent. They sent it for further study by a Japanese linguist.

They did however trace a family called Mori. They were known to the navy and army Intelligence and were being investigated by the F.B.I. When they denied all knowledge of the call they were probably telling the truth. It presumably came from Vice-Consul Morimura who had perhaps shortened his name, or it may have been misheard by the American eavesdroppers. These frequent Tokyo requests concerning Honolulu and Manila, with demands for specific details forty-eight hours before Pearl Harbor, should have alerted them. Also interest was no longer being displayed in American seaports. The call from Mori to Japan with its suspicious flower code and its interest in ships and planes was aimed directly at Hawaii.

On Friday, as well as telephoning, the Honolulu consulate cabled to Tokyo, 'No barrage balloons sighted. Battleships are without crinolines. No indications of air or sea alert.' Morimura was getting reckless because either he knew the end was near or he was being severely pressed for details.

All this activity was regarded as a series of unimportant isolated incidents. In spite of being able to read Code Purple, every American commander from the President downwards was lulled by the heavy radio signal traffic in the Inland Sea and the reports of big Japanese southward troop movements. They had no doubt there were going to be large-scale operations. But these would be thousands of miles away in south-east Asia.

While the Americans in Pearl Harbor kept their happy illusions, Nagumo's six carriers steamed in parallel lines with the battleships *Kirishima* and *Hiei* astern. The heavy cruisers *Tone* and *Chikuma* protected them several miles away on either side.

As they sailed towards Hawaii, the gales and high seas became worse and even the great carriers pitched and rolled like dinghies. Signal flags were shredded to ribbons. Men were washed overboard but the fleet did not stop. It could not spare the time to search for drowning sailors in this fateful, split-second operation.

Then fog came down. Red-eyed lookouts peered through the damp grey blanket until they became dizzy but the fleet did not slacken speed. Held back by the slowness of the supply ships and the need for fuel economy, the force made its way slowly towards Hawaii at thirteen knots. But as it plunged on through the eerie silent fog, helmsmen had to keep their steering speed with hair-breadth exactness as there was a constant danger of collisions. However the fog had its advantages. It helped to hide the fleet.

Below decks pilots studied maps and the Pearl Harbor mock-ups until they knew Oahu better than most Hawaiians. Japanese secret intelligence—called A information—relayed news in code every few hours of the activities of the American fleet in Pearl Harbor. It now came mostly from the Honolulu consulate.

Aboard Admiral Chuichi Nagumo's carriers, as they fought their way through storm and fog, a nervous twenty-four-hour watch was kept in the radio rooms on transmissions from Hawaii. Had their secret leaked out? Lieutenant-Commander Ono, staff communications officer, ceaselessly monitored Hawaiian stations KGU and KGNB but the Americans obviously had no inkling of the coming attack. As the hostile armada approached, the Honolulu transmitters continued to chatter away in their usual peacetime manner.

As they crept nearer Hawaii, the carriers began intercepting messages from American patrol planes. Cryptographers aboard *Akagi* could read most of their 'soft' code messages or plot the planes' positions by radio bearings. They knew the number of patrol planes in the air at all times. No planes or ships were sighted. The Americans were patrolling south-west of Oahu—in the opposite direction from which the Japanese were approaching. Nagumo decided it was too risky to fly his own air patrols but posted double lookouts.

As Nagumo's carriers sailed towards their historic attack, the twenty-seven big Japanese submarines converged on Hawaii from the south in advance of the carriers to reconnoitre Hawaiian waters. That is why the submarines were named Advance Force.

Nagano and his Naval Headquarters planners were still gloomy about Yamamoto's plan. They still estimated there was only a fifty per cent chance of a successful attack by Nagumo's planes. That was why they considered it vital for the submarine force to launch underwater attacks at the same time as the air raids were made on Hawaii.

When they reached Hawaiian waters, the submarines floated on the sea at night. During the day they cruised submerged to periscope depth. When they were joined by the five midget-carrying submarines their final orders were:

(1) To watch the movements of the U.S. fleets round Pearl Harbor.

(2) To despatch Target A from their decks and observe the results.

(3) To attack U.S. warships, if any.

(4) To rescue crews of midget submarines and shot-down Japanese flyers.

On Friday night all the submarines took up scouting positions round Pearl Harbor. The nearest was eight miles from the harbour and the farthest a hundred miles away.

Three submarines were placed in a line a hundred miles ahead of Nagumo's carriers for the final dash towards Pearl Harbor. On the surface they could steam at twenty-three knots. If they sighted any planes or ships they were to submerge. As soon as it was safe to re-surface they would radio information to Nagumo's carriers.

Commented Admiral Fukudome, now Naval Headquarters Chief of Staff, 'No obstacles were encountered in the movements of any of the operational forces. The weather eventually turned out favourably and the secrecy of the operation was safely maintained by the Grace of Heaven. Although fear no longer existed that a change of plan would be necessary, there was one factor that we could not determine until the last moment. This was whether the U.S. fleet would be in Pearl Harbor at the time of the attack.'

The Japanese believed that four American carriers, *Yorktown*, *Hornet*, *Lexington* and *Enterprise*, were based at Hawaii at this time. In fact only *Lexington* and *Enterprise* were based there and they had left port as Nagumo approached. *Yorktown* and *Hornet* were in the Atlantic.

Yamamoto however did have correct information—presumably from a Japanese spy on the west coast—that *Saratoga* was in San Diego and would shortly rejoin the Pacific Fleet. This was his only piece of accurate information about the carriers.

There was still a great unsuspecting prize awaiting Nagumo's bombers. In the great U.S. naval base of Pearl Harbor were: eight battleships, two heavy cruisers, six light cruisers, twenty-nine destroyers, five submarines, one gunboat, eight destroyer-mine-layers, one minelayer, four destroyer-minesweepers, six mine-sweepers and twenty-four auxiliaries.

Luck was still with Nagumo's fleet. The day after Yamamoto sent his climb-the-highest-mountain message, the sea became calm and they were able to spend a whole day fuelling from tankers. When the last tanker had pumped oil aboard, Nagumo's carriers increased speed to twenty-six knots and raced through calm seas towards Pearl Harbor. That same morning Halsey with the *Enterprise* set sail from Wake Island to return to Oahu.

Saturday was a nerve-racking day for Nagumo. On the carriers' decks planes were lined up wing to wing, while maintenance crews swarmed over them giving them their final detailed checks. Early in the morning Imperial Headquarters in Tokyo broadcast the latest information from Pearl Harbor to the carriers. It was fairly accurate. Ensign Yoshikawa was doing his job up to the last minute. The Headquarters message said there were seven battleships and seven cruisers in Pearl Harbor but no carriers. Each pilot altered his information pad accordingly. But there were still twenty-four hours —time for them to enter port.

At one time Yamamoto had hoped that up to six carriers might be among the American ships to be trapped at Pearl Harbor. He now knew the *Saratoga* was on the west coast of the United States, but not knowing *Hornet* and *Yorktown* had been transferred to the Atlantic he still thought there should be at least three carriers in Pearl Harbor. On Saturday evening came another message from Tokyo: 'No carriers in Pearl Harbor, but there are eight battleships and fifteen cruisers.'

On Saturday night the nearest Japanese submarines out at sea from Pearl Harbor could see the neon lights on Waikiki Beach and hear radios playing dance music. The gunnery officer of *I–24*, who had once visited Hawaii during a training cruise, was especially interested. He stood on the deck of the giant submarine in the dark and pointed out various ways to get into the entrance of Pearl Harbor to Captain Sasaki commanding the midget submarines.

That evening one of the twenty-seven Japanese submarines now surrounding Pearl Harbor, *I–72*, raised its periscope at the mouth of the Lahaina anchorage. This deep anchorage was used for training. If the Pacific Fleet had been there it would have offered an easy target. But the *I–72* signalled, 'American fleet not in

Lahaina'. Where were the American carriers? Were the Japanese about to risk their necks and their carriers for practically nothing?

Admiral Nagumo's intelligence officer, Lieutenant-Commander Ono, collated the latest reports. Five of the eight American battleships had reached port the previous Saturday. There was one more which had remained in harbour all this time, perhaps in dry dock. The five ships which had arrived on the previous Saturday had been there a week. They might sail.

On the whereabouts of carriers, Ono's information was pessimistic. He now knew *Enterprise* had left harbour a week before accompanied by two battleships, two heavy cruisers and twelve destroyers. The two battleships had sailed back yesterday but *Enterprise* had not yet returned. He was hopeful she might return that day. He still felt that they stood a good chance of catching her early Sunday morning.

The carrier *Lexington* had left with five heavy cruisers on Friday. *Wasp* was known to be in the Atlantic. But where were *Yorktown* and *Hornet* which belonged to the Pacific Fleet? They must be somewhere in the area.

Nagumo's Chief of Staff, Admiral Kusaka, a leading expert on the U.S. Pacific Fleet, was now certain they had little chance of catching *Enterprise* or any other carriers. His view was that the American carriers would be unlikely to enter Pearl Harbor on a Saturday. They would stay at sea over the weekend. But for the same reason he did not think the battleships would leave over the weekend. All eight battleships would be in harbour the next day when they attacked.

But information was still coming in from the busy Honolulu consulate. Just before nine o'clock on Saturday night, Hawaii transmitted Ensign Yoshikawa's last message to Tokyo which read:

A Information 1800. Ships in harbour as of 6 December: nine battleships, three cruisers, three seaplane tenders, seventeen destroyers. In dock: four cruisers, three destroyers. All carriers and heavy cruisers at sea. *Enterprise* and *Lexington* have sailed from Pearl Harbor. No indication any change U.S. fleet. Oahu quiet.

That same evening, another very significant message arrived in Washington. It was the Japanese reply to the U.S. note which was intercepted by the Americans while being transmitted. Thirteen parts of a fourteen-part Japanese memorandum sent in Purple were intercepted, decoded and made ready for distribution by U.S. military intelligence by 9 p.m. That evening President Roosevelt despatched an earnest appeal to the Emperor of Japan for the preservation of peace in the Pacific which was ignored.

Late in the evening, Nagumo read Yoshikawa's message retransmitted from Tokyo in his operations room aboard *Akagi*. It ended, 'Imperial staff convinced of success.' Admiral Nagumo was not so convinced. One fact was clear: Kimmel had brought most of his fleet into harbour for the weekend as usual—except the carriers.

Unfortunately for him Tokyo's information did not contain the fact that one big American carrier, *Enterprise*, was temptingly near. At dawn on Saturday when she was 200 miles west of Oahu, Halsey flew off a number of his planes to land on Ford Island. They were to be caught by Nagumo's carrier planes at breakfast-time next day.

Admiral Nagumo called his officers into the operations room to give them this appraisal of the situation:

1. Enemy strength in the Hawaiian area consists of nine battleships, two carriers, about ten heavy and six light cruisers. The carriers and heavy cruisers seem to be at sea but the others are in harbour.

2. There is no indication the enemy has been alerted but that is no reason to relax our security.

3. Unless an unforeseen situation develops, our attack will be launched upon Pearl Harbor.

Then Commander Shibuya, staff officer in charge of submarine operations, explained to the officers aboard *Akagi* the plan for submarines. He told them about the big submarine screen and the plan for the midgets to penetrate Pearl Harbor during darkness before the attack. But no matter how good an opportunity might arise, all submarines had orders not to strike until the planes had done so.

This order probably saved the other American carrier, *Lexington*. That Saturday Admiral J. H. Newton's task force, which included *Lexington*, the heavy cruisers *Chicago*, *Portland* and *Astoria*, and five destroyers, was cruising near Midway.

A patrolling Japanese submarine the *I-74*, sister ship of the one which had reported no carriers in Lahaina, sighted the *Lexington*. But, obeying her orders, *I-74* did not attack. She trailed the unsuspecting *Lexington* all night. When dawn came, just as Nagumo's bombers were taking off and she would soon have been free to sink her, the sea was empty. She had lost the carrier during the night.

As the long Saturday evening drew on, Nagumo's flagship *Akagi* pitched and rolled in worsening weather while he sat with Admiral Kusaka, his chief of staff, and other officers, poring over his intelligence information. It was now certain beyond all doubt following Yoshikawa's last message that the American carriers were at sea —while all the battleships remained in harbour.

Should Nagumo go on? It was a very lonely moment for him. Such a decision must always be left to the commander at sea. No one—neither Yamamoto nor anyone else—could help him any longer. Theoretically he still could have abandoned the operation. In fact he had no choice but to carry out the attack as planned. The American battleships, although secondary to the carriers, were still a priority target. There also remained the faint possibility that some of the American carriers might have returned to Pearl Harbor by the time he launched his planes.

Just after nine o'clock when his striking force was 400 miles north of Pearl Harbor, he summoned all hands onto the flight decks. Thousands of officers and men stood at attention to hear Admiral Yamamoto's war message read out: 'The rise or fall of the Empire depends upon this battle. Everyone will do his duty to the utmost.' Again it was an echo of Togo—and Nelson.

Then Japanese sailors wept and cheered when a huge battle-flag broke on *Akagi*'s masthead. It was Admiral Togo's flag that had been run up on his flagship *Mikasa* thirty-six years earlier in the Straits of Tsushima before his victory over the Tsar's fleet. The hoisting of this flag was the idea of the former ensign who had fought with Togo in that battle and lost two of his fingers—Admiral Yamamoto.

Group commanders made patriotic speeches, there were choking cries of *banzai*. Everyone, even to the humblest stoker, was conscious this coming attack on America was an even more historic moment in Japanese naval history than Togo's defeat of the Russians.

Then *Akagi* hoisted the signal, 'Speed twenty-six knots, course south'. As the sailors cheered and the carriers climbed to full speed ahead, the pilots crowded into the operations room for a final briefing. Each carried a blown-up photograph of Pearl Harbor on which he marked off the latest location of each American ship.

In the early hours of Sunday, a last short Imperial G.H.Q.

intelligence report came in. Nagumo on the bridge grabbed it eagerly from the signal officer. Then he threw it down on the chart table. It said: 'No carriers repeat no carriers in Pearl Harbor.'

It was a cloudy black night as the carriers steamed towards their launching point 270 miles north of Pearl Harbor. The wind sprang up and heavy seas battered the big ships. It now looked as though luck was deserting them. In this weather it might be difficult to launch planes.

Nagumo's carriers were still five hours away from their launching point, steaming fast, when at 1 a.m. the five parent submarines dived. The securing clamps were cast off, the midgets floated off their decks and were on their way to Pearl Harbor. Four submarines were released within minutes of one another. The fifth, delayed by mechanical trouble, followed them two hours later.

The two-man crews' orders were to enter Pearl Harbor and find targets of opportunity. Then they would regain their parent submarines at a rendezvous seven miles west of Lanai Island.

But no midget crews expected to return. The officer commanding one midget carefully laid out all his private possessions with messages of farewell to his parents. He gave money to his orderly with directions for forwarding his private effects. These preparations were fully justified, as he was never heard of again.

The entrance to Pearl Harbor was shallow and narrow with the channel well protected with submarine nets. The midgets' only chance was to get through in the wake of an American ship.

At 3.45 a.m. with less than three hours to go before Nagumo's carriers launched their planes, the U.S. minesweeper *Antares*, towing a steel barge, was waiting outside the harbour boom for a tug to come and meet her when she sighted a small submarine 150 yards away. With its conning tower awash and its periscope slightly raised, it was apparently trailing her in the direction of Pearl Harbor.

Just before dawn the U.S. coastal minesweeper *Condor* also picked up the white wake of a periscope near the Pearl Harbor entrance buoys. As U.S. submarines were prohibited from operating submerged in the area, she immediately reported it to the destroyer *Ward* on patrol at the harbour entrance.

The *Ward* moved into the attack and patrol planes from 14 Squadron at Kaneohe dropped two smoke pots to mark the submarine. *Ward* dropped depth charges and so did the plane. They were the first shots of the Pacific war.

Although *Ward* promptly reported her encounter, no one was very interested. The matter was still being idly chatted about over the telephone at Ford Island when the first Japanese bombers dived on the conversationalists.

The harbour gates were opened at 04.58 to allow the passage of the *Antares* and another minesweeper. There was so little interest in prowling unidentified submarines that they were left open. No one thought the presence of unidentified, but not totally confirmed, submarines indicated any possibility of an attack on Pearl Harbor.

The duty destroyer U.S.S. *Monaghan* was not ordered to close the gates until 8.40 a.m. That fateful morning the Pearl Harbor entrance was open for nearly four hours to any daring Japanese submarine commander. The Japanese navy believe that three slipped in as ordered. Certainly the Americans sighted the conning towers of the two midgets in the north channel. One was sunk by *Monaghan* which, after closing the gates too late, rammed and depth-charged it.

While these small significant events were taking place near the mouth of Pearl Harbor, Nagumo was not happy. He knew the shoe-string spy system Japan had set up and had not much faith in it. Was Headquarters information entirely accurate? He felt he must satisfy himself definitely that there were no American carriers in the crowded anchorages at Pearl Harbor. So he took a big chance.

At 5 a.m. in the inky pre-dawn darkness, while the great ships wallowed in the rough seas, the heavy cruisers *Chikuma* and *Tone* each catapulted a float plane to reconnoitre Pearl Harbor. As they droned away in the darkness, planes were lining up on the carriers. Waves were now so high that they constantly crashed over the flight decks. Maintenance crews, fighting for breath in the gale, slid about the slippery, shifting decks clinging to their planes to keep them from being washed overboard.

An hour later, at 6 a.m., it was darker than ever and the sea showed no signs of abating. The wave-washed flight decks were still pitching badly. Under these conditions it was going to take a long time to launch planes. Although he had still not heard from the scout planes, Nagumo decided he must launch immediately, otherwise vital surprise might be lost.

By this decision Nagumo, ignoring the split-second timing decided in Tokyo for the declaration of war, achieved even more surprise than he had anticipated. Instead of the minimum thirty minutes to which the naval staff had finally agreed, there would now be hardly any time between the declaration of war and his bombers arriving over Pearl Harbor.

Nagumo summoned Commander Mitsuo Fuchida into *Agagi*'s dimly lit briefing room. One of Japan's most experienced flyers with twenty-five years' service in the Imperial Navy, he was to lead the attack. When he reported to Admiral Nagumo and the flagship commander, Captain Hasegawa, the rest of the pilots aboard the other carriers went into the operations room for their last orders. On a blackboard was written the positions of the ships in Pearl Harbor according to intelligence reports received up to a few hours previously from patrolling submarines and spies in Honolulu. There was no further information, nothing further to say. Nagumo held out his hand to Fuchida and said, 'Take off according to plan.'

As Fuchida climbed into his red-and-yellow striped bomber with the armour-piercing shell slung underneath, the senior petty officer of the maintenance crew handed him a white *hashimaki*—a cloth headband—as a symbol he must be prepared to die. As he fastened this to his flying helmet, the carriers swung round into the north wind and Nagumo's battle-flag was run up alongside Togo's tattered banner, still fluttering at *Akagi*'s masthead. A green light made a dim circle in the darkness, to signal the first plane to start its run along the dark pitching deck. As it swung away into the black sky excited sailors shouted repeated *banzais*.

The flyers, exalted by their 'divine mission', roared safely one after another off the decks, and Nagumo realized his fears had been unjustified. In spite of the black night and stormy seas, within fifteen minutes the first wave of 183 fighters, bombers and torpedo planes took off from the six carriers. They circled over the fleet and set course south for Pearl Harbor. It was 6.15 a.m.

9

Tora, Tora . . .

ALTHOUGH Nagumo had expected to lose some planes at take-off because of the high waves and strong winds, every plane was launched successfully. The Japanese estimated the first wave should reach the coast of Oahu in little over an hour. Fuchida's planes immediately climbed above the cloud layer at 10,000 feet. As they flew on their deadly mission, the cloud began to thin and a brilliant morning sun shone through. It was dawn.

Nagumo's anxiety to be certain about the carriers in harbour nearly betrayed him. Only American peacetime complacency saved him. In a remote aircraft warning station at Opana, Privates Joseph Locard and George Elliott were on duty from 4 to 7 a.m. From 6.45 a.m. onwards they plotted an unidentified plane approaching Oahu. This was one of the two reconnaissance planes from the cruisers *Chikuma* and *Tone*, making a dangerous last-minute check to make certain there were no carriers.

Private Locard thought the machine was at fault but when he checked it he found it was operating correctly. At 7.02 a.m. the radar also plotted a large number of planes approaching Oahu 130 miles away to the north.

These two groups of strange planes worried Locard and Elliott so much that after an agitated debate at 7.20 a.m. they called the aircraft warning centre. The only officer on duty until 8 a.m. was Lieutenant Kermit A. Tyler. He was an air force officer who was attached to the radar post for training and observation. When Private Locard telephoned, he thought he was being alarmist. He told him to forget it. He said the planes must be a patrol of Hickam Field bombers or perhaps a flight of B–17s which was due in from the mainland.

The large group of planes which Lieutenant Tyler dismissed as a flight of B–17s were Commander Fuchida's first-wave attack. He flew in front of his own group of forty-nine level bombers carrying 1,600-lb armour-piercing converted shells.

To his starboard and slightly below him flew Lieutenant-Commander Shigeharu Murata—also of the flagship *Akagi*—with forty Kate torpedo planes, the main battleship attack force. To port and slightly above Fuchida was Lieutenant-Commander Kuichi Takahashi from the carrier *Shikoku* with fifty-one Val dive bombers each carrying a 500-lb bomb. Above the three bomber formations, to protect them from American interception, was a fighter escort of forty-three Zeros commanded by Lieutenant-Commander Shigeru Itaya from *Akagi*.

While the two American privates were plotting him on the radar screen, Fuchida tuned in to some light music from the Honolulu radio station. He turned his antennae in the direction from which the broadcast was coming and found he was five degrees off. He corrected his course and the rest of the bombers and fighters followed him.

Then the radio gave a weather report: 'Partly cloudy, but clouds mostly over mountains.'

Good visibility? That meant they would see the targets clearly! Their stepped formation flew on towards their objective, taking advantage of every cloud cover.

There were two plans for the attack. If complete surprise was achieved Murata's torpedo planes were to strike first. Than Fuchida's group of level bombers would follow them in. At the same time Takahashi's dive bombers were to turn their attention to the air bases at Hickam and Ford Island near the anchorage.

If there was American resistance, Takahashi's divers were to deliver the opening attack. When they screamed down without warning this was bound to cause panic and confusion at once and then attract American fire. Fuchida's level bombers would bomb the American anti-aircraft guns as soon as they opened up. Then in the middle of the confusion the third wave of torpedo planes would swoop down and attack the battleships.

Each attack was to be signalled by a flare. 'One Black Dragon' signalled a surprise attack. If surprise were lost, Fuchida would fire 'Two Black Dragons'.

The surprise attack, scheduled to last only ten minutes, was timed like this:

At 7.55 dive bombers would swoop on Hickam and Wheeler Fields. Two minutes later torpedo planes would dive on the battleships.

At eight o'clock, five minutes after the first dive-bombing attack, Zeros would strafe air bases.

Five minutes later Fuchida's level bombers would round off the attack by bombing the battleships.

An hour and forty minutes after they had taken off from the carriers, through a gap in the clouds Fuchida's pilots saw a long, crinkly line beneath them. It was surf breaking on the northern shore of Oahu. The time was 7.40 a.m.

A few minutes later Pearl Harbor and Honolulu stood out like grey shadows in the pink-stained morning mist. Peering through the light mist veil the pilots could make out the ships of the Pacific Fleet, anchored in pairs, like soldiers on parade. As Fuchida's men craned forward eagerly to count them, not a trace of smoke came from the harbour or battleships. Everyone seemed asleep.

The people most astonished at the American fleet's soporific negligence were Fuchida and his pilots. He described the scene later like this:

'Below me lay the whole U.S. Pacific Fleet in a formation I would not have dared to dream of in my most optimistic dreams. I have seen all German ships assembled in Kiel harbour. I have also seen the French battleships in Brest. And finally I have frequently seen our own warships assembled for review before the Emperor, but I have never seen ships, even in the deepest peace, anchored at a distance less than 500 to 1,000 yards from each other. A war fleet must always be on the alert since surprise attacks can never be fully ruled out. But this picture down there was hard to comprehend. Had these Americans never heard of Port Arthur?'

As they flew round Oahu to attack Pearl Harbor from the south their radios were anxiously tuned in for reports from the two float planes to tell them what their final targets were.

Someone else was also twiddling his radio knob. Ensign Yoshikawa, disguised as Vice-Consul Murimara, was switched on to Tokyo short-wave radio. Twice during the weather forecast the announcer reported 'East Wind Rain'—the code signal for an attack on American territory.

Yoshikawa began burning his code book and other intelligence material. Shortly afterwards he heard the bombs drop. When the F.B.I. came for him he had only a rough sketch of Pearl Harbor in his possession.

That Sunday morning it was lunchtime in Washington. Secretary of War Stimson, Secretary of State Cordell Hull, and Navy Secretary Knox met in the State Department to talk over the Japanese problem. Hull insisted that the Japanese were planning some devilry. He said, 'These fellows mean to fight. We will have to be prepared.' When they broke up the conference for lunch, Fuchida's planes were just approaching the shores of Oahu.

In Tokyo it was nearly 3 a.m. and lights were burning in Naval Headquarters where Admiral Nagano waited anxiously for news of the attack he had reluctantly approved. In his flagship *Nagato* in the Inland Sea, Yamamoto waited in his operations room, looking constantly at his watch. This was the only gesture that revealed his anxiety. He seemed the calmest man in a room of tense, agitated officers although not only his career, but the fate of Japan, depended upon Fuchida's bombers thousands of miles away circling above Pearl Harbor, about to begin their all-out attempt to destroy the American Pacific Fleet.

It was the beginning of a fine sunny morning over Oahu. As well as the great unstirring Pearl Harbor navy base, Fuchida could see civilian planes circling John Rodgers commercial airport near Honolulu. He decided he could wait no longer for the float plane reports. As they had not reported he decided to go ahead and, pushing back his canopy, fired 'One Black Dragon'—a surprise attack.

As soon as they received Fuchida's signal, Takahashi and his fifty-one dive bombers climbed to 15,000 feet and divided into two groups, ready to swoop down. One, led by himself, headed for Ford Island and Hickam Field. The second group, led by Lieutenant Akira Sakamoto, dived towards Wheeler air base.

Commander Murata's torpedo bombers swung from behind the clouds and plunged down almost to sea level to begin their attack on the unsuspecting American battleships. At the same time Itaya's fighters climbed as high and as fast as they could, ready to destroy any American fighters which appeared. Fuchida's level bombers kept height but flew just under the clouds to study their targets clearly.

As the commanding officer at Kaneohe air base drank his morning coffee he heard an increasing hum of a large number of planes. When they came into view he glanced at them, idly thinking they were a flight due in from the west coast. Then he suddenly noticed they circled to the left instead of the right which was the rule in the area.

Something was wrong. He jumped in his car and drove away towards the hangars. He looked at his watch. It was 7.48 a.m.

Pearl Harbor was now clearly visible to the Japanese pilots. Fuchida peered at it through his binoculars and counted eight big battleships at anchor.

His planes were now all in position ready to go. He turned to his radio operator and ordered him to tap out the pre-arranged attack code signal, '*To, to, to* . . .' The time in Pearl Harbor was 07.49.

Although Kaneohe's C.O. realized something was wrong, everything else seemed calm and peaceful. No American fighters rose into the air. Not a gun flashed from the ground.

Just as they were splitting up for the attack *Chikuma*'s plane reported there were ten battleships, one heavy cruiser and ten light cruisers in Pearl Harbor. One minute later *Tone*'s plane confirmed there were no carriers there.

The Pacific Fleet was in its usual state of peacetime readiness for ships in port—four hours' notice. A handful of duty men were cleaning brass and wiping overnight dew from the warships' guns. Officers breakfasting in their wardrooms could hear the church bells for eight o'clock mass ringing across the harbour. At Kaneohe Bay naval air station three planes of Patrol Squadron 14 were in the air, having taken off before sunrise for a routine patrol. The rest of the squadron was in readiness—and Squadron 11 was on standby. In front of the hangars they were warming up the C.O.'s Kingfisher scout plane. Four Catalina PBY flying boats were anchored in the bay. The warning signal for eight o'clock colours was being given on the American ships as Takahashi's divers appeared over Ford Island and pushed their sticks forward for their swing downwards.

The first attack was made by Lieutenant Akira Sakamoto, who swung down with twenty-five Val dive bombers in a screaming assault on Wheeler air base, which Japanese intelligence had reported was the main centre of American fighter operations in Hawaii. Sakamoto's task was to smash the American planes on the ground.

Immediately behind Sakamoto's group, Lieutenant-Commander Kuichi Takahashi led the remaining twenty-six dive bombers over Hickam Field, the heavy bomber base of the American Air Force. Some veered away to attack the navy fighter base on Ford Island, where Halsey's carrier planes had landed the day before.

Two minutes after the Kaneohe C.O. saw Fuchida's planes circle the wrong way, the first bomb fell on Wheeler Field. A few seconds later Takahashi, flying towards Hickam Field, saw the heavy bombers lined up invitingly on the apron. All his planes peeled off and dived one after another. Within less than a minute flames and explosions from burning aircraft sent huge columns of smoke billowing over Hickam Field, Wheeler Field and Ford Island.

At five minutes to eight, Rear-Admiral W. R. Furlong, commander of the Pacific Fleet Mine Force, began his morning constitutional along the deck of the U.S.S. *Ogalalla*, tied up alongside the cruiser *Helena*. He took no notice of a group of nine planes flying low over Ford Island. Planes were continually in the air at the base. But these were part of Sakamoto's attack. Even when a loud explosion shook his ship he thought it was an accidental bomb that had been dropped. What Admiral Furlong in fact heard were the first Japanese bombs to fall on United States soil.

At that moment stupefied officers and men began to notice the red ball insignia on the wings of the diving aircraft. They looked at one another in amazement, then back again disbelieving—Japanese planes!

Ironically enough it fell to Rear-Admiral Patrick N. L. Bellinger, the officer who had complained so bitterly about the lack of preparedness nearly a year earlier, to broadcast the message from Ford Island that shook the United States as nothing else in that country's history had ever done. 'Air raid on Pearl Harbor—this is no drill,' he said. A few seconds later Admiral Kimmel, C.-in-C. Pacific Fleet, broadcast the same message.

When Navy Secretary Knox in Washington heard it he exclaimed: 'My God! This can't be true! They must mean the Philippines!'

Admiral Nagumo in his carrier 200 miles away and Yamamoto aboard his flagship in the Inland Sea both waited tensely for news. So as he turned towards Barber's Point to start his own level bombing run, Fuchida ordered his radio operator to send '*Tora, tora, tora*'. In Japanese, the word *tora* means tiger. This code word was based on a Japanese saying, 'A tiger goes out 2,000 miles and returns without fail.'

Surprise was complete. No American fighters appeared in the air. Everyone aboard the ships in harbour appeared to be still asleep. While the bombs exploded with a shattering noise, the Honolulu radio continued to broadcast dance music.

When Fuchida's signal was received aboard his flagship *Akagi*, Nagumo at once relayed it to Japan. But it had already reached there. It was received aboard *Nagato* by Yamamoto and in Tokyo directly from Fuchida's plane. By some freak of air-wave conditions this low-powered transmission from his bomber was heard thousands of miles away across the Pacific in Japan.

This radio message was the curtain raiser for war all across the Pacific and Indian Oceans. Immediately it was received, Japanese aircraft launched their attacks against the enemy over thousands of miles of front.

When the radio tower picked up Fuchida's message it was shot down the pneumatic tube at once to Yamamoto in the operations room in *Nagato*. As soon as a staff officer read out the news a tremendous hubbub broke out. Only Yamamoto remained impassive. His only reaction was to say to an aide, 'Check the time of the attack carefully. It is very important to know when the attack began. It seems to have come earlier than we expected.'

At first the staff officers could not understand what he was talking about. It was only later that they realized he was concerned about the interval of time which should have expired between the ultimatum and the attack. Yamamoto had no knowledge that the Japanese note had not yet been delivered in Washington. This was due to Japanese carelessness and ineptitude. During this crisis period their Washington Embassy had orders to keep a twenty-four-hour watch in the message room. Whatever time of night a top-priority Purple message arrived they had orders to wake up both ambassadors.

Perhaps because the crisis had been going on so long it had made them careless. The fourteenth and last part of the Japanese memorandum was intercepted by the Americans in the early hours of the morning and was ready for distribution by intelligence at 8 a.m. It closed with this statement: 'The Japanese Government regrets to have to notify hereby the American Government it cannot but consider it is impossible to reach an agreement in further negotiation.'

This last and most important part of the Japanese note, although it was transmitted during the night, was not shown to the ambassadors until breakfast-time on Sunday. The work of translating the note took more time than had been anticipated as it was 5,000 words long. Ironically enough, the American interceptors were five hours ahead of the Japanese in translating their own message.

There is no doubt that if the Ambassadors Nomura and Kurusu had been aware that war was to begin immediately they would not have been so negligent. But they knew neither the timing nor the location of the attack. If they had been informed the Americans would have intercepted the message—and been warned.

Because of their ignorance they took the ultimatum much more casually than they should. Kurusu twice objected to the typing and wording—after all it was a most important message!—and sent requests for delay to the State Department. It was planned to deliver the note at 1 p.m., Washington time. When Ambassador Kichisaburo Nomura rushed round to the State Department with the note it was 2.20 p.m.

Fuchida had begun his attack on Pearl Harbor thirty-five minutes earlier. If the note had been presented on time it would have given the Americans more than the thirty minutes warning upon which Yamamoto had insisted. As it was, Japan entered the war without a formal declaration. But then this was not the first time in her history she had done this.

Neither did Yamamoto manage to check the time that day. The radio room immediately became jammed with messages about attacks on Malaya and along the whole southern front. All day monitors intercepted information from American sources. The Americans gave excited uncoded details of the size of the Pearl Harbor attack and the damage it had done and the Japanese picked them up. The intercepted American radio calls confirmed what Yamamoto knew already from his own intelligence—there were no carriers in Pearl Harbor. Nagumo had not been able to tell them this before because he kept radio silence until after the attack. Although they felt the information they had sent Nagumo was fairly accurate up to then most of the staff officers had still hoped at least one carrier would be in Pearl Harbor.

As Fuchida's radio operator tapped out his 'surprise achieved' message, Lieutenant-Commander Shigeharu Murata's forty Kate torpedo bombers began their run towards the battleships anchored east of Ford Island.

One of the leading torpedo planes was piloted by Lieutenant Inichi Goto, second in command to Murata. When he flew over Ewa air base on his run in to Pearl Harbor he saw the lined-up fighters and exclaimed, 'What a juicy target!' As he went down to 1,500 feet, he passed over another juicy target—Hickam Field with the bombers lined up unsuspecting and inviting ready for Takahashi's dive bombers.

It was a clear day with little cloud to obscure the target when Murata and Goto split their planes into two parallel lines for the attack. Each was eager to strike the first blow against the Pacific Fleet. Goto's target was the *Oklahoma*. As he dropped down to his attack position his intensive training came into play. He carefully checked altitude, speed and degree of approach before he launched his torpedo. He knew that either he or Murata leading the other column of bombers would be the first to drop a torpedo.

Suddenly as he settled his angle and speed half a dozen black shapes streaked down in front of him. They were Japanese dive bombers which had misunderstood Fuchida's 'Black Dragon' signal. They thought surprise had been lost and it was their duty to attack the battleships first. Goto recalls, 'I felt nothing but fury. I thought the divers were trying to steal our thunder after all our careful training. I could not believe it was a mistake.'

However he remained on course and the battleship's super-structure and masts flashed past him like fence-stakes as he flew at deck level to launch his torpedo. The ship seemed deserted. He could see no one on deck. But he was concentrating so hard on his correct torpedo aim that he did not notice details too clearly.

When he released his torpedo, he went into a climbing turn across the battleship, too low and fast for machine-gun bullets to reach him. Then he turned and looked back to watch the white wake of his torpedo foaming towards the battleship. Almost immediately there came a flash and an explosion and a huge fountain of water shot up higher than the deck. He shouted excitedly through the intercom, 'We hit her!'

As he circled round to have another look, machine-gun tracers came streaking past him and he swerved away. 'The Americans were better prepared and reacted much faster after such a shock than I would ever have thought possible,' he reported.

Another account of what it was like in the air above Pearl Harbor on that morning was given by torpedo bomber pilot Chief Flight Petty Officer Juzo Mori, from the carrier *Soryu*, who said:

I did not expect to survive the attack. Since the bombing waves from *Akagi* and *Kaga* had already passed over, the attack by *Soryu*'s planes was met with intense anti-aircraft fire from the enemy fleet. My bomber shook from the impact of enemy machine-gun bullets and shrapnel.

I flew directly over the enemy battleships along Ford Island, and then banked into a wide left turn. I chose as my objective a battleship anchored some distance from the main group of vessels which were being attacked by the *Soryu*'s torpedo aircraft. It appeared to be the only battleship yet undamaged.

It was imperative that my bombing approach be absolutely correct. I had been warned that the harbour depth was no more than forty-five feet. The slightest deviation in speed or height would send the released torpedo plunging into the sea bottom or jumping above the water. All our effort would go for naught.

By this time I was hardly conscious of what I was doing. I was reacting from habit instilled by long training, moving like an automaton. I was down to 200 feet when suddenly the battleship towered ahead of my bomber like a great mountain peak. I pulled back on the release with all my strength. The plane lurched and faltered as flak struck the wings and fuselage. My head snapped back and I felt as though a heavy beam had struck against it.

I was acutely conscious of the enemy anti-aircraft fire. Enemy shells appeared to be coming from all directions. I was so frightened that my clothes were soaking in perspiration.

Suddenly there was an enemy plane directly in front of me. As my plane was armed only with a single rearward-firing 7·7 mm machine-gun it was almost helpless in aerial combat. As I was going to die, I decided I would take the enemy with me. I swung the bomber over hard and headed directly for him. The pilot appeared startled at my manœuvre and fled. I asked myself: 'Is this what is called war?'

These torpedo-bomber attacks caused massive explosions. Boiling waterspouts foamed up and black smoke floated into the air from the battleships. High above the battle Lieutenant-Commander Shigeru Itaya's forty-three Zeros searched in vain for American fighters. As they did not find a single one Itaya decided it was safe to swoop down and ground-strafe.

Service crews were being ferried to four seaplanes at Kaneohe Bay when his Zeros roared down. A second later, there were hissing boiling geysers in the water and four planes lay burning on the water with wounded or dying American airmen splashing feebly around them. The petty officer turning over the propeller to warm up the C.O.'s Kingfisher was killed.

Itaya's fighters swept to the end of the bay and then turned and came back strafing again. They attacked Ewa Marine air base, skimming over the tree-tops and diving down to twenty feet to put in short bursts of machine-gun fire. Within fifteen minutes all the Marine aircraft were shot up or set on fire. Thirty-three out of the forty-nine planes at Ewa blazed and exploded and the remaining sixteen were too damaged to fly. Then Itaya's pilots turned their attention to the Marines themselves.

The counter measures were heroic but pitiful. The fire of a solitary machine-gun met Itaya's Zeros. This gun had been dragged from the armoury by John Finn, the chief ordnance man, who mounted it with the cover of a garbage can as a shield. Some of the Marines fired pistols at Itaya's pilots. Then others set up machine-guns. In between attacks attempts were made to clear the burning wreckage. Cars were driven on to runways to prevent landings which were never attempted.

The majority of casualties occurred while the Americans were trying to save undamaged planes. Only nine of the thirty-six planes at Kaneohe escaped destruction and six of those were damaged. The only three intact were the routine flight patrolling south of Oahu looking for unidentified ships.

The commander of Patrol Wing One reported that the conduct throughout the attack was magnificent, in fact too much so. Had they not set up machine-guns to fire back at the strafing planes the Americans would have lost less men. Due to their reckless resistance, two of Itaya's planes were destroyed and several more went off with heavy gas leaks as they suddenly vanished as quickly as they came.

It was time to launch the big level bombing attacks. Fuchida formed his ten squadrons, each plane carrying an armour-piercing shell, into a single column at intervals of 600 feet. By this time the Americans had recovered from their shock. As they began their bomb run, American ships opened fire with their anti-aircraft guns. Then the shore batteries joined in the defensive shelling. Dark grey puffs of exploding shells began to burst round the Japanese planes. Near misses made their planes shudder and jump.

Fuchida's pilots were taken aback by the rapidity of the American counter-attack. It came less than five minutes after the first bomb had fallen. They could hardly believe that American reaction could have been so quick. For the Japanese character, although quick in attack, is slow to adjust to the defensive.

Commander Fuchida led his forty-nine Kate bombers towards the *Nevada* moored at the northern end of Battleship Row at Ford Island. Anti-aircraft fire worried them as they circled the target. Some managed to make their runs at once. Others, put off by the heavy fire, tried three times before dropping their bombs.

One pilot who during training had often been reprimanded for poorly timed bomb release again dropped his bomb before time. Ignoring the dark, peppery puffs of anti-aircraft fire, Fuchida swooped towards him and shook his fist. Then he noticed the pilot's plane was losing gas so he wrote on a small blackboard, 'What happened?' and held it towards the plane. The pilot answered on another blackboard, 'Fuselage hit.'

Fuchida ordered him to return at once to the carriers. He refused, scribbling on the blackboard, 'Fuel tank destroyed. Will follow you.' Although Fuchida knew it was certain death to try and fly a crippled plane through the increasing American fire, he waved his hand, giving him permission. The pilot went into a full dive towards the battleships and was blown up by a shell burst.

Fuchida said about his own bomb run:

I lay flat on the floor to watch the fall of bombs through a peep-hole. Four bombs in perfect pattern plummeted like the devils of doom. The target was so far away that I wondered for a moment if they would reach it. The bombs grew smaller and smaller until I was holding my breath for fear of losing sight of them. I forgot everything in the thrill of watching them fall towards the target. They became small as poppyseeds and finally disappeared from my view just as tiny white spurts of smoke appeared on or near the ship. I shouted 'two hits' and rose from the floor of the plane.

While some of Fuchida's planes circled over Honolulu, the other bomber groups made their runs. The anti-aircraft fire was getting heavier every second. As every available gun belched flame at them, most of the planes made three tries before letting their bombs go.

Suddenly there was a colossal explosion in Battleship Row and a column of dark red smoke rose thousands of feet in the air. The shock-wave reached Fuchida's plane, bouncing it around like a ping-pong ball. Several direct hits by heavy bombs had exploded the battleship *Arizona*'s boilers and forward magazine. Smoke also began to curl up from the battleship *Maryland*. Two bombs had hit her but they did little damage.

While Fuchida was attacking two other things were happening. The big Japanese submarines moved closer towards Pearl Harbor to torpedo any ships which tried to escape. The submarines' task was made difficult by the rough waves which had made it so tricky for planes to take off from Nagumo's carriers. They were felt by the big 2,000-ton I-class submarines down to a depth of ninety feet, where they rolled five degrees.

The heavy seas made it difficult to break the surface. One had so much difficulty she did not manage to surface until broad daylight. Then the trimming tanks were flooded but she refused to sink. From the conning tower the crew saw two American float planes. But they took no action. The U.S. planes reported a Japanese submarine ten miles south of Barber's Point but everyone was too occupied with the air attack to hunt it.

The second wave was now arriving. While Fuchida was still on his way to Pearl Harbor, Lieutenant-Commander Shigekazu Shimazaki, flight commander of *Zuikaku*, took off from the carriers with a second force of 170 aircraft. Shimazaki's planes arrived off Kahuku Point at 8.40 a.m. But because of the number of passes his bombers were making at the target Fuchida was still attacking. Shimazaki's second wave was ordered to circle for fifteen minutes to avoid colliding with Fuchida's planes. While circling they too felt the shock wave from the *Arizona*.

After Fuchida's attack had lasted about an hour, he ordered all his planes back to the carriers. Their losses were three fighters, a dive bomber and five torpedo planes. As Fuchida's bombers swung to return to the carriers they waggled their wings at the second-wave planes waiting their turn to attack.

Fuchida did not fly back with his planes. His bombs gone, he climbed high to watch the result of the second-wave attack. Lieutenant Masaharu Suganami, leader of *Soryu*'s Zeros, who had convoyed Fuchida's bombers, also remained over Oahu Island to watch the second attack. It was a hazardous act with a fighter's small range. He returned to his carrier with only a few gallons of fuel left in his tanks.

When Fuchida's attack was over Nagumo sent a signal to Yamamoto confirming what he already knew—there were no carriers in Pearl Harbor. Rear-Admiral Kamahito Kuroshima, his operations officer, swiftly wrote out a signal and showed it to Yamamoto for approval. It read, 'Seek out American carriers. They must be destroyed.'

Yamamoto shook his head. 'Don't send it,' he said. 'Nagumo is thousands of miles away. He may have information we do not have. He must fight his own battle. I have complete faith in him.' There was nothing else Yamamoto could do. He had to trust the man on the spot.

Fuchida had left Pearl Harbor and the air bases wrecked and burning by his strafings and bombings, and there were still no American fighter planes in the air. But anti-aircraft fire had greatly intensified when just before nine o'clock Shimazaki ordered his 170 planes to attack. His was by far the more dangerous task, as the Americans, although reeling, were now fighting back furiously. Unlike Fuchida, he had no torpedo bombers but commanded fifty-four Kate level bombers. They made for the air bases.

The second-wave dive-bomber group led by Lieutenant-Commander Takashige Egusa, *Soryu*'s flight commander, was much bigger. It consisted of eighty Val divers armed with 500-lb bombs. Egusa's pilots were the hand-picked *élite* of the Japanese carrier pilots. They had been specially selected and trained to destroy the American carriers in an all-out blow. Cheated of these, they decided to dive on those battleships which had suffered least from Fuchida's attacks.

Egusa led his dive bombers over the mountains and turned back into the fierce barrage. He chose as his targets the ships which were putting up the stiffest fire because they had obviously suffered least from the first-wave bombers.

Billowing smoke from the burning ships and harbour installations made it difficult for the planes to find their target. But as they dived on the American battleships Egusa's pilots followed his plane with its red-painted tail as if they were still training in Kagoshima. Explosion followed explosion, and red flames, boiling spray and thick black smoke sprang into the air.

While Egusa's skilled pilots wrecked the remaining big battleships, most of Shimazaki's level bombers concentrated on Hickam Field. The rest attacked Ford Island and Kaneohe air base. None of these planes were lost to anti-aircraft fire although nearly half of them were holed.

Fighter cover for the second wave was provided by thirty-six Zeros. No American fighters rose to tangle with them because the first wave had shot up most of them on the ground.

One Zero pilot, Iyozo Fujita, went up to 18,000 feet with Zero commander Iida to look for American fighters. They flew round twice but found no American planes. But American ground fire was much fiercer than they expected and their planes were followed by 'shells bursting like flowers'.

As Shimazaki's level bombers flew out of anti-aircraft range to make their attack, Fujita followed Iida and the other Zeros in a strafing attack on Kaneohe air base. When Iida ordered an attack, Iyozo Fujita became so excited at his first taste of action that his machine-gun bullets splashed harmlessly into the water.

Twenty-seven-year-old Lieutenant Iida was one of Japan's leading fighter pilots who had fought in China for two years. When he led his inexperienced pilots into a second attack, the Zeros, ignoring machine-gun bullets from the ground, dived on the hangars and set them on fire.

As he circled over Kaneohe making sure that all the fighters were safely back in formation a bullet hit Iida's plane. Fuel and smoke started pouring from it. Iida flew close to Fujita and put his hand over his mouth to show that fumes were choking him. Then he waggled his wings and made a downwards gesture with his hands. Then he put his plane into a vertical dive towards the airfield, and Fujita watched helplessly as it crashed and exploded on the ground between two hangars. Iida, one of the first Japanese casualties of the war, had kept to the agreement the pilots had made in Tankan Bay.

Shimazaki's second attack, like Fuchida's, lasted about an hour. It successfully hit the least-damaged battleships and attacked the undamaged cruisers and destroyers. Owing to the increased anti-aircraft fire its casualties were higher—six fighters and fourteen of Egusa's dive bombers were lost.

While Shimazaki headed back to the carriers, Fuchida still circled Pearl Harbor photographing the damage. He counted four battleships definitely sunk and three severely damaged. Another battleship appeared to be slightly damaged. Extensive damage had also been inflicted on other ships. The aircraft bases at Ford Island and Wheeler Field were both in flames.

Yamamoto in full regalia as Admiral of the Fleet in the Japanese Imperial Navy.

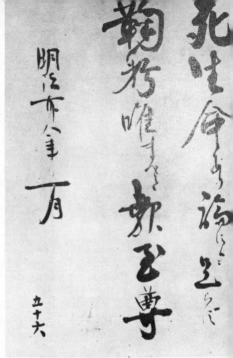

日露戦争出征前父貞吉翁に贈りし少尉補代の写真

左写真裏に書かれた決意の筆

Above left: A photograph presented to his father by the young ensign Isoroku before going into service during the Russo-Japanese War. *Above:* on the back of the photograph, at the left, are the date—January, 1905—and the name Isoroku; the epigram at the right declares that he is not afraid of death and is proud to go to war. *Left:* Wedding picture, 1918.

Opposite page:
Above: Sightseeing in Washington, 1926.
Below: Yamamoto (at left) in 1926, as he took over in Washington from the retiring Japanese naval attaché, Captain Kiyoshi Hasegawa. With the Japanese captains are Curtis Dwight Wilbur, the U.S. Secretary of the Navy, and Admiral E. W. Eberle, Chief of Naval Operations.

Yamamoto in Washington, 1926. *Above:* in his office.
Below: a formal portrait.

In England, 1934. In the photo above, Yamamoto is at the left.

Aerial photo of Pearl Harbor, looking south-west, October, 1941. In the centre is Ford Island, with anchored American ships in Battleship Row.

Above: A Japanese propaganda photo, captioned: "The moment at which the Hawaii surprise attack is about to take off from the carrier...On the faces of those who go forth to conquer and those who send them off there floats only that beautiful smile which transcends death."

Opposite page:
Above: Ford Island seen from a Japanese Sea Eagle. The American battleships on the far side of the island are under low-level attack. *Below:* A Japanese close-up of Battleship Row. The white streaks at the left and in the centre are torpedo tracks, and beside the *Maryland* (left-hand ship of the pair in the centre) a column of water indicates a direct hit.

Photos: U.S. Navy Department

Above: A drawing found in a Japanese plane shot down over Pearl Harbor. The inscription at the left reads: "Hear! The voice of the moment of death. Wake up, you fools!"
Left: Battleship Row seen from overhead after the attack. The *Maryland* has capsized.
Below: Fire and smoke rage on the *Arizona*.

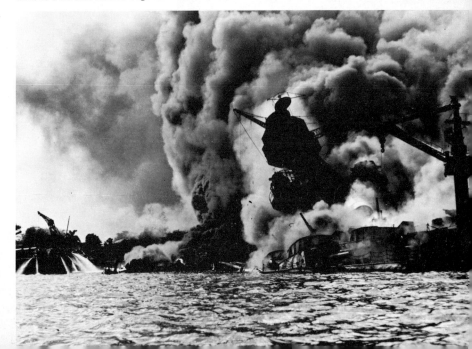

With a Zero fighter at Rabaul base in 1942.

Aboard a submarine.

Left: Yamamoto during the Pacific War, boarding a submarine en route to a frontline base.

Top: An American carrier under attack by low-flying Japanese torpedo aircraft at Midway. *Above:* The Japanese heavy cruiser *Mogami* after attack by Task Force 16 at Midway. *Below:* A blazing Japanese plane crashes into the stack of the U.S.S. *Hornet* off Santa Cruz. *Opposite:* The signal bridge of the *Hornet* after the crash.

Above: Yamamoto addressing naval pilots at Rabaul just before his death. *Below:* After the State funeral. Yamamoto's wife is at the left, his son third from right.

Although their losses were very small against the huge damage they had inflicted on the American fleet, many of the Japanese second wave were hit. Most of them managed to fly back to the carriers.

Iyozo Fujita's experience was typical. He was escorting a group of Egusa's dive bombers back to the carriers when an American plane appeared in front of him. He tried to jettison his long-range gas tanks but could not. As he swung away another plane came towards him from the side. He shot that down in flames but the first plane came at him head on.

He had repeatedly been told in training that 'to turn away makes certain of defeat'. So he determined to ram the plane if necessary. It was the American who turned away first, but as he did so he sent a burst of machine-gun bullets at Fujita which shattered his windscreen and peppered the back of his seat an inch from his head.

Fujita's plane was full of holes, his engine kept cutting out and his oil pressure dropped dangerously. Below him he could make out Japanese submarine periscopes waiting hungrily for American ships to sail out of Pearl Harbor.

At first he thought he would crash land on the sea and hope to be picked up by a submarine. Then he decided this was too risky and he would try to make the carriers. He did, but as his plane shuddered to a stop on *Akagi*'s deck his oil-pressure gauge read zero. Then the engine fell out—but Iyozo Fujita was unhurt.

When he landed Admiral Nagumo was getting a first-hand account of the battle from Fuchida. 'Four battleships definitely sunk,' he said. 'One sank instantly, another capsized. Two others settled on the bottom of the bay.'

What damage had been inflicted on airfield and air bases? Fuchida reported there were still many targets remaining which should be hit. He said, 'In spite of growing opposition I recommend another attack.'

This led to an immediate clash of opinion. Watched by the returning pilots, Genda and Fuchida began arguing animatedly on the bridge. Genda was not in favour of risking planes and carriers in a third attack, although the returning planes were refuelling at once on the flight decks in case.

The argument was still going on as the last plane landed. At one o'clock Nagumo, having heard all the flight commanders' reports, decided they could not do much more damage without greater risk.

He decided to call it a day. At 1.30 p.m. a signal flag was run up at *Akagi*'s masthead giving the carriers orders to set a northerly course. They began to steam away as swiftly as they had come.

Nagumo's decision was based mainly on the opinion of his chief of staff, Rear-Admiral Ryunosuke Kusaka, who backed Genda in opposing another attack. His point was that radio interceptions indicated that the Americans still had a large number of bombers in operational condition. To remain within range of American land-based planes was risky, especially in view of the limited 250-mile range of their own air searches. Nor could they depend upon Japanese submarine patrols operating in Hawaiian waters. They had given Nagumo hardly any information at all.

But his main reason for advising a quick withdrawal was that any hope of finding the American carriers had been reluctantly abandoned. To stay longer without a chance to hit these targets was not worth the danger involved.

There was no doubt they had done very well. Out of the total of 353 planes which set off from the six carriers, only nine fighters, fifteen dive bombers and five torpedo planes with their crews—fifty-five officers and men—were missing.

Against these almost negligible losses Nagumo's intelligence officers estimated that eight battleships—virtually the entire battleship strength of the U.S. Pacific Fleet—were sunk or severely damaged. Pilots reported the battleships *Arizona*, *California* and *West Virginia* sunk, the *Oklahoma* capsized, the *Nevada* heavily damaged, and the *Maryland*, *Pennsylvania* and *Tennessee* damaged.

They also claimed the destroyers *Cassin* and *Downes* burned and heavily damaged. *Shaw* was heavily damaged, and so too was the repair ship *Vestal*. The minelayer *Ogalalla* had been sunk, the seaplane tender *Curtiss* damaged and the auxiliary *Utah* capsized.

The factors which influenced Admiral Nagumo's decision not to attack Pearl Harbor for a third time have never been properly documented because he committed hara-kiri in the summer of 1944 during the battle of Saipan. Only one document briefly summarizes his reasons:

1. The first attack had inflicted all the damage we had hoped for. Another attack could not be expected greatly to increase the extent of that damage.
2. Enemy fire had been surprisingly prompt even though we

took them by surprise. Another attack would meet strong opposition. This would make our losses disproportionate to the additional destruction which might be inflicted.

3. Intercepted enemy messages indicated at least fifty large planes still operational. Also we did not know the whereabouts of the enemy carriers, cruisers and submarines.

While Nagumo's carriers sailed away, the mission at Pearl Harbor accomplished, the big mother submarines cruised at periscope depth still waiting to pick up the midget crews. Because of the confusion caused by the bombing it was extremely difficult to determine what had happened to the midget submarines. None of the five boats ever returned to report.

Although some were sighted by American ships and planes, three managed to get through the channel entrance, including the one following *Antares*. The fourth midget, commanded by Ensign Kazuo Sakamaki and a late-starter through mechanical trouble, ran aground twice through a faulty gyro and could not fire its torpedoes. It drifted all round Ford Island and ran onto a reef near the entrance channel. At 8.17 a.m. it was spotted there by the U.S.S. *Helm* which opened fire. While being fired upon, it slipped off the reef and submerged.

Another midget, commanded by Lieutenant Yokoyama, slipped into harbour at dawn and lay submerged all day until nightfall as its original orders had directed.

At 6.50 p.m. Commander Nakaoka, commanding the big submarine *I-68*, surfaced near the Pearl Harbor entrance buoy. As he did so a huge explosion came from the direction of the battleship *Arizona* and smoke curled up into the evening sky. Protected by the dark, Nakaoka stayed on the surface to watch developments.

Thirty minutes later his radio operator picked up a radio signal from Lieutenant Yokoyama saying, 'I have succeeded.' This radio signal was also received by Admiral Shimizu aboard the submarine flagship, *Katori*.

For their own safety, whatever success they achieved, all the midgets had orders not to give themselves away by signalling while still in the harbour. As thirty minutes had elapsed between the explosion and the radio message, Commander Nakaoka assumed the midget had managed in that time to get out of harbour. But where was she? Admiral Shimizu ordered another big submarine,

I–69, to join *I–68* and wait around the harbour mouth to rescue the gallant Yokoyama and his shipmate.

At nine o'clock that evening Commander Watanabe arrived with *I–69* and surfaced hurriedly to recharge his batteries. Smoke lay like a cloud all over Pearl Harbor and in the middle of it he saw a spiralling blazing column marking the end of the *Arizona*. He reported later, 'Pearl Harbor shone red in the sky like a thing of fire.'

While he was watching this spectacular sight the three patrolling American destroyers *Blue*, *Ramsey* and *Breeze* found him. Watanabe dived at once as they peppered him with depth charges. He knew the American depth-charge setting was in the neighbourhood of 100 feet, so by diving deeper he could evade them. He put *I–69* to 200 feet although her ordinary diving capacity was set at 100 feet. The depth charges rocked and damaged her even at that depth.

Then her sister boat, *I–68*, also waiting for Yokoyama, got into trouble. She too was seen by an American destroyer. When she dived down to the seabed she was caught in a submarine net.

When she managed to free herself, the crew found that the depth charges had caused leaks in her hull. The leaks became so dangerous that Commander Nakaoka decided he must surface and, if necessary, fight it out. When he broke the surface it was a pitch black night and the American destroyers had given up the chase.

There were many big Japanese submarines lurking round Pearl Harbor that night. *I–16* dived to over 200 feet near the harbour mouth when she heard a destroyer. She received three depth charges directly over her but was so far below them she was untouched. This submarine remained submerged for twenty-five hours.

Next morning Ensign Kazuo Sakamaki, overcome by fumes, managed to struggle ashore after beaching his midget. He was taken prisoner and his submarine salvaged. A U.S. navy chart recovered from it showed detailed navigational information carefully translated into Japanese. The submarine also carried a simple code to transmit information to the big I-class submarines still waiting outside Pearl Harbor to try and pick up Yokoyama, Sakamaki, or any other midget crews.

After four days there was no sign of the midgets, so the submarines abandoned all idea of recovering the crews and set sail for the Marshalls. Yokoyama was never heard of again. Presumably he was sunk by the American destroyers as he tried to escape from the harbour.

The I-class submarines arrived in Kwajalein in the Marshall Islands, in time for the big Japanese festival of New Year when every Japanese becomes a year older. A vast crowd of Polynesians put on a dancing display for the navy and everyone drank a great deal of *sake*.

Although Pearl Harbor was planned as a two-pronged attack, all the damage was done by carrier planes and the submarine operation was a failure. As a result the submarine service lost face. Their failure caused them to be put low on the list for essential materials and funds. Later in the war demands for radar were ignored and many of the submarines were reduced to the role of supplying cut-off garrisons in the Solomons battles.

The only submariners who came gloriously out of Pearl Harbor were the midget crews. The nine men who lost their lives in the tiny two-man submarines were promoted two ranks, given posthumous decorations and glorified as national war heroes. The only one who missed promotion and canonization was Ensign Kazuo Sakamaki, the captured sole survivor.

The Japanese navy public relations described their feat as 'the glorious incomparable attack on Pearl Harbor by the Special Attack Units at the time of the iconoclastic blow against the outrageous Americans who disregarded our great motive and mission of world peace.'

When Nagumo endeavoured to obtain similar promotion for the fifty-five airmen lost in the attack on Pearl Harbor he was turned down on the ground there were too many. There was a lot of ill-feeling about this. What made Nagumo's carrier pilots particularly angry was that the Imperial General Staff gave midget submarine commander Yokoyama full credit for sinking the battleship *Arizona*. They pointed out there was a repair ship moored outboard of *Arizona*, so a submarine torpedo could not possibly have hit her. They also claimed that *Arizona* exploded immediately after Shimazaki's second wave of high-level bombers had registered two direct hits on it. The General Staff, however, preferred to rely upon Yokoyama's verified radio signal.

The pilots' irate feelings were typified by a remark from *Soryu*'s air officer, Commander Kusumoto, who even went so far as to allege that 'the top echelons in Tokyo seem to be deliberately trying to discourage our victorious naval flyers'.

10

No Sampans for Halsey

WHILE Nagumo disappeared at top speed as suddenly and mysteriously as he had come, complete confusion remained at Pearl Harbor. All kinds of theories were advanced as to where the Japanese carriers had gone. The fact that the Japanese planes had flown round Oahu to approach Pearl Harbor from the south strengthened the opinion that this was the direction from which they had come.

The diligent Opana radar station, which had followed them in, once again correctly tracked the Japanese planes retreating northwards. And once again their superiors failed to inform Pacific Fleet headquarters.

Several shot-down Japanese pilots as well as the midget submariner, Ensign Kazuo Sakamaki, gave quite accurate information about Nagumo's fleet. Yet in the confusion and panic the C.-in-C. Pacific Fleet was not informed of the interrogation.

A direction-finding bearing on a radio transmission from one of Nagumo's carriers, showing it was almost due north of Pearl Harbor, was misinterpreted. By some bad luck the interpreter made it 178 degrees—or almost due south.

Admiral Kimmel guessed right. At 9.42 a.m., as the attack was drawing to a close, he informed outlying sources, 'There is some indication of a Japanese fleet, north-west of Oahu.' He ordered Admiral Halsey to intercept the Japanese fleet, whose composition and position were completely unknown. That was to ask even 'Bull' Halsey for the impossible.

The light cruisers *Detroit*, *St Louis* and *Phoenix*, with destroyers and fast minesweepers, sailed out of Pearl Harbor to join Admiral Halsey's *Enterprise* in the search for 'sampans'—Nagumo's carriers.

It was the false radio bearing that led Kimmel finally to conclude that the Japanese had sailed southwards towards their advance naval base in the Marshall Islands. Light cruisers and destroyers from

Newton's *Lexington* task force returning from Midway were ordered south at dusk in a forlorn effort to catch the Japanese carriers.

A few hours after the news was received in Washington, Admiral Stark ordered the carrier *Yorktown* and the battleships *New Mexico, Mississippi* and *Idaho* from the Atlantic to the Pacific. The carrier⁴ *Saratoga*, about to enter San Diego, was also ordered to sail to Pearl Harbor at once.

While these frantic but useless searches were going on the Americans took stock of the disaster. They found that the Japanese pilots had done most damage to the battleships which were their main target. The battleships moored east of Ford Island suffered the worst.

The *Arizona*, moored inboard of the repair ship *Vestal*, which was too small to offer much protection, was a total loss. Surrounded by burning oil the battleship, claimed by both Japanese pilots and midget submariners, sank, taking with her more than 1,000 men.

As the ships were moored in pairs the outboard vessels suffered severely from torpedoes. The *Oklahoma*, moored outboard of the *Maryland*, received three torpedo hits in the first minutes of the attack. She at once began to capsize and was only raised later to clear the harbour.

The *West Virginia*, outboard of the *Tennessee*, was also torpedoed but prompt counter-flooding prevented her from capsizing. She settled to the bottom with only a moderate list. The *Tennessee* also took two bomb hits but suffered only medium damage. The *Maryland* escaped with only a couple of bomb hits. The *California*, moored singly, was hit by two torpedoes and a bomb. She settled slowly into the Pearl Harbor mud in an upright position. The *Nevada*, also moored alone in Battleship Row, was the only ship to get under way under a hail of bombs. She finally beached herself to avoid being sunk in the channel. The *Pennsylvania*, flagship of the Pacific Fleet, was in dry dock where torpedoes could not touch her. She also put up such a heavy barrage of anti-aircraft fire that she received only a single bomb hit.

The planes, parked in compact rows as a precaution against sabotage, suffered badly. The navy lost eighty planes. Out of the army's 231 planes only seventy-nine were usable after the attack.

Yet Pearl Harbor was much less of a disaster than it appeared at first. The old battleships which were sunk were too slow either to stand up to Japan's newer and faster battleships or to escort the fast American carriers. The attack forced the United States to adopt carrier warfare, which in the long run was to give her victory.

Nagumo made a very grave error when he overlooked 4,500,000 barrels of oil in tank farms near the harbour. It was only 2,000,000 barrels less than the whole Japanese navy supply at the outbreak of war. This carefully accumulated fuel reserve would have taken many months to replace, and without it the Pacific Fleet could not have operated from Pearl Harbor.

But the greatest piece of bad luck for the Japanese was that the three American carriers were not in Pearl Harbor when Nagumo attacked. *Saratoga* was on the west coast, *Lexington* was still delivering planes to Midway and *Enterprise* was returning after delivering planes to Wake Island. This was what soured the 'victory' of Pearl Harbor for Yamamoto and his flyers.

When Nagumo's flying officers gathered in the operations room aboard his flagship *Akagi* to analyse the results of the attack, their main anxiety was still to find and destroy the American carriers which had eluded them. They surmised rightly that some of the missing carriers were to the south of Oahu engaged in training exercises. If Nagumo's carriers, instead of returning by the northern route, sailed south to the Marshalls, carrying out continual air searches, perhaps they would locate the American carriers. Staff officers quickly pointed out that this was impossible. They were short of fuel, and tankers were already heading for a pre-arranged fuelling point on the northern withdrawal route. If they sailed south they would miss them.

Next day Nagumo dropped his speed down to fifteen knots to conserve fuel. About 550 miles from Midway his carriers turned west until they were well beyond the range of American planes patrolling from the atoll. The carriers *Soryu* and *Hiryu*, and the heavy cruisers *Tone* and *Chikuma*, with the destroyers *Urakaze* and *Tanikaze*, were detached to support the scheduled invasion of Wake Island. Between 21 and 23 December they made almost continuous strikes against Wake. The other carriers steamed on through heavy seas towards Japan.

It did not become clear to the Americans until Monday evening— thirty-six hours after the attack—that the Japanese attack had come from the north. *Minneapolis*, with a force of light cruisers, searched all day in that direction although Admiral Kimmel knew it was too late to catch up with the Japanese carriers.

The fact that the haphazard, clueless searches were unsuccessful was fortunate for the United States. Neither *Enterprise* nor *Lexington* would have been any match for Nagumo. Not only did he have six carriers escorted by battleships and heavy cruisers but his crews were half-jubilant and half-disappointed. Flying officers talked about nothing else but the chance to sink the carriers they had missed at Pearl Harbor.

Even if Nagumo had met *Lexington* and *Enterprise* together he could have put 350 planes in the air against their 131. With a superiority of nearly three-to-one there is no doubt he would have sunk the American carriers.

The wave of American hatred against Japan after Yamamoto's lightning blow was unparalleled in modern history. When the news of Pearl Harbor broke, some maddened patriots chopped down four Japanese cherry trees in Washington Tidal Basin. The Japanese deer in New York Central Park Zoo were saved from destruction only because someone very quickwittedly put up freshly painted signs reading 'Asiatic deer'.

If the American public was shocked by the announcement of Pearl Harbor the Japanese were more so. A totally unexpected broadcast on Sunday morning said without preliminary, 'At midnight today [Tokyo time] our army and navy opened hostilities with American and British forces.'

People listened open-mouthed. They were unable to comprehend the announcement. Many of them thought it was a hoax. They knew that diplomatic relations between their country and the United States had been strained since the summer when the American Government had frozen Japanese assets in the United States. They also vaguely knew from their newspapers the negotiations in Washington had not been going well. The ordinary Japanese-in-the-street, like so many people of other nations, found it difficult to follow all this international tension. Then without warning came the announcement of total war! Surely it was a mistake? Shortly after the first broadcast came the solemn reading over the radio of the Imperial Rescript declaring war. The Emperor had spoken. Japan really was at war.

Neither the navy nor the army shared the shock and alarm of the civilians. On the first day of war, officers jammed the message rooms of Imperial Headquarters in Tokyo anxiously awaiting the first reports. An unending stream of radio signals described the victories

won. Even the apprehensions of senior officers faded with the increasing number of glowing reports. The first hours of war revealed victories which far exceeded the most optimistic pre-war estimates. No country simultaneously launched so many battles of such magnitude or so completely defeated its enemies as the Japanese did in their carefully planned operations stretching 6,000 miles from Hawaii to Malaya.

In some ways Pearl Harbor was the worst thing that could have happened to the Japanese. Before the attack they were not confident of success. As one of Nagumo's pilots put it, 'We felt as if we were about to pull the eagle's tail feathers.' Now their initial fears changed to wild joy, and officers jubilantly cheered each new message of conquest.

But easily the most stirring news was Yamamoto's daring, magnificently planned and executed attack—the greatest air operation ever seen up to this time. In a single blow 353 planes from six aircraft carriers had completely wrecked the powerful battleship fleet of the United States. For the loss of fifty-five Japanese flyers, 2,000 officers and men had been killed in this unannounced attack.

Without firing a single gun, Yamamoto had almost completely destroyed the most formidable warships of the United States Pacific Fleet. A new era in naval warfare had begun. Ever since modern navies had been built the battleship had been regarded as the queen of the sea. Now this was no longer true.

Another amazing factor about the Hawaiian operation was that the planes were so skilfully employed that less than half of them actually attacked the battleships. Although 353 aircraft took part, only 154 were assigned to attack the American warships. The remaining 199 aircraft were ordered to strafe and bomb the Hawaiian airfields.

Pearl Harbor in particular caused young officers to clamour for combat duty. Rumours spread among the naval flyers in training that the war would end within a month with a smashing victory for Japan. This would mean they would be robbed of their chance to fight the enemy.

The tremendous industrial potential of Japan's enemies meant nothing to them. They were fully convinced the war would end before they could join in. But many senior officers, with a more intimate knowledge of the long-range consequences, felt very anxious about the future. One of them was Yamamoto.

And, for different reasons, so did the American naval chief, Admiral Stark. For Yamamoto by his bold unorthodox use of sea and air power had put the United States on the defensive at once. The day after Pearl Harbor Stark issued a basic war plan in which he ruled that the primary duties of the Pacific Fleet were now defensive. They must prevent any further Japanese advance in the western hemisphere.

Stark's plan was in fact the original Rainbow Five Plan. This called in time for the capture of the Marshall and Caroline Islands so that an advance naval base could be set up at Truk. This would support the Royal Navy south of the Equator and westwards to the Solomon Islands.

That was the long-range plan. But what about the more immediate future? Kimmel thought the Japanese carriers might be replenishing their fuel and ammunition in their Marshall bases preparatory to another attack on Pearl Harbor. Or were fast battleships already escorting transports to Oahu or some other Hawaiian island? Perhaps they would range farther. Attacks on San Francisco or the Panama Canal were not impossible.

The attack by *Hiryu* and *Soryu* on planes on Wake Island, which was a stepping stone to Midway, made any of these seem probable. At least Admiral Stark thought so. He informed Kimmel that he expected Midway and Hawaii to be occupied before the Japanese closed on Oahu. Midway might be lost. Nor could the shattered fleet defend Guam or the Philippines. But Johnston, Palmyra and Samoa must be held at all costs.

Meanwhile *Enterprise*, having searched unsuccessfully to the west for the Japanese carriers, entered Pearl Harbor on Monday afternoon. She refuelled all night and set off at dawn to hunt submarines. Intelligence reported correctly that Japanese I-class submarines were sailing to the west coast of America. Halsey spent a lively five days searching, 'wasting too many depth charges on neutral fish'.

It was not such a wild-goose chase as he thought. Nine I-class submarines out of the twenty-seven which had sailed from the Inland Sea before Pearl Harbor had in fact gone to the west coast of America. Some of the 2,000-ton undersea cruisers encountered the American fleet. Three days after Pearl Harbor just before dawn on 10 December a plane from *Enterprise*, piloted by Lieutenant Edward L. Anderson, patrolling 200 miles north-east of Oahu, spotted the *I-70* and dive-bombed her so she was unable to submerge. Later in the day another *Enterprise* pilot, Lieutenant Clarence D. Dickinson, found the submarine surfaced with men and wreckage around it. He dive-bombed and sank it.

The same day *Enterprise*, while recovering her planes, saw another submarine dead ahead. When a destroyer raced up to depth-charge it it crash dived at once.

Next day a torpedo passed twenty yards astern of the *Enterprise*. These small engagements were the only contact by American planes or ships with Yamamoto's great fleet.

In mid-December Kimmel, partially blamed for the Pearl Harbor disaster, was superseded by a blue-eyed Texan, Admiral Chester W. Nimitz, whose defensive tasks were sharply defined as:

1. Holding the Hawaii–Midway line and maintaining communications with America.

2. Maintaining communications between the United States and Australia.

This meant America was determined to stop further Japanese encroachments but not to attack—she could not. Yamamoto had seen to that.

However the architect of Pearl Harbor was not as overjoyed as other naval officers about its success. Although the operation brilliantly achieved its aim to prevent the U.S. Pacific Fleet from interfering with Japanese attacks to seize oil resources, its failure to find the American carriers bothered Yamamoto. Ironically enough, his worry was even greater because his own successful attack had demonstrated just how vital and formidable carriers were going to be in the coming Pacific war.

As the Japanese carriers cruised back to home waters the same problem constantly exercised the minds of all his pilots. Commander Genda, Nagumo's air operations officer, was particularly concerned about the missing carriers. Like Kimmel, he thought Nagumo's fleet should put into Truk lagoon, refuel and sail out at once to find them. Genda also thought invasion operations should start against Midway Island, 1,100 miles south-west of Pearl Harbor. His view coincided with Admiral Kimmel's that it was necessary to strike again quickly and this scheme seemed the best way to follow up the Pearl Harbor success. His idea was put into operation—six months later. It was to lead to Japan's greatest defeat, at Midway.

Nagumo still sailed on towards home. The carriers sighted the coast of Japan just before Christmas. *Akagi* and *Kaga* arrived in Kure in the Inland Sea on Christmas Eve. Next day they were joined by *Shokaku* and *Zuikaku*. Three days later *Hiryu* and *Soryu* sailed in from Wake Island. Every carrier crew received a tremendous ovation for having delivered such a blow for the Emperor.

Upon their return, they found the Japanese naval staff so complacent and elated over the destruction of the battleships at Pearl Harbor that they were lukewarm towards any plan for a prompt follow-up against the American carriers. There were, however, many criticisms, particularly among Yamamoto's own staff, about Nagumo's failure to inflict any damage on the American carriers or make a third attack which would have destroyed the oil storage tanks on Oahu.

Nagumo's answer was that he had obeyed orders. He had destroyed the battleships and other military installations at Pearl Harbor. This was not the reply of an imaginative leader, which indeed he was not. In fact he was not even a carrier man. He was a torpedo expert. He had been given command of the big carriers because he was the senior admiral.

Yamamoto's fiery operations officer, Admiral Kuroshima, who had been prevented from sending him a signal to find the carriers, put it to Yamamoto bluntly that he should transfer Nagumo after what he regarded as the partial failure of Pearl Harbor.

Yamamoto would not agree for a curious reason. He said, 'How can I? He is an old-fashioned *samurai* type. If I move him he will commit hara-kiri because he will consider it such a disgrace.'

Was the village schoolmaster's son a little in social awe of the ineffectual but aristocratic admiral who served under him? For by keeping Nagumo, Yamamoto went a long way towards dooming himself and his navy.

The only forces still left in touch with the Americans were Yamamoto's nine big submarines patrolling off the coast between Seattle and San Diego. By Christmas-time, in spite of their long range, they were running short of fuel. Before they left to refuel they were very anxious to give the American people a Christmas present.

They wanted to send a message saying, 'Roosevelt is the enemy of peace. He must take full blame for this war.' This Christmas message was to be transmitted on the American naval wavelengths in their own code so they could easily pick it up. They also wanted to place it in missiles to be fired on American coastal towns.

Everyone in the Japanese submarine fleet, including their C.-in-C., Admiral Shimizu, was enthusiastic about the idea of wishing Roosevelt an unhappy Christmas. There was one snag. No one spoke good enough English to translate the message. They decided to ask Naval Headquarters in Tokyo, where there were many English speakers, to write it for them.

The admirals in Tokyo proclaimed themselves profoundly shocked by the idea. In spite of their sneak attack on Pearl Harbor they said, 'Americans are Christians and even if they are enemies you must not mock their holy day. They must not be wantonly attacked during their Christmas period.'

Although they felt the stuffy old admirals could not see a joke, the submarine commanders reluctantly dropped the idea. Only one submarine disobeyed. She shelled San Diego on Christmas Eve, setting some fuel tanks on fire.

In the same period the submarines scored their first success. On 11 January the *I–6* torpedoed the 33,000-ton carrier *Saratoga* 500 miles off Oahu. Three fire rooms were damaged and six men killed and, although she managed to reach Pearl Harbor under her own power, she had to return to the United States for major repairs.

Another submarine inadvertently gave away a closely guarded secret in another part of the world. On 10 January, the *I–124*, commanded by Lieutenant-Commander Koichi Kishigame, sailed from Dabao in Indonesia to lay mines outside Port Darwin in Australia. She laid twenty-seven mines in the harbour mouth and then patrolled outside looking for Allied shipping.

At nine o'clock on the evening of 19 January, Commander Kishigame signalled he was following a merchant ship and a cruiser entering the harbour. After that there was silence. The *I–124* was sunk by depth charges in 150 feet of water off Darwin.

Australian divers went down and found her nameplate. Then relays of other divers followed, armed with oxy-acetylene torches to cut open her hull. Patrol boats stood by while bubbles from the underwater torches and the divers' breathing apparatus floated up to the surface. Soon objects from the sunken submarine, attached to lines by the divers, were being hauled to the surface. One of them was a thick black book heavily weighted with lead. It was a Japanese naval code book which confirmed the findings of Colonel William F. Friedman.

*   *   *

Whether Pearl Harbor, although a short-range success, was a long-range mistake, will be debated as long as naval history is written. The Emperor of Japan proclaimed he had no doubts when he sent this message to Yamamoto forty-eight hours after the operation:

At the very outbreak of this war our Combined Fleet has displayed a brilliant strategy and fought bravely. At Hawaii it has heavily crushed the enemy's fleet and air strength. We have received a report of this signal achievement ourself. Moreover we extend our deepest praise to our fighting forces, officers and men alike. If they strive harder and harder we foresee a magnificent future for our Empire.

In the opinion of Admiral Thomas S. Hart, Commander-in-Chief of the Asiatic Fleet at the time, Nagumo made a vital error in not pressing on with the third attack. His view was that the loss of the oil installations would have probably delayed the American counter offensive in the Pacific much longer than the sinking of her battleships.

The American naval historian S. E. Morison says emphatically that strategically Pearl Harbor was a ridiculous and stupid operation. His view:

If the Japanese had not carried out their attack on Pearl Harbor the Rainbow Five operational plan, which was to begin with a declaration of war, would have been carried out. The U.S. Pacific Fleet would have attacked Japanese positions in the Marshall and Caroline archipelagos including Truk Island.

This means that if the Hawaii operation had not been conducted by the Japanese the U.S. fleet would instead have launched an offensive. The Japanese navy accordingly could have launched its long-cherished counter operation by calmly remaining in waiting. The Japanese navy had for thirty years been arduously engaged in studying and training for the so-called 'counter-attack decisive battle against the U.S. fleet'. This American onslaught was to be countered and destroyed in the seas adjacent to Japan as the only sure way of gaining a victory. No offensive operation against Hawaii had ever been contemplated in the past.

Is Morison's view correct? Admiral William V. Pratt, one of the most illustrious figures of the modern U.S. Navy, totally disagrees. In a letter to Admiral Hichisaburo Nomura, Japan's joint ambassador and naval negotiator in Washington at the time of Pearl Harbor, an intimate friend of his, he described Yamamoto's attack on Pearl Harbor as 'a most thoroughly planned and daring project—a strategical success of rare precedence in history.'

Admiral Shigeru Fukudome, Yamamoto's chief of staff at the time it was planned, commented, 'We plunged into a desperate war disregarding the issue whether we won or lost. But it was not until February 1944 that the U.S. fleet began its real advance across the Pacific. This gave us two years and two months to prepare for the American assault.'

Fukudome's view of Pearl Harbor and the war is typically Japanese. They did not expect complete defeat but they were not optimistic —only fanatically keyed up. Fukudome said afterwards, 'We thought victory was a ninety per cent possibility. There was also a ten per cent possibility of national death.'

The bold attack by Yamamoto on America's biggest Pacific base was undoubtedly greatly helped to success by the laxity of the American defences. What was the greatest American weakness at Pearl Harbor? Complete carelessness – the Americans thought the Japanese would never dare to attack it.

As Admiral King commented, 'An unwarranted feeling of immunity from attack seems to have pervaded all ranks at Pearl Harbor, both army and navy.'

If the alert had been given at 7 a.m. when the Opana radar picked up Nagumo's scout plane it would have given the Americans fifty minutes' grace before Fuchida's bombers dived into the attack. This would have been plenty of time for aircraft to take to the air and ships to disperse. The battleships could have been getting up steam if not already under way.

What was the reason for the incredible laxity of the American commanders? The Congress Investigating Committee has this to say in its report:

The estimate of the situation made by Admiral Kimmel and Army Commander General Short was not altogether incredible in the light of the inevitable lassitude born of over twenty years of peace. Both of them insisted they received no information that Hawaii was to be attacked. Yet a commander in the field cannot presume to expect that he will be advised of the exact time and place an enemy will attack. As outpost commanders it was their responsibility to be prepared against surprise and the worst possible intelligence.

Yamamoto's intelligence about the U.S. fleet was nearly as scanty. When he attacked he was still not sure if the American ships were fitted with torpedo nets. In case nets nullified his torpedo attacks, he depended very much upon the large number of high-level bombers commanded by the skilful, seasoned Fuchida. Poor intelligence also caused Admiral Nagumo to risk detection by sending out scout planes an hour ahead of Fuchida's first-wave bombers, which were detected by the Opana radar station. Yamamoto's ring of information-seeking submarines operating round Pearl Harbor before the attack could also have been easily detected if the defences had been more alert.

Before Pearl Harbor only a handful of American naval officers had ever heard of Admiral Isoroku Yamamoto, C.-in-C. of the Japanese Combined Fleet. After that fateful Sunday morning his name was on everyone's lips. To every American he was the embodiment of the evil enemy, the stab-in-the-back aggressor, the peculiarly personal foe. He remained so until the Americans managed to kill him—in an act of personal revenge. For not only was he the man who had planned the treacherous blow at Pearl Harbor but, to add insult to injury, he was believed to be arrogantly planning to dictate peace in the White House.

The story of the famous boast about dictating terms in the White House began as a broadcast intended for Japanese internal consumption only. It was picked up by American monitors and reached the American Press ten days after Pearl Harbor. It made wonderful hate propaganda.

The broadcast relayed a letter published in the Tokyo daily *Yomiuri*, which Yamamoto was supposed to have sent to a close friend on 24 January 1941 in which he said, 'Any time war breaks out between Japan and the United States I shall not be content to capture Guam and the Philippines and to occupy Hawaii and San Francisco. I am looking forward to dictating peace to the United States at the White House in Washington.'

This broadcast was believed implicitly and is still believed in America by many people. It was also believed by the Japanese, as it was meant to be. For it was put out by the military-controlled Press to bolster up Japanese morale shaken and stunned by the news of the outbreak of war.

Yamamoto did write a letter on that date. But, as so often happens with unscrupulous wartime propaganda, his words were plucked out of context and twisted. Yamamoto's real letter had quite a different meaning. It was not to a 'close friend' but to an acquaintance, Ryoichi Sasakawa, an extreme right-wing Trade Unionist, leader of the ultra-nationalist All-Japan Labour Class Federation.

It said:

24 January 1941

Dear Sir,

I trust you are in the best of health. I deeply appreciate the trip of inspection you made to the South Seas. In this age when armchair arguments are being glibly bandied about in the name of State politics your sober attitude in going to so much trouble to be loyal to your own opinion is to be most highly commended. But it embarrasses me not a little to hear you say that you 'feel at ease in the knowledge that Yamamoto is out at sea with his fleet'.

All I am doing is to devote my utmost by day and night towards building up our strength, ever bearing in mind the Imperial admonition, 'Despise not an enemy because he is weak; fear him not because he is strong'. I am counting only on the loyalty of the 100,000 officers and men who are going about their duties in silence and without boasting.

Should hostilities break out between Japan and the United States it is not enough that we take Guam and the Philippines or even Hawaii and San Francisco. We would have to march into Washington and sign the treaty in the White House. I wonder if our politicians who speak so lightly of a Japanese–American war have confidence as to the outcome and are prepared to make the necessary sacrifices?

With best wishes for your good health,

Respectfully yours,

I.Y.

The admiral was pointing out to Sasakawa that war with America was not so simple as political warmongers might think. It was easier to start a war than finish one. However much territory the Japanese took, final victory might finally elude them. He never swerved from this view.

This opinion he openly displayed on the eve of Pearl Harbor.

On 11 November 1941 he sent a letter to his friend, retired Vice-Admiral Teikichi Hori. It was less than four weeks before Pearl Harbor and Nagumo's carriers were already concentrating in the Inland Sea when he wrote:

Friend Hori, My family I leave to your guidance while I am away.

1. I recognize that the general situation has already come to the worst. How miserable it is to have to say as did Admiral Yamanashi, 'This is fate.'

2. But then further arguments pro and con will avail nothing. Now that we have reached the stage where 'the Emperor alone must grieve over the state of affairs in the land', the only thing that can save the situation is the final Imperial decision. But how difficult that will be in view of the present situation in the country.

3. What a strange position I find myself in now—having to make a decision diametrically opposed to my own personal opinion with no choice but to push full-speed in pursuance of that decision. Is that, too, fate?

4. And what a bad start we've made with one serious occurrence after another resulting from blunders from the very beginning of the year!

With cordial regards, Yours, Isoroku.

Ten days after Pearl Harbor, when his victory was being celebrated hysterically all over Japan, he remained unmoved and pessimistic. He wrote to his sister, Kazuko; 'Well, war has begun at last. But in spite of all the clamour that is going on we could lose it. I can only do my best.'

Even the Emperor's personal letter of congratulation, although as a good Japanese he was awed by it, failed to cheer him up. As the victories piled up Yamamoto remained uneasy and unhappy. When Admiral Yonai, one of Japan's most revered elder admirals, gave a party for him in Tokyo to celebrate Pearl Harbor he was not very merry. On the same day he wrote to a friend:

This war will give us much trouble in the future. The fact that we have had a small success at Pearl Harbor is nothing. The fact that we have succeeded so easily has pleased people. Personally I do not think it is a good thing to whip up propaganda to encourage the nation. People should think things over and realize how serious the situation is.

*   *   *

In this period Yamamoto's warships fought one bitter battle in which they were completely victorious. The battle of the Java Sea, fought by cruisers against cruisers, was the biggest surface engagement since Jutland.

At the end of February 1942, the Japanese began gathering convoys in preparation for encircling Java and completing their hold on the Dutch East Indies. They had nearly a hundred transports for this big, vital operation, for which the overall commander was Admiral Sokichi Takagi. His flagship was the heavy cruiser *Haguro*, accompanied by her sister ship *Nachi*. He also had the light cruisers *Jintsu* and *Naka* and destroyer groups, making seventeen ships in all. Their task was to protect two great convoys. One consisted of fifty-six transports and cargo vessels under the command of Rear-Admiral Jisabura Ozawa, and escorted by *Jintsu* and seven destroyers. Rear-Admiral Shoji Nishimura waited in the Macassar Strait with forty-one transports covered by the light cruiser *Naka* and seven more destroyers.

To prevent this great convoy landing on Java, the Allies had only a mixed and partly damaged fleet commanded by a gallant, gangling dark-haired Dutch admiral, Karel Doorman. He could not scrape together much of a force to meet the Japanese. Apart from his flagship, the Dutch cruiser *De Ruyter*, he had the British cruiser *Exeter*, the American *Houston*, two light cruisers the Australian *Perth* and the Dutch *Java* and ten destroyers, of three different nationalities. His only course of action was to lead this small fleet out to try to smash the two convoys one at a time. For several days Doorman cruised round the Java Sea frantically searching for Takagi's ships but found nothing.

On the morning of 27 February he was half-way across the Java Sea making towards Surabaya to refuel. His whole fleet was in poor shape. His men had been at action stations continuously for thirty-seven hours and he had just radioed, 'Exhaustion point far exceeded', when there came a report of a big convoy of Japanese transports approaching. There was only one thing to do. Doorman, with his motley fleet and tired crews, turned and headed for the Japanese ships.

At 4.12 p.m. the British destroyer *Electra*, searching ahead of Doorman's cruisers, found seven Japanese destroyers and the cruiser *Jintsu*. When she radioed, 'Enemy sighted,' she did not know that Takagi's two big cruisers were only a few miles away.

The Allied fleet, with *De Ruyter* in the van, formed into a battle line. The Japanese ships also turned into battle formation. At 25,000 yards, *Houston* and *Exeter* opened fire and flames spouted from the leading Japanese destroyers. The Allied ships were firing much more rapidly than the Japanese, three salvoes to the Japanese two. It looked as though they would soon destroy the light cruiser and her escorting destroyers.

Doorman decided to close to 20,000 yards, but as he steamed forward to shorten the range the two Japanese heavy cruisers, *Haguro* and *Nachi*, appeared. Between them they had twenty eight-inch guns while Doorman's cruisers could only bring twelve eight-inch guns to bear. While *Jintsu* concentrated on the other ships, the two big cruisers fired on the vulnerable light cruiser *Perth*. She could not reply because her guns had too short a range.

Then the Japanese light cruiser *Naka* steamed forward with six destroyers to fire torpedoes. These deadly Japanese weapons, with a range of 30,000 yards, were propelled by oxygen fuel which left no bubbling wake to warn their victims of their approach. Within the next few minutes fifty torpedoes were launched by the Japanese destroyers and cruisers. They all missed. The Japanese in their excitement released them too far away even for their great range.

Under the thickening curtain of smoke and the flames of exploding shells and burning ships, Doorman was fighting the battle blindfold, as only the *Exeter* was fitted with radar. Takagi was also without radar but three Japanese float planes flew lazily in the blue sky above the smoky, flame-shot cauldron of battle. Whenever they caught a glimpse of one of Doorman's warships scurrying through the battle haze with her guns ablaze they reported her position to Takagi. Instantly Japanese fire was brought to bear on her.

The British destroyers *Electra* and *Jupiter* dashed forward into the heavy smoke to try and prevent the Japanese destroyers closing the range and firing more torpedoes. The little *Electra* fired on the cruiser *Jintsu* and hit her several times. It was a desperately brave action but she was doomed as soon as *Jintsu* brought her bigger guns to bear. There was an enormous explosion, a gush of flames and *Electra* was no more.

Haguro was now fighting a fierce duel with *Exeter*. Great geysers of boiling spray shot up as shells narrowly missed each ship. Then just after five o'clock a shell smacked into *Exeter*'s boiler room. The exploding boilers shook her from end to end and her speed dropped to five knots. As *Exeter* swung away from the Japanese, *Perth* steamed forward to place a protective smoke screen round her.

In the smoke and confusion of battle the other British ships, seeing *Exeter* turn, and not realizing how badly she was hit, assumed she was obeying an order from Doorman. They followed her—an action leading to confusion and near-collision. As the Allied cruisers milled around aimlessly, the Japanese destroyers seized their chance. They steamed forward at full speed and their torpedoes began snaking in among the reeling ships. However, by good luck and skilful seamanship, all Doorman's vessels dodged them except one Dutch destroyer which suddenly puffed smoke and flame, snapped in half and sank.

The flamboyant Eastern sunset was now beginning to change into sudden tropical darkness. The crippled *Exeter*, her flames a halo round her dark bulk, must make a perfect night target. Sighting her bright glow, the Japanese would smash her into the sea within a few minutes. Doorman ordered her to sail as fast as she was able back to Surabaya.

With *Exeter* gone, he re-formed his battered line of ships to continue the fight. He sailed ahead of them headlong into the blinding smoke, blotched with red gun flashes and yellow explosions. When *Haguro* and *Nachi* suddenly appeared like grey ghosts, in a break in the smoke, Doorman ordered every gun to bear on them. As his shells spattered round them, Takagi suddenly sighted the Surabaya lighthouse and realized that in the fury of battle he had sailed too near the coast for the safety of his ships.

It was 6.30 p.m. and getting too dark to fight, so he turned and steamed at full speed out to sea. Both sides took advantage of the lull in the battle to give their bone-weary crews a hasty meal. Aboard the Allied cruisers, smoke-grimed sailors lay sprawled on deck drinking fruit juice or tea and eating tinned sausages. The equally battle-blackened but much less exhausted crews aboard the Japanese ships hungrily gobbled dried fish and boiled rice.

While the sailors of both fleets were wearily eating, the indomitable Doorman was thinking of ways to tackle the Japanese cruisers again. If he could only smash them he could sink the transports at leisure and prevent the invasion of Java. While he pondered, an explosion and a sheet of flame came from the British destroyer *Jupiter*, which immediately sank. At first Doorman thought it was the Japanese attacking again. Then he discovered she had hit a Dutch mine which had been laid that afternoon without his knowledge.

Although his four remaining cruisers were in no real fighting condition, the dogged Doorman was still determined to find the Japanese. At 11 o'clock on a black cloudy night he ran straight into Takagi, who was withdrawing with his two heavy cruisers. The latter rapidly launched twelve torpedoes at the nearly point-blank range of 10,000 yards. Several of them hit *De Ruyter*, which suddenly blazed like a blow torch in the darkness. The Dutch light cruiser *Java* shuddered with gigantic explosions and plunged into the black water. The furiously blazing *De Ruyter* was now a perfect lit-up target and as other torpedoes slammed into her she began to break up. Doorman frantically signalled to the rest of his ships, 'Retire to harbour of Batavia.' Then a series of explosions convulsed his ship and she slipped under the sea taking the heroic Dutch admiral with her.

In twenty minutes it was all over. The only survivors, *Houston* and *Perth*, began to steam away from Takagi. He did not pursue them through the dark night. He had no need. His ships were practically undamaged and his convoys were safe to sail on to Java. The battle was won and the Japanese naval cordon was tightening.

The remnants of the Allied fleet had to try to escape before they were cornered and sunk. Next day, 28 February, the damaged *Exeter* tried to break out. Her only chance was to sail through the fourteen-mile Sunda Strait dividing Java from Sumatra. Escorted by an American and a British destroyer, she limped out of Surabaya to try to escape the Japanese net.

A few hours later the less damaged *Houston* and *Perth* followed her. They made much faster speed than the crippled *Exeter* and tried to sneak through the narrow Sunda Strait on a humid, moonlit night. Lurking near was a big Japanese naval force, including the aircraft carrier *Ryujo*, a group of destroyers, and two more cruisers, *Mogami* and *Mikuma*. They were being held in reserve in case the Allies brought up carriers or any other big warships to resist the landings.

At 10.30 p.m. *Mogami* and *Mikuma* saw *Houston* and *Perth* and opened fire at once. A shell from *Mogami* smashed into *Perth*'s seamen's mess just as a torpedo exploded in her boiler room. She began to lose speed, and oil and water gushed over her decks. Then *Mikuma* began to fire on *Houston* and one of her heavy shells exploded in the after engine room, causing clouds of choking steam and scalding the stokers to death.

It was just after midnight when *Perth*, lurching from side to side as if in pain, rolled over for the last time and dived beneath the waves.

Houston, with half her boilers blown out, was down to six knots. A bugle sounded 'Abandon ship' and the survivors of her crew jumped to join the survivors of *Perth* swimming in the oily, dark, wreckage-strewn sea. Orange flames licked her from stem to stern and black smoke streamed from her as she turned slowly over and disappeared. It was 12.45 a.m.

It had been a confused deadly battle in the moonlight. *Mikuma*'s crew in the excitement of their first action had fired a few wild torpedoes. One of them hit the headquarters ship of the invading 16th Japanese army. The commanding general, Hitoshi Imamura, leapt into the oil-covered sea and, surrounded by half-drowned American and Australian sailors, swam ashore clinging to a spar.

While *Perth* and *Houston* were being battered to death by the Japanese cruisers, the slow-moving *Exeter* was sixty miles south of Borneo limping towards her own fate in the Sunda Strait. As she steamed painfully towards the narrow waters her commander, Captain O. L. Gordon, did not hold out much hope, for she could neither manœuvre nor fully protect herself.

He knew the end had come when in broad daylight at 9.35 a.m. next morning he fell within range of the heavy cruisers *Haguro* and *Nachi*. Then *Mikuma* and *Mogami* appeared steaming fast from the other side. *Exeter* frantically loosed torpedoes at them but the range was too great and the Japanese vessels avoided them easily. The four heavy cruisers began mercilessly to batter the crippled ship with eight-inch shells and torpedoes.

Exeter, famous for her victory over the German *Graf Spee* early in the European war, fought savagely for her life. Although shell after shell crashed into her, she fought for over an hour. At 11.20 a.m., as she drifted helplessly on the water, an eight-inch shell smashed her last steam pipe. She stopped dead, her engines idle, her steering smashed, her guns silent and useless. She was listing heavily with yellow flames and black smoke spouting into the peaceful blue sky when Captain Gordon gave the order to abandon ship and sink her. There was no need. The white ensign was still flying at her masthead when her stern rose and she plunged under the waves in a cloud of steam. Japanese destroyers picked up 300 of her officers and crew.

Only four small warships, American destroyers of the old four-stack type, successfully escaped this sea massacre and reached Australia. They managed to sneak unchallenged through the shallower waters of Bali Strait which the cruisers, with their deeper draught, could not negotiate.

With the last of Doorman's warships starting to rust at the bottom of the seas around Java, the invading troops were able to land almost unmolested. Java with its oil wells was safely in Japanese hands. Yamamoto now had enough fuel to fight as long as his ships could float.

A Day in June

11

Nagumo Sails to Ceylon

EARLY in 1942 Japan's victories were almost complete. She had grabbed everything she wanted. She held the Dutch East Indies with their oil, the great British base of Singapore was in her hands, and Yamamoto had crippled the U.S. Pacific Fleet. Only in the Philippines were the Americans fighting a last-stand rearguard action.

But how was Japan to continue the war? Her easy lightning victories left her military leaders a little groggy, like a successful boxer who has scored an unexpected quick knockout. But, unlike a boxing champion, Japan had to go on fighting.

At the end of 1941 neither the navy nor the army had any agreed long-range strategic plan. Should Japan concentrate on holding what she had won? Or should she remain on the offensive, aiming to conquer still more new territories? If so, where? Should she strike westwards against India and Britain? Or in Hawaii and the Pacific against the United States? Which would be the most effective? And which would be the easiest, not only to conquer but to supply and hold against counter-attack?

All future war planning depended upon Yamamoto. Theoretically naval strategy was the prerogative of the Naval General Staff functioning as part of Imperial Headquarters. Admiral Osami Nagano, Chief of the Naval General Staff, had the power to issue orders to Yamamoto as Commander-in-Chief Combined Fleet. In practice, after Pearl Harbor, Yamamoto and his officers shaped future fleet plans. The Naval General Staff's only function was to act as an umpire when disagreements arose—and very often not even that.

Everyone realized that Yamamoto must take the second big step in the naval war. The great success of his Pearl Harbor attack, mounted against strong opposition from the Naval General Staff, made his influence paramount and unquestioned. Unlike their serious, austere commander-in-chief, Yamamoto's staff officers exuded an air of smug self-confidence. It was nicknamed 'victory disease' by more clear-thinking naval officers. But the Naval General Staff handled them tactfully and delicately. After all they had been proved right—and the Tokyo desk admirals wrong.

In spite of the widespread complacent jubilation, Yamamoto fully appreciated that the Imperial Navy could not stand still. In the middle of January he ordered his chief of staff, Matomi Ugaki, to prepare a blueprint for the fleet's next action.

Ugaki knew he had not much time. In two months—in the middle of March—the first phase of offensive operations, triggered off at Pearl Harbor, would end.

But the enemy, both British and American, would soon recover and start planning the heaviest counter-attacks of which they were capable. If a decision on future strategy was not reached by the end of February the Imperial Navy would just drift. In a situation like that they could easily be caught napping by the Americans.

Admiral Ugaki locked himself in his cabin aboard the battleship *Nagato,* anchored in Hiroshima Bay. He spent four days there alone. His only visitor was a steward who brought him his meals of rice and green tea. When he emerged from his lengthy meditation he told Yamamoto the fleet must remain vigorously on the offensive. He suggested three possible moves—an attack on Australia, India or Hawaii.

Ugaki proclaimed himself personally in favour of a move against Hawaii. No one was surprised at this as he had always been a Hawaii-first man.

He gave these reasons for his decision:

1. Because of the vastly superior national resources of the United States time was working against Japan. Unless Japan quickly resumed the offensive, she would be incapable of doing anything except wait for the inevitable counter-attack.

2. If Germany succeeded in conquering England, the British fleet might reinforce America in the Pacific. This would double the pressure upon the Japanese navy. The surest way to avert this threat was to sink the American fleet before the situation arose. Then the Royal Navy could be dealt with separately. The destruction of these two big navies offered the only possible chance of speedily ending the war.

3. Seizure of Hawaii and the loss of the American fleet would constitute the most damaging blows to the United States.

4. A decisive fleet engagement in waters close to Hawaii had the best chance of success. In such a battle the Japanese fleet had a three-to-one advantage in aircraft carriers and an overwhelming superiority in battleships.

Yamamoto's staff officers had many doubts about Admiral Ugaki's plan. For instance the fleet could not sail straight there. The vital American base at Midway which acted as a sentinel for Hawaii must first be taken.

Three unanswered problems stood out:

1. The Japanese could not expect to achieve surprise as they did ,at Pearl Harbor.
2. They had not enough air strength to gain control of the skies over so large an area as the Hawaiian Islands.
3. In a battle between ships and shore batteries, the odds would be heavily against the battleships.

But other officers, apart from Ugaki, were also studying Japan's naval plans. One of them was the senior fleet operations officer, Rear-Admiral Kamahito Kuroshima, who came out as an advocate of the go-west plans—to destroy the British fleet and capture Ceylon. This would give Japan control over the Indian Ocean and shield the Dutch East Indies and Malaya. It might also lead to an early junction with German forces in the Middle East. Ugaki's capture of Hawaii and Kuroshima's anti-British plan were given to the staff to study. No one could agree and the argument raged right through February.

When a four-day war game to consider both plans was staged aboard Yamamoto's new flagship, the recently completed *Yamato*, it led to no firm decision. Afterwards a joint conference was held in Tokyo to discuss the plans with the army commanders. This was necessary because troops would have to be switched from Burma and Malaya for an attack on Ceylon. Army commanders, still obsessed with a possible attack on the Soviet Union, were opposed to releasing any troops to capture further territory. That was the end of Kuro-shima's Ceylon plan.

While Yamamoto's admirals pondered in their darkened cabins in Hiroshima Bay, the Naval General Staff planners in Tokyo had also been busy. They wanted to attack Australia. Captain Sadatoshi Tomioka on the staff of Rear-Admiral Shigeru Fukudome, Chief of

Operations, rightly argued that Australia must become the springboard for a counter-offensive against Japan. This meant there was an urgent need to have it under Japanese control—or at least cut it off from the United States.

The Australia-first plan was even more speedily rejected by the army than Kuroshima's proposed occupation of Ceylon. Ten combat divisions was the minimum required for the invasion of Australia, and the Army High Command said emphatically they could not spare them.

The truth was they were not interested in any of these plans. They knew Germany was planning a big attack against Russia in the Caucasus and confidently expected a German victory. If this happened they in their turn wanted to stab their ancient enemy, Russia, in the back. They planned to throw in large forces against the Soviet Union on the Siberian border if Hitler's armies forced the Russians back.

Faced with this army attitude towards the invasion of Australia the Naval General Staff were forced back on a much less ambitious plan. This was to isolate Australia by gradually extending Japanese control over the near-by Pacific islands—New Guinea, the Solomons, New Caledonia and Fiji.

While the admirals in Hiroshima Bay and Tokyo argued about the relative merits of invading Hawaii, Ceylon or Australia, Yamamoto, realizing the army's reluctance to commit a single soldier, decided there was one operation he could carry out on his own which would not need the army's assistance.

Although no further territorial conquests would be agreed for the moment by the army, Yamamoto decided that the British Eastern Fleet must be dealt with next. This would leave the way open to the second-phase operations wherever they were to be aimed. If the Japanese approached Australia or Ceylon, the Royal Navy would have to be met and fought. Yamamoto decided to strike first.

At the end of March Nagumo steamed towards Ceylon with a fleet nearly as big as the one which attacked Hawaii. He had five large carriers, *Akagi*, *Hiryu*, *Soryu*, *Shokaku* and *Zuikaku*. They were the carriers which had attacked Pearl Harbor, except that *Kaga* had been left behind in Japan for repairs. With them sailed three battleships, *Hiei*, *Kirishima* and *Haruna*, six cruisers and twenty destroyers.

On 1 April Admiral Sir James Somerville, commanding Britain's hastily assembled Eastern Fleet, received information that a strong

Japanese force of three battleships and four or five carriers was heading for Ceylon. The British were about to get their first taste of Yamamoto's carrier warfare with which the Imperial Navy had had such success.

To meet Nagumo's rapidly approaching fleet, Admiral Somerville had five veteran battleships, three aircraft carriers—two modern, one old—two heavy cruisers, six light cruisers and fifteen destroyers. Two of the cruisers were Dutch. Somerville formed his rather elderly fleet into two task forces. From his twenty-four-knot battleship *Warspite*, he commanded the carriers *Indomitable* and *Formidable*, the cruisers *Cornwall* and *Dorsetshire*, the old light cruisers *Emerald* and *Enterprise*, and six destroyers.

Admiral A. V. Willis, from the old twenty-one-knot battleship *Resolution*, commanded the battleships *Ramillies*, *Revenge*, *Royal Sovereign*, and the old carrier *Hermes*. Some of his ships were veterans of World War One, and Somerville later confessed, 'It was a marvel they still kept running.'

At dawn on 4 April, Nagumo's carriers were steaming in radio silence 500 miles off Ceylon. They hoped to repeat the Pearl Harbor surprise and catch the British Eastern Fleet unprepared at anchor. Warned by the Pearl Harbor disaster, however, the British air patrols were constantly alert.

At 10 a.m. a patrolling Catalina flying boat saw the Japanese carriers and radioed to Colombo. Six Hiryu fighters swooped on the plane and quickly shot it down. The crew was picked up by the destroyer *Isokaze*. But their message had been received in Colombo.

Next day, thirty minutes before dawn, the five carriers reached their launching position 200 miles south of Ceylon and the attack wave of thirty-six fighters, fifty-four dive bombers and ninety high-level bombers began to take off. They were again under the command of Mitsuo Fuchida, who expected trouble because of the flying boat which had almost certainly got a message through. He received confirmation of this shortly after he took off.

As they flew through broken cloud towards Ceylon they saw below them a formation of six British Swordfish torpedo planes on their way to attack the Japanese carriers. The British pilots did not notice the Japanese above them. Fuchida signalled Zero leader Lieutenant-Commander Itaya, another Pearl Harbor veteran, to close up. He motioned downwards to the slow-flying Swordfish. Itaya nodded and swung off to lead his fighters against the unsuspecting British. The lumbering Swordfish were jumped on out of the sun and all shot down.

There was now no doubt that British fighters were waiting to attack them. To mislead the British defences, Fuchida led his planes round the island as he had done at Pearl Harbor and then swung in to bomb Colombo.

When the carrier pilots looked down they saw Colombo glistening after a recent rain squall. There were no fighters in the air and a big airfield south-east of the city was empty. This meant the British had taken off to intercept them.

As Fuchida lined up his planes into bombing formation over Colombo, thirty-three Hurricanes and Fulmars which had been patrolling out of sight screamed down on his aircraft. While they tangled with Itaya's faster, more manœuvrable Zeros, Fuchida's fifty-four dive bombers swooped down on ships in the harbour. No warships were anchored there but it was crammed with merchant vessels. As bombs rained round them, sending up great white fountains of foam, four cargo ships began to sink. At the same time Fuchida's ninety level bombers began to attack the airfield and the railways.

As bombs fell, shattering hangars and railway sidings, Fuchida picked up a terse message from *Tone*'s float plane searching in the Bay of Bengal. It said, 'Two British heavy cruisers sighted heading south.' They were the *Cornwall* and *Dorsetshire*, the vanguard of Somerville's old ships, sailing towards the carriers.

Fuchida abruptly called off the Colombo attack. Although the three Japanese battleships could easily deal with two cruisers, there were other British warships around. If the British were going to attack Nagumo's carriers all their planes must return at once so that the bombers could refuel and take off to sink the British ships while the fighters patrolled to protect their own carriers.

While they were heading for home more Hurricanes swooped out of cloud upon the bombers. Itaya's Zeros peeled off to engage them while Fuchida's planes streaked back towards the carriers. The Japanese lost heavily in this running fight—with twenty-four planes shot down for sixteen British fighters.

When Fuchida landed on Akagi, a second wave of forty dive bombers under Lieutenant-Commander Egusa were already on their way towards the British cruisers. Egusa, Japan's greatest dive bomber pilot, led a picked squadron specially trained to destroy aircraft carriers. A few minutes later he radioed, 'Enemy sighted'.

Twenty minutes later he identified the cruisers as the *Dorsetshire* and *Cornwall*. When his bombers climbed to get into their diving position there was not a breath of wind. This enabled them to aim their bombs with devastating accuracy and ninety per cent of them fell on the target. The *Dorsetshire*, having taken seventeen direct hits from 500-lb bombs, rolled over and sank. Ten minutes later the *Cornwall* also slid under the waves. Most of their crews were picked up by circling British destroyers.

Somerville on the bridge of the *Warspite* off Ceylon studied a stream of radio reports detailing the course of the battle. Then came silence and destroyer signals telling him of the sinking of the two cruisers. This attack by forty dive bombers, even before the 180 planes which had just attacked Colombo had had time to land on their parent carriers, indicated that three or more carriers were operating. This was the first time he had received direct confirmation of the shot-down Catalina's report. As he had no hope of defeating this much stronger fleet, Somerville decided prudence was a virtue. This was in direct contrast to the time when as Flag Officer Force H, based on Gibraltar, he had unhesitatingly sought action with superior Italian forces.

This time he decided withdrawal was the only sensible course if he was not going to risk sinking most of his slow old fleet. In the words of Churchill in a secret speech to the House of Commons on 23 April 1942, the Eastern Fleet 'withdrew into the wastes of the Indian Ocean'. In fact Somerville sailed to the remote Maldive Islands south of Ceylon.

While Somerville was deciding discretion was the better part of valour, Nagumo on *Akagi*'s bridge was pondering another signal. When *Tone*'s float plane reported the two British cruisers he realized they were steaming towards the exact spot where his carriers had originally intended to launch their planes. This original course had been given out by code message. Then Nagumo suddenly decided to alter course. As he was so near British territory and did not want to risk a radio signal being picked up and used for direction finding, this change was given to the fleet by flag signal. This meant the British could not possibly know he had changed course. But why were they sailing so accurately to cut across his original course? Was it a coincidence? Or did they know he was on that course? Could this possibly mean they were able to read the Japanese naval code?

Nagumo dismissed this idea as unthinkable. However he mentioned the situation in his report of the battle. Although this was the first instance of an enemy fleet being in the exact position to intercept —which was to prove so disastrous at Midway two months later— Tokyo read his report and instantly dismissed the code-breaking possibility just as he had done. They decided it was only a coincidence.

For the next three days the five Japanese carriers with their escorting battleships and cruisers sailed around, deliberately letting themselves be seen by R.A.F. reconnaissance planes. By this method Nagumo hoped to entice Somerville's fleet into a decisive daylight battle.

Somerville refused to fall into the trap. If he engaged in a daylight battle, hundreds of Japanese planes would pound his ships into the Indian Ocean. He wanted what the Japanese also often tried to achieve—a night surface action. His British sailors were as well trained as any Japanese in night fighting. But, more important, if he could use his superior fifteen-inch guns against the Japanese fourteen-inch guns they would give him an excellent chance of victory. Equally Nagumo, fully aware of the menace of the bigger British guns, was not going to be forced to fight at night.

After three days, realizing the Royal Navy was not going to fight on his terms, he ordered his carriers to retire southwards beyond the range of Ceylon-based air patrols. This again was a bluff. He wanted the British to think he had given up and relax their vigilance. After the lesson of Pearl Harbor and with the knowledge that big Japanese carriers were still lurking unseen in the Indian Ocean, the British remained nervously and constantly alert.

Then Nagumo swung his carriers round for an attack on Trincomalee in Ceylon. Since the loss of Singapore this was now the most important British Eastern naval base. As dawn broke on 9 April, Fuchida again led the bombers. As he neared the coast, British radar detected his approaching planes and Hurricanes swarmed up. When the Japanese reached the harbour heavy A.A. batteries fired at them.

Yet Fuchida's attack was highly effective. Dive bombers and torpedo planes sank three warships, the *Monitor* and the smaller *Erebus* and *Sadaing*, while his own level bombers with their 1,500-lb bombs concentrated on the airfield. Carrier-type aircraft, lined up in rows on the apron, were set on fire. A munitions depot exploded like a firework display.

In the landlocked inlets of the jungle-fringed harbour were still two light cruisers, a group of destroyers and ten cargo ships. As Fuchida had not enough bombs left for an effective attack upon them, he radioed *Akagi* giving details of the ships and suggested Egusa's second wave of dive bombers be sent to deal with them.

Nagumo had just ordered Egusa to take off when one of *Haruna*'s float planes returning from a search sighted a British carrier cruising in the Bay of Bengal accompanied by a cruiser and a corvette. Egusa was ordered to switch his attack to them. As his dive bombers disappeared in search of the British carrier, all planes aboard the five Japanese carriers were hastily refuelled and rearmed in case Egusa's divers failed to sink her. Overhead flew a full combat patrol to beat off British planes.

When Egusa's dive bombers began to circle the British carrier, they identified her as *Hermes*, but could not understand why there were no planes on her deck and no fighters circling above her in protective patrol. As they took their positions to dive they could hear the *Hermes* calling repeatedly to Trincomalee asking if fighters had been despatched. Her fighters never arrived. They were the planes which Fuchida had destroyed on Trincomalee airfield a few hours before.

Except for A.A. fire, *Hermes* was completely at the mercy of Egusa's bombs. She took nine direct hits in succession and, twenty-eight minutes after the first bomb fell, she rolled over and sank. Down with her went her escorting vessels, the veteran Australian cruiser *Vampire* and the corvette *Hollyhock*.

While the *Hermes* was being attacked *Akagi*'s loudspeakers suddenly blared 'Ack-Ack action!' There was a crash of exploding bombs and four white columns rose to starboard and two to port of the flagship. Nine Blenheims were seen in formation overhead. The Japanese warships opened fire and Zeros scrambled off the decks to aid the combat patrol. The Blenheims turned for home without having scored a single hit. They were followed by the Zeros who shot down five of them.

When Egusa's planes landed after sinking *Hermes*, Nagumo decided to call it a day. Total Japanese losses in the Trincomalee attack were five bombers and six fighters.

Four days later his five carriers steamed past the Straits of Malacca on their way home to Japan. The Ceylon operation, which the British believed was a curtain-raiser for a seaborne invasion of India, was over. It turned out to be another hit-and-run operation exactly like Pearl Harbor because the Japanese army considered itself fully extended and the invasion of India would have taken many more divisions than they could spare. As no decision about the second phase operations had yet been taken by Imperial Headquarters in Tokyo, Yamamoto had decided to fill in the time by attacking his other big opponent—the Royal Navy.

This was his last foray into the Indian Ocean. No major Japanese warship operated west of Singapore again. For Yamamoto did not want to risk his irreplaceable carriers in such distant waters. Also he had now decided upon his plan of action. He would strike again in the Pacific.

12

Doolittle and Plan A.F.

YAMAMOTO had taken no part in the two-month controversy over the Hawaii–Ceylon–Australia invasion plans, merely studying them without comment. Then suddenly, while Nagumo was on his way to Ceylon, he came out partially in favour of Admiral Ugaki's Hawaiian plan.

He said that Midway, which was only 1,130 miles from Hawaii, must be seized and used as an advance base for air and submarine patrols. This was not the real prize at which he aimed. He was convinced—and he was proved to be absolutely right—that any attack on Midway must lure out the fullest strength of the American fleet, giving him a chance to catch the carriers that had escaped him at Pearl Harbor.

Yamamoto's plan was really an extension of his old dream. He thought the destruction of the American carriers and the seizure of Midway with its threat to Hawaii would undermine America's will to fight and pave the way for a negotiated peace.

At the beginning of April his planning officer, Commander Yasuji Watanabe, went to Tokyo to present Plan A.F.—the Midway plan—to the Naval General Staff for their approval.

The opposition was even greater than it had been at the time of Pearl Harbor. When Watanabe put the plan to his opposite number, Commander Tatsukichi Miyo of Naval Operations, he opposed it so bitterly that several times Watanabe was on the verge of angry tears.

Miyo's objections were: Midway was only just over 1,100 miles from the American base at Hawaii, and after Pearl Harbor the Americans would not be caught napping again. Large numbers of aircraft based on Hawaii would support American carriers in defence of the island.

He totally disagreed with Yamamoto's confident prediction that America would gamble away the last of her remaining fleet to defend Midway. Even if they captured Midway, argued Commander Miyo, the atoll was so small and far from Japan that it would be snatched back by an American surprise attack at any time. To prevent this happening a huge number of planes would have to be on constant scouting patrol. They would need large quantities of fuel. Over a long period this alone might prove beyond Japan's capabilities.

He was also opposed to Yamamoto's idea that Midway would be an excellent advance base to watch for American carriers sailing towards Japan. The existing range of Japanese patrol aircraft was only 700 miles, which would not be of much use in the largest ocean.

Neither would Commander Miyo go along with the negotiated peace theory. He pointed out that Midway was too far away in the Pacific to be any threat to the continental United States. Its capture would have little effect on American morale.

Yamamoto's overall plan also called for the simultaneous invasion of Port Moresby in New Guinea and Tulagi in the Solomons. These operations were already past the planning stage and were waiting only for Nagumo's carriers to return from Ceylon to reinforce the naval covering forces.

Commander Miyo put forward an alternative plan to these. He suggested a move against New Caledonia, Fiji and Samoa. Although they were farther from Japan than Midway they were equally distant from Hawaii. An attack there would be much more likely to draw out the American fleet than one on Midway. Australia would feel herself seriously threatened by these invasions so near her own coasts and must appeal to the American navy for help. In these engagements the U.S. fleet would be a long way from home.

The fierce, near-tearful arguments went on all day between the two commanders in the single-storey wooden headquarters in Tokyo. Neither side would give way. On the other hand neither completely rejected the other's plan.

Next day the Naval General Staff worked out that seventy per cent of Yamamoto's estimated requirements for Midway could be met. After that was established, during the next forty-eight hours conferences went to a higher level. Yamamoto's envoy, Commander Watanabe, had long talks with Admiral Seiishi Ito, Deputy Chief of the Naval General Staff, and his head of operations, Rear-Admiral Fukudome.

Both these staff admirals rejected Yamamoto's Midway plan. When their refusals became final and unyielding Watanabe excused himself and telephoned Yamamoto aboard his flagship. When he suggested a compromise Admiral Yamamoto flatly refused. It was

Midway or nothing. Commander Watanabe returned to the waiting admirals in the conference room with this message from Yamamoto:

> The success of our entire strategy in the Pacific will be determined by whether we succeed in destroying the United States fleet, particularly its carrier task forces. By launching the proposed operations against Midway we can succeed in drawing out the enemy's carrier strength and destroying it in decisive battle. If the enemy should avoid our challenge we shall still have an important gain as we will have advanced our defensive perimeter to Midway and the western Aleutians without obstruction.

The most important admiral in Japan's navy, the man who had planned and successfully carried out Pearl Harbor, had spoken. They heard the message in silence.

Admiral Fukudome turned inquiringly to Vice-Admiral Ito. Ito hesitated for a moment. Then he quietly nodded. Midway was on.

Why was Yamamoto so determined about the Midway operation? He could not forget the United States had seven first-class carriers. Not one of them had been at Pearl Harbor. The only damage he had been able to inflict on them up to then had occurred when one of his big 2,000-ton Japanese submarines, the *I-6*, had hit *Saratoga*.

Yamamoto also had a 3,000-mile perimeter stretching across the Pacific. He had little doubt it would soon be breached by American task forces. There was only one way to stop that—the U.S. carriers must be sought out and destroyed. To do this he appreciated he must risk one of the major naval battles in world history. If she did not fight a decisive sea battle soon Japan would face a long war which he was certain she must lose.

He would not agree to the Naval Headquarters plan to attack in Fiji or New Caledonia because he did not think the United States would risk a decisive battle so far away. They must have a better bait dangled nearer home. Midway was the answer.

He was right about the Americans. They had accepted the fall of Guam and Wake, but they could not tolerate a Japanese advance beyond the 180th meridian. If the Japanese tried to occupy the Aleutians and Midway, the U.S. Navy was determined to throw in everything they had to stop them.

Yamamoto knew the Midway plan carried a great risk for his ships because it is twice as far from Japan's Inland Sea to Midway as it is from Pearl Harbor. On the other hand he was not impressed by the

Naval General Staff's anxiety about America's possible attempts to recapture the atoll. He regarded that as another possible heaven-sent opportunity for Japan. Even if the invasion of Midway did not lead to a full-scale naval battle of Japan's choosing, an American attempt to retake the atoll would give him one more chance to destroy the U.S. Navy.

But where were the American carriers? What had happened to their carrier fleet after Pearl Harbor? While the planners argued, Yamamoto sent two thirty-one-ton Kawanishi flying boats off on a long-range reconnaissance of Hawaii. This new type of long-range four-engined flying boat, later nicknamed Emily by American Intelligence, could fly 5,000 miles without a bomb load at a cruising speed of 160 knots. With a full bomb load of two tons it could still fly 3,000 miles. In February only two had been test-flown at the Japanese navy base at Yokosuka. No others would be ready before August.

On 15 February the two Emilys left Yokosuka and flew to the Japanese base of Kwajalein in the Marshalls for refuelling and bomb loads. On their long Pacific trip to Hawaii they were to be refuelled once again off French Frigate Shoals near Midway by I-class submarines.

Favourable weather over the ocean was needed for refuelling by submarines at sea. Although not so successful as the Americans at code-cracking, Japan had succeeded in breaking American naval weather codes. They could read the daily weather reports from Midway, Johnston and Hawaii.

At the beginning of March Yamamoto received a message: 'The Americans changed their weather code on 1 March. We can no longer construct a weather map based on their reports as before. We are now endeavouring to break the new code.'

The flying boats were due to take off on the last leg of their trip to Hawaii. The refuelling submarines had already arrived at French Frigate Shoals where they reported calm seas. Next day Japanese scout planes flew near Wake Island to check on the weather for the flying boats.

After a personal briefing by Vice-Admiral Shigeyoshi Inouye, C.-in-C. of the Fourth Fleet, the two Emilys took off at dawn on 3 March. At 6.30 that evening they saw their refuelling submarines, *I-15* and *I-19*, anchored inside the reef at French Frigate Shoals off Sand Island. When the planes alighted on the sea, stiff winds and a moderate swell parted them from their mooring ropes. Refuelling continued with a struggle in fairly rough seas long after dark until each plane had taken aboard 3,000 gallons of fuel.

A full moon was shining when the flight commander, Lieutenant Toshio Hashizume, took off from French Frigate Shoals. When he picked up the Hawaiian coast a misty tropical rain was falling, but the two Emilys flying at 15,000 feet were soon able to identify Kaena Point lighthouse.

At 2.10 a.m. Hashizume reckoned he was over Pearl Harbor so he dropped his bombs. The air-raid alarm sounded as his four bombs exploded on the uninhabited slopes of Mount Tantalus six miles from Honolulu. The only damage he did was to a clump of algaroba trees.

Twenty minutes later the pilot of the second Emily, Lieutenant Tomano, his view completely obscured by clouds, also dropped his bombs over what he thought was Pearl Harbor. He was a little more accurate than Hashizume but his bombs landed harmlessly in the sea outside the harbour.

In spite of this ineffectual and indiscriminate piece of terror bombing, their real purpose—reconnaissance—had not been achieved. The clouds were so low and dense that they returned having seen practically nothing.

Yamamoto sent them off again on a photographic reconnaissance of Midway and Johnston Island. Hashizume was given the Midway job. As his heavy four-engined plane approached, American Marine fighters were alerted by radar. Hashizume was shot down. Tomano, who flew to Johnston Island, was luckier. There were no fighters and he obtained excellent pictures.

Although the Emily long-range reconnaissance had been largely a flop, with no information supplied about Hawaii or Midway, Yamamoto was determined to press on with his plan. He wanted to attack in the first week of June when the moon was full. This led to more bickerings and disagreements. The Naval General Staff wanted D-Day to be postponed until the end of June to allow more time for preparations. Yamamoto again would not agree. He felt a month's delay might seriously reduce the chances of success.

There were also rows with his senior commanders. Vice-Admiral Shigeyoshi Inouye, commander of the Fourth Fleet in the south-west Pacific, was a bitter opponent of the Midway plan. When Yamamoto flew a staff officer to Inouye's headquarters at Truk atoll to discuss transporting supplies to Midway after its occupation, Admiral

Inouye said bluntly he had no confidence in the plan. His main objection was that he did not think his fleet could continue to supply the island. The argument became so heated that Yamamoto's officer angrily left the room saying, 'I will report to the Commander-in-Chief that he cannot rely on his Fourth Fleet.'

The Naval General Staff, who had once more been coerced into giving their reluctant consent, also made it plain that they still remained very doubtful of the success of the operation.

While these arguments were going on, the two admirals who were to lead the Midway operation, Vice-Admiral Kondo of the Second Fleet and Vice-Admiral Nagumo of the First Air Fleet, knew nothing about the plans. Until mid-April Nagumo was still returning from Ceylon and Kondo's surface ships were actively engaged in other southern operations. Yamamoto did not wish to withdraw them just to study blueprints of Midway planning.

This was his first error. His vital battle plan was drawn up by staff officers without first-hand knowledge of the fighting efficiency of the two fleets which would lead the operation. His chief of staff, Rear-Admiral Ryunosuke Kusaka, pointed out that the carriers had just finished a long series of operations. Pilots and crews were exhausted. He suggested there ought to be two months' delay so combat pilots could be withdrawn to train the new flyers ready for the coming battle.

Yamamoto refused. Every week counted. American strength was almost equally divided between the Atlantic and Pacific oceans and he wanted to sink the Pacific half before it became too strong.

Despite Japan's incredible successes everywhere, Yamamoto could not rid himself of one particular fear – that the Americans might raid Tokyo. He had an even more nightmarish thought: these raids might even include an attack on the Imperial Palace of the sacred Emperor.

It was unthinkable that the Emperor's safety should be endangered by as much as a single American plane flying over Tokyo. Defence against air attack was nominally the army's job. But since the only bombers that could reach Japan at this stage would have to be launched from American carriers, Yamamoto was very conscious that it was his duty to destroy any American carrier striking force at sea before it could bomb Japan. It became an obsession with him that Tokyo, the Imperial city, must be kept absolutely safe from air attack as part of his foremost duty to protect the Emperor.

What made him especially fanatical about this was that he fully realized that his own surprise carrier-borne attack on Pearl Harbor had created a model for the Americans. His stay at Harvard and his later term in Washington as naval attaché had given him a deep understanding of the American national character. He had no doubt that Nimitz's fleet would attempt to strike back at Japan with carriers as soon as they could. The problem that concerned him was: when and how?

His officers thought him eccentric because wherever he was he kept asking for the latest Tokyo weather report. Nor could they understand why he always appeared more cheerful if the reports were bad —for bad weather gave extra protection against bombers.

Apart from the safety of the Emperor he had another gnawing anxiety about American air raids on Japan. He could not forget that during the Russo–Japanese war a Russian fleet suddenly appeared outside Tokyo bay. This caused many of Tokyo's inhabitants to flee to the mountains in a panic. When the Russians appeared, angry mobs also stoned the home of Kamimura, the vice-admiral responsible for Japanese home waters.

Yamamoto was not worried that this might happen to him. Personal safety was of little importance to a man who had constantly courted assassination before the war by his public stand against warmongers. But he knew his own people. He was fully aware of the temperamental instability of the Japanese character. What perturbed him was that an air raid over Tokyo might lead to short-range panic and long-range falling off of civilian morale.

Japan had no radar. So how was he to guard against penetration by an American carrier force? He established a picket boat line 600–700 miles off the Japanese coast and extending for 1,000 miles. This primitive early-warning line was supplemented by daily long-range patrols by naval aircraft.

His fear of an attack on Tokyo was sharply increased on 3 March when Halsey's carrier *Enterprise* struck at Marcus Island. Yamamoto instantly realized the significance of this blow. For little Marcus Island was only 1,000 miles from Tokyo. It was much too near for comfort.

Was this the curtain-raiser for air raids on Japan? Yamamoto wasted no time. He ordered two carriers, *Zuikaku* and *Shokaku*, patrolling in the south-west Pacific to return at once. He also recalled the land-based 21st Air Flotilla from south-east Asia and stationed it near Tokyo. Added to the already heavy air defences along Japan's coasts, these reinforcements made him feel happier for the Emperor's safety. Yet six weeks after the attack on Marcus Island Yamamoto's apprehensions were fully justified.

At dawn on the morning of 18 April the fishing boat *Nitto Maru* was on her station in the early-warning line 720 miles from Tokyo Bay when the lookout called the captain on deck. He pointed at a fleet of big unidentified ships steaming at high speed towards Japan. The captain, excitedly studying the dim, far-off, fast-moving shadows through his glasses, thought he recognized three aircraft carriers.

There were in fact two carriers—*Enterprise* and *Hornet*. Aboard *Hornet* were Lieutenant-Colonel James Doolittle's flyers with their B.25s on their way to attack Tokyo and other big Japanese cities.

At the same time as the little *Nitto Maru* saw them the American carriers sighted her. There was a hasty conference aboard the *Hornet*. The American plan called for the B.25s to take off that afternoon when the carriers were 500 miles off the Japanese coast. This would enable them to reach their targets in darkness.

Now that they had been detected and reported, this plan must be scratched. If they did not take off at once the whole Japanese air force would pounce on them. To take off immediately meant a more dangerous daylight attack, but at least they would arrive before the Japanese could muster their forces.

At 6.30 a.m., when Yamamoto received a radio message from *Nitto Maru* which confirmed his worst fears, Doolittle's B.25s were already taking off—200 miles farther away from Japan than had been planned.

Yet Yamamoto was not unduly alarmed when he received *Nitto Maru*'s report. As he and his staff pored over their charts aboard his flagship in the Inland Sea and marked the American position, they estimated American carrier planes could not approach within launching range before dawn the next morning. That gave the defences ample time to deal with them.

Yamamoto rapidly issued his orders. Admiral Kondo's Second Fleet, which had entered Yokosuka naval base the day before with four big battleships, was ordered hastily back to sea to intercept the American carriers. Thirty-two medium bombers of the newly arrived 21st Air Flotilla, escorted by twelve Zero fighters, took off from their base near Tokyo heading for the Americans. They flew out into the

Pacific to the limit of their range but never found them. The reason was that when they took off Doolittle's planes were already nearing the Japanese coast; and the big battleships had hardly put to sea when Yamamoto received an unbelievable message: 'Tokyo bombed!'

How could it be possible? No carrier planes had a range like this. Then came further staggering reports of attacks on Yokohama, Kawasaki, and the naval base of Yokosuka. Later reports told of attacks farther south on Nagoya, Yokkaichi, Wakayama and Kobe. The defences were caught completely unprepared. As Doolittle and his flyers flew in at wave-top height much earlier than expected, every Japanese fighter missed them.

At first as these reports poured in Yamamoto and his staff were baffled by what was happening. More detailed reports revealed the raid was apparently the work of only twenty planes.

But what planes? Yamamoto was even more puzzled when he received the answer. The planes were positively identified as B.25 land bombers, not carrier planes at all. They had a far greater operational range than any naval plane.

Although these medium bombers were able to fly much farther than carrier planes, they still did not have enough range to take off from the nearest American base. Could they possibly have been launched by the carriers sighted by *Nitto Maru* more than 700 miles off-shore? If so, how were they to get back? Heavy planes like that, even if they managed to take off, could never land on a carrier. Or was the attack a one-way suicide operation?

Reports came that the American planes had turned south. Five were sighted flying off the tip of Kyushu, Japan's southernmost island. Did they have orders to land on the sea somewhere off Japan's south coast where American submarines were waiting to pick up their crews?

Then Japanese army units in China radioed that some American planes had crash-landed near Nanchang. Japanese Intelligence however still could not confirm whether the raiders had flown from the carriers seen by *Nitto Maru*.

Yamamoto and his admirals measured their charts. Except for the forbidding Aleutians, shrouded in bad weather, where was the nearest American outpost to Tokyo? It was Midway Island, 2,250 miles to the east.

Was this the Shangri-la that President Roosevelt meant when he joked about the place the bombers had come from? Whether it was or not, it was a sentry for Hawaii, 1,130 miles farther on.

Two days after Doolittle's raid, Nagumo's five carriers sailed in from their victorious Ceylon sweep and anchored in the Inland sea, At the same time the Naval General Staff suddenly became enthusiastic about Yamamoto's plan for Midway. Doolittle decided them.

13

Carriers in the Coral Sea

WHILE the Midway operation was being prepared, an event which was to help dictate its outcome was taking place nearly 3,000 miles away on the shores of New Guinea.

Following Nagumo's successful foray into the Indian Ocean, Yamamoto's planned landings in the Solomon Islands and New Guinea went ahead. Their major goal was the capture of Port Moresby in New Guinea because it was the only air base from which Allied aircraft continued to strike at the still advancing Japanese forces.

In January 1942 the Japanese took Rabaul in New Britain and decided to seize Port Moresby. The original plan was to 'seize important points' in Australia as far down Queensland as Townsville. When the Japanese army refused to co-operate in the Australian invasion, it was decided to put into operation a less ambitious plan to land forces on the New Hebrides and New Caledonia to cut off Australia. This would bring northern Australian ports and airfields within range of Japanese warships and bombers. It might even force Australia out of the war.

Tulagi across the channel from Guadalcanal in the southern Solomons was also to be invaded and made into a seaplane base to cover the flank of the Port Moresby operation. The occupation of Port Moresby and Tulagi was originally planned for March.

The United States read the Japanese top-secret signals and knew all Japan's plans. But how were they to gather sufficient forces in time to meet the threat to Port Moresby? For America and Britain were determined to resist the new Japanese move. If they held on to Port Moresby it would not only spell security for Australia but the port could be used as a springboard for future offensives.

Carriers were in short supply. *Saratoga*, which had been torpedoed in January, was still being repaired in Puget Sound. *Enterprise* and *Hornet*, steaming back from the Doolittle Tokyo raid, were not due into Pearl Harbor until 25 April. They could not possibly reach the Coral Sea in time.

But *Yorktown,* the core of Admiral Fletcher's task force, was in the South Pacific. To join him, Rear-Admiral Aubrey W. Fitch, flying his flag in *Lexington,* sailed from Pearl Harbor. From New Caledonia came the *Chicago,* and the British Rear-Admiral J. C. Crace sailed with the Australian cruisers *Australia* and *Hobart* towards the southwest Pacific.

This gathering of forces also became known to Japanese Intelligence. They reported to Yamamoto that an American aircraft carrier might be in the area, seriously threatening the projected Solomons and New Guinea invasions. Then came further reports estimating the American fleet to be two carriers, four heavy cruisers, four light cruisers and a dozen destroyers. Yamamoto postponed the operation until early in May.

He ordered the two powerful carriers *Shokaku* and *Zuikaku,* commanded by Rear-Admiral Chuichi Hara of the Nagumo force, returning to Japan after the Indian Ocean operation, to steam at full speed for the Solomon Islands. He also diverted the 12,000-ton light carrier *Shoho,* a converted submarine tender, for the operation.

Shokaku and *Zuikaku,* which could deal with any American warships attempting to stop the operation, reached the Fourth Fleet's home base at Truk atoll just before the end of April. The Japanese plan was for the smaller carrier *Shoho* to cover the landing on Tulagi and later protect the Port Moresby invasion force sailing out of Rabaul. Vice-Admiral Shigeyoshi Inouye, commander of the Fourth Fleet in the central Pacific, was assigned to command the whole force.

As he knew the Japanese carriers were scheduled to take part in the Midway operation planned for June, Inouye lost no time. He planned to seize Tulagi on 3 May and carry out the main assault on Port Moresby a week later.

Inouye now had a big fleet of seventy ships under his command. As well as the two heavy carriers and the light carrier *Shoho,* it included a seaplane tender, six heavy cruisers, four light cruisers, fifteen destroyers and fourteen troop transports.

Against Inouye's fleet were ranged two American carriers, one British battleship, two American battleships, four heavy cruisers, four light cruisers and seventeen destroyers. The fire power of the

Allied fleet was much greater than the British had had against Nagumo in the Indian Ocean. But Japanese confidence was high because they had already seen the outstanding superiority of the Zero fighters which swept aside all opposition. Aboard their carriers Japanese pilots looked forward eagerly and optimistically to their first battle against the American carriers.

Both American and Japanese carriers and their escorts sailed at top speed towards the Coral Sea which, ringed with glittering coral beaches and dancing green palms, was like a picture of the romantic South Seas come true. For centuries its calm tropical peace had been disturbed only by trading schooners or the occasional short, savage squabbling of painted Polynesian war canoes. Now the first great naval clash between East and West was about to take place. The Coral Sea was to become the stage for the world's first big carrier battle.

When the Japanese invasion convoys sailed from Rabaul they were covered by two fleets. The light carrier *Shoho* with four heavy cruisers, *Aoba*, *Kako*, *Furutake* and *Kinugasa*, commanded by Rear-Admiral Aritomo Goto, left Truk on 30 April. When the Japanese warships started to move from Truk to pick up their transports the Americans guessed the probable point of attack for this huge force was Port Moresby—or perhaps even Australia.

Next day, 1 May, the Japanese striking force commanded by Vice-Admiral Takeo Takagi, made up of *Zuikaku* and *Shokaku*, the two heavy cruisers *Miyoko* and *Haguro* and six destroyers, sailed. The Japanese, in accordance with Inouye's plan, first sailed to Tulagi in the Solomons. The small harbour of Tulagi—to become part of a bitter battle a few months later—fell without any opposition and the fleet moved out for the second stage of the operation, the attack on Port Moresby.

On 3 May *Yorktown* and *Lexington* spotted the Japanese transports concentrating in Tulagi, and *Lexington* was ordered to attack them. Before dawn on 4 May Admiral Fletcher began to launch his planes for the 120-mile flight over Guadalcanal Island with its 6,000-ft mountain peaks and on to Tulagi. Once over the jungle-covered hills the torpedo planes went down to water level for the final twelve miles to the harbour.

Tulagi harbour was full of Inouye's transports guarded by three cruisers and four destroyers. Their first warning came from the high-pitched roar of the American dive bombers. Then the low-flying torpedo bombers released their loads and white foaming wakes criss-crossed the harbour.

Torpedo explosions sent small craft into the air and flames shot skywards as a destroyer listed under two bombs. A 20,000-ton transport went down and 1,000-lb bombs plunged into the decks of a heavy cruiser. Two destroyers turned over and sank. A seaplane tender was hit but limped out of the harbour trailing oil. Another destroyer and two supply ships went down.

By the time the American second wave came in, the Japanese had rallied and began firing frantically at them. Seaplane fighters soared off the bay to attack. American planes found a Japanese destroyer trying to escape and left her wallowing, steam and smoke curling from her hatches and oil pouring from ragged holes in her hull. The American pilots claimed fourteen Japanese ships sunk or damaged. American losses were three planes.

Yamamoto was delighted when he received reports of these fierce attacks for they proved without any doubt that American aircraft carriers were in the area. The first battle between American and Japanese carriers would not be long delayed.

He ordered Rear-Admiral Chuichi Hara, commanding the Japanese carriers, to swing round the Solomons to try and catch the American carriers. The Port Moresby convoy of fourteen transports continued on its way, closely covered by Rear-Admiral Goto's cruisers and the small carrier *Shoho*.

On the morning of 6 May *Yorktown* joined up with *Lexington*. Admiral Aubrey W. Fitch aboard *Lexington*, and with long experience in carriers, was to direct air operations.

Just as *Yorktown* and *Lexington* met, the Japanese carriers *Shokaku* and *Zuikaku* sailed into the Coral Sea. The Americans also received a depressing news item: Corregidor fell on 6 May.

The four opposing admirals, Takagi and Hara, Fitch and Fletcher, began searching frantically for each other's carriers. They groped towards each other like two giant blind boxers. Each had bad luck at first.

At 8.10 a.m. on 6 May a Japanese flying boat sighted *Yorktown* and *Lexington* but failed to get word through to Admiral Takagi. That same evening Hara almost succeeded in surprising Fitch's carriers at their most vulnerable moment, when they were refuelling. He was within seventy miles of the American carriers and rapidly overhauling them when he suddenly changed course.

Fletcher and Fitch were also conducting air searches for the two Japanese carriers. But most of their planes had to turn back because of high winds and squally weather.

Then an American Fortress from Port Moresby found and attacked Admiral Goto's convoy. This meant that Japanese troop transports were in danger of being attacked at any moment by other American bombers, so Admiral Inouye ordered the convoy to make a quick change of course to escape.

Now that the Allied fleet knew the whereabouts of the Japanese troop transports they prepared to attack. At dawn on 7 May Fletcher detached three cruisers and three destroyers under Admiral Crace to intercept Goto with the Moresby invasion force.

An hour later Admiral Takagi received reports of two American carrier forces forty-five miles from each other. One report was correct—that was Fletcher with *Yorktown*. The other was not. It was Crace's combined American and Australian squadron with the Australian cruisers *Australia* and *Hobart*, the American cruiser *Chicago* and two destroyers—but no battleships. Thirty-three bombers with an escort of eleven Zeros took off from Rabaul to attack them.

At 12.30 p.m. they reported sinking an American battleship, causing serious damage to a British battleship and leaving one cruiser burning in the water. The Japanese lost four bombers.

In fact not a single Japanese torpedo or bomb struck any of the ships. The quick-moving cruisers and destroyers proved too slippery a target for the Japanese pilots. But one significant factor was revealed by the failure of the Japanese attacks. The bombers which attacked Admiral Crace's fleet were manned by hastily recruited replacements. Their efficiency was far below that of the Pearl Harbor pilots or of the flying crews who sank the *Prince of Wales* and *Repulse*. This was the first action which showed Yamamoto that his fully trained pilot reserves were inadequate, a problem foreseen by the training officer, Lieutenant Takekatsu Tawaka, at Kasumigaura flying school.

Fletcher expected *Yorktown* and Fitch's *Lexington* to come under attack during the day. He had accurate information that three Japanese carriers were involved in the operation. But neither he nor his opponents Takagi and Hara were certain where the other was. As the Japanese had still not found the second American carrier, Takagi ordered all his three carriers to send up scout planes. They did not have to search far. At 5.32 a.m. a Kate bomber sighted 'an American carrier'.

Although the Japanese admiral thought he had found Fletcher's *Yorktown*, the bomber's report was incorrect. What he had found was the tanker *Neosho* and the destroyer *Sims*. They were 200 miles south of the carrier *Shokaku*. Admiral Hara immediately launched every available aeroplane from his two big carriers to attack the American 'carrier'.

At 6.10 a.m. Lieutenant-Commander Kuichi Takahashi, who had commanded the dive bombers at Pearl Harbor, led a force from *Zuikaku* and *Shokaku* of seventy-eight bombers, torpedo planes and fighters. They were hardly airborne when Admiral Hara received later reports from other search planes. The first carrier report was untrue. It was too late to divert the attack. An irreplaceable opportunity to strike the first blow at the American carriers was lost.

For thirty minutes later, while Takahashi's planes were racing towards the American 'carrier', a reconnaissance seaplane from Admiral Goto's convoy sighted 'another large carrier' steaming 280 miles north-west of them. This time it really was an American carrier. But as all the planes from *Zuikaku* and *Shokaku* were still in the air on their way to the first 'carrier', an attack could not yet be launched against her.

At 9.35 a.m., when Takahashi reached the place where the 'carrier' had been reported, all he found was the large tanker and destroyer. He at once launched a full-scale attack on them. The destroyer *Sims* went down with most of her crew. The *Neosho* took seven hits but remained afloat. Her survivors were taken off four days later.

Mistaking the oiler for a carrier proved costly. But the Americans also made their own mistake. At 8.15 a.m. an American scout plane reported 'two carriers and four heavy cruisers sighted'.

Ninety-three planes were at once launched from the two American carriers. When the scout plane returned it was discovered that his report had been wrongly decoded. He had only reported two cruisers with two destroyers. Fletcher however decided to let the attack proceed. The risk was rewarded. At 10.22 a.m. a Japanese carrier was reported only thirty-five miles away from the cruisers. She was the *Shoho*. The planes at once altered course and flew towards her.

At the same time as Takahashi's planes were returning to *Shokaku* and *Zuikaku* after their attack on *Neosho*, lookouts on *Shoho* reported American aircraft approaching. There were only a few fighters circling over her, as most of her Zeros were protecting the troop transports on their way to Port Moresby.

It was 11 a.m. when the American pilots saw *Shoho* and began their attack. She turned into the wind to try and launch her planes as the bombers from *Yorktown* and *Lexington* plunged down on her. *Shoho* reeled under thirteen bomb and seven torpedo hits. After listing and staggering crazily, she went to the bottom at 11.35 a.m. It was the first sinking—in fact the first attack—ever made by American pilots on an enemy carrier.

Fletcher decided not to launch any more planes until the other two big Japanese carriers were pinpointed. He was now certain that Takagi knew his position and would soon attack. He wanted to be ready for him. Fletcher's assessment was right. When nearly a hundred American planes swooped down on *Shoho*, Admiral Takagi knew that two large American carriers were near. Although the Japanese tried very hard to attack them that day they made a series of fantastic errors.

When Takahashi landed from his wasted mission he was ordered to load up with bombs and torpedoes again, ready to attack the American carriers. But it was not an easy task. It was late afternoon and getting dark—and few pilots had any training in night landings.

Also the normally calm Coral Sea began to heave with tropical squalls, and high winds began to batter the Japanese carriers. Takagi and his carrier commander, Hara, became desperate as night approached. In spite of the weather somehow they must sink the American carriers before they could destroy the Moresby landing force.

Although Takahashi's planes from *Zuikaku* and *Shokaku* had refuelled and were ready to take off again, Hara hesitated. He knew that if he sent them off now, untrained pilots would have to grope their way back and land in darkness.

But the situation was critical. The Americans must be sunk. He decided to risk it but only with his best flyers. At 4.30 in the afternoon, while it was overcast but still light, the seasoned Takahashi took off once again with twelve dive bombers and twelve torpedo bombers flown by his most experienced pilots. He had orders to attack at twilight when it would be difficult for the American anti-aircraft gunners to see his planes in the fading light.

It was a gamble which very nearly came off. As soon as Takahashi's planes took off they flew into heavy rain squalls. Shortly afterwards as it became dark they struggled to keep formation in increasing mist. Thick blanketing clouds made it impossible to find the American vessels, so Takahashi gave the order to jettison bombs and torpedoes, to lighten their load and make their return flight less hazardous.

Suddenly in the squally black night *Lexington*'s radar picked up aircraft circling above her. They were Takahashi's planes. Having flown two missions since early morning they were tired out. Lost and dazed, they did not realize that an American carrier was passing directly beneath them. It could not have been worse luck for the Japanese air crews. After flying blindly about in squalls and heavy cloud, they had by pure chance found an American carrier. *Lexington* was cruising along without suspecting danger—and only a short time before they had thrown their bombs and torpedoes into the sea. The Americans tracked them for a short while by radar, then attacked suddenly with Grumman Wildcat fighters.

The Val dive bombers, unusually manœuvrable for their size, turned sharply to meet the diving Wildcats. But the lumbering Kate bombers were easy targets even without their torpedoes. In the brief battle the Wildcats shot down eight of the fifteen torpedo bombers and one Val dive bomber. The Americans had an enormous advantage as, unlike the Japanese, they were fitted with radar and could follow the Japanese bombers' movements through the black clouds.

An hour later the surviving Japanese flyers made an even more fantastic error. One exhausted pilot made out an aircraft carrier below him in the swirling dark mists. As he flew nearer he thought he recognized the shape of *Zuikaku*. He thankfully dived towards her and the remaining fifteen bombers switched on their signal and blinker lights and followed him in to land. It was in fact the second American carrier, *Yorktown*.

As the first aircraft began his descent towards the carrier deck the pilot suddenly realized it was unfamiliar. It was an American carrier! The Americans also thought it was one of their own planes for, as his bomber approached, not a single gun fired. The Japanese pilot frantically gunned his engine and swerved away at full speed followed by his astonished squadron. Only then did the startled American gunners open fire. It was too late. The Japanese disappeared into the darkness.

By now the tired-out Japanese pilots were completely bewildered.

This ill-fated abortive twilight attack swung the balance against the Japanese carriers. Apart from the nine planes shot down by Wildcats, nine other inexperienced and exhausted pilots plunged into the sea attempting night landings when they at last found their carrier. Hara recovered only six of his twenty-four planes.

But they had done at least one part of their job. They had found both American carriers and reported they were only fifty to sixty miles away. The two fleets were in fact a hundred miles apart.

For the four admirals, Takagi, Hara, Fitch and Fletcher, in their pitching carriers in the wind-whipped Coral Sea, the night of 7 May seemed endless. Each side was now aware of the nearness of the other. Each admiral had the uneasy feeling that the enemy was too close—and might deliver a body blow without warning.

The Japanese were especially taut, as it had been a bad day for them. American bombers had destroyed the *Shoho*, the first Japanese aircraft carrier to be lost in the war. In their turn they had failed to attack the American carriers and had succeeded only in sinking a harmless oiler.

The American admirals Fletcher and Fitch were just as jittery. Takahashi's planes flying over *Lexington* and then trying to land on *Yorktown* made them realize how very close the Japanese carriers must be.

When Takahashi landed and reported the positions of the American carriers, Takagi considered a night battleship attack. So did Fitch. Both rejected the idea as too risky. The main battle of the Coral Sea was postponed for twelve hours.

As the Japanese flyers grimly prepared for the next day's battle the atmosphere aboard their two big carriers, *Shokaku* and *Zuikaku*, became more tense every hour. They knew whoever found the enemy first next morning would have the advantage. Before the grey stormy dawn came up over the Coral Sea, both sides launched search planes to search through the clouds for the enemy.

When both *Shokaku* and *Zuikaku* sent out float planes to look for the Americans, their pilots waited anxiously for their reports. For there had to be victory that day. At 8.24 a.m. one of their scout planes piloted by Warrant Officer Kenzo Kanno radioed back that he had sighted two American carriers and a battleship 235 miles from the Japanese fleet.

Within a few moments an American reconnaissance plane dived out of the clouds and found the Japanese carriers steaming through the dark mists. Each side began to launch planes almost simultaneously. It was just after nine o'clock when planes from *Lexington* and *Yorktown* took off into the swirling clouds and driving rain.

A few minutes earlier Takahashi took off with eighteen fighters, thirty-three dive bombers and eighteen torpedo bombers to fly towards the American ships he had passed over the night before.

As the two groups of planes, American and Japanese, raced towards each other's carriers several hundred miles apart, the great battle began. It could not have been fought on more even terms. Each force had two big carriers. Admiral Fitch had 121 planes, Admiral Takagi 122. The Americans were stronger in bombers, the Japanese had more fighter and torpedo planes. The Japanese pilots also had more combat experience and better torpedoes.

Warrant Officer Kanno continued to shadow *Yorktown* and *Lexington* and report by radio every detail to *Shokaku*. The Americans did not spot him. Ten minutes after his first report, Kanno gave a more exact position for the Americans. Takahashi's sixty-nine planes were now in the air. When the message was radioed to him he changed his course on Kanno's information.

For the first time since the four carriers entered the Coral Sea the Japanese had a little luck. While their ships were still concealed under clouds and rain squalls, the weather began to clear as the Japanese planes flew towards the American carriers.

When Takahashi was less than twenty miles away he could see the dark lozenge shapes of the two American carriers etched clearly in the now clear bright morning. As Takahashi divided his planes into two torpedo groups and one bomber formation there were no American fighters in the sky.

Warrant Officer Kanno who was still shadowing the two American carriers turned for home as his fuel began to run low. As he did so, he spotted Takahashi's approaching planes. In spite of his detailed minute-by-minute reports, it seemed to him as if they would miss the carrier. Kanno flew alongside and waved to Takahashi to follow him. When he did this he placed himself and his crew beyond the point of no return. He would now have insufficient fuel to return to his own carrier 200 miles away.

As he now had little hope of survival, Kanno decided to lead the attack. The Americans, whose radar had picked up the Japanese seventy miles away, could now see the enemy bombers glittering silver in the sun. Hundreds of puffs of black anti-aircraft shell bursts began to blotch the blue sky, while Wildcats spun off the decks to shoot down Takahashi's aircraft. When Takahashi gave the signal to attack he dived after Kanno into this hell of shrapnel, heading for *Yorktown*'s decks. Seconds later both their planes blew up, the blazing wreckage plunging into the sea near *Yorktown*.

The Japanese swooped on *Yorktown* first, then *Lexington*. It was approaching noon as the battle raged. The hot tropic sun glared down on the diving, dodging planes and the bomb-scarred decks. The placid translucent waters of the calm Coral Sea were churned up by exploding bombs and shrapnel.

Lieutenant-Commander Shigekazu Shimazaki, commander of the second wave at Pearl Harbor, who led *Zuikaku*'s air group into battle, gave this description of the attack:

> Never in all my years in combat had I ever imagined a battle like this! Our fighters and American Wildcats dived and climbed in the middle of our formations.
>
> Burning and shattered planes of both sides plunged from the skies. Amidst this fantastic rainfall of anti-aircraft shells and spinning planes, I dived almost to the water's surface and sent my torpedo into the *Lexington*.
>
> I had to fly just above the waves to escape the enemy shells. I was flying below the level of the flight deck and I almost struck the bow of the ship. I could see American sailors staring at my plane as it rushed by.

Charles Dorton, a yeoman third class aboard *Lexington*, saw the attack differently:

> The pilots of the Japanese torpedo planes seemed nervous. You could see them plainly as they swept in towards the ship through our machine-gun fire.
>
> Things began to happen fast. Anti-aircraft racket was awful. The sky was filled with shrapnel. One Japanese torpedo plane was hit by our machine-gun fire when it was 200 yards away. And only sixty feet above the water. The Japanese didn't have a chance to launch his 'fish' but turned and kept coming right at us. He crashed into the ship near the port forward gun battery. Our boys quickly shoved the wreck off into the water before it could catch fire and explode the torpedo.

Yorktown successfully dodged all the Japanese torpedoes, but a single 800-lb bomb landed near the island superstructure on her flight deck. It tore a hole in three lower decks, causing extensive damage. Two near-misses also made her leak badly.

The larger and less manœuvrable *Lexington* was attacked on both bows simultaneously. She took two torpedoes and two bombs which flooded three boiler rooms.

Her engines were unharmed and her speed did not fall below twenty-four knots but she turned away listing. The list was quickly corrected by shifting oil, and fires which broke out were quickly under control. To her fighter pilots flying above her she appeared undamaged. But her fuel pipes had been damaged. This was to doom her.

Shortly after Takahashi took off to attack the Americans, eighty American planes began flying towards *Shokaku* and *Zuikaku*. *Yorktown* sent off twenty-four bombers with nine slower torpedo planes. Ten minutes later *Lexington* launched her dive bombers and torpedo planes.

Only half the Americans who took off saw action. Not having a heroic Kanno on their side, *Lexington*'s twenty-two divers failed to find the target. Only her eleven torpedo planes and four level bombers reached the Japanese carriers.

At 10.30 a.m. *Yorktown*'s dive bombers found them. *Zuikaku*'s captain saw the dive bombers coming out of the thick grey clouds and at once steamed full ahead into a near-by rain squall and dodged them. Still visible, *Shokaku* took the full fury of both divers and torpedo planes. She managed fairly easily to avoid the slow American torpedoes but two bombs shattered her decks. Then a third crashed onto her. Her steering gear was damaged and she was able to manœuvre only with difficulty.

Shokaku's captain, with smoking bomb craters in his flight deck, was worried about how he could land his aircraft when they returned from attacking *Yorktown* and *Lexington*. He signalled his plight to *Zuikaku*'s captain who ordered planes on deck to be rolled overboard to clear space for emergency landings for his own and *Shokaku*'s aircraft upon their return.

Shokaku was burning, sending up columns of black smoke and moving erratically, when those *Lexington* planes which did find the target dived through the dark clouds. Suddenly through the mists they saw her sister ship, *Zuikaku*, loom up. The level bombers aimed their 1,000-pounders at her and torpedo planes dived down to sea level and managed to release five torpedoes towards her. She manœuvred swiftly and steamed back under cloud cover undamaged.

This swift unsuccessful attack on *Zuikaku* virtually ended the battle. The exchange of bombs and torpedoes had taken little over an hour. The battle of the Coral Sea was the first in the history of naval warfare in which great ships fought without ever coming into contact with one another. *Lexington* never saw the carriers that launched the planes which damaged her severely, nor did *Shokaku*. Their own planes were 200 miles away at the time, attacking the unseen enemy carriers.

The commander of *Lexington* gave this laconic account of the battle:

At dawn on 8 May our scouting forces located two Japanese aircraft carriers and several other enemy ships hidden in a rain squall about 200 miles away. It was evident to us the enemy had contacted us about the same time, so we sent out two raiding squadrons and prepared for an attack.

We found one of the Japs, the *Shokaku*, about 11 a.m. She was pounded with heavy 1,000-lb bombs and hit with five torpedoes. Then the Japanese attacked us. We counted eleven torpedo wakes coming in our direction. We avoided all but two. Then Jap dive bombers got us with three bombs, one of heavy calibre. There were a lot of close misses. Many men on the flight deck were killed by fragments.

It was only midday when the battle was over. The burning Pacific sun was high in the sky as the planes from both sides began their homeward flights. Many of them were holed and damaged. They were returning to a burning Japanese carrier and an American carrier which was doomed. When the American planes began to land on their carriers they appeared to have won the battle. Both their carriers were still operational. *Lexington* did not seem badly damaged, while the blazing *Shokaku* was out of the battle. *Yorktown* and *Zuikaku* were both intact.

In spite of dumping spare planes overboard in frantic efforts to make more deck space, *Zuikaku* was unable to take on all the planes of her damaged sister carrier. Many of them still circling round were radioed to come down on the sea. Destroyers raced alongside to pick up the pilots.

The Japanese planes had suffered badly. *Zuikaku* had twenty-four

Zeros, but only nine Val dive bombers and six Kate torpedo planes operational—a quarter of the bombers aboard both carriers before the battle. More than twenty-six bombers, nearly half Takahashi's force, had been lost attacking *Yorktown* and *Lexington*. But Admiral Fitch could still put thirty-seven attack planes and twelve fighters into the air.

Yet the Japanese admirals were jubilant. The reports of the returning flyers led Admirals Takagi and Hara to believe the attack was a total success. They all claimed both *Lexington* and *Yorktown* had been sent to the bottom and a battleship or cruiser had been damaged.

Takahashi's second-in-command reporting his death gave these brief details: 'Starting off at 09.20 hours we made determined torpedo and bomb attacks against one *Saratoga*-type and one *Yorktown*-type aircraft carrier. At least nine torpedoes and more than ten 550-lb bombs struck the former ship. The latter was hit with three torpedoes and eight to ten 550-lb bombs. We damaged two other vessels.'

With both American carriers believed to have been eliminated, the tide of battle appeared to have veered strongly in favour of the Japanese. Although *Shoho* was lost and *Shokaku* severely damaged, *Zuikaku* remained unharmed. Admirals Takagi and Hara seemed in an excellent position to complete the Americans' destruction.

The American admirals, Fletcher and Fitch, did not know how badly off the Japanese were but they wanted to continue the battle. They were planning a fresh attack after their planes had refuelled and re-armed.

Ever since the Japanese planes had vanished, the crew of *Lexington*, grim, sweating and tired under the hot sun, had been fighting the numerous fires the bombs and torpedoes had started in the listing carrier. Within half an hour the smoke-grimed damage control squads had her back on even keel and three out of four fires were under control. Only one fire still smouldered. Everything seemed fairly shipshape and they were looking forward to a break for chow.

Five minutes later at one o'clock the ship was shaken by a shattering roar below decks. A spark from a generator had touched off a leaking fuel pipe. Even then the danger did not seem serious, and returning bombers and fighters continued to land on *Lexington*'s deck. Then heavy fires spurted up and flames began to lick rapidly towards the flight deck. Although the fire fighters fought them as tenaciously as ever, they began to get out of control. *Yorktown* was ordered to take aboard the last *Lexington* planes returning from the attack on the Japanese carriers. Those which had already landed on Lexington had to be left to burn.

Flames began to creep everywhere over the great 33,000-ton ship, one of the two biggest carriers in the world. Fire spread to the hangar deck and every few minutes ammunition stores began to explode, rocking the whole ship. Engineers below stuck to their posts although the intense heat blistered the paint on the bulkheads around them. They were ordered on deck just before the telephone communications system failed. Had the order been delayed for a few seconds the engine-room crew would never have come out alive.

With *Lexington*'s communications gone and fires and explosions getting worse every minute, destroyers drew alongside to take her crew off. The sun was going down when the order came to abandon ship. The men took the order in a calm and disciplined fashion. Some left their shoes in neat rows on the flight deck before sliding down ropes to the cruisers and destroyers waiting under the shadow of the blazing ship. The storekeeper gave away the ship's supply of ice cream and some men filled their hats with it before they slid down the ropes. Not a single life was lost as the men climbed into the boats. The ship's eight per cent casualties were sustained in Japanese air attacks.

The last man to go was *Lexington*'s commander. As he stood on the edge of the flight deck more gasoline blew up with a huge explosion which shook the ship. As debris was blown hundreds of feet into the air, he quickly slid down a rope into the water. A boat picked him up and carried him to a cruiser standing by.

But *Lexington* was still afloat. To prevent her from falling into Japanese hands a destroyer sent five torpedoes into her. It was just before eight o'clock, eight hours after Takahashi's planes had attacked her. A sheet of flame covered her from stem to stern as, spurting smoke and steam, she slid under the calm waters of the Coral Sea.

At five o'clock that evening, three hours before *Lexington* sank, Vice-Admiral Inouye, overall Japanese battle commander at Rabaul, made a questionable decision. He ordered Takagi to break off the action and retire. He also ordered the Port Moresby invasion ships back to Rabaul.

Why did Inouye decide to break off the battle? He rightly was wary of his pilots' reports that they had sunk both American carriers. He also was worried because so few aircraft remained aboard the only operational carrier, *Zuikaku*. With one carrier lost and another incapable of fighting further, he felt he had not enough air strength left to protect the invasion convoy if any American carriers remained afloat.

It was not a bold decision. It can perhaps best be explained by the fact that Inouye did not understand carrier warfare. Neither he nor Admiral Takagi had any experience in carrier-based air operations. Real leadership on the Japanese side in the battle of the Coral Sea was exerted only on the level of junior commanders like Takahashi, who led the air attack.

Early next day a search plane found oil and floating wreckage where *Lexington* had sunk during the night. But what of *Yorktown*? The Japanese were certain she was sunk but no one could find out definitely. Hara signalled; '*Yorktown* carrier received hits by more than eight bombs and three torpedoes. She was left burning, listing heavily to port. She is believed to have sunk although there is no confirmation yet of her destruction.'

Inouye gave up too soon. If he had been more aggressive he might have caught up and destroyed the damaged *Yorktown* which was making all speed to Hawaii for repairs.

Admiral Yamamoto was delighted at the reported sinkings of two American carriers. At first, acting upon his usual system of leaving it to the local commanders to fight the battle, he made no suggestions. But when reports that Admiral Inouye had broken off the battle reached him in the Inland Sea at midnight he became very angry. He decided he must interfere. He despatched a peremptory message to Inouye ordering him to send his remaining carrier and all other warships to chase and smash the American ships.

When the Japanese ships turned and searched, as ordered, it was too late. *Yorktown* and the other American ships were safely out of reach. The Japanese finally sailed away from the Coral Sea on the night of 10 May—more than forty-eight hours after the last bomb had been dropped.

The battle of the Coral Sea had one most important effect upon the Americans. It destroyed for ever for them the Pearl Harbor-induced, morale-sapping myth that the Japanese navy was invincible.

It had several more vital results. The most important was that the invasion of Port Moresby was called off. Also, when Inouye blundered by not pursuing the Americans his action sent ripples far beyond the Coral Sea. If he had managed to catch the crippled *Yorktown* she could not have joined in the battle of Midway a month later. Her unexpected appearance there contributed strongly to the Imperial Navy's shattering defeat. Before the Japanese eventually sank her, *Yorktown*'s planes sealed the fate of their own carrier flagship, *Akagi*.

The Coral Sea battle had another far-reaching result. On 17 May, when *Shokaku* limped into Kure naval base, repair crews watched her in silence. She had the unhappy distinction of being the most heavily damaged Japanese warship to put in there since the beginning of the war. The Japanese navy began to feel a dent in the invincible armour they had been wearing since Pearl Harbor.

Shokaku was also a striking and ominous example of carrier vulnerability. Three medium bombs had rendered her incapable of flight operations. It would take at least a month to complete her repairs. This meant she could not participate in the Midway operation.

Zuikaku, which followed *Shokaku* into port a few days later, had escaped much damage. But she had lost most of her pilots. This was also to make it impossible for her to take part in Midway.

For only a week now remained before Admiral Nagumo was due to sail. Even if aircraft and air crews were promptly replaced, they would not be well enough trained to fight in the battle.

The crews of his other four carriers, *Akagi*, *Kaga*, *Soryu* and *Hiryu*, were rather inclined to sneer when the two carriers *Shokaku* and *Zuikaku* sailed into the Inland Sea. They felt they had let the side down by their indifferent performance in the drawn battle of the Coral Sea.

Without *Zuikaku* and *Shokaku*, Nagumo was deprived of one-third of his air power. This margin was to make the difference between victory and defeat.

But Yamamoto remained optimistic about the impending battle. Nagumo still had his four battle-tested carriers, while he believed two American carriers had been sunk in the Coral Sea. He was completely confident of his ability to crush any American fleet he might meet. Even the ever-cautious Naval General Staff which had thought the Midway venture too risky, just as they had opposed Pearl Harbor before it, now seemed happy about the outcome.

While Yamamoto was planning the last details of the coming battle, relying on optimistic false information, *Yorktown* was limping back to Hawaii. When she arrived repair crews in Pearl Harbor worked flat-out round the clock to make her ready for sea. Within forty-eight hours she was ready to join the Midway battle. This achievement was in striking contrast to Japan's tortoise-like repairs to *Shokaku*. She was not ready for sea until weeks after Midway.

The difference was largely due to the attitudes of the two opposing commanders-in-chief. Nimitz knew *Yorktown* was vital and must be ready. Yamamoto on the other hand thought he had carriers to spare.

14

The Great Armada

WHILE the two carriers *Zuikaku* and *Shokaku* were fighting the Coral Sea battle, preparations were being rushed forward for the bigger decisive battle for Midway atoll. In May mock torpedo and bombing attacks were carried out at Iwakuni in the Inland Sea. The 21,000-ton *Settsu*, an old decommissioned battleship, was used as a target. Many of the pilots' practice attacks proved so disappointing that staff officers supervising the training openly wondered how such poor flyers would ever equal the feats of their seniors at Pearl Harbor and the Coral Sea battle. Even their flying formations were ragged, as they were not given enough time to practise them.

It was not all the pilots' fault. Yamamoto was rushing their flying programme because of his anxiety to destroy the American fleet before it could be built up. Not only were they pushed ahead with inadequate training but they had the minimum facilities. Most of Nagumo's carriers were undergoing repairs and maintenance after their long voyages, so the only available ship on which to practise take-off and landing was the carrier *Kaga*, which had been left behind when he sailed to Ceylon.

The fledgeling flyers had to queue up to learn the bare rudiments of carrier landings and very few of them were taught the essentials of the hazardous night-landing technique. Only the more seasoned flyers, veterans of Pearl Harbor and Ceylon, were given a chance to make a dusk landing. The rest had to sail to Midway risking the fact that they might be forced to land at night. There was no doubt they were entering a world-shaking battle grossly undertrained.

There were also other significant signs of coming disaster. After four months of brilliant victories, the Imperial Navy persisted in regarding the Coral Sea battle as only an unimportant setback. The Midway and Aleutian operations had been agreed before it was fought, and no one saw this drawn battle as in any way affecting their plans. They overlooked the fact that after the Battle of the Coral Sea the invasion of Port Moresby was postponed indefinitely.

On the other hand, they had every excuse for regarding the Coral Sea battle as a minor event. Their overconfidence was based on their faith in the air arm, in whose creation Yamamoto, their revered Commander-in-Chief, had played so intimate a part. Surely he could continue to rely upon it. For the navy's tale of victory was like a conquering admiral's dream. The Americans and their allies had been swept from the vast spaces of the Pacific and Indian Oceans at a ridiculously low cost in ships, planes and men. Why should these victories not continue?

In May, aboard his newly launched flagship *Yamato*, Admiral Yamamoto called staff officers to a conference to weigh the gains and losses from the beginning of the war to the Coral Sea. The scoreboard was enough to give the most timid and cautious admiral confidence:

1. Pearl Harbor. Japan's carrier planes sank or disabled the United States battleships *Nevada, California, Arizona, West Virginia, Maryland* and *Oklahoma*, and heavily damaged the battleships *Pennsylvania* and *Tennessee*. They also sent to the bottom the old target ship *Utah*, the cruiser *Helena* and two destroyers. The Americans had also suffered heavy damage to shore installations and the loss of many aircraft.

2. Malaya. Japan's land-based bombers sank the new British battleship *Prince of Wales* and battle cruiser *Repulse*.

3. Java sea. Japanese warships sank the Dutch cruisers *De Ruyter* and *Java*, the Australian cruiser *Perth*, the American cruiser *Houston*, the British cruiser *Exeter* and five destroyers.

Barely a month before the conference, Nagumo's bombers had sunk the British cruisers *Cornwall* and *Dorsetshire* in the Bay of Bengal. Four days later, off Trincomalee, the same planes had claimed their first enemy aircraft carrier, the British *Hermes*. Yet at the beginning of May their total losses were only six destroyers.

In the first week in May the Coral Sea battle had altered the balance sheet a little with the loss of the carrier *Shoho* and heavy damage to the big carrier *Shokaku*. But in the same battle Japanese carrier aircraft had sunk the big American carrier *Lexington* and heavily damaged or destroyed the *Yorktown*. Compared with the Allies, Japan had suffered very lightly indeed.

Yamamoto hurried into the Midway venture because of his unswerving conviction that the balance of military strength must shift against Japan two years after Pearl Harbor. By then America's giant industrial power would easily overwhelm Japan's small output. Having missed the carriers at Pearl Harbor he felt he had only one chance—to strike a series of massive and devastating blows.

Unless Japan could defeat the American fleet in a decisive battle as soon as possible she was lost. There can be no doubt however that his normally clear judgment was warped by the Doolittle raid. Although the Japanese newspapers jeered at it as the 'Do Nothing Raid', it made Yamamoto's preoccupation with keeping the Imperial capital of the Mikado immune from air attack even more intense.

He made no secret that his attitude towards the war remained unchanged. He wanted it to end quickly. He confided to Rear-Admiral Yamaguchi that, if the Midway battle succeeded in destroying the U.S. Pacific Fleet, he intended to press Tojo strongly to make overtures for a negotiated peace.

He had two specific objects in choosing Midway and the Aleutians. In Japanese hands, Midway could be a powerful springboard for Pacific attacks towards America. On the other hand, Kiska and Attu islands at the western end of the Aleutian chain could be stepping stones towards Japan. Their occupation would help to prevent American task forces attacking the Japanese homeland.

Admiral Yamamoto was certain the U.S. fleet could be forced to a gigantic showdown at Midway. He also had no doubt the battle he sought so eagerly must determine the final outcome of the Pacific war.

Never for a moment did he consider the battle might go against him. Why should it? He began to weld the whole Japanese navy into an enormous armada under his personal command to take part in one huge operation spread over the northern and central Pacific. There was nothing small in his planning. It was on a titanic scale.

The largest fleet in the history of naval warfare was ordered to assemble for the attack. The spearhead was to be his four big carriers, *Akagi*, *Kaga*, *Hiryu* and *Soryu*, under the command of Vice-Admiral Chuichi Nagumo as they had been at Pearl Harbor. Nagumo's experienced, unbeaten Pearl Harbor carriers were screened by the two fast battleships *Kirishima* and *Hiei*, three cruisers and eleven destroyers.

In addition to the four big carriers, four more carriers were ready for battle. Two of them, *Ryujo* and the new *Junyo*, commanded by

Rear-Admiral Kakuji Kakuda, would attack Dutch Harbor to support the Aleutian landings. This whole operation would act as a diversion to draw American attention away from Midway.

Two more, *Hosho* the oldest and smallest carrier, and *Zuiho*—sister ship of *Shoho* sunk in the Coral Sea—were to provide air cover for Yamamoto's giant battleships, called the main body, which were to take part in the fight. The main body alone was a gigantic fleet of seven of the world's biggest battleships including *Yamato* from which Yamamoto would direct the battle. She and her new 64,000-ton sister ship *Musashi*, both mounting eighteen eleven-inch guns, were the most formidable surface warships in the world.

Altogether Yamamoto had 200 ships, among them eleven battleships, eight carriers, twenty-two cruisers, sixty-five destroyers, and twenty-one submarines, and there were 700 planes. The vessels exceeded a million and a half tons and were manned by 100,000 officers and men, many of them veterans of the Pacific and Indian Oceans. They were to be deployed as follows:

Yamamoto's battleships—600 miles north-west of Midway.
Nagumo's carriers—300 miles east of Yamamoto.

The Midway occupation force of twelve transports was commanded by Vice-Admiral Nobutake Kondo, who had participated in the conquest of the Philippines and the Indies. With him were two battleships, four heavy cruisers and seven destroyers. The landing forces were also closely escorted by a cruiser and ten destroyers.

When Yamamoto had collected all his fleet together his superiority in carriers alone was nearly three to one. After the sinking of *Lexington*, the U.S. Pacific Fleet could only muster *Yorktown*, *Hornet* and *Enterprise* against his four large carriers and four light carriers. The worst prospect that faced him was that the Americans would refuse battle with such an invincible armada. But even if they did, there would always be another day.

His only drawback was that Intelligence had no clue as to where the American carriers might be. Their information was pure guesswork. Some argued there might be three American carriers near Midway. Others guessed there would be none. They had been certain that *Hornet* and *Enterprise* were back at Pearl Harbor. Yet several days after the Coral Sea battle reports came in that they had been sighted a long way from Pearl Harbor—in the South Pacific. If these two carriers were still in the South Pacific this would make the capture of Midway easier, but it would prevent Yamamoto's greater objective —the destruction of the American carriers. He still believed his pilots had sunk not only *Lexington* but *Yorktown*. However, his staff officers did allow for a possible third carrier in case there had been a hasty reinforcement. Or, as was correct, *Yorktown* might have managed to get back to Hawaii.

On 3 June—twenty-four hours before the Midway invasion— the two carriers *Ryujo* and *Junyo* would strike at the Aleutians. Then troops would land on Adak, Attu and Kiska. This was intended to confuse the American command about his aims. He had no plans for remaining in the Aleutians. He intended to withdraw his invasion forces in mid-September before the onset of winter.

Next day at dawn Nagumo's big carriers would bomb Midway and destroy the planes based there. Having softened up Midway all day, on the night of 4 June 5,000 troops would wade ashore to take the atoll.

The vital part of Yamamoto's plan was his submarines, which he proposed to send ahead of his giant fleet. One boat was to scout Midway while four took positions off the Aleutians. Two would station themselves off America's west coast. The most important submarine lines were to cover Pearl Harbor. Four submarines would lie 500 miles west of Oahu and another seven boats across the route between Pearl and Midway. These were to be on station by 1 June.

Yamamoto placed them west and north of Hawaii, so when the Pacific Fleet left Pearl Harbor it must cross one or two lines of his submarines. In the absence of any other information, this would give him ample warning of what American ships were against him. After radioing their reports the submarines could then attack and inflict the first losses on the American fleet.

The plan for the Japanese carriers was to try and get them between the Pacific Fleet and their base at Pearl Harbor. When they were cut off from their base Yamamoto's big battleships of the main body, kept at a safe distance to avoid air attack, would close in for an easy kill.

In spite of the awe-inspiring scope of the planning, many staff officers remained unhappy with the decision to leave the undamaged *Zuikaku* behind. Their opinion was that in such an all-out blow the remaining pilots from *Shokaku* should have been posted aboard *Zuikaku* to give her a full complement for the Midway fleet. If their advice had been taken this extra carrier might have altered the whole aspect of the Midway battle. But Yamamoto decided to keep her in reserve.

It was quite a sound decision because he had no doubt the two great fleets, his main body battleships and Nagumo's carriers, would easily complete the task he had begun at Pearl Harbor. They were quite capable of totally destroying the U.S. fleet before it was reinforced by new construction.

On 1 May, aboard the *Yamato*, moored to a red buoy in Hashira anchorage, Admiral Yamamoto and his senior officers were hurriedly putting the finishing touches to his Midway plan. The ship-to-shore telephone cable from the flagship was busy twenty-four hours a day with messages from the Naval General Staff in Tokyo or calls to Kure naval base about ship repairs, maintenance and supplies.

The two vice-admirals, carrier commander Nagumo and Kondo, who was to escort the invading transports, reported aboard the bustling flagship. When Yamamoto told them for the first time the details of Plan A.F.—the Midway operation—the two admirals had completely different reactions. Nagumo was openly indifferent both about the plan and the location of the next operation. His carriers had fought unscathed and victorious from Pearl Harbor to Ceylon and he was fully confident—even over-confident—of his pilots' ability to carry out any mission anywhere.

One of Nagumo's carrier division commanders, Rear-Admiral Tamon Yamaguchi, was much more enthusiastic about Yamamoto's plan. Like Yamamoto himself, he had served as naval attaché in Washington. He agreed whole-heartedly that the United States fleet must be brought to battle at the earliest opportunity. The flying crews shared Yamaguchi's attitude, as they saw in Midway a chance to destroy the American carriers they had missed at Pearl Harbor.

Vice-Admiral Kondo, who had not met Yamamoto since the start of the war, did not share their enthusiasm. He made no secret of his misgivings about the Midway plan. He thought the Americans would employ substantial shore-based air strength and might also bring up their whole carrier fleet.

Having already had all this out with the Naval General Staff and won, Admiral Yamamoto was in no mood to listen to his subordinate Kondo. He told him curtly the Midway plan had been drawn up after prolonged study by the senior staff officers. He had no intention of changing it. If there was a similar surprise to that at Pearl Harbor, there was no fear of defeat.

Admiral Kondo was not satisfied. It would be his responsibility to supply Midway after its capture. He asked Yamamoto's chief of staff, Rear-Admiral Matomi Ugaki, how this was going to be done.

Ugaki finally admitted it might become impossible to supply the occupation forces. If so, they would be evacuated after destroying American military installations. This convinced Kondo the whole operation was pointless.

The same day Admiral Ugaki began a four-day series of war games, not only for Midway but for the second phase of the war. They were the biggest war games since the rehearsal for the Pearl Harbor attack six months before. All the senior officers who were to take part in the attack on Midway attended. The problems set were as follows:

1. In early June the Combined Fleet will capture Midway. Part of it will seize the western Aleutians.

2. Most of the battleships will return to Japan, but the remainder of the Midway invasion naval forces will resume operations early in July for the capture of strategic points in New Caledonia and the Fiji Islands.

3. The Nagumo force will later carry out air strikes against Sydney and other points on the south-east coast of Australia.

4. At the beginning of August, Nagumo with other forces will launch operations against Johnston Island and Hawaii, employing the full strength of the Combined Fleet.

Every mock operation from Midway to the assault on Hawaii was carried out with ease. But this was only because Admiral Ugaki, the presiding officer, frequently set aside rulings made by the umpires. All verdicts on the air fighting were altered in favour of Japan.

In one war game Nagumo's fleet was bombed by American aircraft while its own planes were in the air attacking Midway. One umpire, Lieutenant-Commander Okumiya, an air staff officer, ruled there had been nine enemy hits on the Japanese carriers. Both *Akagi* and *Kaga* were listed as sunk. But Admiral Ugaki reduced the number of enemy hits to three, with only *Kaga* being sunk and *Akagi* slightly damaged.

One of Nagumo's staff officers was asked in a discussion following

this mock operation what he would do if American carriers appeared while they were making their air attack on Midway. This was
precisely what happened in the actual battle. He made such a vague
reply that even Admiral Ugaki cautioned him. This incident revealed
that many of Nagumo's staff officers were not following what was
going on.

As a result, at the end of the war games Admiral Kondo, backed by
most of the other admirals, urged that the invasion day be postponed
to allow more time for the training of pilots and staff officers as well
as for other battle preparations. Once again Yamamoto refused to
listen to Kondo. He insisted that early June was the only time when
there would be enough moonlight for night movements off the invasion beaches.

Another aspect that perturbed many staff officers was that they felt
that the Midway plan was based on an obsolete concept. Unaware of
Yamamoto's thinking, they thought he was making battleships and
not carriers the core of the fleet's fighting strength. It seemed to them
that the carriers were being left naked without the battleships to
screen and support them. The battleships, which could throw up an
extra barrage of anti-aircraft fire to fight off air attacks on the carriers,
were to be 300 miles away from them. Many officers could not see
how battleships so far to the rear could help in the operation at all.

Admiral Yamaguchi, although enthusiastic for the Midway operation, was one. He proposed the fleet should be reorganized into three
task forces with battleships and destroyers screening the carriers.
This suggestion was not approved by Yamamoto, who was certain
the carriers would fight better on their own.

The war games broke up with many important problems unsolved
and many officers dissatisfied. The only people who were not unduly
worried were Nagumo and his flying crews. They believed themselves
capable of smashing the U.S. Pacific Fleet single-handed.

Since the battle of Midway there have been many hindsight criticisms of Yamamoto's decision to station himself and his battleships
300 miles from Nagumo's carriers. Many Western naval authorities
have agreed with the Japanese staff officers that he should have been
up with his carriers to give them extra protection from his guns.
In fact, the Japanese battleship anti-aircraft armament was so inadequate that their protection would have been little help. Their own
anti-aircraft shield was so thin they would probably have been a
liability and might have been damaged by American planes.

Yamamoto also knew that the battle must be fought by carrier against carrier, as in the Coral Sea but on a much greater scale. In this type of engagement battleships would only get in the way and be more of a nuisance than a help. They would be much better placed at the rear between the Aleutians and Midway fleets to give what support was needed by either as the battle developed. Only when the carriers had slugged it out could any other moves take place.

Yamamoto intended to play these later moves by ear according to the extent of the American defeat. He had no fleet plan beyond Midway. When the American carriers had been eliminated there would be plenty of time to think of the next move. It should be temptingly easy. For instance Hawaii and the whole of America's west coast would be exposed to the guns of his great battleships. In his view nothing would be better calculated to put Americans in the mood for a negotiated peace.

Only one ingredient was needed for his massive scheme—victory. But surely that must be automatically his. Even if the Americans brought all their Pacific carriers against him it would still be a two-to-one battle even without calling on the two carriers with his Aleutians force.

Yamamoto surveyed the future after victory with grim satisfaction. He would be undisputed master of the vast Pacific ocean. His big battleships could range at will where he liked. He could attack wherever he pleased. American reinforcements trying to reach Hawaii would be sunk.

He could roam like an iron-clad pirate the whole length of America's west coast, shelling and burning from San Francisco to Seattle. He could even land parties of troops there to ravage and burn where they liked. It was going to be a spine-chilling summer for the United States of America. He was confident this would be such a blow to civilian morale that they must negotiate.

15

Next, the American Coast

WHAT sort of a place was Midway that made Yamamoto collect the greatest armada in the history of the world to invade it? The hot, sandy, uninhabited Pacific atoll is at the end of the Hawaiian chain, just over 1,100 miles from Pearl Harbor. It is only six miles across with two tiny islands, Sand and Eastern, just inside the lagoon. Sand Island, with its highest point rising only to thirty-nine feet, is two miles long. Eastern, where the runways were situated, is half the size of Sand Island.

Midway, anchored like an outsize stationary aircraft carrier half-way across the Pacific, is far more important than a hundred larger, lusher islands. It is strategically invaluable. For nearly a hundred years, the U.S. Navy had realized this. As long ago as 1867 they spent fifty thousand dollars dredging out an anchorage on the atoll. Then for the next thirty years no American went near it. The only visitors were occasional trading schooners which put into the lagoon to collect tropical bird feathers for hats.

Although in 1904 a cable station was built on Sand Island, it was not until thirty years later when war loomed in the Pacific that the United States began to take an urgent interest in these two Pacific Islands. Also the air age, in which Midway was to play such a crucial part, was coming fast. In the 'thirties technicians of Pan-American arrived to develop a seaplane base on the atoll.

In 1938 Rear-Admiral Arthur J. Hepburn led a party of naval officers to study the possibilities of Midway. He reported to Congress that as an air base Midway was second in importance only to Pearl Harbor. His advice was taken seriously. Two years before the outbreak of the Pacific war, America had installations on Midway worth twenty million dollars (seven million pounds).

It was to wrest this tiny, strategically vital Pacific atoll from the Americans that Yamamoto was preparing to give battle with all his vast strength.

During May, in Hashira anchorage south of Hiroshima, surrounded by hilly little islands bristling with camouflaged anti-aircraft batteries, gathered the greatest concentration of ships ever seen in the Pacific. It was a perfect natural hiding place well away from the international merchant shipping routes and could accommodate the entire Japanese navy. As every day passed more and more warships dropped anchor. Small yellow fleet auxiliaries with tall funnels shuttled between warships bringing supplies.

The cherry blossom faded as spring turned into summer. But the two carriers *Ryujo* and *Junyo* were loading heavy winter clothing. Sailors speculated excitedly whether they were going to Arctic waters. Or was it a deception plan? But in this closely guarded, secret Japanese anchorage that was hardly likely or necessary. The two carriers were in fact part of the northern force bound for the Aleutians.

The harbour now held most of the Japanese navy—a total of sixty-eight big warships. The battleship divisions under Yamamoto himself consisted of seven of Japan's biggest warships, *Yamato*, *Nagato*, *Mutsu*, *Ise*, *Hyuga*, *Fuso* and *Yamashiro*. These great battleships had been anchored in Hashira since the outbreak of war awaiting a decisive surface battle. Nagumo's flyers sarcastically referred to them as the 'Hashira Fleet'.

Torpedo nets ringed each of these giants. The Japanese navy had demonstrated at Pearl Harbor what happened to unprotected ships if torpedo bombers attacked. They were not going to be caught in their turn.

On 18 May, a week after the war games finished, Colonel Kiyono Ichiki, who was to command the army assault troops detailed to take Midway, boarded *Yamato* to be given all the latest details of the operational plan by Admiral Yamamoto. He was the last officer to be briefed.

After his visit the great armada began to move. Forty-eight hours after his talk with Yamamoto, Colonel Ichiki sailed with twelve transports carrying his Midway landing forces. The day after Ichiki left, the northern force, led by the sister carriers *Ryujo* and *Junyo*, sailed out of the Inland Sea for the Aleutians invasion.

The giant battleships and carriers which were to steam directly from the Inland Sea to the battle area still had up to a week to wait. Admiral Yamamoto decided not to waste this time. On the same day as the Aleutians force sailed he led his main body of battleships with

Admiral Kondo's Second Fleet and Admiral Nagumo's carriers through the mine-free channel in the Bungo Strait into the open sea. For two days they engaged in fleet manœuvres, the biggest undertaken since the outbreak of war. They were also the last ever to be staged in the open sea by the Japanese Imperial Navy.

When they arrived back in Hashira anchorage on 25 May, Vice-Admiral Takagi who had commanded the Japanese fleet in the Coral Sea battle reported to Yamamoto. He gave all commanders a detailed lecture on the engagement. Through lack of information, he painted a much rosier picture than was actually the truth. He was certain that *Yorktown*, if not sunk, was so badly damaged she could not take part in the Midway battle. He could not know about the near-miracle the Pearl Harbor repair groups were going to perform.

A feeling of excitement ran through the big ships as everything became ready for the battle. Senior officers were invited aboard his flagship by Admiral Yamamoto to toast the success of the forthcoming operation. They drank *sake* from special cups presented to Yamamoto by Emperor Hirohito. 27 May was Navy Day, when Japanese sailors celebrated Admiral Togo's great victory over the Russian fleet in the battle of Tsushima.

Officers and ratings felt that once again Japan's national naval hero, whose flag was hoisted before Pearl Harbor, was to be associated with this coming battle. Everyone aboard the great fleet was certain that this was the day they would sail.

It was eight o'clock on a warm May morning when cries of *banzai* suddenly resounded round the harbour. A signal flag was fluttering at *Akagi*'s masthead. It gave the long-expected order to sail.

The destroyers cut foaming swathes as they began to move towards the harbour entrance. Anchor chains rattled as the cruisers and battleships made ready to follow them. The bulky carriers *Akagi*, *Kaga*, *Hiryu* and *Soryu*, which had helped to smash the American battleships at Pearl Harbor, began to move. Nagumo's flyers were on their way to spearhead the Japanese Imperial Navy in its greatest battle. It was the first and last great massed carrier battle ever to be fought. It was to be the most decisive and significant naval action since Trafalgar nearly a century and a half before. For whoever lost this battle must lose the Pacific war.

As the carriers steamed out of the anchorage the crews of Yamamoto's battleships, not due to follow them until two days later, lined the rails waving their caps. Two hours after he had flown his signal,

Nagumo aboard his flagship *Akagi* headed towards Bungo Channel at sixteen knots on a fine sunny day with a gentle breeze.

The twenty-one ships formed a single column for their passage through the channel. The light cruiser *Nagara*, flagship of Rear-Admiral Susumu Kimura, was in the van. Behind her sailed Rear-Admiral Hiroaki Abe's cruisers. With *Tone*, his flagship, and her sister ship *Chikuma* were the fast battleships *Haruna* and *Kirishima*. Behind *Kirishima* came the big carriers *Akagi* and *Kaga* under Admiral Nagumo's direct command with Rear-Admiral Tamon Yamaguchi's *Hiryu* and *Soryu* bringing up the rear.

As they passed groups of Japanese fishing boats their crews waved excitedly as the mightiest armada ever seen in the Pacific steamed proudly by. Aboard the warships, sailors who had come on deck to catch a last glimpse of Japan's rapidly fading coastline waved happily back.

The officers were not so cheerful. Many of them were worried that news of the fleet's sailing might have leaked out. They felt there had been too much over-confidence which had led to slack security. With so many ships docking in Kure for repairs or to load supplies not a single person in the town could help knowing the Japanese fleet was preparing for a mighty battle. Everyone could also see that some of the ships were rather obviously being fitted out for cold-weather latitudes.

The officers would have been much more anxious if they had known that some of the ships had sent messages to one another which had even mentioned their destination. One message, admittedly given in code, was in response to a request asking where sailors' and officers' mail was to be forwarded. Confidently and very stupidly came back the reply: Midway.

When the carriers began to sail out of the Bungo Channel into the blue waters of the Pacific, tension increased as Japanese naval Intelligence reported a dozen American submarines operating close to the coast. They could not attack the formidable fleet but they could send back information about it. Occasionally the Japanese would monitor their radio reports to Hawaii. They knew the sailing of the armada had been reported to Nimitz in Pearl Harbor because two American submarines sent soft-code messages reporting the passage of the carriers. Although the Japanese fleet intercepted them they still remained confident no one could guess where they were going.

As they headed into the Pacific the armada changed into a circular formation. *Nagara*, the lead ship, was still out in front. Behind her the four carriers steamed surrounded by two wide circles of screening ships with twelve destroyers forming the outer circle.

As the destroyers spread out watchfully everyone stood to his anti-submarine post and lookouts strained their eyes. Patrol planes swooped overhead but no American submarines were sighted. For the first time since they had left Hashira anchorage at breakfast-time the Japanese admirals relaxed.

Forty-eight hours later Yamamoto's seven battleships left the Inland Sea accompanied by the small carriers, *Hosho* and *Zuiho*, and screened by three light cruisers and twelve destroyers. Vice-Admiral Kondo's Second Fleet, consisting of the battleships *Kongo* and *Hiei*, with several cruisers and destroyers, accompanied Yamamoto's ships for the first two days of their voyage. Then they sailed away to rendezvous with Ichiki's transports ploughing their slow way towards Midway.

As his battleships zigzagged along their plotted route, Yamamoto was apparently ignorant of or indifferent to the fact that a dozen American submarines might be shadowing him. He was certain the United States had no knowledge he was sailing towards Midway.

His own knowledge of the movements of the U.S. fleet still remained scanty. Two days after his gigantic fleet sailed out of the Inland Sea Lieutenant Tomano, the survivor of the ill-fated earlier reconnaissance to Midway and Johnston Island, was told to make another full-moon reconnaissance of Pearl Harbor. Before his Midway attack Yamamoto wanted to know the Pacific Fleet's strength in their main base.

When a Japanese refuelling submarine arrived at French Frigate Shoals her lookout saw through the periscope American aircraft and destroyers patrolling there. Her captain signalled that refuelling was impossible. Instead of moving the submarine to near-by Necker Island to refuel, the Japanese naval staff cancelled Tomano's flight.

It was another incredible piece of careless over-confidence. If Tomano had refuelled and flown on to Hawaii, he might have sighted the American carriers sailing from Pearl Harbor to Midway. This would have warned Admiral Yamamoto of the bitter opposition he was going to meet.

For, as Yamamoto had predicted, the U.S. Pacific Fleet was determined to oppose the invasion of Midway with all its available strength. Midway was too important as the sentinel for Hawaii and the Americans were going to fight for it.

Admiral Chester W. Nimitz, C.-in-C. of the Pacific Fleet, was aware of Yamamoto's intentions a month before he sailed. With Japan's most secret cypher broken by the U.S. Navy, as soon as Yamamoto's staff began sending code signals arranging details of Plan A.F., the Americans picked them up and deciphered them.

As Yamamoto's great armada gathered in the Inland Sea American Intelligence's Black Chamber at Pearl Harbor consistently monitored and decoded their secret messages. At first the Americans were not absolutely sure whether D-Day would be at the end of May or early June. Nor did they know whether the attack was intended for Midway or Oahu.

Nimitz was certain from the beginning that the Japanese were after Midway. But he must be sure. Commander Joseph R. Rochefort of the Black Chamber had a good idea. He suggested sending an uncoded radio message from Midway saying its distillation plant had broken down.

Forty-eight hours later the Black Chamber cryptanalysts intercepted a Japanese despatch. It informed Japanese commanders that Midway was short of fresh water. This completed American information about Yamamoto's plan. Nimitz now knew the Japanese objective, the approximate composition of their forces, the direction of approach and the approximate date of attack.

Although forewarned of Yamamoto's intentions and able therefore to prepare for them, which was half the battle won, Nimitz was uncomfortably aware the American chances of victory were still slight. The knowledge they had gained was a tremendous advantage. It should make an American victory possible—but only barely possible. There was one gigantic drawback. Nimitz knew approximately the size of the armada approaching. His information was cold comfort to him because he knew he was able to raise only a much smaller fleet to meet it. The Japanese fleet was superior in every way.

Another problem faced him. Should he concentrate all his forces on Midway and let the Aleutians go? Or should he reinforce them at the expense of Midway?

In the end he decided he could spare little to meet Yamamoto's Aleutians fleet. He sent an inadequate force of five cruisers, fourteen destroyers and six submarines, under the command of Rear-Admiral Robert A. Theobald, to face the two Japanese carriers *Ryujo* and *Junyo*.

Nimitz's second problem was that Midway atoll with its two small islands could not support enough men to repel the impending attack. Also he had very little time. While Ugaki was organizing the war games in Japan, Nimitz flew to Midway personally to supervise the strengthening of the atoll's defences. The Marine garrison was reinforced by 2,000 men, and many more anti-aircraft batteries were installed. The beaches and approach waters were heavily mined.

The Marine squadrons were equipped with twenty-six fighters, mostly old Brewster Buffaloes. There were also thirty-four bombers, either Douglas Dauntlesses or Vindicators. Nimitz increased Midway plane strength by sixteen Marine dive bombers, seven Wildcat fighters, eighteen army B.17s, and four B.26s specially rigged for torpedo attacks, for which they were unsuited. Most of the pilots of these attack planes were as inexperienced as Yamamoto's men who were practising landings on *Kaga*'s flight deck. The American pilots had been rushed out from flight school and not one of them had had any practice at dive bombing. There were also thirty PBYs—Catalina search planes.

This haphazard collection of planes, the best Nimitz could scrape together, brought the total of aircraft on Midway up to 120. None of them were much good. The only really effective planes on the island were six TBFs, the first of that type to reach the Pacific.

On the day Nagumo's carriers sailed for the atoll Nimitz wrote to Midway's commanders, Marine Lieutenant-Colonel Harold D. Shannon and Commander Cyril T. Simard, that D-Day was expected on 4 June. This gave them just over a week to put the last touches to their defences.

Midway became a thicket of guns, mines and barbed wire. But there were still not many troops to meet Colonel Ichiki's 5,000 Japanese assault troops. Shannon's garrison was 2,138 Marines. Simard had 1,494 flyers and troops—of whom 1,000 were navy men. The Marines would undoubtedly give the invading Japanese a warm reception, but the fate of Midway depended entirely upon the Pacific Fleet.

The American carrier situation was critical. *Lexington* had been sunk and *Yorktown* badly damaged in the Coral Sea battle. It did not look as if she could be repaired in time to defend Midway. *Saratoga* was still at San Diego undergoing repairs for torpedo damage inflicted by the Japanese submarine *I-6* in January. Repair crews working day and night managed to make her ready for the impending battle but Nimitz decided he could not count on her.

The Pacific Fleet was so short of ships that he could not raise a proper escort to protect *Saratoga* and he dare not risk another submarine attack on her. It was 1 June before she left San Diego naval base and steamed across the Pacific at top speed with a heavy escort. She arrived in Pearl Harbor on 6 June—exactly twenty-four hours after the Midway battle was over.

With *Lexington* sunk and *Yorktown* and *Saratoga* doubtful starters, Nimitz was left with only *Hornet* and *Enterprise*. Yamamoto's information that they had been switched to the South Pacific was correct. While on their way back from the Doolittle raid in April they had been ordered to join in operations in the Coral Sea.

Now Nimitz urgently signalled them to return at once and join the damaged *Yorktown* in Pearl Harbor. On the same day as Nagumo's four carriers sailed from the Inland Sea, *Hornet* and *Enterprise* arrived in Pearl Harbor. Next afternoon *Yorktown* came creeping in and went into dry dock. Repair crews—1,400 of them—swung into action in a furious race against time.

Then another unexpected problem faced Nimitz. 'Bull' Halsey, his most aggressive carrier admiral, fell ill, worn out with the strain of months of combat patrol after Pearl Harbor. Nimitz was only too painfully conscious of the task that faced him. He must choose the best carrier admiral America could produce. His choice fell on Rear-Admiral Raymond A. Spruance, a cruiser task force commander. Quiet, courageous and cautious, Spruance was exactly the opposite of the flamboyant Halsey. But his unassuming manner concealed a cool mind and sound judgment. He was not to let Nimitz down.

Yamamoto might not have been so absolutely certain of victory if he had known that on the same day as he led his seven giant battleships out of Hashira anchorage, Admiral Spruance sailed from Pearl Harbor with *Hornet* and *Enterprise*, screened by six cruisers and nine destroyers. He set course for Midway.

While Nimitz was pouring reinforcements into Midway and placing his fleet to meet the coming attack, Yamamoto's Intelligence still believed it was defended by only 750 Marines although they were well equipped with coastal guns and anti-aircraft artillery. They admitted that Midway's air defence might possibly be doubled by reinforcements from Hawaii if Japanese intentions became known.

As they neared the atoll, Yamamoto issued an estimate of American strength in Midway, Hawaii and the Aleutians, based on Japanese Intelligence reports. This said it was believed there were twenty-four patrol flying boats, twelve army bombers and twenty fighters on Midway. Several patrol boats and a number of submarines were also believed to be stationed near the island. They reported that in the Aleutians there was little American naval and air strength, and no important military installations apart from Dutch Harbor.

After his two carriers sailed Nimitz was at the receiving end of a near-miracle. Badly damaged *Yorktown* was scheduled to be in dock for three months. The Pearl Harbor repair crews, fully aware America was facing the greatest threat in her history, performed a truly astonishing feat. Somehow they managed to compress three months' work into two days.

Twenty-four hours after Spruance sailed, *Yorktown* was ready for sea. She fuelled, took on a quickly organized air crew and sailed only two days after the other carriers. Rear-Admiral Frank Jack Fletcher flew his flag in her. Three days later, he joined up with Spruance who flew his flag in *Enterprise*. Then Fletcher, as senior admiral, took command as the three carriers made for a point north-east of Midway.

As his carriers sailed towards Midway, Nimitz knew the die was cast. They were all he had. The only other possible reinforcements were some old battleships on the west coast. They were too slow to make it on time. And even if they tried, so depleted was the U.S. Navy that he had not enough destroyers to screen them on their long voyage across the Pacific.

Nimitz's three carriers were not only standing between Yamamoto and Midway. If he lost the atoll the next place to be attacked would be Hawaii. Worse—the west coast of America would be open to Yamamoto and his battleships. He fully understood the desperate historic significance of the coming clash when he remarked, 'Those three carriers are all that stand between the Japanese fleet and the American coastline.'

He was also painfully aware that his carriers were sailing to do battle with twice the number of Japanese carriers, backed by some of the biggest battleships in the world, commanded by an audacious and unorthodox Japanese commander-in-chief.

It was an appalling task that faced Fletcher and Spruance. Nimitz's orders to them were clear: 'You will be governed by the principle of calculated risk. This means the avoidance of exposure of your force to attack by superior enemy forces without good prospects of inflicting greater damage on the enemy.'

Fletcher and Spruance faced up to the gloomy prospects of annihilation by the Japanese which would make the Pacific their pond—and leave a thousand miles of America's west coast at their mercy. But the luck which had been with Yamamoto at Pearl Harbor was beginning to desert him. His line of I-class submarines which were to report the movements of the American carriers let him down. They had been on long patrols and unceasing active duty since Pearl Harbor and for this new big operation most of them needed repairs and maintenance.

Unlike the American repair gangs, the Japanese did not perform small miracles with the repairs. The Japanese submarines, due to be on station on 31 May, were exactly twenty-five hours late.

The delay was crucial. The submarines arrived too late to warn Yamamoto of the presence of the American carriers. *Hornet* and *Enterprise* crossed the Japanese submarine patrol line between Pearl Harbor and Midway on 29 May. The Japanese submarines were not due to take station until two days later, so they would have missed them anyway. However, if they had been on station on the day planned, they would have seen *Yorktown*, which crossed their line on the night of 31 May. Then there would have been no surprise at Midway—and the result might have been quite different. Instead, the submarines arrived on 1 June when all three American carriers were safely across their patrol line.

Nimitz had another imponderable advantage over Yamamoto which was to prove a decisive factor in the coming battle. He remained ashore at Pearl Harbor retaining overall command. This way he could co-ordinate instantly the movements of ships, submarines and the Midway-based planes. While he was doing this Yamamoto, maintaining radio silence in his elephantine flagship, was to become a helpless spectator at his own battle.

Whatever happened in the coming battle, in one respect Midway was the reverse of Pearl Harbor. As a result of the constant stream of intercepted Japanese secret messages, Yamamoto had lost any shadow of surprise. Every American ship was placed in the best position to repel his invasion of the key atoll.

Nimitz had also learnt the bitter lesson of Pearl Harbor. He and his admirals were certain air power was the key to the battle. They decided to concentrate everything on Nagumo's rapidly approaching carriers.

If Yamamoto had known this he would have welcomed it. For he shared their view. The whole purpose of Midway was to precipitate a full-scale carrier battle with the Americans. With his seasoned, courageous pilots and greater number of carriers he had no doubt of the outcome.

16

Decision at 8.30 a.m.

NOT only did Yamamoto's armada sail almost completely in the dark about the strength and position of the American carriers, but what little information the Japanese did glean was often lost through misunderstanding or inefficiency.

For instance on 30 May shortly after he sailed, Tokyo high radio tower monitored signals pointing to brisk American activity in the Hawaiian area especially among patrol planes. This pointed strongly to the fact that a powerful American force might be sailing from Pearl Harbor for Midway. This information was passed on to Yamamoto's flagship.

Immediately Yamamoto received the message he showed it to Rear-Admiral Kamahito Kuroshima, his operations officer, and said, 'This must be sent to Nagumo at once.' But Kuroshima disagreed, saying he was certain Nagumo must have picked it up too. To send it would mean breaking radio silence which might imperil the whole operation.

Yamamoto replied, 'It doesn't matter. This is the one time we must risk it. There may be carriers among them. If so they must be attacked. We must be sure he knows at once.'

Kuroshima did not see the necessity for such an enormous risk, so, on his own responsibility, he did not pass the message on. He overlooked the fact that *Akagi*'s less powerful receivers could not pick up messages so easily. This decision probably lost Yamamoto the battle. His carriers sailed ahead in complete ignorance of Fletcher's three-carrier task force steaming to intercept them.

Although he advanced into battle with no actual information about Nimitz's ships, the questions were constantly in Nagumo's mind: Were they still in Pearl Harbor? Had they sailed to protect Midway? Or were they in the South Pacific?

He did pick up one signal from the Naval General Staff in Tokyo which made him believe the South Pacific theory. The message said there was a lot of American fleet activity in the Solomons, suggesting the American carriers were still there. This meant Nimitz could not have suspected the Japanese intentions. Otherwise he would have recalled all carriers to Pearl Harbor—which was exactly what he had done.

After sending out this erroneous assessment, Tokyo tower then intercepted many 'urgent' calls in the Hawaii–Midway area. Again they were not passed on to Nagumo, and he was left to believe there were no American carriers poised to oppose him.

Nagumo's carriers did not have an easy voyage from the Inland Sea. On 2 June they ran into a heavy sea mist which by dawn next day became an impenetrable fog blanket. The thick fog placed the big carriers, which were on a zigzag course to avoid submarines, in danger of collision. Powerful searchlights tried to pierce the gloom while Admiral Nagumo paced the bridge gazing with smarting eyes into the fog. Beside him stood *Akagi*'s commander, Captain Taijiro Aoki, who had not left the bridge since they sailed.

As Nagumo peered anxiously into the fog he had greater worries than his flag captain. He constantly asked his operations officer, Captain Oishi, if there was any news of Nimitz's fleet. He was told there was nothing new. Yet the giant flagship *Yamato*, hundreds of miles to his rear, was receiving constant 'urgent' messages from Nimitz and his admirals, passed on by the big Tokyo naval listening post. Although they did not pass him any messages, Yamamoto's staff were blissfully unaware that Nagumo was convinced that the big American carriers were still in the Solomons thousands of miles away.

That was why he decided to go ahead with the attack on Midway as planned. His carriers were still groping their way through the fog which made it impossible to use visual signals, the only kind which could not possibly be intercepted. Because of the full moon and the transports sailing to invade, Nagumo was tied to a strict timetable. He decided to risk using *Akagi*'s low-powered radio to send out an order to the fleet to change course towards Midway. If the Americans picked it up it would alert them and all surprise would be lost. He only hoped such a low-powered transmission would be heard by his ships alone.

In fact the flagship *Yamato* heard his message clearly. This was the only confirmation to reach Yamamoto that his carriers were going to attack as planned. Fortunately for Nagumo the Americans on Midway did not pick up this vital message sent out just before the battle.

Their failure was certainly not due to lack of alertness. Nimitz's monitoring crews were piano-wire taut listening for every single Japanese transmission. It was probably due to freak radio transmission, just as Fuchida's message had somehow reached Tokyo direct from his plane over Pearl Harbor.

When he gave the order to change course for the attack, Nagumo was still completely in the dark about American movements and the size of the American fleet. He made three guesses—all of which proved completely wrong. They were:

1. The Americans are not aware of our plan and have not detected our task force.

2. There is no evidence of an American task force in our vicinity.

3. It is possible to attack Midway, destroy land-based planes there and support the landing operation. Then we will turn round to meet any approaching American task force and destroy it.

At first Nagumo's carriers could not obey his order to speed towards Midway because the fog was too heavy. But that afternoon, 3 June, it lifted and the carriers began to head for Midway at twenty-four knots.

The four carriers were still the centre of a heavy protective shield. Alongside them cruised the battleships *Haruna* and *Kirishima*, the heavy cruisers *Tone* and *Chikuma*, and the light cruiser *Nagara*. Twelve destroyers circled round constantly alert.

All the ships' crews were jumpy, as they knew zero hour was rapidly approaching. On the bridge no one spoke except to give an order. The calmest people were the young pilots who sprawled about below decks laughing and playing cards.

As they approached Midway two American planes flew near them and then disappeared. Although Nagumo was criminally short of vital information he must also take a great deal of the blame for sailing into battle blindfold. Did he not think these planes had reported his warships—just as the submarines that had been reported earlier must have warned Nimitz?

Yet he persisted in his belief that 'there are no American carriers in the waters near Midway'. Why was he so sure on the morning of the

battle that the Americans were unaware of his rapidly approaching
carriers?

Following so soon upon the aggressive action by the American
carriers in the Coral Sea Nagumo's attitude was remarkable. But he
was not the only Japanese admiral to ignore the dangers of the new
pattern of warfare revealed by the first big carrier clash in which
Shoho had been sunk and *Shokaku* severely damaged. Nagumo and
his staff seemed so drunk with their unshaken series of victories that
they brushed all ominous portents aside. In fact the Coral Sea,
instead of warning them, had the reverse effect. The Japanese claims
of two American carriers destroyed tended to make them even more
confident and careless.

Nagumo lacked radar and the facility to read the enemy's secret
code and had not been warned as he should have been about
American activities. Yet there was one routine way in which he might
have discovered the whereabouts of the American carriers. It was
simple, old-fashioned air reconnaissance, but he did not use it. As his
carriers approached Midway he did not bother to send ahead a single
scout plane.

There can be only one explanation. He and his officers were so
cloaked in smug self-confidence that they thought they had nothing
to fear. It is difficult to believe that the men who had carried through
the brilliant, painstaking plan for Pearl Harbor only six months
before were the same people who sailed into this slaphappy Midway
operation.

The Americans were much more alert. Before dawn each morning
Midway-based Catalina flying boats—PBYs—took off to range the
Pacific, seeking Yamamoto's armada. Although the maximum limit
of their searches was 700 miles from Midway, any Japanese carrier
due to attack the following dawn must arrive about that distance away
by nightfall. This would enable her, after steaming at top speed all
night, to be within range to launch her planes before daylight next day.

On the morning of 3 June Ensign Jack Reid of Paducah, Kentucky,
was at the 700 miles limit of his patrol when he dived his PBY out of
the clouds to take a final look. Below him he saw half a dozen Japanese transports escorted by six cruisers. He began a close search and
fifty miles away he flew over four more heavy cruisers escorting large
merchant ships and transports.

This was Colonel Ichiki's invading force protected by Admiral
Kondo's big fleet. The Japanese had sixteen transports carrying

1,500 Marines to land on Sand Island and 1,000 soldiers to invade Eastern Island. There were also two construction battalions to rebuild the damaged airfield.

Reid radioed his discovery back to Midway. This was the first definite news of the approach of the Japanese armada. It confirmed Nimitz's information. Until that moment he could not be sure that all the intercepted code messages had not been fed to him as part of a deception plan. The mysterious Japanese fleet movements were aimed at Midway. They were also going to invade.

That afternoon, when there was no further news of the Japanese transports, more Catalinas took off from Midway to make a night attack on Ichiki's troopships. As they swooped down through broken clouds in the bright moonlight the Catalinas spotted a dozen hazy shapes cruising at high speed. They cut their engines and glided silently downwards in the first torpedo attack delivered by a flying boat in any war. As they skimmed along noiselessly just above water level they pulled their torpedo releases and nosed into a steep climb. There was an explosion and black smoke blotted out the ships. Immediately the moonlit sky was lit up by heavy anti-aircraft fire from Kondo's protecting cruisers and destroyers.

One Catalina went down on the way back. The pilot, Dagwood Propst, and his crew kept the plane afloat by bailing out with their helmets while their rubber rafts lay inflated at the ready. They spent two days and two nights floating on the waves and the Midway battle had been decided before another Catalina sighted them and landed beside them to take them off. Their hopelessly swamped plane was sunk by gunfire.

While Midway-based PBYs attacked Ichiki's transports, the three American carriers kept their position 300 miles from Midway. Kondo's fleet, mighty as it was, was not their target. They were waiting for Nagumo's carriers. There was still no news of them but Spruance and Fletcher expected the Japanese carriers to approach from the north-west under cover of bad weather. This was exactly what Nagumo's carriers were doing as they sailed at top speed for Midway.

As zero hour approached, the Japanese confidence rose. Imperial Headquarters still estimated that the atoll was guarded by only 750 troops and sixty planes. They considered that Ichiki's landing party of 2,800 Japanese troops, covered by 300 planes from Nagumo's four carriers, could overwhelm them easily.

This Imperial Headquarters report was as wrong as Nagumo's estimate that there would be no carriers in the area. As Yamamoto's ships drew near in his great bid for control of the Pacific, Nimitz by hasty last-minute reinforcements had packed nearly 5,000 troops and over 100 planes onto Midway. The latter figure did not include the planes on Fletcher's three carriers. However the battle went, Ichiki's soldiers and marines were almost certain to be massacred.

When the Japanese carriers were 250 miles north-west of Midway, *Akagi*'s loudspeakers ordered all air crews on deck. It was 2.45 a.m. on 4 June and a dark warm morning in mid-Pacific. When they scrambled out of their cabins the decks were already loud with the roar of plane motors warming up.

As the crews reported to the operations rooms on all the carriers, flames spurted from exhausts and navigation lights glowed in the pre-dawn dark. The roar of the engines aroused Commander Minoru Genda, air staff operations officer, who had been confined to his cabin with stomach trouble. When he made his way to the bridge and was seen standing next to Admiral Nagumo the confidence of the air crews rose even higher. For Genda was the greatest naval air expert in Japan. He had been at the heart of the Pearl Harbor planning and ever since then had remained aboard *Akagi* directing the series of successful operations launched by the carriers.

Nagumo himself briefed *Akagi*'s pilots and once again revealed his overconfidence when he told them: 'Although the enemy is lacking in fighting spirit he will probably come out to the attack as our invasion proceeds.'

As battle loomed, Nagumo for the first time began behaving cautiously. Although he did not expect American carriers near Midway, he sent only half his planes to attack the atoll. He held back his best pilots in case of any counter-attack by American carriers.

Although he was still convinced there were no American carriers in the area, he also finally decided to put up an air search. Japanese air patrols were normally very meticulous. This one was casual and haphazard.

A plane from *Akagi* was to fly south for 300 miles, then turn and fly sixty miles east. A *Kaga* plane was to fly the same pattern south-east. Two planes each from the heavy cruisers *Tone* and *Chikuma* were to fly 300 miles, turn left and fly sixty miles, and then return. The last plane, from *Haruna*, was to fly only 150 miles, then turn left and fly forty miles before returning.

This search, despatched half an hour before sunrise, would have given vital information if it had worked out as planned. It did not. The carriers *Akagi* and *Kaga* launched their search planes on schedule at 4.30 a.m. But *Tone's* two planes were delayed for thirty minutes by catapult trouble. A plane from *Chikuma* developed engine trouble and turned back at 6.35 a.m. Most of the other scout planes ran into bad weather and returned half-way through their search.

Here the luck of war was still against the Japanese. If the *Chikuma* scout plane which developed engine trouble had been able to continue its search it would have flown directly over the American carriers and Nagumo would have been warned in time. The belated take-off of *Tone's* two planes was also unfortunate. If they had taken off on time instead of half an hour late, they too might have found the American carriers and given an early alarm.

It was still not dawn when the floodlights on *Akagi's* flight deck were switched on and the first bomber gathered speed and roared into the night. As other planes followed and climbed into the scurrying clouds the flagship's crew cheered. The other carriers, *Kaga*, *Hiryu* and *Soryu*, also switched on their floodlights as their planes began to take off. Within fifteen minutes the four carriers launched 108 planes. The slight south-west wind and calm sea enabled them to hold course easily while launching. The planes circled over them and flew east towards the dawn.

The time was 4.45 a.m. on 4 June. The most crucial battle for the control of the Pacific was about to begin.

The first attack wave of 108 planes was commanded by Lieutenant Joichi Tomonaga. This was his first battle in the Pacific. He had flown in China air battles but had reported to *Hiryu* only just before she sailed.

Under his personal control were thirty-six level bombers from *Soryu* and *Hiryu*. The thirty-six dive bombers from *Akagi* and *Kaga* were led by Lieutenant Shoichi Ogawa from *Kaga*. The fighter escort of thirty-six Zeros, nine from each carrier, was led by Lieutenant Masaharu Suganamai of *Soryu*. Unlike Tomonaga, they were both seasoned Pacific pilots who had been with Nagumo at Pearl Harbor and every carrier action since.

Before Nagumo launched his seven scout planes, the American search aircraft from Midway had already taken off on their pre-dawn patrol. An hour after the Japanese carrier planes took off, a

PBY pilot reported in plain English: 'Many planes heading Midway distance 150.' Tomonaga's pilots were half-way to the atoll.

Five minutes later blobs on the scanner at the Marine radar station on Sand Island showed the planes approaching ninety-three miles away. The B.17 bombers were told to take off and circle to prevent them from being destroyed on the ground.

But where were the Japanese carriers? Two minutes later came the answer. The same Catalina reported: 'Enemy carriers sighted 150 miles.' Then another Catalina pilot reported: 'Two carriers and battleships 180 miles from Midway.'

Immediately all available Midway planes, including the four B.26s carrying torpedoes and the six newly arrived TBFs, took off to attack Nagumo's carriers. They were joined by twenty Brewster Buffaloes and seven Grumman Wildcats. The circling B.17s were also directed to the Japanese carriers.

As Tomonaga approached Midway with his thirty-six Vals and thirty-six Kates he knew he must have been spotted but he remained confident as he droned on through the dark pre-dawn sky. He knew he must meet heavy American resistance but he had great faith in the fighters protecting his bombers—even though there were only thirty-six of them escorting twice their number.

Unknown to Tomonaga, the PBY which had first sighted his planes was still shadowing them. They were thirty miles away from Midway and it was still not yet dawn. Suddenly the shadowing flying boat dropped a flare and lit up Tomonaga's squadron hidden in the darkness. Marine fighters circling above in the clouds dived on the Japanese planes and started a running fight. As the air battle raged all round them, Tomonaga's bombers flew on, still keeping perfect formation.

When twenty-seven American fighters, led by Major Parks, plunged on the Japanese bombers they found themselves battling with formidable aircraft. They could not shake the tenacious, fast-moving planes off their tails. As they turned and weaved desperately they realized they were up against a new type of fighter. This was not the famous Zero with rounded wingtips which had been such a sensational success at the beginning of the Pacific war. This was a new and even more manœuvrable aircraft with tapering wings. It was an improved Zero which became known as the Zeke.

The twenty-seven Marine fighters not only were outnumbered by the thirty-six Japanese Zekes but were no match for them individually. The Japanese fighter commander, Lieutenant Suganamai, easily prevented the Americans from reaching his bombers. The inexperienced American pilots were shot up and driven off by the greatly superior Zekes.

While the fighters unsuccessfully fought the new Zekes, Tomonaga and his seventy-two planes began to make their bomb runs over the sandy atoll. At 6.30 a.m. the first bomb fell. In spite of heavy anti-aircraft fire from the reinforced defences, within the next half-hour bombs hit the power house, set fuel tanks on fire and destroyed a hangar. But the heavy American anti-aircraft fire daunted the Japanese pilots, many of whom were as inexperienced as the American flyers. It made their bombing wild. They aimed for airstrips, stores and barracks but many of their bombs just fell on sand. Circling over the burning fuel tanks and barracks, Tomonaga realized that the damage his bombers had done was far from effective. He radioed that a second strike was necessary.

In fact he had done more damage than he thought. The fuel supply system was so badly hit that all subsequent fuelling had to be carried out by hand. The seaplane hangar and fuel storage tanks on Sand Island were destroyed. Yet in spite of this concentrated bombing in such a small area the Americans had only twenty killed and wounded.

The runways were damaged but not put out of action and the surviving Marine fighters were able to land on them. They were a dispiriting sight to a garrison waiting to repel the Japanese invasion. Out of the twenty-seven planes only ten returned. Seventeen had been shot down, including the flight commander, Major Parks. Those that managed to stagger back had been so badly mauled that only two of them were fit for further combat. But their desperate fight—the first of many to be fought in the burning skies above Midway on that June morning—had not been in vain. When the survivors landed, with their aircraft peppered with holes and their pilots wounded, they did not know that their fierce resistance had helped to harass Tomonaga's bombers enough to put them off accurate aim.

After the fight each side made excited, excessive claims. The Americans said they had shot down fifty-three Japanese planes during the attack, ten by anti-aircraft fire and the rest in aerial combat. In fact only five of Tomonaga's planes failed to return to the carriers. He lost two Kates, one Val, and two Zekes, mainly from anti-aircraft fire. On their side Japanese flyers claimed forty-two American planes destroyed. In fact twenty-seven took part in the battle—but only two returned undamaged.

The battle was now beginning to expand. While Tomonaga bombed Midway, Nagumo was receiving a confusing succession of reported contacts with both flying boats and small numbers of unidentified planes. There was no doubt now that the Americans were shadowing the Japanese fleet. Zekes patrolling above the carriers tried to shoot them down but failed to catch them as they skilfully weaved in and out of the clouds.

Although Tomonaga had radioed his partial failure, the atoll must be neutralized before the invasion forces started wading up the beaches. Tomonaga's bombers were only Nagumo's second string. His first team, commanded by veterans from Pearl Harbor, had been kept in reserve in case any American carriers appeared.

The sun was just rising as the second attack wave of 108 planes was hauled onto the flight decks. This was a most formidable force commanded by an experienced group of Japan's greatest flyers. Lieutenant-Commander Shigeharu Murata of *Akagi*, who had led the successful torpedo plane attack at Pearl Harbor at deck height, led the fifty-four torpedo bombers. The new narrow-winged Zeke fighters were led by Lieutenant-Commander Shigeru Itaya of *Akagi*, another Pearl Harbor veteran. The spearhead of thirty-six dive bombers was led by Lieutenant-Commander Takashige Egusa from *Soryu*. He was the Imperial Navy's leading expert in dive bombing and a frustrated man. His *élite* pilots had been carefully trained to destroy the American carriers in Pearl Harbor at one blow. They had sunk the British carrier *Hermes* in the Indian Ocean but that was small consolation for losing the mighty American carriers. If any American carriers now appeared the opportunity for which Egusa had waited and trained for years might be near at hand.

While Egusa's dive bombers and Murata's planes, armed with torpedoes, sat on deck ready for action should any American carriers or battleships appear, Tomonaga's message came in from Midway saying that another strike on the island was necessary.

A few minutes later twenty-seven Midway-based bombers raced in two waves at low altitude to attack Nagumo's carriers. This convinced Nagumo that Tomonaga was right. Midway was still fighting and must be crushed.

When the two waves approached, the Japanese carriers zigzagged frantically and threw up heavy anti-aircraft fire. The American TBF pilots skimmed over the waves to press home their attacks with great courage but their lumbering aircraft fell an easy prey to the quick-turning Zekes and the fleet's accurate gunfire. The first attack became a massacre. Several torpedoes foamed towards *Akagi* but she swung away and they all missed. American planes fell flaming into the ocean and not a single torpedo struck the carriers.

Major Lofton R. Henderson's Marine dive-bombing squadron started a cold courageous attack on the carriers. His pilots, fresh from flying school, had no training in dive bombing. They were forced to make a more dangerous glide bombing attack, which made them sitting ducks to swooping Zekes and murderously concentrated anti-aircraft fire. As the American glide bombers made for *Hiryu* this method of attack puzzled the Japanese. It was too high for torpedoes, too low for dive bombers.

As they came gliding lower, the battleship *Kirishima* loosed her main batteries at them. Black shell bursts dotted the sky around them but they still came on. Then *Akagi* went into action and shot down two, but three more came on and released their bombs. Major Henderson's damaged bomber skimmed straight over *Akagi*, nearly grazing the bridge as he tried to dive his plane into *Kaga*. He burst into flames and plunged into the sea. The Japanese log reported: 'A U.S. dive bomber apparently hit by A.A. fire crashed into the sea close to *Kaga* on the port side near the island superstructure.'

Of the sixteen Marine planes which had taken off from Midway, with pilots inexperienced in dive bombing, only half returned, and six of those were damaged beyond repair.

Midway's attack on the Japanese carriers was courageous but piecemeal and ineffective. Yet it had one valuable result. It distracted the Japanese at a critical moment, delaying their launching of the second wave of planes.

Nagumo's search planes had now been gone for over two hours and should have reached a radius of 200 miles. As they had reported no American ships much less carriers, Nagumo thought it safe to relax even his scanty precautions. As all the planes attacking him were land-based, there could be no carriers near. These continual land-based attacks convinced Nagumo that Midway must be struck again quickly.

At 7.14 a.m. while his Zekes were still shooting down the remnants of Henderson's glide bombers, Nagumo decided it was safe to attack Midway again. He issued his fateful order: 'Planes in second wave

stand by to carry out another attack on Midway. Re-equip your-
selves with bombs.'

Just then *Tone*'s search plane, about to turn and fly back to the
carriers, made out a group of American ships far below him. Excitedly he radioed, 'Enemy sighted.' Were there carriers among
them? When Nagumo received this he hastily sent a signal out asking,
'What type?'

It was a nerve-racking moment. The second-wave planes, originally
armed for an attack on American carriers, had now been ordered to
prepare instead for another strike on Midway. The torpedo bombers
were being reloaded with bombs as the four carriers feverishly prepared for another attack on the atoll.

Just after eight o'clock *Tone*'s plane, replying to *Akagi*'s query
about the type of ships, radioed, 'Enemy have five cruisers and five
destroyers.'

When Chief of Staff Kusaka read this message on the bridge of
Akagi and handed it to Nagumo they were both relieved. No carriers!
Cruisers and destroyers could be safely taken care of at leisure. Their
first task was to finish off the air strength at Midway which was still
considerable.

Then at 8.30 a.m., just as the last attacking American planes disappeared, *Tone*'s scout plane reported, 'Enemy force accompanied by
what appears to be an aircraft carrier in the rear.' This information
staggered everyone—but identification was not yet certain.

If *Tone*'s information was correct and the Americans did have a
carrier—why had carrier-type aircraft not yet joined in the attack on
Nagumo's fleet? And why had not the scores of Japanese submarines stationed between Hawaii and Midway warned of its
presence? Nagumo did not know they had arrived twenty-five hours
late on station after the American carriers had crossed their patrol
line.

Another message from *Tone*'s plane reported, 'Two additional
enemy ships apparently cruisers sighted 250 miles from Midway speed
twenty knots. Carrier believed to be *Yorktown* with group.'

Admiral Nagumo now knew he was up against a big American fleet
with at least one carrier. What was he to do? Should he attack these
ships before he launched another strike on Midway?

Tomonaga's planes were coming back from Midway and a quick
decision was imperative. Most of his fighters were nearly out of fuel
and some of the returning planes were also in distress. If they were

not allowed to land at once many of them would plunge into the sea.

This moment was ultimately to decide more than the battle. Upon his decision, made on that warm day in June in mid-Pacific, rested the future of the Japanese fleet. Yet what a crucial choice Nagumo had before him. Should the planes be moved to the hangar decks to make way for Tomonaga's landing aircraft? That would make it impossible to launch an attack until later.

Should he send his dive bombers immediately against the American ships? And should he also launch the torpedo bombers even though they were now armed with bombs? They would also have to attack without fighter cover.

Or should he order the bombers on deck to circle out of danger until enough fighters could land, refuel and take off again to provide escort? This would mean the planes back from Midway would have to be kept in the air until the bombers had cleared the deck. Damaged planes would have to take their chance. If they could not keep on flying they would have to crash-land into the sea, where destroyers would rescue their crews.

Why did he not launch the divers immediately even without fighter protection? In all-out carrier warfare the risk of sending out unprotected bombers must be accepted. The Americans were already taking desperate risks. Why not Nagumo? The plain fact was that he did not appreciate the urgency of the decision facing him. Who can blame him? He still had only an unconfirmed report of *one* American carrier. Why should he send his planes to the same fate as the unescorted American planes which his carriers had just shot down?

He now realized how right Yamamoto had been. To save Midway the Americans were throwing in everything they had. Yet it still did not appear to be much. Up to now their attacks had proved notably unsuccessful and had been easily driven off. Nagumo's mighty carriers were unscathed.

When he looked at them from the bridge of *Akagi*, steaming proudly in the calm Pacific awaiting his orders, who can blame him for feeling confident? The carriers, 250 yards long, as big as a city block, seemed unsinkable. The might of his great fleet and the feeling of superiority that Pearl Harbor had induced not only in him but in the whole Imperial Navy, had much to do with his ignoring one glaring danger signal—the lone American carrier which *Tone*'s float plane had reported.

After *Tone*'s radio message about 'one' carrier, no further news came from the search planes. And the shore-based planes on Midway were still a problem. There were many more of them than Intelligence had reported. Would they attack again?

Although Nagumo was nervously aware that his carriers, their decks crammed with planes, were perilously within striking range of the atoll, he decided Midway must wait. First he must destroy the American carriers.

Nagumo's junior, Rear-Admiral Tamon Yamaguchi, the man everyone in the Imperial Navy forecast would one day succeed Yamamoto, had also been closely following the reports from *Tone*'s scout plane aboard his flagship *Hiryu*. When he read the message about 'one carrier' it alarmed him. Nagumo's failure to take prompt action against it struck him as dangerous. He sent a message to him saying, 'Consider it advisable to launch attack force immediately.'

But Nagumo had made up his mind. He considered that to attack without fighter protection was too great a risk. When all Tomonaga's planes had landed safely, he would set course to destroy the Americans with a massive blow. To do this he must switch back from bombs to torpedoes. Nagumo's decision, taken shortly after 8.30 a.m., looked perfect on paper.

Aboard the carriers the weary maintenance crews, dressed only in tropical shorts, began lowering the torpedo bombers from the flight deck to the hangar deck to make room for Tomonaga's returning planes. They had not long begun their first switch from torpedoes to bombs. Now they were faced with Nagumo's order, 'Change back to torpedoes.' They began to lift the heavy bombs from the planes. As there was no time to lower them into the magazines they piled them up on the decks. These highly explosive bombs stacked carelessly round the carrier were to be another big factor in the coming disaster.

While the sweating Japanese carrier crews hurriedly tried to replace the second-wave bombs with torpedoes, Tomonaga's planes came into sight. One bomber landed on a single wheel and the pilot, Lieutenant Hiroharu Kadone, lost consciousness the moment his plane stopped. On the flight towards Midway he had been hit in the leg by a machine-gun bullet. He flew on with the formation and made the attack before returning to the carrier.

Tomonaga managed to land safely although his own plane was hit in the left fuel tank. He reported the death of Lieutenant Rokuro Kikuchi from *Hiryu*. When his plane caught fire after being struck by an A.A. shell over Midway, Kikuchi opened his canopy, waved a cheerful farewell to his comrades, and plunged down to his death. With Tomonaga's returning bombers were thirty-four out of the thirty-six fighters which had set off. Nagumo gave orders to refuel them at once so that they could join the other thirty-six held in reserve with the second wave.

It was now a clear, sunny day in the central Pacific with a few high clouds. As Nagumo gazed from his bridge there was not an American plane in sight. The survivors of the Midway defenders had flown off in their shrapnel-torn planes. The first round had clearly gone to him. Tomonaga's planes seemed to have gone a good way towards smashing Midway while the atoll defenders had sacrificed half their planes without damaging any Japanese warships. As Nimitz observed, 'Most of Midway's fighters, torpedo planes and dive bombers, the only types capable of making a high percentage of hits on ships, were gone. Without American carriers Midway was at the Japanese mercy.'

Nagumo now felt ready to deal with the reported American carrier. He sent a radio message to Yamamoto saying, 'Enemy composed one carrier five cruisers five destroyers sighted 240 miles from Midway. We are heading for it.'

At the same time the blinker from *Akagi* signalled all ships, 'After taking on returning planes proceed to contact and destroy enemy task force.' Four minutes later the last of the Midway dive bombers landed on the decks of *Akagi* and *Kaga*. Seven minutes after them the twelve remaining fighters put down on the carriers.

Akagi turned and signalled for maximum battle speed. Within a few minutes the carriers were steaming at thirty knots. As their bow waves curled higher and the big ships shuddered with the sudden surge of speed they were a daunting sight. There were twenty-one of them, including the four carriers whose planes were being refuelled and re-armed to destroy the Americans. Above them in the placid blue sky eighteen Zekes circled above in protective combat patrol. The small number of fighters in the air was to prove another decisive factor in the coming battle.

It was 9.20 a.m. It had taken almost two hours to arm and then re-arm the carrier planes. But now they were almost ready for take-off. *Akagi* and *Kaga* each had three fighters and twenty-seven torpedo planes on their decks. Three fighters and eighteen torpedo planes apiece were ready for launching in *Hiryu* and *Soryu*.

The first signal to take off to attack the American fleet was about to be given when the ships' lookouts once again yelled, 'American planes approaching!' Maintenance crews, already working frantically to get the planes in the air, redoubled their last-minute efforts. Every plane must take off at once. As the first group of fast manœuvrable Zekes swung into the air a few ragged thin cries of *banzai* followed them from the perspiring, grimy sailors.

Nagumo's carriers were at last in a major battle. None of their crews or pilots had any doubt the American Pacific Fleet was about to be destroyed. Nagumo and Captain Taijiro Aoki, *Akagi's* commander, did not share their optimism. Radio reports coming in every second told of the large number of American aircraft heading towards the carriers. They looked at each other, puzzled and alarmed. These planes obviously came from more than one carrier.

Nagumo immediately ordered *Soryu* to launch her fast reconnaissance plane to find out how many American carriers there were.

17

Death of Three Carriers

THE three American carriers were continuously informed of Nagumo's movements by the watchful, cloud-dodging flying boats. Admiral Fletcher read their reports and waited for the most advantageous time to pounce.

At midnight on 3 June as the carriers sailed through a clear Pacific night Midway's Catalinas reported they had sighted Nagumo's carriers. They also signalled that a strong Japanese fleet was approaching Midway in five columns. Aboard *Hornet*, pilots of Torpedo Squadron 8 filed into the ready room to hear the news from the Chief of Staff, Captain Miles Browning. They pencilled on pads the latest position of the Japanese fleet chalked on the blackboard. Outside their planes were being warmed up.

At sun-up halyard flags reported the patrol planes were still in contact. It was just getting light when the Midway scout planes reported the Japanese had two carriers with them 200 miles away. Then the teletype on *Hornet* stuttered out reports from Midway that the Japanese were bombing the atoll. Admiral Frank Jack Fletcher, aboard *Yorktown* and commanding the three-carrier force, immediately sent *Hornet* and *Enterprise* to sail towards them with orders to 'Attack enemy carriers when definitely located'. *Yorktown* waited to land the planes from her morning search.

Spruance steamed ahead with *Enterprise* and *Hornet* to bring the Japanese within striking range of his torpedo bombers. The two carriers separated, dividing the screening vessels between them. This was a lesson learned from the battle of the Coral Sea when *Lexington* and *Yorktown* had drawn apart under fierce attacks and split up their protective screen. The result had been a near disaster — the sinking of *Lexington* and serious damage to *Yorktown*.

At 6.40 a.m. *Yorktown* search planes landed safely and she turned to steam after *Enterprise* and *Hornet*. At seven o'clock, as Midway's first Marine planes were diving on Nagumo's carriers, Spruance decided the time and distance were right. He was only 150 miles from Nagumo. He ordered his dive bombers and torpedo planes to take off. His plan was to deliver his first blow at the most vulnerable time when Tomonaga's Midway attack planes were coming in to land on the Japanese carrier decks.

First *Hornet* turned into the wind to launch her attack group, Torpedo Squadron 8. She also sent thirty-five bombers and ten fighters in addition to the fifteen torpedo planes of Squadron 8. Quickly *Enterprise* swung round to follow. She launched thirty-three dive bombers, fourteen torpedo planes and ten fighters—100-plus planes altogether.

There was none of the excited cheering of the Japanese carrier crews as the planes disappeared, racing towards Nagumo. The American crews watched them silently. They were only too conscious of the magnitude of their task.

Admiral Fletcher knew from his Japanese code interceptions that he must expect four or five Japanese carriers. When the float planes reported only two he hesitated to commit *Yorktown*'s planes. Where were the other enemy carriers?

As the 100-plane attack flew towards the Japanese carriers in the bright sunny morning the pilots aboard *Yorktown* waited in their ready room. Then came a teletype from *Enterprise* reporting, 'Enemy naval units now within striking distance. Expected striking time 09.00.' Under each *Yorktown* pilot's chair was a drawer containing his helmet, goggles, gloves and a pistol. When they heard the *Enterprise* message they silently reached down and pulled them out.

It was a little after 8.30 a.m. when Fletcher decided he could not miss so tempting a target. He launched seventeen dive bombers, twelve torpedo planes and six fighters. This was only half *Yorktown*'s aircraft. He still kept the rest in reserve because Intelligence had led him to expect more carriers as Yamamoto's spearhead. As they had not yet been sighted, Fletcher sent off more search planes to look for them.

Fifty minutes after *Yorktown*'s planes took off to join the battle, the first wave from *Enterprise* and *Hornet* spotted two big columns of smoke just beyond the horizon. They had found Nagumo. The first all-out clash between American and Japanese carrier fleets, for which the Coral Sea had been only a curtain-raiser, was about to begin.

Torpedo Squadron 8 counted three carriers, six cruisers and ten destroyers. The carriers' decks were loaded with planes apparently being refuelled and re-armed. Then they definitely identified *Soryu*. They radioed all this information back to the American carriers. Then their squadron leader, Lieutenant-Commander John Charles Waldron, radioed his position and said he was going to attack. This was the last message ever received from the gallant Torpedo 8.

To Nagumo's carriers, Waldron's torpedo bombers first appeared as tiny dark specks a little above the horizon off *Akagi*'s starboard bow. When Waldron wiggled his wings as a signal to start the attack the high-circling Zekes swooped down. The rattle of the American rear-gunners' machine-gun fire was punctuated by the louder, slower thump-thump of the Zeke cannons.

Waldron was still eight miles from Nagumo's fleet. All the Japanese sailors could see was their distant wings flashing like silver petals in the sun. Occasionally one of the silver specks burst into flame and, trailing black smoke, plunged into the water. But the survivors of Waldron's squadron came determinedly on into the concentrated curtain of fire from the carriers and their protecting warships.

At 9.30 a.m. as they came skimming over the waves a Japanese lookout yelled, 'Enemy torpedo bombers starboard coming in low!' This was immediately followed by another cry, 'Enemy torpedo bombers approaching to port!'

As they flew in to attack to starboard they first came within range of the fast cruiser *Chikuma* at 3,500 yards. At once *Akagi* and the other three carriers began twisting violently and furiously firing their anti-aircraft guns.

Flying in two columns, Torpedo 8 [*Hornet*] closed in from both sides just above the water and flew like darts straight for Nagumo's flagship *Akagi*. They were without fighter protection. *Hornet*'s fighters, which were supposed to protect their carrier's torpedo squadron, joined up with *Enterprise* fighters by mistake. Climbing to 20,000 feet these fighters were above the Japanese carriers when Waldron made his ill-starred attack. As they did not receive any pre-arranged signal for help from Waldron, who was far too pressed to give it, the fighters continued to circle above the battle. It made the Zekes' task as easy as duck shooting. While the Japanese fighters were annihilating Torpedo 8, their own fighters circled over the Japanese carriers and returned when their fuel ran low without having fired a single shot.

But the battered remnants of the two lines of American torpedo planes managed to reach their release points. Amid the smoke and crash of gunfire, Nagumo's crews watched for the wake of their torpedoes. Then at the last moment a handful of planes zoomed overhead and made for *Hiryu* astern of *Akagi*. As Waldron's planes flew mast-high past *Akagi* her gunners redoubled their sweeping fire and more Zekes bore down on them, trying to shoot them into the water.

Of the eight American torpedo planes which came in from starboard only half were left. Only five remained of the original seven planes to port. But they charged on *Hiryu* as she redoubled her anti-aircraft fire.

The Zekes tore down to sea level after Waldron's planes. Torpedo 8 had no chance. The unprotected, slow and clumsy torpedo planes could not escape the Japanese guns and fighters. They were flying so close to the water that hitting it was like smashing into a stone wall. On *Akagi*'s flight deck there was wild cheering as one after another the Americans went down.

Suddenly it was all over. The last shrapnel-torn American plane crashed into the sea without damaging *Hiryu*. The Zeke combat patrol leader radioed, 'All fifteen enemy torpedo bombers shot down.'

It was true. Only one member of the squadron, Ensign George (Tex) Gay, escaped. While he was skimming the water 800 yards away from *Hiryu* his radio operator was killed and he was shot in the left arm. He managed to release the emergency lever of his torpedo by holding the stick between his knees and using his uninjured hand. Then he flipped and cleared the carrier's bow by ten feet. As he roared over the flight deck Japanese ran in all directions to avoid his plane which they thought was crashing.

As he zoomed up again four Zekes dived on him and shot him down into the sea a quarter of a mile from the carrier. He escaped further injury but his plane began to sink. He opened the hood and grabbed his black rubber seat cushion. As he did so he heard an explosion which he thought was his torpedo exploding on *Hiryu*.

He held the cushion over his head pretending to be a piece of floating wreckage to protect himself from Japanese machine-gunners. No one bothered with him. The Japanese were too busy elsewhere. He floated there until dark, having a hazardous grandstand view of the great sea battle that blazed all day.

Gay, still alive, was picked up by a PBY at 2.30 next afternoon. He was the only survivor of the gallant Torpedo 8. But Waldron and his men did not die in vain. If it had not been for their suicidal attack, Nagumo's planes, still refuelling on the carriers' decks, would have had time to take off. They could have reversed the tide of battle.

When Winston Churchill heard of their annihilation he broke down and wept. Yet Torpedo 8 would not have suffered so badly if their inexperienced fighter escort had not inadvertently abandoned them.

Fifteen minutes after *Hornet*'s Torpedo 8 attack, *Enterprise*'s torpedo planes arrived, followed by *Yorktown*'s. Like Torpedo 8, they were without fighter protection, which was still circling uselessly 20,000 feet above them.

Excitement was at its height on the Japanese carriers as the planes swooped down to launch their torpedoes. Waves of low-level Douglas TBD Devastator torpedo bombers lumbered in through the anti-aircraft fire. As they battled fiercely to break through the curtain of shellfire, the Zekes followed them recklessly to within a few feet of the water, trying to shoot them down before they could reach the wildly veering, evasive carriers.

Like Torpedo 8, the second wave registered no hits on the fast, expertly handled carriers. But the bravery of the American pilots was superb. Forty-one torpedo planes took off from the three carriers and only six returned safely. These low-flying Douglases made a sacrifice more effective than they knew. When in the heat of the battle they drew the deadly Zekes down to wave level the Japanese carriers were left wide open to attack. While fighting the Douglases off, the Japanese forgot to look up. Hidden in the high clouds, following the torpedo planes were the American dive bombers.

They nearly missed Nagumo. An American scout plane had correctly radioed the Japanese position but, after his report was received, Nagumo changed course. The Japanese were not where the Americans expected to find them.

Hornet's thirty-five dive bombers failed entirely to sight the Japanese. They continued on a false course until their fuel ran low. Then twenty-one returned to the carrier. The remaining fourteen headed for Midway, where three crashed. Their accompanying fighters with their shorter range force-landed in the sea when their fuel was exhausted.

Enterprise's dive bombers, like *Hornet*'s, also failed to find the Japanese in the position given to them. They searched the area but the ocean was calm, peaceful—and deserted. There was not a Japanese ship in sight. Lieutenant-Commander Clarence Wade

McClusky, their commander, had to decide whether their information was incorrect. Or had Nagumo changed course?

The narrow margin of luck by which great battles are decided now began to turn slightly towards the Americans. The Japanese admiral Nagumo had made a wrong decision by not getting all his planes off as soon as the presence of an American carrier was reported to him. Now an American lieutenant-commander high above the Pacific made a right decision. McClusky decided the Japanese carriers must have changed course and turned northwards. Captain George Murray, commander of *Enterprise*, called it 'the most important decision of the entire action'.

When McClusky signalled his bombers to turn north it was not only a lucky but a courageous decision. For his bombers had already used up half their fuel. If the Japanese carriers were not found soon their planes would run out of gasoline and drop one by one into the Pacific.

A little after ten o'clock—twenty-five minutes after he gave the change-course order—McClusky saw a faint white streak below him. It was the wake of a long Japanese destroyer. Then three long stick-like vessels slid from under the broken cloud. They were zigzagging, surrounded by a score of escort vessels which looked like darting water beetles. Tiny flames and little dots all round them showed they were under attack.

They were the Japanese carriers trying to beat off the low-level torpedo bombers. McClusky peered out of his cockpit and identified *Soryu* in the lead with *Kaga* and *Akagi* trailing a little behind on each side. He did not see *Hiryu* in the rear because she was still obscured by cloud.

Aboard the Japanese carriers the smoke was beginning to clear as the last torpedo plane was staggering away, chased by Zekes. The gun crews sat down, suddenly worn out after the fierce action. Nagumo had every reason to be pleased with the brisk morning's work. Wave after wave of American planes of all types had been beaten off without doing any damage to his carriers. Now it was his turn. He was ready to deal with the American carriers. All his aircraft were refuelled and equipped with armour-piercing bombs and torpedoes. He gave orders to launch when ready. Engines began to roar in the warm-up as the four big Japanese carriers turned into the wind.

The first Zeke was just roaring off *Akagi*'s deck when a lookout shrieked a warning. While the guardian Zekes were still near the surface of the water chasing off the last of the torpedo bombers, three of McClusky's planes screamed down on *Akagi* out of the high clouds. Other planes plunged on her sister ship *Kaga*.

When the American dive bombers appeared without warning it was the beginning of the end for Nagumo's carriers. Having no radar to warn him of their approach and with his fighter patrol at wave height shooting at the last of the American torpedo bombers, he was taken completely by surprise.

Only a couple of machine-gunners recovered quickly enough to fire a few quick bursts at the Americans as Japanese planes scurried like frightened chickens to get clear of the carriers. It was no good. As the American Dauntlesses pulled out of their whistling dives, black bombs detached themselves, almost leisurely, from their wings.

There was a blinding flash and two loud explosions aboard *Akagi*. The guns suddenly stuttered into silence, their crews shocked or wounded. When the thick black smoke cleared the American planes were nowhere in sight.

Peering through the eye-smarting smoke, Nagumo and his officers saw a fearful sight. *Akagi* had received two direct hits. One had blown a huge hole in her flight deck. The second had wrenched and twisted the amidship elevator as though by a giant's hand.

The air was filled with burning splinters, the odour of petrol and hot metal, and the sweetish roast-pork smell of burning human flesh. Charred smoking corpses and mutilated sailors lay strewn over her deck. Badly burnt men lay screaming, others feebly moaning before they became silent and dead. Then bombs, left lying on deck after the hasty reloading, began to explode. They shook the bridge where Nagumo stood motionless with his chief of staff, Admiral Kusaka, and Captain Aoki, *Akagi*'s commander.

Thick smoke swirled up to the bridge, making it difficult for them to see and the air was hot with yellow flames. As the fire licked along the flight deck more torpedoes and bombs began to explode and sailors fled from their fire-fighting apparatus half-blinded. Spreading flames began to sear the bridge, their heat and smoke making it uninhabitable. Through the blackness Nagumo could see something even worse—two glowing red smudges where *Kaga* and *Soryu* were. He knew then that they too had been hit.

Kaga, *Akagi*'s sister ship, was hit by McClusky's planes almost simultaneously with *Akagi*. She had thirty planes on her flight deck all armed and fuelled. They too were awaiting the take-off signal when the American dive bombers shot out of the clouds.

McClusky's planes were too busy diving in their quick devastating attack and get-away to know what was going on aboard the other carriers. But at the same time as they struck *Kaga* and *Akagi*, unknown to them, the SPDs from the carrier *Yorktown* hit *Soryu*.

Yorktown's planes had been launched more than an hour later than McClusky's. *Hornet*'s planes had missed Nagumo's carriers completely and McClusky had only found them after a lucky decision to change course. But when the *Yorktown* dive bombers took off to find the Japanese the weather was clearing rapidly. Clear blue skies with wisps of very high cloud helped them to find Nagumo easily. Their attack followed immediately after McClusky's dive bombers. When they came out of the clouds, McClusky's planes were diving on *Akagi* and *Kaga*, so *Yorktown*'s planes concentrated on the third undamaged carrier *Soryu*.

When she saw what had happened to her flagship, the light cruiser *Nagara* came alongside to help with the fire-fighting. Kusaka urged Nagumo to board her. But the admiral, his face blackened with smoke, his eyes bloodshot, refused to leave his flagship. Captain Aoki pleaded with him saying, 'Admiral, please go. I will take care of the ship.'

As he spoke there were more explosions and the companionway up to the bridge crashed in flames. Now the only means of escape was by rope from the bridge window.

Nagumo, realizing the fires were out of control and he could no longer direct the battle from the blazing carrier, climbed through the window. Helped by his flag lieutenant, Lieutenant-Commander Nishibayashi, he swung down an already smouldering rope to *Nagara*'s boat alongside.

The time was 10.46 a.m. It was only twenty-two minutes since McClusky's first bomber had come plummeting like a sparrowhawk out of the clouds. As Nagumo left his ship the blast of explosions came every few seconds sending the fire-fighting sailors sprawling, stunned, wounded or dead. The metal companionways between decks became red hot and half-choked sailors began to jump overboard from the blazing decks.

In spite of urgent calls from Captain Aoki on the bridge, *Akagi* was not answering her rudder and there was no response from the engine room. Then the ship stopped with her bows still pointing into the wind as though she was getting ready to launch the planes which were burning and exploding on her deck. The dynamos died and the lights went out. Without electricity the fire pumps could no longer operate. Fire-fighting parties, wearing gas masks, rolled hoses down to the burning lower decks. As they staggered over the torn and charred corpses of their comrades, explosions every few seconds wounded or killed more of them. Others took their place, struggling to stop the fire, only to be killed by the next explosion.

Doctors and medical orderlies worked in suffocating heat and blinding smoke. The clothing of wounded men began to smoulder as they lay on the deck. Some of them began to scream as, lying with broken bones on the burning decks, they started to fry alive. The lucky ones were strapped to bamboo stretchers and lowered over the side. Although fire had cut off the signal tubes to the bridge the engine rooms below were still undamaged. Hot smoke filtering through the intakes made stokers fall back, gasping and clutching at their throats. Commander Tampo, *Akagi*'s chief engineer, clambered up a red-hot ladder and staggered through flames and smoke to the bridge to tell Captain Aoki his men were dying. Aoki gave the order for all engine-room crew to come on deck. An orderly slid down a burning rope and ran along the blazing, smoke-blackened decks to tell them. He never returned. No one escaped from the engine room.

The confusion that now reigned among the Japanese carriers was demonstrated just after midday when a signal came from Yamaguchi in *Hiryu* to *Akagi* saying, 'If any of your planes can take off have them transferred to *Hiryu*.'

Take off? All *Akagi*'s planes were burning or had blown up and she was at that moment transferring the last of her air crews to the destroyers. At 4.15 p.m. Commander Tampo reported to the captain that there was no possibility of the ship steaming under her own power. As the last of the wounded were carried into the boats, the giant carrier was blazing from stem to stern. Captain Aoki finally decided to abandon ship. When the order came at last, sailors leapt into the sea, littered with floating corpses and wreckage, and swam away from the blazing carrier. Destroyers *Arashi* and *Nowake* circled round trying to pick them up from the oil-streaked sea.

It was 7.20 p.m. when Captain Aoki, the last man to leave, boarded one of the destroyers. He immediately radioed Yamamoto for permission to sink the crippled flagship to stop her falling into American hands. But Yamamoto could not bring himself to order the proud flagship *Akagi* to be torpedoed by its crew. He signalled Aoki, 'Delay disposition.'

When he received Yamamoto's message, Captain Aoki ordered a boat crew to take him back to his ship. Alone, he climbed up a rope ladder to the bows, the only area still free from fire. There he lashed himself to an anchor to await the end.

When *Akagi*'s navigator, Commander Miura, heard what he had done he boarded the carrier to try and persuade Aoki not to go down with his ship. He argued with him, surrounded by flames and smoke, and at last managed to persuade him not to commit hara-kiri and come back with him aboard a destroyer.

Akagi's sister ship, *Kaga*, was even more badly hit when nine American dive bombers swooped on her. The first three made near-misses but then four scored direct hits. One after another the bombs smashed into her flight deck.

One landed near the bridge, killing everyone on it, including her commander, Captain Jisaku Okada. His second-in-command, Commander Takahisa Amagi, immediately took over the carrier. The helmsman, blinded by a bomb flash, fell shrieking, holding his eyes, and let her run wild. Thick black smoke curled from her fires into the placid blue Pacific sky as she began to wander erratically over the water like a stunned duck.

Shattered glass on the bridge and smoke from bomb damage reduced visibility to zero, but her position was far from hopeless. Commander Amagi immediately ordered the crew to begin clearing the decks and fighting the fires. With her steersman blinded and her captain killed, she was still drifting like a dead leaf in a drain but her engines and rudder were intact.

Amagi appeared to be getting everything under control when a small truck filled with gasoline for fuelling planes blew up on the flight deck. Its flames rapidly spread and began to lick the whole length of the carrier. Amagi was forced off the bridge onto the boat deck. The damage-control crew which he had organized still fought desperately to halt the spreading flames. But realizing the end was near he ordered the Emperor's portrait to be lowered reverently down to the destroyer *Hagikaze*.

Three and a half hours after the dive bombers had swooped, Commander Amagi, still in command of the blazing carrier, saw a submarine periscope a few thousand yards away from his ship. This was the American submarine *Nautilus*, commanded by Lieutenant-Commander William H. Brockman, which had been lurking round the fringes of the battle waiting for a chance to strike.

Amagi watched helplessly as three white torpedo wakes streaked towards his carrier. Her commander could do nothing but await her fate. Disabled as she was, she could not swerve to dodge them. *Kaga*'s two protecting destroyers, *Hagikaze* and *Maikaze,* raced round, dropping depth charges on the crash-diving *Nautilus*.

Two of her torpedoes missed. The third struck, glanced off the side, and miraculously broke up without exploding. Instead of sinking the ship it saved the lives of some of her crew. Several sailors, blown overboard by the gas-truck explosion, grabbed the floating section of the torpedo and clung to it. They were picked up by a Japanese destroyer.

Fires still raging in *Kaga* had now turned her into a blazing, unmanageable hulk. When at 4.40 p.m. Commander Amagi gave the order to abandon ship many of her crew slid down ropes to the two destroyers.

Two hours later Amagi, watching her anxiously from a destroyer, thought the flames seemed to be dying down. He immediately led a fire-fighting party back in the hope of saving her. But when they climbed aboard they were driven back by the heat. No one could stand on her red-hot decks, so Amagi ordered his party to return to the destroyer.

It was fortunate he did so because shortly afterwards the burning hull was wrenched by two terrific explosions. The *Nautilus*, which was still lurking around untouched by Japanese depth charges, had fired two more torpedoes which had hit *Kaga*'s fuel tanks. As the destroyers raced around again trying to find the American submarine, *Kaga* suddenly rolled over and sank in a hiss of steam and smoke.

Ensign Gay, floating in the warm Pacific under his cushion, watched the end of the burning *Kaga*. Over a hundred of her crew were still huddled on her deck when the two explosions tore her apart. Others were trapped below decks. When she went down, a third of her crew of 800 went down with her.

The third Japanese carrier, *Soryu*, suffered a similar fate. Her planes were standing on the decks ready for take-off when her commander, Captain Yanagimoto, heard four explosions aboard *Kaga*. Then he and his crew saw fires break out aboard her as thick clouds of billowing black smoke spiralled slowly upwards into the blue sky.

Two minutes later his own lookouts screamed a warning as thirteen *Yorktown* planes appeared out of the clouds and dived down on *Soryu*. The *Yorktown* divers did even greater destruction than McClusky's bombers. One bomb hit the forward part of *Soryu*'s flight deck. Then two more bombs crashed amidships, wrecking the entire deck. They set fire to planes waiting to take off and their petrol tanks exploded like heavy artillery. Explosions from the unloaded bombs carelessly stacked on deck, and torpedoes slung under the re-armed planes, began to make the ship shudder from end to end. Her crew felt she must shake herself to pieces and sink at once. Within five minutes she was enveloped in smoke and flames.

Ten minutes after the bombs dropped her main engine stopped and her rudder did not answer. Then a tremendous explosion below decks blasted many of the crew into the water. Other sailors jumped over-board as flames began to scorch their clothes. The destroyers *Hamakaze* and *Isokaze*, circling round the blazing carrier, picked up as many as they could. But most of the sailors just floated away, dead.

One oil-blackened swimmer who was rescued turned out not to be a Japanese. He was an American torpedo pilot who was dragged aboard a Japanese destroyer, shocked and half-drowned. He was at once taken aboard *Nagara*, Nagumo's temporary flagship, and inter-rogated.

Nagumo sent this radio signal to Yamamoto:

Statement obtained from Ensign (Air) from *Yorktown*. Carriers involved are *Yorktown*, *Enterprise* and *Hornet*. Six cruisers and ten destroyers. *Yorktown* accompanied by two cruisers, three de-stroyers acting independently of others.

Sortie from Pearl Harbor morning of 31 May. Arrived in vicinity of Midway 1 June. Patrolling north-westerly course ever since. No capital ships in Pearl up to 31 May. Prisoner long at base has no knowledge of capital ship movements.

The fact that this ensign came from *Yorktown* was almost incred-ible. Surely she had been sunk in the Coral Sea battle? This was the first time Nagumo knew there were three American carriers in the battle—*Enterprise*, *Hornet* and *Yorktown*. The information came so late it was almost useless, because by this time three of his own carriers were doomed.

Twenty minutes after the *Yorktown* attack, *Soryu* was ablaze from stem to stern with constant explosions and blinding, choking smoke. Captain Yanagimoto ordered, 'Abandon ship' but remained on the bridge of his blazing carrier. He was determined to go down with her.

No commander in the Japanese navy was more popular with his men and they were determined not to let him commit hara-kiri. Before they slid down the ropes to the waiting destroyers, they deputed the biggest among them, a navy wrestling champion, Chief Petty Officer Abe, to go and reason with him. They gave Abe secret instructions to drag their captain to safety by force if necessary. When Abe climbed up to *Soryu*'s bridge, Captain Yanagimoto was standing motionless, sword in hand, silhouetted against the roaring red flames.

The sight unnerved Abe but he saluted and said, 'Captain, I have come to take you to safety. The men are waiting for you. Please accompany me to the destroyer, sir.' His only reply was the roaring of the fire. Yanagimoto did not look at him. He did not appear to have even heard him.

He remained motionless as a statue, gazing expressionlessly over the bows of his burning ship. Abe started towards him to carry him bodily to the waiting boat. Only then did his captain turn towards him. Navy discipline proved too strong. The stern expression on Yanagimoto's face halted Abe. He hesitated, saluted and, with tears in his eyes, turned slowly away. As he slid down the rope to the waiting boat alongside he heard a loud voice above the roaring flame. It was his captain singing '*Kimigayo*', the Japanese national anthem.

At 7.13 p.m. *Soryu* settled in the water and sank. As well as her captain, 718 men went down with her.

18

The End for 'Yorktown' and 'Flying Dragon'

THE three Japanese carriers were already burning and sinking before Nagumo knew how many American carriers were opposing him. Then he only found out by a lucky chance when one of his rescue destroyers picked up an American pilot who talked. But where were they? He had still not heard from *Soryu*'s search plane. For the Japanese jinx was still working. *Soryu*'s plane quickly found the three carriers and tried to send back a radio report, but could not because his radio had failed.

The rest of Nagumo's ships closed in a circle round the sole surviving carrier, *Hiryu*—Flying Dragon—and prepared to continue the battle. *Hiryu* was the flagship of Rear-Admiral Tamon Yamaguchi, a much more resolute and clear-thinking commander than his senior admiral, Nagumo. He was one of the ablest officers in the Japanese navy, and had graduated second in his class at the Naval Academy. He was also a graduate of Princeton and former chief of Japanese naval Intelligence in the United States.

When Nagumo transferred from his blazing flagship *Akagi* to the light cruiser *Nagara*, Yamaguchi took over air operations. He wasted no time before launching an immediate attack on the American carriers. At 10.40 a.m. he ordered Lieutenant Michio Kobayashi, a Pearl Harbor veteran, to take off with eighteen Val dive bombers and six escorting Zekes.

The *Yorktown* planes which had sunk *Hiryu*'s sister carrier, *Soryu*, were on their way back. About noon when she was preparing to recover her bombers and refuel her fighters her radar picked up Kobayashi's planes fifty miles away. Refuelling was hastily abandoned and planes on the flight deck were quickly launched with orders to clear off out of trouble. The returning bombers were waved away. A cruiser steamed up to either bow to add fire power to her defences.

Combat air patrols from *Enterprise* and *Hornet* flew towards *Yorktown* to help in her defence, making a total of twenty-eight fighters.

As Kobayashi flew towards the American carrier at 18,000 feet, lookouts on *Yorktown* saw the Japanese planes floating like tiny matchsticks in the clear sky. As they came down to 10,000 feet to start their attack Kobayashi saw American torpedo bombers returning to the carrier. He waved his Zekes forward. They dived on the bombers, chased by the American combat air patrols. In the fierce dogfight, two Zekes were lost.

As the Japanese bombers came nearer, American fighters from the three carriers tore in to try and break up their formation while the anti-aircraft guns aboard the carriers and the cruiser fired ceaselessly.

It was almost complete annihilation for the eighteen dive bombers. Ten of Kobayashi's planes were shot down into the sea. But there were just not enough American fighters to stop a handful of the divers getting through. As the survivors fought their way through the curtain of shells, two more were shot down by carrier gunfire. The remaining six dived on *Yorktown*. One dropped his bomb harmlessly in the water and crashed after it. Thirteen bombers were now shot down—but five made it. That was enough. Three landed bombs on *Yorktown*. One went down the smoke stack into the engine room, disabling two boilers and extinguishing the fires in all the others except one.

That bomb stopped the ship. Another exploded on the flight deck, blowing a big hole in the middle of it. A third blew up near the magazines which were hastily flooded to prevent fires.

While Kobayashi's pilots were bombing *Yorktown*, *Soryu*'s reconnaissance plane flew back to find its carrier blazing from end to end, so the pilot landed on *Hiryu*'s deck and reported at once to Admiral Yamaguchi. He told him what Nagumo learned from the shot-down American airman—that the Americans had three carriers, *Enterprise*, *Hornet* and *Yorktown*.

Admiral Yamaguchi rapidly reassessed the situation in view of this startling new information. *Hiryu* was alone facing three American carriers, only one of which may have been damaged by his first-wave attack. He wasted no time in taking the action he had urged on Nagumo by radio earlier in the battle.

He decided to launch every available plane at once. He ordered all the planes he had left—ten torpedo bombers and six fighters—to take off and attack the American carriers. Chosen to lead the attack once again was Lieutenant Joichi Tomonaga, who had led the strike on Midway. He did not hesitate when he received the order although his plane's left-wing fuel tank, damaged by an A.A. shell over Midway, had not yet been repaired. He ordered the flight crews to refuel his remaining tank. They gazed at him silently as they went to obey his order. It meant that, whatever happened, he would not be able to return. He was deliberately flying on a one-way mission.

At 12.45 p.m. sixteen planes, led by a man who knew he would not return, rose from *Hiryu*'s flight deck and headed for the American carriers. On their flight towards the U.S. Fleet they passed a little group of five planes. It was all that was left of Kobayashi's sixteen dive bombers. They did not include Kobayashi's plane, as he was among the thirteen lost.

When the five pilots landed on *Hiryu* they claimed six bombs had been dropped on an American carrier. They reported she had stopped and was sending up great columns of smoke. Weeding out their over-optimistic reports, Yamaguchi sensibly concluded that the American carrier must have been hit by at least two bombs and severely damaged.

What he did not know was that damage-control parties in *Yorktown* worked so effectively that in less than two hours—by two o'clock in the afternoon—the carrier was again able to make eighteen knots under her own power. The engine room and deck were repaired with astonishing speed. The crew ran emergency steam lines round the wreckage and pulled the carrier's speed up to fifteen knots, then eighteen. She even ran up a brand-new ensign to replace the one torn and stained by fire and smoke.

She was steaming along at eighteen knots refuelling the rest of her fighters when about 2.30 p.m. her radar began tracking Tomonaga's torpedo group only forty miles away. Once more refuelling was suspended and the combat air patrol scrambled into the air.

So speedily had *Yorktown*'s repairs been effected that when Tomonaga sighted an American carrier surrounded by escort ships he thought she was another undamaged carrier. He could not believe it was *Yorktown*.

His orders were to attack undamaged carriers, so he prepared to dive on her. Tomonaga and his second-in-command, Lieutenant-Commander Toshio Hashimoto, split into two lines to attack *Yorktown*. She was still trying to launch her fighters when they came down to 150 feet and flew to within 600 yards to deliver their torpedoes.

American fighters shot down some of the Japanese before they came within range of the ship's guns, while two guard cruisers from Spruance's force threw up a formidable barrage. But a few determined pilots succeeded in penetrating it. One of them was Tomonaga.

Signalling his pilots to follow him, he dived his yellow-tailed plane straight through the anti-aircraft fire to launch his torpedoes. Then, knowing he could never get back, he crashed his plane on to *Yorktown*, where it blew up in a sheet of flame. A long dark smudge of brown smoke on *Yorktown*'s deck marked his pyre.

Tomonaga's action, similar to that of Flight Warrant Officer Kanno in the battle of the Coral Sea, did much to raise the morale of the Japanese pilots which had been badly shattered by the three burning and sinking carriers they had left behind.

Yorktown kept twisting from side to side but could not escape the low-flying, fanatically brave torpedo pilots. Inspired to great heights of courage by Tomonaga's example, they flew unflinchingly through the barrage. Swooping from an altitude of 9,000 feet to wave height the rest of his planes headed straight for her.

Two of their torpedoes struck. The second one seemed to strike amidships in exactly the same hole as that made by the first. Hashimoto launched his torpedo and flew under the bows of *Yorktown* to escape the furious anti-aircraft fire. But as he flew away thick yellow smoke and flames, mingled with foaming water, vomited up from the carrier. The great 20,000-ton hull jumped like a startled horse. An American sailor said, 'She seemed to leap out of the water. Then she sank back, all life gone.' It was 2.45 p.m.

At that same moment, Nagumo and Yamaguchi received a laconic radio message from Hashimoto, now in command of the bombers, saying, 'Two torpedo hits on this carrier.' A few minutes later another signal said, 'Believed to be of the *Yorktown* class.'

This second raid by *Hiryu* planes was the last Japanese effort against American ships in the battle of Midway. Only five torpedo bombers and three fighters—half the number launched—got back to *Hiryu*. They landed at 6.30 p.m. to give Admiral Yamaguchi details of their attack. The surviving pilots claimed a carrier severely damaged. This, with the previous attack on *Yorktown*, made him think that two American carriers were mortally hurt. He had no inkling it was *Yorktown* his pilots had struck again. But their two torpedo hits, added to the damage inflicted by Kobayashi's earlier dive-bomb attacks, doomed her.

While the survivors of Tomonaga's torpedo bombers flew away from *Yorktown*, one of her scout planes which had been searching the Pacific for three hours found Yamaguchi's *Hiryu*. He reported it was a hundred miles away. Evening was coming on after a gigantic battle fought since dawn. It was all or nothing now.

Admiral Fletcher ordered an immediate strike. At 4 p.m., *Enterprise* began launching twenty-four Dauntless dive bombers, of which ten were refugees unable to land on *Yorktown*. The *Hornet* also launched sixteen. They set off without fighter escort because Fletcher, worried by the repeated attacks on his carriers, kept his fighters back to protect them against any more bombers.

When the Dauntlesses had been flying for an hour they saw three curling towers of smoke silhouetted against the reddening evening sky. They marked the hulks of *Kaga* and *Soryu*, and the still-burning *Akagi*. The dive bombers ignored the smoking wrecks with a few destroyers standing by them. They swung northwards to catch the rest of the fleet fleeing in a tight circle round their last carrier, *Hiryu*.

Hiryu had now made three air attacks, including one on Midway, and had hardly any planes left. At 4.30 p.m., as the last plane of Tomonaga's group that had attacked *Yorktown* was returning, her aircraft had been reduced to six fighters, five dive bombers and four torpedo bombers.

The pilots, who had been fighting since dawn, tottered out of their cockpits, expressionless as scarecrows. Even worse was the condition of *Hiryu*'s crew. They were asleep on their feet. In addition to her own constant attacks, since sunrise seventy-nine planes had attacked *Hiryu*. The carrier had successfully dodged twenty-six torpedoes and seventy bombs aimed at her.

But Yamaguchi, aggressive and desperate, fully realizing the plight Yamamoto's fleet was now in, was still determined to make an all-out effort to destroy the American carriers. He decided to make a last attempt at dusk. The uncertain light would give his few remaining planes a better chance to make a surprise attack on the Americans. This had been tried with great loss of pilots in the Coral Sea but he decided that he had no alternative but to risk it again.

At five o'clock, half an hour after Tomonaga's last plane landed, sweet riceballs were served to the hungry, exhausted, battle-battered *Hiryu* crew. A handful of them had just finished refuelling the pitifully few planes for Yamaguchi's twilight attack.

It was three minutes after the mess call. The duty men were grate-
fully shovelling the rice down with chopsticks as the carrier was turning into the wind to begin launching, when suddenly *Enterprise*
bombers dived out of the sun. As *Hiryu* had no radar, once again
there had been no long-range warning of their approach. Her commander, Captain Tomeo Kaku, swung the ship to starboard as the
bombers came down. The Americans lost three planes to anti-aircraft
fire and Zekes. But although *Hiryu* twisted like a giant eel, more
American planes dived through the barrage and four bombs exploded
simultaneously on her deck.

The forward elevator was blasted against the bridge, blotting out the
view and preventing navigation. Flames leapt rapidly amongst the
loaded planes ready to take off. One after another they began to
explode, starting enormous fires. Men staggered, blinded, round the
decks, falling over bodies, scorched by flames, suffocating from heat
and smoke. Columns of black smoke arose as the carrier lost speed
and stopped.

Within minutes of the first of the twenty-four dive bombers from
Enterprise finding Yamaguchi's flagship she became a helpless hulk
torn with flaming explosions. Her damage was so great that the last
half-dozen pilots in the *Enterprise* bombing line-up saw that she was
already doomed and turned away to bomb one of her escorting
battleships, *Haruna*.

When the survivors of Tomonaga's squadron came back from
attacking *Yorktown* to land on *Hiryu*, she was burning from end to
end. The returning Japanese planes circled her helplessly like fledge-
lings watching a burning nest. They flew round in circles, still guarding her. The fighters savagely attacked the Americans and fought
some of them off. Then one by one, as their fuel ran out, they plunged
like wounded birds into the sea.

When the second half of the American strike—the sixteen Dauntlesses from *Hornet*—arrived thirty minutes later they did not bother
with the flaming *Hiryu* but dropped their bombs on the battleship
Haruna and the cruiser *Chikuma*. All *Hornet*'s planes returned.

Hiryu as well as four direct hits had also taken two near-misses.
Although great fires were still burning she managed to resume com-
munication with the engine room and began to steam at high speed
to avoid any more American planes. At 6 p.m., as the flames were
still spreading, she stopped to allow the cruiser *Chikuma* to come
alongside and help with the fire fighting. For several hours it looked

as though *Hiryu*'s fires might be brought under control. Then came another explosion and the flames fanned out even more furiously. It became evident that the ship could not be saved. The Emperor's portrait was transferred to a destroyer.

The American admirals Fletcher and Spruance, however, were not having it all their own way. Kobayashi and Tomonaga, diving to their deaths, had finished *Yorktown*. As his opposing admiral, Nagumo, had been forced to do a few hours earlier, Fletcher had to leave his damaged flagship. He transferred to the heavy cruiser *Astoria*. There he received a report from Spruance about the attack on *Hiryu* which ended, 'Have you any instructions for further operations?'

'Negative,' replied Fletcher. 'Will conform to your movements.' This left the command of the carriers to Spruance. It was a wise decision, for carrier operations can be properly controlled only from a carrier where the admiral can personally question his returning flyers. Spruance, his flagship *Enterprise* undamaged, was in a much better position to continue the fight.

Yorktown, now a darkened hulk gushing steam, drifted in erratic ever-slowing circles to port. As there was no power left for shifting fuel or counter-flooding, she began to turn slowly on to her side with a handful of planes clinging like insects to her slanting decks. As the list increased to twenty-six degrees and her port scuppers became awash, stretcher bearers threaded through her steepening passage-ways collecting wounded. At 2.55 p.m. Captain Elliott Buckmaster gave an order. Up went the blue-and-white flag, 'Abandon ship'.

Men lingered by the rails talking, reluctant to leave their great carrier. Sailors paddled life rafts around picking up shipmates, shouting, 'Taxi'. Almost all her 2,000 crew were saved.

Last to go was her commander, Captain Buckmaster, with his little, brown-skinned Filipino mess-boy. He lowered the boy on a line. By the time he reached the water the boy was hysterical. The captain slid down after him, dragged him to a raft and pushed him aboard.

As evening approached the escorting American cruisers withdrew, leaving their destroyer *Hughes* to guard *Yorktown* or sink her to avoid capture. She was still listing at about twenty-four degrees and looked as though she might capsize at any moment.

The late afternoon was beautiful with a calm sea and a flamboyant sunset. An American pilot patrolling above *Hornet* and *Enterprise* looked back at the stricken *Yorktown*, alone except for the destroyer

Hughes. His eyes filled with tears as he gazed down on her 'floating helplessly like a dying queen'.

Yorktown was dying and so was her adversary *Hiryu.* Just before midnight *Hiryu*, now shipping a lot of water, stopped dead with a list of fifteen degrees. Her steering system had gone and most of her fire pumps were out of action. Several desperate attempts by rescue parties to fight their way to the engine rooms through smoke and flames were driven back. It was obvious *Hiryu* was lost. As she lay like *Yorktown*, helpless and dead on the water, a squadron of American B.17s attacked her. Great fountains of spray foamed up all round her but every bomb missed.

A brilliant Pacific moon provided a blackcloth to the leaping flames and lazily climbing black smoke when at 2.30 a.m. Admiral Yamaguchi ordered Captain Tomeo Kaku to summon all hands. Etched against the scarlet flames, he addressed the 900 crew through a loudspeaker from the bridge saying, 'As officer commanding this carrier division I am solely responsible for the loss of *Hiryu* and *Soryu*. I shall remain on board to the end. But I command all of you to leave the ship and continue your loyal service to His Majesty the Emperor.'

Then Yamaguchi took off his black admiral's cap and gave it to his Flag Lieutenant, Commander Ito, as a memento. In return Ito gave him a piece of cloth to lash himself to the bridge and make sure he would go down with the ship. Then amid thunderous *banzai*s *Hiryu*'s flag and the admiral's were ceremoniously lowered. When they saw these flags being hauled down, Yamaguchi's officers begged permission to die with him but he ordered them aboard the destroyer *Kazagumo* standing alongside. Captain Kaku refused to board the destroyer, insisting on staying aboard the blazing carrier with his admiral. Before the officers left, he and the admiral drank a silent farewell toast with them in water from a cup.

As soon as the destroyer reported this to Admiral Hiroaki Abe, the cruiser division commander, he climbed aboard *Hiryu* and went at once to the bridge. He tried to persuade Admiral Yamaguchi and Captain Kaku to leave the ship. They shook their heads in refusal as they stood side by side on the bridge waving goodbye to the last of *Hiryu*'s crew climbing down rope ladders to the boats.

Then Admiral Yamaguchi turned and gave his final order to Abe, 'When everyone is off the ship, torpedo her. She must not fall into the hands of the Americans.' Abe saluted silently, turned, and swung himself overboard. When every man had left the ship he ordered his destroyers clear of *Hiryu*.

Admiral Yamaguchi's decision to go down with her was as great a tragedy for the Imperial Navy as the loss of *Hiryu*. After Yamamoto, he was his country's greatest sailor and there was no doubt he would have succeeded him as commander-in-chief.

But when he strapped himself to the bridge to await the end the battle was over. Nagumo's carrier planes had not even knocked out Midway. America had complete control of the air over the Pacific.

Not until just before dawn did *Akagi* and *Hiryu* sink within minutes of each other. At midnight *Akagi*'s dead engines, staffed by dead men, suddenly came to life and turned her in a circle for nearly two hours until they stopped for ever. Still she did not sink. At midnight Yamamoto received a message that an American task force was approaching ninety miles to the east of *Akagi*. A quick decision became necessary to destroy the blazing hulk that was once Nagumo's mighty flagship.

At 3.50 a.m. Admiral Yamamoto finally gave the fateful order to scuttle the great carrier. He signalled to her standby destroyers, 'Dispose'. Commander Hagotaro Koga, captain of the destroyer *Nowake*, wept uncontrollably as he fired his torpedoes into the carrier. It was a particularly melancholy task for him as it was his first target of the war.

Seven minutes later the carrier slid under the sea. A great fountain of water sprayed on to the ring of destroyers as a terrific underwater explosion occurred. It was 4.55 a.m.—a few minutes before sunrise. With her died 263 members of her crew.

Burning *Hiryu*, guarded by the destroyers *Kazagumo* and *Ugumo*, was also finished. The first streaks of dawn were in the sky when torpedoes from her destroyers crashed into her. The big carrier started to go down at once. She was sinking sixty miles north of *Akagi*'s grave as the destroyers steamed away.

Yet an hour and twenty minutes later a plane from the light carrier *Hosho* discovered *Hiryu* still afloat with men clinging to her sloping deck. The plane took pictures of the smouldering derelict and radioed the news. Immediately every effort was ordered to rescue any survivors. A destroyer went to search for her and seaplanes were launched. But *Hiryu* was never seen by the Japanese again.

In fact she remained afloat until 8.20 a.m. The men seen on the deck were survivors of the engine-room crew trapped below who had escaped when the destroyers' torpedoes blew open a gaping hole. When the carrier sank some were picked up by an American ship. *Hiryu's* last battle cost the lives of 416 of her crew in addition to the admiral and captain who chose to die with her.

While the great Japanese carriers were sinking or being scuttled during the night, some strange things were happening to *Yorktown*, still floating rudderless, engine-less, and dead on the calm sea.

In the middle of the night the destroyer *Hughes* standing by heard a machine-gun fired from her port side. A party went aboard and rescued two wounded men who had fired the machine-gun for help. They also handed over three secret coding devices they had discovered which had been overlooked in the hasty 'abandon ship'.

At sunrise a fighter pilot paddled up to the destroyer *Hughes* on his raft and was picked up. When the sun came up *Yorktown* was still afloat, so the destroyer *Hamman* went alongside her to put aboard a salvage party of 160 *Yorktown* officers and men. In the half-light of dawn no one noticed a Japanese search plane dodging in and out of the clouds.

At noon the minesweeper *Viereo* arrived. She had been ordered by Nimitz to tow *Yorktown* back to Pearl Harbor. She started to pull the carrier towards Hawaii at only three knots. Even at that speed *Yorktown* was too much for the little vessel. She was scarcely making steerage way. The salvage party worked frantically, pumping out flooded compartments and cutting guns from her lower side to right and lighten her. They made considerable progress, reducing her list by two degrees and lowering the water level in some flooded compartments.

The *Hamman* was secured along *Yorktown's* starboard side supplying power for the pumps. Apart from *Hamman* and *Hughes*, five other destroyers circled her to guard against submarine attack.

But the Japanese flying boat which had observed her plight had reported to Yamamoto. Lieutenant-Commander Yahachi Tanabe, commanding the submarine *I–168* off Midway, received a report that an American carrier was damaged and adrift not more than 150 miles away from him. He was ordered to sink her. The long-range *I–168* was the Japanese submarine which arrived at French Frigate Shoals to refuel the Japanese patrol plane only to find an American seaplane tender and other American craft already there.

Tanabe threaded his way carefully through the heavy American patrol-boat cordon round Midway and headed at twenty-one knots for the *Yorktown*. He arrived at 1 p.m. to see seven U.S. destroyers swarming round the crippled carrier. *I–168* passed under the first line of destroyers undetected and came up to periscope depth. Tanabe noted that the carrier seemed to be a little down by the stern. A close periscope inspection showed she was in tow—the *Viereo* was still trying to pull her to Pearl Harbor. Tanabe waited his opportunity and then fired four torpedoes. As he dived there was a rumbling explosion, and a shout of exultation went up in the submarine.

When the wakes of four torpedoes were sighted *Hamman* had no time to pull clear. One torpedo hit her, cutting her in two. Geysers of oil, water and torn wreckage spouted high in the air. The convulsive heave of *Hamman*'s decks snapped sailors' limbs, and stunned men were thrown overboard or sucked down into the rapidly flooding compartments. She sank almost at once and exploded under water. The concussion killed some swimmers outright. Others, with blood pouring from their eyes, nose and mouth, slowly turned over and sank. Two other torpedoes exploded against *Yorktown*.

When her battered hulk absorbed the two shocks her tall tripod foremast whipped like a sapling. The first shock levelled her list but Captain Buckmaster knew she was doomed. He mustered what was left of her working party once again and abandoned ship.

Not every one of them was able to escape. Five decks below, two carpenter's mates and a petty officer were trapped surrounded by mounting water. It was hopeless to try and get them out. Someone telephoned down, 'Do you know what kind of a fix you're in?' 'Sure,' they called back. 'We know you can't get us out but we've got a helluva good acey-deucey game down here right now.'

While Buckmaster was once again getting his men off *Yorktown* the remaining six American destroyers furiously attacked Tanabe's boat. There were sixty near-misses on his submarine. One depth charge lifted the boat several feet and caused her to shudder from end to end. She was crippled, unable to move, with no pumps working. The lights went out, leaving the boat in pitch darkness. The batteries were damaged and poisonous gas began to escape. Tanabe and his men, crawling and gasping half-choked in the darkness, knew they must surface if they were to live.

As Tanabe gave the order to surface three more depth charges came crashing down. Again the boat shuddered as if she were going to burst. When the crash of the explosions died away the submarine was standing almost on end as if half-way up a hill.

Men groped about in the choking poisonous darkness trying to find the smashed batteries and stop the flow of chlorine gas. Others staggered about with stores and equipment trying to restore her to an even keel. At last the damaged battery was isolated and the switch closed.

The propellers started to move and the lights came on again. But they could still hear the noise of the destroyers' engines overhead. Water was pouring in faster than ever. There was only one grim expedient left. They must surface and fight it out no matter what the odds.

When the grey porpoise bulk of Tanabe's big submarine broke surface three destroyers, picking up survivors from *Hamman*, spotted her. They swung towards her, firing their guns from 5,000 yards away. *I–168* dodged about on the surface while trying to pump in more compressed air. The American shells began to straddle so closely it was certain she would soon be sunk.

Tanabe decided he must risk a crash dive again and lie still, waiting until it was dark. Then he would surface, pump in more air, and hope to escape attention. American destroyers kept passing directly overhead but fired only a few more depth charges. They had fired so many that they were running out.

At 8 p.m. *I–168*'s repairs were complete. Her crew listened intently but the sound of propellers had died away. When she surfaced again there were no destroyers. The Americans obviously thought they had killed Tanabe's submarine. He managed to sail her at sixteen knots back to the Inland Sea for repairs.

His victim, *Yorktown*, still remained afloat, riding low in the water. Early next morning she suddenly turned over and sank in 3,000 fathoms of water. As her bows slid under the men on the destroyers saluted.

Her captain, Elliott Buckmaster, said, 'At daybreak she had a terrible list to starboard. Her flight deck was in the water. She went down with her battle flags flying till they touched the water.'

19

The Lost Fighter

WHILE Nagumo's carriers were blazing and sinking in the warm
waters of the central Pacific, the northern operation against the
Aleutian Islands was proving a most abortive affair.

Just before midnight on 3 June—the day before the Midway
attacks—Rear-Admiral Kajuji Kakuta's aircraft carriers, *Ryujo* and
Junyo, approached Dutch Harbor. Their secret advance towards the
Aleutians was to be the opening blow of Yamamoto's attempt to
control the Pacific.

Japanese carriers had not operated so far north in the Pacific
before and they were not certain what weather conditions to expect.
They soon found out as they approached Dutch Harbor. *Ryujo*,
leading the task force, edged forward cautiously in below-freezing
temperatures with constant drifting fog.

As zero hour approached, Captain Tadao Kato, aboard the flagship *Ryujo*, was huddled into a heavy fur coat giving last-minute
orders. The staff aviation officer, Lieutenant-Commander Masatake
Okumiya, looked at the sky with growing anxiety.

If he could have read *Chicago Times*' reporter Keith Wheeler's
despatch describing the region he would have heartily agreed with it.
'This strange war is proceeding on its eerie course in the latitudes of
the midnight sun,' wrote Wheeler. 'The unending fogs ranging up and
down the bleak Aleutian rocks from Dutch Harbor, 800 miles past
Kiska and Attu, make it as grim a game of blind-man's buff as was
ever contrived by man. Daylight runs twenty hours a day and the
nights are never really dark, but the fog is always there. It lies like a
tattered blanket over sea and land everywhere.'

Okumiya knew the Japanese were remarkably ill equipped for the
attack. The pilots' maps were thirty years old. Their only other guide
was a single blurred photograph of Dutch Harbor which was just as
outdated. Could they ever find their targets with this poor equipment
in such bad weather?

Half an hour after midnight it was foggy but there was already a half-light in these Alaskan latitudes. The bad northern weather which enabled Kakuda's two carriers to approach the Aleutians unseen by watchful American submarines, picket boats and planes, now turned against him. When the Japanese were 165 miles from Dutch Harbor he decided to launch thirty-five planes.

Lashed by cold winds and driving rain, six Zekes and twelve Val dive bombers, commanded by Lieutenant Yoshio Shiga, took off from *Junyo* to attack the American positions. They flew blindly about in the fog. Then increasingly violent storms forced them to abandon their mission and return to the carrier.

But six Zekes and eleven Kate bombers, led by Lieutenant Masayuki Yamaguchi from the *Ryujo*, fought their way in heavy rain and thick fog towards the Aleutians. The sky cleared directly they arrived over Dutch Harbor, and the Americans were taken by complete surprise. The Kates bombed the radio station and the piers. The Zekes, with no American fighters to meet them, strafed flying boats tied to the harbour buoys. They lost only two planes.

Their attack was made easy because Nimitz, fully committed in the central Pacific, could not spare a carrier to defend the far-off Aleutians. Admiral Theobald's task force, ordered to defend the Dutch Harbor–Cold Bay area, had no air cover except land-based planes. And he had few of them. The Navy had twenty PBY search planes and sixty-five fighter planes mostly at their westerly base, a secret field at Otter Point on Umnak. His principal striking power was twenty B.26 army bombers based at Kodiak, Cold Bay and Umnak. To provide early warning of the Japanese approach, Theobald stationed six submarines and twenty small patrol vessels 200 miles from Dutch Harbor into the Bering Sea.

On their return flight from Dutch Harbor, Yamaguchi's planes sighted five American destroyers in Makushin Bay. Admiral Kakuda at once launched another wave to attack them. As they took off the weather became thicker and American P.40s from Otter Point shot down four. The rest turned back in swirling clouds and rain. None reached Makushin Bay. But when American P.40 fighters took off to attack *Junyo*'s planes they revealed to the Japanese the army's secret airfield at Otter Point. This discovery caused Kakuta to cancel the landing on Adak. Bad weather was hindering them enough, without their taking on the further risk of landing on a place only 350 miles from the just-revealed American airfield at Otter Point. Instead he decided upon a second attack on Dutch Harbor.

At four o'clock in the afternoon, as the Japanese carriers were steaming towards Dutch Harbor for this second attack, a group of American planes found them. None of these, PBYs rigged with torpedoes and B.26s, were much good against the ships. The pilots attacked with great gallantry but achieved only a few near-misses and lost three planes.

They did not prevent Kakuda launching another wave of nine fighters, eleven dive bombers and six level bombers. In spite of the bad weather, they arrived over Dutch Harbor in the late afternoon. In half an hour they set fire to the new fuel oil tanks containing 22,000 barrels of oil, a ship, a warehouse and an aircraft hangar.

Soon after he launched his second Dutch Harbor strike, a radio message told Kakuda of the disaster at Midway. It was followed by a second message from Yamamoto ordering him to bring his carriers south to join him immediately.

It took Kakuda two hours to land all his planes and change course to join the main fleet. He had hardly set off when Yamamoto changed his mind and ordered the occupation forces to proceed with the Aleutian landings. His reason was obvious: Japan must have some sort of a victory, however trivial, to offset the Midway defeat.

Soon after noon on 6 June, 12,250 men of a special naval landing force landed unopposed on the tiny, uninhabited island of Kiska. They captured a handful of men running the United States weather station there.

Next day in the Arctic twilight another 1,200 Japanese troops landed on Attu. Their haul was even smaller. They captured thirty-nine Aleuts and an American missionary and his wife.

In Japan the Government trumpeted the victories in the Aleutians and the occupation of two small, unimportant, foggy islands. These victory claims in the far north were a deliberate smoke screen to conceal from the Japanese nation the shattering carrier losses and defeat at Midway.

In the whistling cold, misty Aleutians the Japanese bad luck still held. Something much more vital than a tiny Japanese victory happened there. Neither Yamamoto nor the Japanese Government learned anything about it, but it was to have a far-reaching effect on later battles in the Pacific.

After the second attack on Dutch Harbor, Flight Petty Officer

Tadayoshi Koga noticed that his Zeke was trailing a thin spray of fuel. He informed his squadron leader that he did not have enough fuel to return to *Ryujo* and would have to land somewhere. Koga flew low over a small island east of Dutch Harbor, where he had seen an emergency landing field planned by the Americans for their own crippled aircraft.

The other Zeke pilots flew round above Koga as he made his approach to the emergency landing field. Immediately his wheels touched the ground his aircraft tipped over. They thought he had been killed and his plane wrecked.

A Japanese submarine was sent to the island and surfaced to sail right round it but she could not see any wreckage. There was no sign of the plane or the pilot on the island's bleak surface of tundra.

Later an American plane flying over the island noticed Koga's plane. A patrol was sent out which discovered his Zeke practically intact. They also found Koga. He had hit his head against the instrument panel when the plane landed and broken his neck.

This was one of the greatest pieces of luck for the Americans. Here was an undamaged specimen of the fighter which had been outshooting and out-manœuvring their own planes. Koga's Zeke was shipped back to the United States, where it was repaired and subjected to exhaustive test flights. It produced several surprises. It was unusually light in weight, but it had a very high performance which was achieved with an engine of only 955 horse-power.

It also had weaknesses. It had a poor diving ability and lacked armour-plate protection. Flight tests also revealed the Zeke had a limited altitude and at high speeds responded sluggishly.

But the greatest prize was that they now knew the smallest secrets of the dreaded Zeke-Zero. Grumman engineers studied the captured Zeke with their operational experience gained from the Wildcat. Immediately blueprints were got out for a fighter containing all the Zeke's advantages—and none of its weaknesses. They reduced the thickness of the fuselage and made every other effort to cut down weight. This Zeke adaptation became the U.S. Navy's Grumman F6F Hellcat. It became one of the most versatile American aircraft in the Pacific.

The new Hellcat, with its 2,000 horse-power engine, was twice as powerful as the Zeke. It not only had a higher maximum speed but could also out-climb, out-dive and out-gun it. It had the Wildcat's strong armour-plating and self-sealing fuel tanks. Yet it still lacked the tight turning ability of the Zeke and its range. But as a close in-fighter the Hellcat completely outperformed the Zeke.

The seemingly trivial incident of losing a single intact Zeke had almost as long-term an effect on the Pacific war as the loss of Nagu-mo's four carriers. The Japanese did not know the aircraft had been captured undamaged. It gave the Americans a unique peep at one of the best, most secret fighters of the war. When they began to manu-facture a fighter specifically guaranteed to overcome the fast man-œuvrable Zekes they did much to hasten Japan's final defeat.

20

Yamamoto Takes Over Too Late

ADMIRAL YAMAMOTO, who had master-minded the great Midway operation, took no part in the battle until it was too late. His flagship *Yamato* was 300 miles from Nagumo's carriers when they steamed ahead to disaster. As he had insisted on radio silence in an attempt to surprise Nimitz, he remained in the dark for hours about the great defeat that Nagumo suffered.

At dawn *Yamato* and the other Japanese battleships, ran into fog so dense that the ships could not see one another. There was still radio silence, so Yamamoto could only speculate whether Nagumo's carriers were also surrounded by fog. If so, would it be too dense for them to attack?

Just after dawn the fog lifted and the sun broke through. Messages from the radio room were handed to Yamamoto standing on the glass-fronted bridge. The first was a signal sent by *Tone*'s seaplane reporting sighting an American flying boat. Yamamoto waited calmly for developments. This meant it would not be long before the American PBYs discovered Nagumo's ships.

Twenty minutes later another message came from *Tone*'s plane reporting that fifteen land-based American planes were approaching Nagumo's carriers. The news again only faintly interested Yamamoto. The Zekes of Nagumo's combat air patrol could easily take care of these few Midway planes.

As no messages came in from Nagumo's flagship *Akagi*, this meant she was still keeping radio silence because everything was going according to plan and she was in no serious danger from the Americans. Yamamoto presumed Tomonaga's first Midway strike had already been safely launched.

Then the flagship radio room intercepted Tomonaga's message reporting the completion of his mission against Midway. When he suggested a second attack, Yamamoto nodded in agreement. American air strength on Midway must be destroyed before the invasion.

He waited confidently for a report that this had happened. His staff talked elatedly among themselves. Just as they had predicted, no American ship was in sight. Complete surprise had been achieved. The operation was going exactly as planned.

At 7.40 a.m. a signal came in to Yamamoto which stopped their jubilant smiles and made them look at one another speculatively. It was a terse flash from *Tone*'s search plane saying, 'Have sighted ten ships apparently enemy.' What was this? Why were there so many American surface ships in the area? Were they perhaps not taken by surprise? And what type of ships were in this American force?

Yamamoto gazed ahead as though trying to estimate the size of it. No one else spoke. It was nearly an hour before another message came from *Tone*'s plane saying, 'American fleet has five cruisers, five destroyers—with one carrier.'

Yamamoto and his staff nearly danced for joy on the bridge. What a piece of luck! They had almost resigned themselves to the idea that there were no American carriers in the area which they could bring into action. Now here was one sailing along like an unsuspecting swan.

Yamamoto looked at the bridge clock. The timing was perfect. Egusa's second attack wave, specially trained to attack American carriers, must now be on deck ready to take off. They would soon make short work of this lone carrier.

Half an hour later all talk abruptly ceased when the loudspeaker relayed another report from a scout plane saying, '100 carrier-borne enemy planes heading for the Nagumo force.' This meant there was more than one American carrier.

Now Yamamoto felt even more confident about the coming battle. Why shouldn't he? He had four carriers. He was certain the Americans could not muster anything like that. His guess was quite correct —they could not. But luck and the backs-to-the-wall courage of the American pilots was at that very moment reversing Japan's numerical superiority.

For two long hours nothing more was heard from Nagumo's carriers. Then at 10.50 a.m. the chief signal officer, Commander Yoshio Wada, silently handed Admiral Yamamoto a radio message. He dare not put it over the loudspeaker.

It was from Rear-Admiral Abe in the cruiser *Tone* telling the fate of Nagumo's carriers. Abe reported, 'Fires raging aboard *Kaga*, *Soryu* and *Akagi* resulting from attacks by enemy carrier and land-based planes. We plan to have *Hiryu* engage enemy carriers. We are temporarily withdrawing to the north to assemble our forces.'

The normally impassive Yamamoto groaned aloud as he read the message. Three of his four carriers, including Nagumo's flagship, were out of action. Only *Hiryu* was left to carry on the fight.

A Japanese sailor described the scene like this: 'The admiral and his staff looked at one another, their mouths tight shut. There was indescribable emptiness, cheerlessness and chagrin.'

Shortly afterwards Yamamoto received Nagumo's message saying he had left his burning flagship and transferred to *Nagara*. It gave full details of the damage to his three carriers. It also informed Admiral Yamamoto that he was proceeding to attack the Americans with all his remaining strength. All was not yet lost, with *Hiryu* still intact.

After his first stunned reaction to the incredible news, Yamamoto acted swiftly. There was only one course open to him. His big battleships must steam towards Midway at once to support Nagumo's carriers. He must take command of the battle personally.

It was a decision he probably should have taken at the outset of the operation. Now it was going to prove too late. Also the bad luck which dogged him throughout the Midway battle appeared again. No sooner had he decided to steam full ahead to join Nagumo than fog came down once more. The other huge battleships were grey shapes scarcely visible from Yamamoto's flagship.

Although speed was vital, it took Yamamoto more than an hour to get his gigantic fleet under way. They began to steam towards Midway at twenty knots, even though the fog was thickening again. They followed a zigzag course to avoid American submarines. This was a most hazardous manœuvre in heavy fog. The danger was ever present that two of the great battleships might collide. Yamamoto decided he must take this risk and push ahead to help Nagumo's shattered carriers. The disaster had made him desperate.

Yamamoto, who had cut himself off from the battle and was powerless to help Nagumo's carriers while they were being smashed, was now steaming full ahead without a properly formulated plan. How could his big ships help to retrieve the situation? There were several possibilities.

As they sailed as fast as they could through the fog, an anxious planning conference went on in the operations room of *Yamato*.

His operations officer, Rear-Admiral Kuroshima, and other

officers kept saying half hysterically, 'Let's fight anyway!' His chief of staff, Admiral Ugaki, was the only calm voice. He disagreed with Kuroshima, who suggested that the big battleships should bombard Midway during the night.

While they argued the merits and drawbacks of this operation for a long time Yamamoto did not speak. Then, pale and tight-lipped, he said, 'O.K. Let's go!' He had decided on a night action. He ordered Vice-Admiral Kondo with his high-speed warships which were escorting the troop transports to Midway to change course at once to try and come to grips with the Americans. This would mean deferring the landing operations. But it could not be helped. Midway and the American fleet must be destroyed.

Yamamoto decided to send the battleship *Hiei* as the spearhead to shell Midway.

At 12.20 p.m. he signalled, 'All forces will attack the enemy in the Midway area.' Half an hour later came a more detailed order, 'Commander Midway forces will dispatch part of his strength to bombard and destroy air bases on Midway. All combat forces from both the Midway and Aleutian area will engage the enemy fleet in decisive battle.' But how soon could Admiral Kakuda with his two carriers, *Ryujo* and *Junyo*, steam south to join the battle? This was vital because, if they arrived in time, the Japanese would still have a superiority in carriers.

Kakuda's reply came at 3.30 p.m. It was not encouraging. Despite dense fog, he had carried out his planned strike on Dutch Harbor. But his ships could not be expected to join the Midway battle before the afternoon of 6 June—forty-eight hours later.

Then at 4.15 p.m. Admiral Yamaguchi radioed from *Hiryu*, 'Pilots report enemy force is apparently composed of three carriers, five large cruisers and fifteen destroyers. Our attacks succeeded in damaging two carriers.'

The fact that Yamaguchi's flyers had succeeded in inflicting some damage on the American carriers was the first piece of good news.

At 5.36 p.m. a search plane from *Chikuma* radioed that the Americans were only ninety miles from Nagumo's fleet—and were withdrawing eastwards. But Yamamoto had already sent Kondo and his fast battleships racing towards them at top speed. A night action might turn the battle in Japan's favour because the Imperial Navy were especially trained for night action. But sunset was at 6.23 p.m. Would Kondo reach them in time?

Then at 5.55 p.m. came the worst news of all. Admiral Nagumo signalled, '*Hiryu* hit by bombs and set on fire 5.30.' His last remaining carrier had gone. The Japanese Midway attack force was blunted —if not completely smashed.

Despite the loss of three carriers in the morning, followed by the disastrous destruction of *Hiryu* in the afternoon, Admiral Yamamoto was determined not to abandon the Midway operation. Although he had temporarily lost control of the air, he did not regard the situation as hopeless. He had with him the carriers *Hosho* and *Zuiho*, and Admiral Kakuda's Aleutians task force had two others.

Hashimoto's laconic message that *Yorktown* was burning made him cling to his plan. At 7.15 p.m.—an hour and twenty minutes after *Hiryu*'s loss—he sent a message to his commanders: 'The enemy fleet which has practically been destroyed is retiring. Combined Fleet units in the vicinity are preparing to pursue the remnants and at the same time occupy Midway.'

This was obviously neither true nor practical with the forces he could immediately muster. Yamamoto of course was not confused as to the real situation. He was just trying to keep up Japanese morale after the shattering loss of all his carriers in the central Pacific.

As the American fleet was withdrawing eastwards fast, any hope of carrying out a night engagement faded considerably. But Yamamoto still persisted in his plan. He wanted not only to continue the fight but to pick up his burning carriers, which were perhaps not completely doomed. He also wanted to capture *Yorktown*, which was still afloat. He could easily deal with her five standby destroyers and tow her back to Japan.

But Nagumo's officers aboard his temporary flagship *Nagara*, having seen their last carrier burst into flames, were in an hysterical and unhappy mood. One staff officer, Oishi, came forward with a fantastic plan that all destroyers standing by the damaged carriers should help in the night engagement. When Admiral Nagumo gave his approval to this suggestion, most other officers were appalled.

There were whispered conferences among his staff. Even the iron Japanese navy discipline became a little strained at their admiral's decision.

If Oishi's night attack failed, the crippled Japanese carriers would have no chance. American carrier planes would swoop to destroy them at dawn. All the crews left aboard the carriers would drown if they sank with no rescuing destroyers at hand.

Then came a blinker message from *Chikuma*. It read, 'Scout plane sighted five enemy carriers, six cruisers and fifteen destroyers thirty miles east of the burning carrier.' The Japanese pilot reported the number of ships correctly but he mistook three cruisers for carriers. Except for *Yorktown* on fire and listing, the two American task forces were still undamaged. They still had the two carriers *Hornet* and *Enterprise*, eight cruisers and fifteen destroyers. But this signal made Nagumo decide that a night action was impossible.

But Yamamoto was determined to carry on the fight. He ordered Tanabe's submarine, *I-168*, to shell Midway and stay there until 2 a.m., when she would be relieved by bombarding cruisers and the battleship *Hiei*.

Meanwhile in Tokyo the Naval General Staff were tensely following the progress of the battle. When the report came in that *Hiryu* had suffered the same fate as *Akagi*, *Kaga* and *Soryu* they realized the operation was doomed.

But did Yamamoto realize it? The Chief of Naval Staff, Admiral Osami Nagano, like Yamamoto, was not too deeply concerned about the loss of Japan's four finest carriers. Even after this disaster, the Imperial Navy still had more warships of every category in the Pacific than the United States. But what did worry him very much was: What would Admiral Yamamoto, smarting under Nagumo's terrible defeat, do next?

American strength on Midway was not destroyed. Also they still had at least one undamaged carrier, if not two. If Yamamoto continued to press home his attack on Midway he might lose the whole Japanese fleet under massive attacks from American carrier and land-based planes.

Yet no orders, no advice, came from Tokyo. It was Admiral Yamamoto's battle. He must fight it as he wished without interference.

Admiral Nagano waited, picking up signals and reading them in complete silence. It was defeat. He knew it. Everyone knew it. But no one was willing to be the first to admit it or call off the operation. That was Yamamoto's decision—and his alone.

Yamamoto now had another problem. Nagumo seemed to have lost his nerve. While things had been going well in the first few months of the war, he had shown high competence. But after the destruction of his flagship *Akagi* he revealed signs of shock and failing judgment. There was no doubt he was bent on retreat.

At 9.30 p.m. he sent Yamamoto an almost panic-stricken despatch based on the false report of *Chikuma*'s scout plane, saying, 'The total strength of the enemy is five carriers, six cruisers and fifteen destroyers. We are retiring to the north-west escorting *Hiryu* at eighteen knots.' The information was obviously exaggerated, as the Americans could not possibly have such a large number of carriers, yet Nagumo repeated the message at 10.50 p.m. Admiral Ugaki, Yamamoto's chief of staff, put everyone's thoughts into words when he threw down the second signal and muttered savagely, 'The Nagumo force has no stomach for a night engagement!'

Yamamoto silently agreed with him. He decided to relieve Nagumo and put Admiral Kondo in charge of the whole attack force. Kondo, who had shown both good judgment and initiative in the crisis, was already on his way to join the battered remnants of Nagumo's fleet and try to provoke a night battle. With him was a formidable fleet of four fast battleships, nine cruisers and nineteen destroyers all geared for a night surface action.

Yamamoto sent an order, 'Commander-in-Chief Second Fleet Kondo will take command of Nagumo forces, excepting *Hiryu*, *Akagi* and the ships escorting them.' This meant that, except for commanding the two blazing, half-sunken hulks of his remaining carriers, Nagumo was relieved from duty.

At midnight the radio transmitter on the flagship *Yamato* was still busily signalling orders to Kakuda to rendezvous as soon as possible with the remnants of Nagumo's fleet. It was also ordering Kondo to prepare for a decisive surface action. Yet even as the signals went out it was becoming increasingly evident that there was little hope of contacting the American fleet before dawn.

In spite of their victory against the Japanese carriers it was a nervous night for both American admirals as they tried to assess the results of that day's tremendous battle. Fletcher's task force, maimed by the loss of *Yorktown*, sheltered behind *Hornet* and *Enterprise*. For although the Japanese carriers had gone, Spruance was still very much afraid of the appearance of Yamamoto's fast big battleships.

In his operations room aboard *Enterprise* he was fully aware that Yamamoto might yet restore the balance by bringing up his giant battleships for a surface engagement. Now he was in tactical command of the American fleet, he was not going to fall into a trap. He decided to sail east during darkness. He said, 'I did not feel justified in risking a night encounter with possibly superior enemy forces. Nor did I wish to be too far from Midway next morning. I wanted to be in a position from which to either follow up the retreating enemy or break up a landing attack on Midway.'

Admiral Spruance did not believe Yamamoto would attempt a landing after losing his four carriers. But the possibility could not be disregarded. While Yamamoto was steaming at full speed towards him with the world's largest battleships determined to fight a surface engagement, Spruance had no idea how near or how strong he was. But Midway must be protected, so he dawdled, sailing a few miles one way then a few miles back. Always he kept the same distance north-east of Midway.

That night was the culmination of a day of deep anxiety and conflicting messages. On 4 June, while one of the greatest naval battles in history was being fought on their doorstep, the American commanders on Midway remained largely in ignorance of what was happening.

During the morning scanty reports reached them that only one Japanese carrier had been damaged. This made the smoking ruins round them inflicted by Tomonaga's first attack a foretaste of disaster. Commander Ramsey, the air operations officer, thought it 'quite possible we will be under heavy bombardment from surface vessels before sunset'.

Lieutenant-Colonel Sweeney, commander of the Fortresses, did not know there were three American carriers near by. He ordered seven of his planes—all he could get ready in time—back to Oahu. There were two reasons for his decision. One was to save them from destruction. The other was to help defend the Hawaiian Islands against the invasion he assumed would immediately follow Midway's fall.

When the seven Fortresses left for Oahu, Midway's air strength was reduced to two fighters, twelve dive bombers, eighteen patrol planes and four serviceable Fortresses. They were determined to fight to the end however hopeless. In the afternoon when Midway learned of the crippling of four Japanese carriers, Colonel Sweeney led his four Fortresses against Nagumo's battered and scattered fleet. Two more hurriedly patched up Fortresses took off an hour later on the same mission. The pilots reported bomb hits. But Nagumo's log acknowledged none. All their bombs missed.

The Fortresses landed with alarming news. Zekes had jumped

them during their attack. Zekes still flying after the fourth carrier had been sunk? Did this mean there was a fifth? In fact the Zekes were orphans from the doomed and burning *Hiryu* fighting to their last drop of fuel before they plunged into the sea.

Eleven Marine dive bombers, commanded by Major Norris, took off at dusk to search for the fifth carrier or any other remaining Japanese ships, but heavy squalls came up with a moonless sky that made their search hopeless. They had difficulty finding their way back. Only the blue blur from their exhausts kept them together until they sighted the oil fires on Midway started by Tomonaga's planes. These guided them home, except Major Norris. He did not return.

Midway decided to mount one more attack that evening in case the smashed Japanese fleet had left any stragglers. Eleven torpedo boats dashed out at 7.30 p.m. to search for them. They also found nothing. The battle had moved too far away.

Both Midway and Spruance were still alarmed by the possibility of a fifth carrier in the vicinity. Tension, which had begun to relax, rapidly built up again. Unconfirmed alarmist reports at once began to circulate.

At nine o'clock a patrol boat falsely reported a landing on the small island of Kure, sixty miles to the west. This seemed to strengthen the report of the Zeke fighters. The invasion again seemed imminent.

Back at Pearl Harbor the Pacific Fleet submarine commander, Rear-Admiral Robert H. English, thought so. He pulled his boats back to a five-mile radius round Midway to prepare for it. At midnight two Catalinas took off armed with torpedoes to attack the approaching ships while the garrison made ready. Eighty-five 500-lb bombs were loaded by hand and 45,000 gallons of petrol were hand-pumped on to planes.

Tension reached its height at 1 a.m. when Lieutenant-Commander Yahachi Tanabe's big submarine, *I-168*, suddenly appeared in the lagoon, fired eight rounds and submerged.

The Midway garrison stood to arms, anxiously waiting for the sight of a great armada looming off-shore. The *I-168* did not fire again. She had just received another assignment. She was ordered to sail and finish off the crippled *Yorktown*.

But when Spruance received a signal that submarine *I-168* was shelling Midway he, too, thought it was the prelude to invasion. This view was confirmed when at 2.15 a.m. the American submarine

Tambor reported 'many unidentified ships' only ninety miles from Midway. They were the heavy cruisers *Mogami* and *Mikuma*, part of the vanguard of the occupation force, now on their way under Yamamoto's orders to relieve the *I–168* and shell the atoll. Spruance thought this might be a landing force. He turned towards Midway at twenty-five knots.

As Spruance began sailing towards the atoll at full speed, Yamamoto was sitting in his operations room on his flagship reassessing his situation. He now knew that the Americans had at least two carriers still operational and Spruance by sailing east had definitely succeeded in avoiding a night action.

Yamamoto also received further depressing news. His fleet was sailing nineteen degrees off course. This meant all hope of a night battle was lost. *Yorktown*, too, was obviously sinking, so he gave up the idea of capturing her. If he continued on his present course his own ships would almost certainly be attacked by planes at dawn. He could not afford to risk further losses after the destruction of his four carriers.

What could he do to snatch victory from disaster? A desperate plan was proposed by his thrusting, fighting-mad operations officer, Rear-Admiral Kuroshima. He suggested the flagship *Yamato* should lead all the battleships to Midway in broad daylight on the following day and shell the shore installations.

Rear-Admiral Matomi Ugaki—the man who had faked the Midway war games in Tokyo—immediately proclaimed it suicide. He said: 'Engaging shore installations with a surface force is stupid. A large number of American planes are still based on Midway. Some of the enemy carriers are still intact. Our battleships will be destroyed by enemy air and submarine attacks before we could even get close enough to use our big guns.'

But was it such a risk? The Japanese fire power, including the great eighteen-inch guns of the battleships, was so huge that it was still far superior to all the American guns either from the U.S. fleet or shore-based on Midway.

Although he had indulged in fantasies at the war games Admiral Ugaki now took a stern and realistic view. He argued that the Japanese Navy must accept the reality of their defeat at Midway. It did not mean they had lost the war. Nor was the loss of the four carriers a complete disaster as, including those nearly completed, the Imperial Navy still had eight carriers. He added, 'In battle, as in chess, it is a fool who lets himself be led into a reckless mood through desperation.'

Ugaki was one of the few sane and level-headed officers. To the majority, to admit to such a crushing defeat was something beyond the limits of their worst nightmares. There was hardly an officer who was not ready to gamble the whole fleet for a chance to save 'face'.

One vital question was in all their minds. It went straight to the core of the Japanese character. Eventually one officer plucked up enough courage to put it into words. 'How can we apologize to His Majesty?' he asked.

Everyone gazed obliquely with unrevealing faces at Yamamoto's masklike features. A great deal depended upon his answer. He said abruptly, 'Leave that to me. I am the only one who must apologize to His Majesty.'

It was only then that they knew for certain that Yamamoto had decided to abandon any further attempts to engage the American fleet—or capture Midway.

It was fifteen minutes after midnight on 5 June when Yamamoto took the first step to acknowledge his defeat. He ordered Vice-Admiral Kondo's fleet, still racing towards a night attack on the American carriers and a bombardment at Midway, to withdraw and join him.

At 2.55 a.m. he issued an order which publicly admitted the great naval defeat. It said, 'Operation A.F.—the Midway operation—is cancelled.' He also ordered Ichiki's troop transports to retire out of Midway air range.

One other smaller but even more humiliating decision remained. He had still not dealt with Captain Aoki's signals requesting permission to sink the burning *Akagi*. Yamamoto might be forced to admit defeat in battle but this postscript to defeat was even more painful. The Japanese navy had never in its history scuttled one of its own warships. He still could not face this decision and ordered the sinking to be delayed. It was not until 3.50 a.m. that he could bring himself to order *Akagi* to be torpedoed by her stand-by destroyers.

All that now remained was the humiliating and hazardous task of rounding up the scattered Japanese fleet and sailing from the battle area without being discovered by watchful American search planes or submarines.

When the twin heavy cruisers *Mogami* and *Mikuma* received the order, 'Operation A.F. is cancelled retire,' they turned away from Midway. The American submarine *Tambor* continued to trail them.

Morale was now so low in the Japanese navy that when their lookouts saw her periscope and shouted a warning, the cruisers collided in their haste to avoid her torpedoes. *Mogami*'s bow was damaged and one of *Mikuma*'s fuel tanks streamed oil, giving the American planes a trail which was to lead to her destruction.

Japanese fleet morale was not improved either when all through the night destroyers arrived with wounded survivors from the four carriers to be put aboard the battleships *Mutsu, Nagato, Haruna* and *Kirishima*. The sea became rough with long swells and it was impossible to bring the destroyers alongside the battleships.

Boats had to be lowered to shuttle the most seriously wounded from destroyer to battleship. All through the pitch-dark night they were pulled aboard by ropes attached to bamboo stretchers. By dawn the sick-bays and crew quarters of the four battleships were jammed with wounded, most of them burn victims.

While they watched this melancholy scene every sailor in the battleships was weighed down with the realization that the Imperial Navy had just suffered a great and crushing defeat. Few of them could console themselves for the loss of the four great carriers by the fact that their main battleship strength remained intact. After what had happened to them they knew better than anyone that big guns were as useless as assegais in the Pacific.

In a clear dawn with a visibility of forty miles—the finest weather since the fleet had left Japan ten days before —Admiral Yamamoto's battleships headed towards the Nagumo and Kondo forces. That day the giant battleships made their closest approach to the Americans since the start of the war. Every ship maintained a strict alert against air raids as they cruised 300 miles north-west of Midway waiting for Kondo's fleet. It was just after sunrise when Kondo's warships were sighted on the horizon and by seven o'clock they had joined forces with Yamamoto.

Five hours later Nagumo's battered ships appeared on the horizon. Standing on the bridge under the hot noonday Pacific sun, Yamamoto watched them approach in silence. Nor did any of his officers speak a word as they gazed at the approaching warships. They bore little resemblance to the proud fleet that had sailed so confidently out of Hashira anchorage only ten days before. Not only were there no carriers left but half their destroyers were missing too. Six of them were still picking up survivors of the battle swimming in their hundreds or clinging to oil-slippery wreckage.

By dawn Spruance was convinced the Japanese were retreating. Between 6.30 a.m. and 8 a.m. Midway planes confirmed his view by reporting that all Japanese vessels within range were withdrawing. The submarine *Tambor*, which was still doggedly trailing the twin cruisers, now identified them as *Mogami* and *Mikuma*. More planes sighted the cruisers *Kumano* and *Suzuya*, steaming fast 175 miles away. There were several other ships over 250 miles away.

When American planes searched for the carriers they had put out of action they found only huge oil patches on the water with oil-blackened men clinging to wreckage. Some of the survivors formed themselves into swimming formations, commanded by officers, to try and beat off sharks. It was *buntai* again—the fierce swim which had ended term at the Naval Academy.

As they swam along there was an occasional flurry of foam and a gasping scream as a shark took one of the outside swimmers. The rest swam on. Sometimes a searching destroyer picked them up. Sometimes they just swam until the sharks got them or they gave up exhausted, and drowned.

Now it was clear the Japanese were in full retreat, Spruance sent every available plane to harry and destroy them. Twelve Marine bombers left on Midway—six Vindicators led by Captain Richard E. Fleming and six Dauntlesses led by Captain Marshall A. Tyler—took off to follow *Mikuma*'s clearly visible oil trail. As the two cruisers limped along with the torn tank their track was unmistakable.

At 8.05 a.m. *Mikuma*'s commander, Sakao Sakiyama, reported 'waves of dive bombers', as through a hail of A.A. fire, the Dauntlesses dived on her sister ship, *Mogami*. They bracketed her with near-misses which shook her from side to side. Then the Vindicators swooped down on *Mikuma*. Fleming's engine was hit by a shell but he held his course and dropped his bomb. Pilots coming in behind him watched his plane flame up as he smashed it into *Mikuma*'s after turret. Fleming was the first Marine flyer to receive the Medal of Honour. Even the enemy paid tribute. Captain Akira Soji of *Mogami* said, 'He was a very brave man.'

The Japanese, busy firing at the marine divers, again fell into the trap of not looking up. A group of high-flying B.17s began to bomb them. They switched their fire hurriedly as the bombs began to burst around the two cruisers. But most of the bombs missed them.

Meanwhile Spruance's carriers were steaming fast to close the gap. It had become a clear day with a smooth sea, and *Enterprise*'s planes soon discovered *Mogami* and *Mikuma* limping along 150 miles away. They made three successive attacks. There were repeated hits on the two damaged cruisers and one bomb fell on the stern of an accompanying destroyer. In their third attack, *Enterprise* and *Hornet* were steaming only ninety miles away from the fleeing Japanese ships. For the first time since the Midway battle had begun the American pilots could see both forces simultaneously.

Although Captain Sakiyama tried to head her for the nearest Japanese base at Wake Island *Mikuma* was sinking fast. At midday, as the third carrier attack flew away, she suddenly turned and went down, taking 1,000 men with her. Her badly wounded captain was picked up out of the water and carried aboard the cruiser *Suzuya*. He died five days later in her sick-bay.

Mikuma was the largest Japanese surface warship to be sunk since the beginning of the war. She had always fought with her sister ship *Mogami*. In fact she perished in *Mogami*'s defence by deliberately drawing down bombers upon herself when *Mogami* was struck by six direct hits.

Mogami, also fighting fiercely to protect herself and her sister ship, received heavy bomb damage and lost her bow, yet she was still able to steam along at twenty knots, listing heavily. She was the last Japanese warship to get clear of the American planes in the Midway battle. Escorted by destroyers she managed to creep back to Truk, but was out of the war for more than a year.

The sinking and battering of these two cruisers was a partial revenge for the battle of the Java Sea. For in that battle they had been responsible for sinking the U.S.S. *Houston* and the Australian cruiser *Perth*.

Next on Spruance's list was the burning Japanese carrier *Hiryu*, which he thought was still afloat. In fact she had sunk hours before. But in the early afternoon twelve B.17s took off from Midway to find her. All they found was the destroyer *Tanikaze* which Nagumo had sent to rescue survivors from *Hiryu* if she were still afloat. *Tanikaze* was steaming back to report *Hiryu*'s fate when the Fortresses swooped on her. They made two attacks, dropping eighty bombs, but the fast-moving destroyer was too quick for them. They achieved only a few near-misses.

The two American carriers *Hornet* and *Enterprise* were now about

130 miles from Midway and the gap between them and the fleeting Japanese was widening. Spruance ordered the bombers to take off armed only with a single 500-lb bomb each. This meant they could carry maximum fuel.

He was so anxious for the biggest kill possible that he held his attack back until three o'clock in the afternoon while his two carriers steamed at full speed to close the range. This late take-off meant his planes could not return before dark and the carriers would have to light up their flight decks to recover them. But Spruance, still believing he was pursuing the fourth Japanese carrier *Hiryu*, accepted the risk. Again all his carrier planes found was the much-harried *Tanikaze*. They attacked her with no more success than the army B.17s.

As they flew back it became dark. *Enterprise* and *Hornet* switched on deck and searchlights to guide them in. This was a big risk because it temporarily made them a sitting target for any Japanese submarine lurking in the area. But Spruance was much more concerned about his pilots, most of whom had never before landed on a carrier at night. They all made the illuminated decks safely except one which came down in the sea. The crew was rescued by a destroyer.

Now it was night and the American carriers were approaching the bad weather area. Spruance decided to call it a day. His fuel was running low and his flyers were exhausted from two days of almost continuous operations. Spruance's information was that there were no Japanese warships for more than 250 miles ahead. But he was not going to risk running into any of Yamamoto's big battleships in the dark where they would pound him to pieces. In addition he was approaching within 700-mile flying range of Wake, where he believed the Japanese had flown a large number of planes ready to land on Midway after its capture.

He felt the Americans had pushed their luck as far as was good for them. So he changed course west to rendezvous with an oiler Admiral Nimitz had set up for his ships.

It was a very wise decision. For Yamamoto, fleeing with his battered fleet, was still spoiling for a fight. His ships were over 600 miles from Midway on the day they were to have invaded it. They looked defeated. His flagship was followed by the cruiser *Nagara*, from whose mast Nagumo's flag seemed to droop in shame.

Yamamoto's one burning intention was to avenge their disaster. The attacks on the *Tanikaze*, *Mogami* and *Mikuma* had given him a plain indication that the American carriers were not far away. He judged correctly that if he turned in that direction he would meet Spruance's carriers. At noon on 5 June he ordered seven cruisers and eight destroyers to sail towards *Mogami* and *Mikuma*'s course. In his flagship *Yamato*, surrounded by his battleships, he followed them to join the battle. He also ordered squadrons of planes from the Marshalls to reinforce Wake's striking power.

If Spruance had not changed course that evening and called off the chase, he would have fallen into Yamamoto's trap before next morning. His two carriers would have had little chance against Yamamoto's mighty battle fleet.

While Spruance fled and Yamamoto pursued, the weather turned bad and fog threatened. This decided both commanders to give up all hope of a further engagement. Although they had won the battle, the American commanders were ignorant of most of Yamamoto's movements as he withdrew. Admiral Spruance still believed the *Hiryu* was afloat. It was not until several days after she sank that a boatload of Japanese sailors from her engine room was picked up and told her story.

The fate of *Mikuma* was also unknown to Spruance. In the late afternoon of 6 June she was photographed lying disabled and dead on the water. American submarines were ordered to finish her off. When they arrived next morning she had gone. They were still not sure whether she had sunk or escaped.

When *Hornet* and *Enterprise* turned away to rendezvous with their refuelling tankers, the greatest sea battle since Trafalgar was over. It had lasted for forty-eight hours but had been won in the five minutes when American dive bombers caught Nagumo unprepared with his carrier decks lined with planes.

Not until several months afterwards did the Americans know what a narrow escape they had had. Only then did they learn that Admiral Yamamoto with seven gigantic battleships, two more carriers and a great fleet of cruisers and destroyers was operating near Midway in support of Nagumo's four carriers. If he had been able to come to grips with the American fleet the battle must have ended differently.

21

The Hidden Wounded

THE Midway defeat was such a shock to Japan that no detail of the operation except the tiny Aleutian landing was allowed to leak out. The fact that all references to the battle were deleted from war diaries and official reports shows how bitterly they took the news. Their only small success had been the capture of two fairly useless Aleutian bases. Admiral Kakuda's northern operation, resumed on Yamamoto's order after its earlier cancellation, was the only one which had gone according to plan. While the remnants of Yamamoto's great fleet were fleeing before the U.S. Pacific Fleet the Japanese took the islands of Attu and Kiska.

The extraordinary lengths to which the Imperial Navy went to preserve the dreadful secret of their defeat are revealed by Captain Mitsuo Fuchida, who led the assault on Pearl Harbor and was at Midway aboard Nagumo's flagship *Akagi*. In a preface to his book about the battle he wrote:

I had a painful taste of the extreme measures taken to preserve secrecy. I was wounded on board *Akagi* and transferred to a hospital ship, *Hikawa Maru*, which brought me to Yokusaka naval base.

I was not moved ashore until after dark when the streets were deserted. I had a leg wound and was taken to hospital on a covered stretcher and carried through the rear entrance.

My room was in complete isolation. No nurses or medical corpsmen were allowed in and I could not communicate with the world outside. All the wounded from Midway were treated like this. It was like being a prisoner of war among your own people. After the Japanese surrender in 1945 all the top secret papers were burned.

Commander Masatake Okumiya, another Pearl Harbor veteran, who was staff aviation officer in the light carrier *Ryujo*, Kakuda's flagship in the Aleutians, commented years later, 'The Pacific war saw air power finally come of age. Battles between great surface fleets were decided without them exchanging a single shot. But it was not until 1951 when a book of mine was published in Japan that the public learned for the first time of the disastrous naval defeat.'

Admiral Nobutake Kondo, who took over from Nagumo after he had lost his nerve at Midway, said, 'Our forces suffered a defeat so decisive and so grave that details of it were kept the guarded secret of a limited circle even within the Japanese navy. Even after the war, few among high-ranking officers were familiar with the details of the Midway operation.'

The Midway failure went much deeper than Yamamoto's decision to withdraw from the battle. He intended to use Midway as a springboard for the conquest of Oahu. He was saving his great fleet for this. If he could have destroyed the remaining American Pacific strength at Midway and completed the job he began at Pearl Harbor, he could easily have taken Oahu. He was convinced the fall of the Hawaiian island would create a situation favourable to a negotiated peace on Japanese terms.

But would it have been such an easy task while any American warship remained afloat? This small atoll, 1,140 miles from Pearl Harbor, would have been exceedingly difficult and wasteful to hold, as the Japanese naval staff pointed out. Although planes stationed there would have had a great reconnaissance value for the Japanese, they would certainly have received more bombs than they dropped. Neither was Midway valuable as a submarine base, especially after the Japanese took Kiska and Attu in the Aleutians.

Battle planning was also faulty from top to bottom and start to finish. None of Yamamoto's senior admirals were fully briefed. They were drawn into battle with the shortest of notice. Even Yamamoto's own deputy and designated successor, Admiral Nobutake Kondo, commander of the Second Fleet, said, 'I was deputy commander of the Combined Fleet in case Yamamoto was unable to act. Yamamoto did not want his fleet commanders, whose energies were fully occupied with the first phase of the operations in so many far-flung theatres, to be bothered with other matters. Even I was not consulted during the Midway planning period and did not learn about the operation until 17 April 1942—the day before the Doolittle raid.'

This faulty preparation extended to the battle itself. Otherwise how could three United States carriers defeat and turn back eight carriers, eleven battleships and an immense number of supporting vessels? Yamamoto had the most formidable single fleet ever seen but he scattered it piecemeal. This was because he never visualized the possibility of defeat, an excellent state of mind for the bold, thrusting commander he was. But when defeat happens, the lack of a secondary plan invariably makes it a much greater disaster.

The Aleutians action was unimportant. It was intended only as a diversion from the main thrust at Midway to destroy American installations and after occupying them for a short time abandon them. On the day of the attack on Dutch Harbor and the first contact in the Midway area—3 June—the Japanese warships were scattered all over the Pacific. The two carriers in the Aleutians might have proved the decisive factor in the central Pacific. Had Midway succeeded, Yamamoto could have snapped up the Aleutian crumb at leisure. Yet without victory at Midway, the Aleutians operation became meaningless.

Nagumo's carriers were 300 miles ahead of Yamamoto's battleships. Once the carriers had been destroyed, Yamamoto was unable to regain the initiative because he could not bring his scattered groups together in time. His main body, for all its gigantic fire power, was an ill-balanced and comparatively useless force.

Many American naval authorities insist that if Yamamoto's big battleships had operated with the carriers their guns would have warded off many attacking American planes and drawn them away from the carriers. Admiral Yamamoto would also have had direct control over the battle instead of powerlessly maintaining radio silence 300 miles away.

But was it such a mistake? The A.A. fire of the Japanese giant battleships was barely enough to protect themselves. They would have been more of a nuisance than a help to the battling carriers. Also Yamamoto could range anywhere from his pivotal position. The only thing he did not allow for was what happened—defeat.

But should not the operation have been delayed until the carriers *Zuikaku* and *Shokaku* were ready to sail and add their strength? Admiral Yamamoto turned down all requests for this, wanting to hurry ahead as the best possible weather and moon conditions for the Midway landings were in early June. The two carriers would never have been ready in time. And who can blame Yamamoto, who knew the potential strength of the U.S. Pacific Fleet, for assuming he already had carriers to spare?

As the battle neared both he and Nagumo must take the blame for faulty intelligence work and poor reconnaissance. Flying-boat reconnaissance of Pearl Harbor—Operation K—was vital to the success of the Midway attack but it was poorly executed. When it was discovered that the big Emily flying boats could not refuel from submarines at French Frigate Shoals no alternative was worked out. The plan was just dropped.

Perhaps the most serious mistake was the handling of the Japanese submarines. Not only were they twenty-five hours late taking up station, but each submarine was assigned to a static position. If they had been ordered to sweep along the line of the Hawaiian Islands north-east of Midway, they might still have found Fletcher and Spruance.

Admiral Nagumo was the only senior Japanese commander to come to grips with the Americans. As Yamamoto had turned himself into a helpless spectator he had to fight the battle alone. Before Yamamoto could take over command of the battle, Nagumo had doomed his four carriers.

Yet if Nagumo had made an earlier search he would almost certainly have discovered the American carriers. When the float planes could not be launched from *Chikuma* and *Tone* he should have ordered up other aircraft. This might have enabled him to strike the first blow instead of taking it.

Nor should he have launched an attack from all four carriers. If he had launched his Midway strike from two carriers and held the other two in reserve he might still have fought off the American dive bombers.

As soon as he knew that the American task force included a carrier, he should have launched every plane he had to attack her even without fighter protection. For he did not have the right to count upon the Americans not attacking him, especially while all his planes were on board being refuelled and re-armed.

Yamaguchi's assessment of this crucial situation was correct. As soon as he heard about the American carriers he attacked at once. Although his own carrier, *Hiryu*, was sunk, he also sank *Yorktown*. This made it one for one.

With all his big carriers gone, even Yamamoto's normally cool judgment seems to have deserted him. The idea of a daylight bombardment of Midway was stupid and desperate. It was the sort of idea that Admiral Nagano, sitting in Tokyo, feared most. Ugaki was right to oppose it.

But was there really nothing left except retreat? Even with the carriers gone, was defeat still certain? The Americans had two carriers left. In spite of Nagumo's alarmist signals, Yamamoto must have been fairly certain that the Americans had no extra carriers to throw into the battle.

On the other hand he had. Kakuda in the Aleutians had two undamaged carriers. Two more, *Zuiho* and *Hosho*, were with his surface fleet.

Why did Yamamoto first cancel the Aleutians operation, then put it on again? Why did he not order Kakuda to join the Midway fleet and forget the Aleutians? Admittedly it would have taken some time to make the rendezvous but, adding Kakuda's two carriers to *Zuiho* and *Hosho*, Yamamoto could have formed a new and formidable four-carrier force which might easily have overwhelmed the Americans who had lost *Yorktown*. Instead, he inexplicably and suddenly acknowledged defeat.

Perhaps Yamamoto's main error was putting to sea at all. He flew his flag in *Yamato* in accordance with the Japanese navy's outworn tradition that the commander-in-chief's duty was to be in the battle. This had no more place in modern warfare than that of a general leading the charge at the head of his troops.

Admiral Nimitz recognized this and stayed ashore. He directed the historic battle from his headquarters at Pearl Harbor. His opponent, afloat in *Yamato*, kept radio silence, afraid of giving away his position. This meant that Yamamoto was unable to communicate with his carriers at the most vital time. If he had been ashore as Nimitz was, he could have maintained close control and given his own leadership throughout the battle.

Apart from Yamamoto's mistakes there is no doubt Nimitz had a priceless advantage. Midway was won by Intelligence. Yamamoto, attempting surprise, was himself surprised. The American code-crackers knew nearly all his moves in advance. Yet even with this ample warning Nimitz was only able to rush three carriers to the scene in time. If he had not been able to read Yamamoto's coded messages he would have had no idea where to send them to intercept the Japanese carriers.

Also, the American forces remained closely concentrated throughout the battle, always showing their maximum strength. This was not the result of brilliance or superior strategy. It was largely dictated by the needs of a smaller and more desperate force.

The other great advantage the Americans had at Midway was that their ships were equipped with radar. This enabled them to receive advance warning of air attack. The Japanese navy lacked this equipment. They did not see the American bombers until a lookout screamed a warning.

Although the Americans showed a much surer touch than in the Coral Sea and their pilots fought with the utmost gallantry, they still had a lot to learn. Better tracking by scout planes and more rapid communications would have turned Yamamoto's defeat into an even greater disaster. With better information Spruance would have realized much earlier that Yamamoto was retreating, and so his final chase after the battle could have done a great deal more damage. As it was, except for *Mikuma*, Yamamoto's big warships escaped practically unscathed.

In spite of the great victory two points emerged which gave the U.S. Pacific Fleet little joy:

1. More determined and prompt damage control might have saved *Yorktown*.

2. The inferiority of American planes was again clearly demonstrated.

Despite the staggering Japanese loss of four carriers, there still remained no doubt that the Zeke's performance exceeded that of any American fighter. The salvage of one intact in the Aleutians was going to redress that balance—but it would take time. Japanese Val dive bombers and Kate torpedo bombers were also at the time two of the world's best aircraft at their jobs.

On the other hand until Midway the Japanese had little regard for the American navy. They had regarded the Coral Sea as a flash in the pan. That is one reason why they were unprepared for the American pilots' courageous attacks. The loss of four aircraft carriers underlined the gravity of their navy's smashing victories across the Pacific and Asia.

The sinking of the big carriers was a blow to *Teikoku Kaigun*— the sea army—from which it never fully recovered. They represented forty-three per cent of the tonnage of Japanese carriers in operation. Even worse was the loss of veteran pilots and the skilled maintenance crews who went down with their ships. From a fighting point of view they represented more than fifty per cent of Japanese carrier strength. It was the most important consequence of the battle.

Only six months after Pearl Harbor the victorious over-confident Japanese navy had suffered a gigantic defeat. With four of his highly mobile carriers sunk, Yamamoto would have to adopt a cautious defensive strategy.

Perhaps the most bitter aspect of the disaster for Yamamoto was the knowledge that it was Japan's first major defeat at sea for 300 years—since the Korean Yi Sun-sin beat the Japanese at the end of the sixteenth century.

The result of Midway was an overwhelming victory for America. Whichever way the Japanese looked at the balance sheet it still read the same. They had sunk the carrier *Yorktown* and the destroyer *Hamman*. But they had lost four carriers and a heavy cruiser, *Mikuma*.

The United States lost 150 planes in this savage battle. But when the Japanese carriers went down their aircraft losses added up to 322 —just over twice the number.

Only 307 Americans died in the battle but 3,500 Japanese sailors, including more than a hundred first-line pilots, lost their lives. The carrier casualties alone were: *Akagi*, 221 killed; *Kaga*, 800; *Hiryu*, 416; *Soryu*, 718.

The crucial five minutes which led to the death of his carriers is perhaps best described in the bleak, understated prose of Nagumo's own report:

On 4 June a *Chikuma* plane failed to sight a large enemy force which should have been sighted. The weather was no friend to our search planes because the enemy was obscured by clouds. When the enemy attack came from behind the clouds it placed us in a very disadvantageous position.

A Morning in April

22

Commander Okamura Lands at Lunga

AT the time of the Coral Sea battle an event took place which no one regarded as important. Yet it was finally to prove as decisive as Midway itself.

A small Japanese naval party, led by Lieutenant-Commander Okamura, landed at the little-used anchorage at Lunga Point on Guadalcanal in the Solomons archipelago. His troops were ludicrously under-equipped to take over the island. Their only arms, apart from rifles, were two old howitzers and three machine-guns. A similar tiny force was landed at Tulagi on the smaller Florida Island in the same Solomons group. Imperial Headquarters regarded the seizure of Guadalcanal and Florida as a local operation of little consequence and did not bother to develop the airstrip.

When Yamamoto was pushed back from Midway he began to look upon Guadalcanal as a vital base from which to attack the Allies. For Guadalcanal, 200 miles south of the equator, is only 1,200 miles from Australia. It was Japan's most southerly conquest. From this small Pacific island he could command the air and sea in the South Pacific and around the north Australian coastline.

Yamamoto began to regard his small naval landing force not as a token, but as a spearhead. From Guadalcanal Japanese planes could cover his warships and transports as they rounded New Guinea to strike at Port Moresby, the Allied stronghold guarding Australia. Bombers based on Guadalcanal could also attack the New Hebrides, New Caledonia and Fiji.

After his defeat at Midway, Yamamoto moved quickly. He ordered some of Colonel Kiyono Ichiki's troops, who had never reached Midway, to land on the island with orders to build a dirt-and-coral airstrip between the two rivers on the north shore.

Even the normally uncomplaining Japanese soldiers hated the place. Guadalcanal, a small island ninety miles long and twenty-five miles wide, looks like a picture-book tropical island. Fringes of coconut palms nod on the sandy beaches, while behind them jungly mountains and quiescent volcanoes rise up to 7,000 feet. In spite of its romantic appearance, it is a very unpleasant and unhealthy spot. The fever-carrying anopheles mosquito breeds in the lagoons, swamps and sluggish streams. The coastal plain at the foot of the central mountains is a boot-sucking morass of dark, steamy, rotting jungle and malarial mud.

Few people had put into its remote harbour since February 1568 when Don Alvaro Mendana first planted the standard of the King of Spain upon this insalubrious island. When the Spaniards left the Pacific it became a British possession.

It was exactly a month after Midway—on 4 July 1942—when a Flying Fortress returning from a mission was blown by a storm off-course towards Guadalcanal. As the plane flew over the island at 23,000 feet her observer took a few photographs on the off-chance.

When these routine pictures were developed, staff officers in Admiral Nimitz's headquarters were astonished at what they revealed. Not only had the Japanese landed troops on Guadalcanal, they were hacking a landing strip out of the jungle. As the Americans studied the photographs, they rapidly appreciated that a Japanese airfield on this little-known Pacific island would be an excellent base for attacking American supply lines in the Pacific. Equally, if America held it, Guadalcanal would be an excellent starting point from which to begin pushing the Japanese back to Tokyo.

It was quickly decided that the first American counter-attack in the Pacific must be made against this island. It had only one aim—to halt the Japanese advance towards Australia. The battle of the Coral Sea had been the first episode in this campaign.

Once the decision was taken events moved rapidly. At the beginning of August, only a month after the Fortress had photographed the airstrip, the First Marine Division was ready to land on Guadalcanal. Nimitz thought this force of Marines would be ample to overwhelm the small Japanese garrison. Like Imperial Headquarters in Tokyo, he saw Guadalcanal as a minor operation which could easily be completed within a week or so. In fact it was to develop into a five-month series of savage major battles on land, sea and air between Americans and Japanese.

Yamamoto realized it was only a matter of time before the Americans discovered he had grabbed Guadalcanal. But he was determined to fight for it because an American air base in the Solomons must challenge his command of the South Pacific which he had built up in eight months of war. He decided to wait and see what the American moves would be. He had much less time to wait than he anticipated.

At night on 7 August a huge convoy with 11,000 U.S. Marines made its way slowly and silently through the Sealark Channel between Guadalcanal and Florida Island to the harbour of Tulagi in the very heart of the Solomons. Cruising in the area, under the command of Admiral Frank Jack Fletcher, were the carriers *Hornet*, *Wasp* and *Enterprise*, and the new battleship *North Carolina*.

At dawn three heavy American cruisers, *Quincy*, *Vincennes* and *Astoria*, and the Australian *Canberra*, steamed towards Guadalcanal. All they could see were coconut palms and white sandy beaches studded with deserted huts. Suddenly the calm of a Pacific morning was shattered as shells and bombs exploded along a fifteen-mile stretch of beach. Not one Japanese shore battery replied and there was only occasional sporadic machine-gun fire. This was because the Ichiki battalion had little else. When the cruiser bombardment of the beaches commenced, Ichiki's men fled to dug-outs and caves in the hills, where they remained watchful and quiet, waiting for the Americans to advance.

In the middle of a typical steamy Solomons morning the American Marines singing their battle hymn began to land on the beaches. On the first day the Marines made no attempt to push on. They spread only a little way through the coconut groves and tall grass to form a perimeter while waiting for their tanks and tractors to land. They slept that night under palm trees in heavy tropical rain, alert for a Japanese counter-attack which never came. Next day they began to climb the steep cliffs and dark, jungle-covered hills hauling machine-guns behind them. It took them two hours to cover a mile.

Then on one hillside they ran into a series of machine-gun nests hidden in limestone caves. Ichiki had begun his murderous defence. Marines slithered forward under a rain of machine-gun fire trying to throw grenades into the mouths of the caves. Other Marines took a hill upon which stood the old British Residency and captured a cricket field just below it.

Ichiki's snipers were now behind every rock and hidden in every tree. The Marines fought their way forward to a ravine honeycombed with pill boxes and dug-outs. This was the main Japanese defence line. Every time they tried to inch forward, annihilating fire poured down upon them. They dug in and waited until reinforcements arrived.

This was the first indication of the kind of desperate opposition the U.S. Marines were to face in the Solomon Islands. The Japanese soldiers, trained to fight the Russians, had little opinion of the American troops. Cheated of a chance to meet them at Midway, they now believed they could easily drive the Marines off Guadalcanal. They felt this was their long-awaited opportunity to prove their superiority.

In the middle of this fierce fighting the American Marines had one surprise visitor. A man wearing crumpled drill walked out of the jungle and greeted them in an impeccable British accent. He was Captain Martin Clemens, the British Commissioner for Guadalcanal, who had been hidden by the islanders when the Japanese invaded.

Thirty-six hours after the U.S. Marines began to move inwards on Florida and Guadalcanal they captured the landing strip and renamed it Henderson Field—after Major Lofton Henderson, hero of the Midway glide-bomb attack.

When he received news of the big American convoy moving across the Pacific, Yamamoto ordered Admiral Nobutake Kondo's Second Fleet and Nagumo's carriers to Rabaul. He was still not yet sure of the Americans' destination. As soon as he heard of the American landings in the Solomons he sailed to Truk from the Inland Sea. On board his flagship *Yamato* in Truk atoll he followed the American moves with something approaching glee. The scattered Solomon Islands were a heaven-sent battleground for his long-sought naval war of attrition against the United States. This could be his revenge for Midway. When the Americans were really committed, he would move into the attack. As a first move he ordered Vice-Admiral Gunichi Mikawa to sail with five heavy cruisers and two light cruisers to attack them.

When Yamamoto ordered Mikawa to hoist his red-and-blue striped flag aboard the cruiser *Chokai* and sail to Guadalcanal the long campaign in the Solomons began.

At six o'clock in the evening of the day after the marines landed Admiral Frank Jack Fletcher, who had lost *Lexington* in the Coral Sea and *Yorktown* at Midway, began to feel increasingly uneasy about the number of Japanese bombers operating over the Solomons. He asked Nimitz if he could withdraw his carriers. They were running short of fuel but he also rightly suspected the wily Yamamoto had brought most of his remaining carriers into the area. He was afraid he might launch a surprise attack on the vulnerable American carriers.

When the carriers sailed, taking the new battleship *North Carolina* with them, they left behind Rear-Admiral Richmond Kelly Turner with five cruisers to protect the Marines. With the departure of the three carriers, Turner was left, in his own picturesque phrase, 'bare arse'. General Vandegrift, commanding the Marines on Guadalcanal, also felt unhappy and naked without air cover. He was particularly disturbed because more than half the supplies of his First Marine Division were still in the ships' holds.

Mikawa's ships sailing at top speed towards Guadalcanal were sighted by an Australian Hudson scout plane. For some inexplicable reason, it maintained radio silence and continued its search before returning to base to report. This mistake enabled Mikawa's cruisers to approach undetected under the cover of darkness. On Guadalcanal, the Marines were asleep in caves dug into the sides of the hills or in hammocks slung between coconut palms. It was so quiet that sailors aboard the cruisers anchored in Sealark Channel could hear the birds calling ashore over the lapping of the waves.

At 1.30 a.m. came the noise of unidentified planes flying overhead. They were seaplanes catapulted by Mikawa's cruisers. Just before reaching Savo Island one plane from his flagship *Chokai* dropped flares right over the Marine transports. Sheltering behind this sudden blinding glare, Mikawa's cruisers raced at twenty-six knots past the American guard destroyers, *Ralph Talbot* and *Blue*. Fifty Japanese guns were trained on the two unsuspecting American destroyers as they slipped past, but the Americans did not see them. After dodging the destroyers, Mikawa sighted Allied ships between Savo and Cape Esperance. When the roar of planes overhead became louder bugles blew aboard the American cruisers. Then came the order through loudspeakers, 'All hands man your battle stations!'

Suddenly Japanese searchlights lit up the American cruisers and shells began to smash into them. The Americans, taken by complete surprise, had no time to fight back. Sailors, blinded and dazed by Mikawa's sudden searchlights, stumbled half-asleep out of their bunks. As the first great explosions reverberated from the sea the Marines on Guadalcanal hastily sprang to arms.

As they did so, crash after crash of explosions made tongues of red flames in the night sky. Hundreds of sailors were flung into the water, some dead, some wounded, some miraculously unhurt.

Then torpedoes began to race across the dark waters. One struck the cruiser *Chicago* and knocked off part of her bow. Twenty shells slashed open the Australian cruiser *Canberra*. Then two torpedoes hit her and she caught fire, developing a ten-degree list. In five minutes she was finished.

Chicago switched on her searchlights to find the Japanese ships but they only lit up empty black seas. The battle had already moved away, leaving her alone and lost.

Mikawa's cruisers were steaming towards the rest of the American ships now lit up by dozens of flares dropped by Japanese aircraft. As they floated overhead, white and brilliant, it was light enough to read a newspaper on the decks of the American cruisers.

Astoria was hit by *Chokai* torpedoes and shells and caught fire. She tried to stagger away at seven knots. Then the Japanese cruiser *Aoba* turned her searchlights onto *Quincy*. Before the horrified crew could man their guns a rain of shells crashed into her. She flailed round crazily and at 2.35 a.m. flung her stern high and went to the bottom. A salvo from the cruiser *Kako* hit *Vincennes* and she too caught fire. The Japanese ships switched off their searchlights as she was so brightly ablaze they could not miss her. Three torpedoes from *Chokai* slammed into her port side and she heeled over and sank forty-five minutes after *Quincy*. Then a Japanese destroyer raced round turning its searchlights on the water and started shooting at American sailors clinging to life rafts.

An hour after he arrived Mikawa disappeared as quickly and as silently as he had come. American destroyers patrolled all night trying to pick up survivors floating in the shark-infested channel. The water was not cold and a couple of men started singing. But the sharks were about. During that nightmare night destroyers constantly machine-gunned the water to drive sharks away from the life rafts. The macabre scene was lit up by flames from the listing *Canberra* which burnt all night. At dawn they picked up the rest of the survivors swimming or clinging to wreckage in the oily waters.

Canberra was still afloat in the morning but so badly damaged she was sunk by American torpedoes. *Astoria* was barely afloat with men trapped below decks. Rescue parties tried to reach them as the ship slid lower and lower in the water. At 11 a.m. water was lapping her decks. Then at midday her magazines exploded and she gave a last lurch. Most of the men on deck managed to jump clear. Fifteen minutes later she heeled over to port and disappeared with a hiss of steam under the sea.

The battle of Savo Island was one of the worst defeats suffered by the American navy, which had been caught completely off balance. In addition to the four cruisers lost, the cruiser *Chicago* and the destroyers *Ralph Talbot* and *Patterson* were damaged. The only damage the Japanese suffered was the destruction of the operations room of Mikawa's flagship, *Chokai*.

In spite of his devastating surprise attack which had destroyed four American cruisers with no loss to himself, Mikawa's victory was not as complete as it might have been. Like every other Japanese admiral after Midway, he was over-cautious about air attacks. Fear of a dawn swoop by Fletcher's three carriers, which he knew to be near Guadalcanal, made him turn away immediately after his attack. He was also obeying the Japanese naval tradition of attacking warships not transports.

With their protecting cruisers nearly all at the bottom of the sea the marine transports in Sealark Channel were defenceless. Most of the Marine reinforcements and supplies were in these ships. Mikawa could have sunk them without any interference. If he had done this, he would effectively have halted American operations in the South Pacific. He would have left the First Marine Division in a serious plight, low on food and ammunition and an easy prey to an Ichiki counter-attack. But instead of sinking them before he left, Mikawa led his cruisers away from Savo and steamed fast back to his base in Rabaul.

Next day the Americans had a slight revenge for the Savo disaster. Off New Ireland an American submarine, *S-44*, commanded by Lieutenant-Commander John R. Moore, caught up with the Japanese cruiser *Kako* and sank her.

Two nights after Savo the fast Japanese battleships *Kongo* and *Haruna* boosted the morale of Ichiki's troops fighting the American Marines on the island by bombarding Henderson Field with their fourteen-inch guns for one and a half hours. They inflicted great damage. This, coupled with Mikawa's attack, set the naval pattern for the Solomons. After that scarcely a day passed when there were not Japanese air raids or bombardments from the sea. Off-shore duels between American bombers and Japanese warships continued incessantly. Most of the Japanese fury was aimed at Henderson Field, where the Marines protecting the airstrip now held a line eight miles in length and five in depth.

Here was fought the battle of the bulldozers. The pace at which the Americans completed Henderson Field, in spite of continual bombardment, astonished the Japanese. Only a week after the Marines landed American planes were flying from the strip.

The bulldozer was a strange new weapon to the Japanese. They had never seen one until Wake Island fell in the first few days of the war. Before they captured it, the Japanese commander there had detailed 300 men to repair the strip. When he experimentally tried the new American machine, he found he could complete the work with a handful of men in a few hours.

Knowing that bulldozers could complete airstrips at lightning speed, Imperial Headquarters kept urging Yamamoto to take full-scale action against the American fleet off Guadalcanal to assist the hard-pressed Ichiki soldiers, who were being slowly forced back yard by yard through the malarial, insect-infested jungle.

Yamamoto refused to give the order for a full-scale naval battle. The most he would do was to issue a 'local decision order' to Naval Headquarters at Rabaul. This left it to Nagumo and his chief of staff, Rear-Admiral Ryunosuke Kusaka, to decide when to sail for battle in Guadalcanal waters, and simply let Nagumo know the wishes of Imperial Headquarters and the opinion of the Combined Fleet.

Why did Yamamoto, usually so decisive in his orders, behave in this seemingly vacillating fashion? It was because after the Midway débâcle he did not wish to risk a full-scale battle with his remaining carriers against Fletcher's big three which he knew were lurking near the Solomons waiting to pounce—unless an opportunity presented itself for a carrier battle which he was certain to win. Instead, he planned to destroy the U.S. fleet piecemeal by a process of attrition. This could only be done, little by little, in small engagements fought at the time and place chosen by the Japanese admiral on the spot. He was confident that his sailors and ships would prove better than the American in this kind of battle. He was not prepared to risk his fleet except to reinforce Guadalcanal. This was already urgently necessary, as not only was the airstrip in American hands but most of Ichiki's men had been killed trying to defend it.

On 24 August four Japanese transports, carrying 1,500 men of the Second Echelon of the Ichiki force together with the Yokusuka Fifth

Special Naval Landing Force, sailed from Rabaul. Yamamoto realized the Americans would mount an all-out attack as soon as they sighted this convoy. To protect the remainder of the Ichiki regiment on its voyage to Guadalcanal he brought up every available Japanese warship. He knew he must risk a major battle because if he could not reinforce Guadalcanal he had lost it.

In spite of his Midway losses he could still bring together a formidable armada. The carriers *Shokaku, Zuikaku* and *Ryujo* were commanded once again by Admiral Nagumo, now recovered from his Midway disaster. They were accompanied by Rear-Admiral Abe's battleships *Hiei* and *Kirishima*, the heavy cruisers *Kumano, Suzuya, Tone* and *Chikuma*, with the light cruiser *Nagara* and fourteen destroyers. This fleet was to refuel at sea, and *Ryujo* with the cruiser *Tone* was to act as a diversionary group under Rear-Admiral Hara of the Coral Sea to lure the Americans away from the transports.

The day before Ichiki's reinforcements sailed from Rabaul, Admiral Fletcher with the three American carriers *Wasp, Enterprise* and *Saratoga* cruising a hundred miles south-east of Guadalcanal was given a false report which led him to believe the Japanese warships were returning to Truk. So he felt safe in detaching *Wasp* for refuelling. This left him only *Enterprise* and *Saratoga*, plus one battleship, four cruisers and ten destroyers, to face three Japanese carriers with a slight preponderance of other ships.

Wasp had already sailed away when an American scout plane sighted the Japanese carriers. It shadowed them for an hour and a half, and, as it departed, dropped a bomb which fell between *Zuikaku* and *Shokaku*. Shortly afterwards a second scout plane dived out of the clouds and dropped a bomb on *Zuikaku*'s flight deck. At the same time Japanese scout planes found *Enterprise* and *Saratoga* 250 miles away.

The second big naval engagement of the Pacific war, the Battle of the Eastern Solomons, was a replica of Midway. Once again it was a carrier battle of planes against ships. Surface craft did not exchange a shot.

At 2 p.m. the first attack group of sixty-seven planes, commanded by Lieutenant-Commander Seki, took off from the Japanese carriers. It was quickly followed by a second wave of forty-eight planes under Lieutenant-Commander Murata, but his pilots made a navigational error and failed to find the Americans.

Seki's aircraft, however, hit *Enterprise*. One bomb bored into the hangar deck and thirty seconds later another bomb hit the same spot. A third bomb fell on the flight deck. As smoke billowed in huge columns and flames began to lick along her decks, *Enterprise* looked as though she were finished. But the now-expert American fire squads quickly brought the flames under control and she was soon making twenty-four knots and able to land planes.

The Japanese pilots gleefully reported they had sunk *Hornet* and avenged Doolittle's April air raid on Tokyo. They made further exaggerated claims that they had sunk, or heavily damaged, three carriers, one battleship and five heavy cruisers. The American announcement simply said, 'Some losses'.

The Japanese losses were not slight. The 20,000-ton *Ryujo* was found by the American planes exactly as Yamamoto had anticipated. They swooped down on her and sent her very quickly to the bottom. *Zuikaku*'s flight deck had been damaged by the scout plane's bomb and *Shokaku* suffered minor damage. Seventy planes and trained crews were lost. On the American side the carrier *Enterprise* was damaged and twenty American planes were missing. But Yamamoto's hope that he could beat off the American fleet had not materialized.

It was a timid, indecisive action. Admirals on both sides had too many recent memories of the Coral Sea and Midway to take all-out risks. As darkness fell Admiral Fletcher withdrew, expecting to resume the battle next day. But the Japanese, with one carrier sunk and another damaged, felt unable to carry on the fight. By next morning they were out of range. They did not know that Fletcher, apart from the damaged *Enterprise*, had only the carrier *Saratoga* left.

Although the carrier battle was not resumed all next day, Marine dive bombers and B.17s continued to attack the Japanese transports as they tried to reach Guadalcanal. At noon the ships carrying Ichiki's reinforcements, unable to stand up to the bombardment any longer, changed course to follow their carriers away from Guadalcanal.

They returned under the cover of darkness and landed 1,500 fresh troops. But this slight delay gave the American Marines much-needed time to strengthen their defences before the reinforced Japanese attacked them.

This first attempt to reinforce Guadalcanal was only the start. Further determined Japanese attempts led to months of hard fighting with small naval and air actions nearly every day. The vastness of area to be fought over, the Pacific with its scattered island chains, meant that big fleets ceased to exist as operational units. The opposing Pacific fleets began to function as strategic pools. Task forces were detached from them as the need arose.

After the East Solomons battle this bitter struggle went in favour of Yamamoto. Not only did it look as though his policy of nibbling attrition was working out, but luck began to swing to his side. For the first time since the beginning of the war Japanese submarines struck some telling blows. On the last day of August the carrier *Saratoga*, which had come undamaged out of the East Solomons battle, was patrolling near the Santa Cruz Islands when she was hit by a Japanese torpedo. After emergency repairs the crippled carrier sailed for Pearl Harbor. Her damage was so extensive that she remained there for three months.

A fortnight later, on 15 September, the carrier *Wasp* also patrolling off the Solomons was sighted at 2.20 p.m. by the Japanese submarine *I-19*, commanded by Lieutenant Takaichi Kinashi. He fired four torpedoes and three hit her in quick succession. Soon yellow flames enveloped her and she developed a heavy starboard list. *Wasp*, burning and exploding, sank at nine o'clock. The battleship *North Carolina* escorting *Wasp* was hit by Kinashi's fourth torpedo and forced to limp back to Pearl Harbor. In three weeks *Enterprise* and *Saratoga* had been put out of action and *Wasp* sunk. This meant that the American South Pacific carrier strength was reduced to one— *Hornet*.

No major battle was fought for nearly two months after this. Nimitz could not afford to risk any more ships and Yamamoto was biding his time. But one urgent, growing problem began to face him. By October there were 15,000 Japanese troops on Guadalcanal who were suffering not only from constant American attacks, but from malaria and malnutrition. The American fleet had such an iron grip on the waters round the island that it was becoming daily more difficult to supply them. Yamamoto would not imperil his ships in daylight as they might be sunk by the growing numbers of American land-based bombers. Yet they must have help.

He started a series of destroyer 'grocery' runs to bring in supplies. On moonless nights, Japanese supply-carrying destroyers began to steam to Guadalcanal at full speed in the hope of avoiding attack. The Americans nicknamed them the Tokyo Night Express.

At midnight a destroyer would arrive at a designated point on the beach. Slung along its gunwales were provisions in metal drums. As it neared shallow waters, the ropes were cut and the drums dropped overboard. At the same time other Japanese warships would start bombarding Guadalcanal to draw attention away from the destroyer's activities. As the destroyer made a fast turn to scuttle back to her base in Bougainville, parties of Japanese soldiers, either in small boats or swimming, seized the ropes and hauled the provisions up on the beach. They worked feverishly to drag the drums ashore before daylight. For as soon as dawn broke, American planes and patrol boats began to machine-gun the working parties.

By day the Japanese destroyers remained anchored in Shortland Bay at Bougainville where they were continually bombed by American planes. When the frequent air-raid alarms sounded they got under way, swinging their bows violently to avoid bombs. The commander of the destroyer squadron, Admiral Tomiji Koyanagi, nicknamed the manœuvres the 'bon dance' after the Japanese festival where swinging lantern dances were performed. So regular were the bombings that the Japanese referred to them as *teikibin*—scheduled trips.

Yet these heavy daily air attacks did not prevent the destroyer operations being a great success. Yamamoto, who knew he must supply the Guadalcanal troops at all costs, estimated half his destroyers would be lost in these trips. His pessimistic prediction did not come true. Not one ship was damaged in the Night Express operation. The reason was that small fast destroyers make a poor target.

The Tokyo Night Express was working well. It could deliver troops and provisions in comparative safety every dark night. Yet it had one disadvantage. It could not carry the heavy equipment or large supplies of ammunition that 15,000 troops needed.

One immovable obstacle impeded Ichiki's men, however bravely they fought or however daringly Yamamoto's destroyers ran in supplies. It was Henderson airfield.

In mid-October Yamamoto decided that he must make a concentrated effort to destroy it. At the same time, the Americans realized the situation could not continue as it was. They were desperate to stop the flow of Japanese reinforcements to Guadalcanal and the fierce nightly bombardments which accompanied them.

They, in their turn, needed to reinforce the island. Rear-Admiral Norman Scott was ordered to sail with his flagship, the cruiser *San Francisco*, and with *Salt Lake City*, the two light cruisers *Boise* and *Helena*, and five destroyers to escort a convoy carrying the 164th American Infantry Division to Guadalcanal.

Just after noon on 11 October American patrol planes sighted Japanese cruisers sailing southwards through the Slot towards Guadalcanal. This was Rear-Admiral Aritomo Goto with the cruisers *Aoba*, *Kinugasa* and *Furutaka* on his way to try and neutralize Henderson Field and pave the way for the landing of troops and supplies. At dusk the ships, the strongest Japanese naval force assembled for two months, were again sighted 110 miles from Guadalcanal.

Admiral Norman Scott sailed to intercept them. At eleven o'clock that night, as Scott's ships neared the channel between Cape Esperance and Savo, the radar screens on *Boise* and *Helena* showed five Japanese ships 18,000 yards away. At the same time search planes from *San Francisco* reported a Japanese transport and two destroyers in Sealark Channel.

The third naval battle of the Solomons, Cape Esperance, began under a new moon, thirteen minutes before midnight. Scott decided to attack the large force of cruisers and destroyers and let the transports escape. The battle began when *Helena* opened fire with her six-inch battery, followed by *Salt Lake City* and *Boise*. Goto's ships were caught completely by surprise.

It was a savage, close-range battle fought in darkness in the narrow waters. The men on Henderson Field, manning their guns, watched as the flames of the short, fierce fight lit the sky. Before the Japanese could recover, the American ships were able to execute the classic naval manœuvre of crossing the T. This meant that each ship was able to fire as it came forward on the top of the T, while the Japanese ships in a single line making the down-stroke screened one another's fire.

The Japanese destroyer *Fubaki* blew up and sank at once. Rear-Admiral Goto, who had commanded the transports at Midway, was killed aboard his flagship *Aoba* when a shell burst near the bridge. At once Captain Kikunori Kijima took command, but *Aoba* was hit forty-four times and caught fire and sank. The shells also smashed into the heavy cruiser *Furutaka*, but she managed to crawl away to sink later. When an American destroyer found her wreckage there were only a few sailors swimming in an oil-streaked sea. The cruiser *Kinugasa*, also damaged by shell fire, was the only survivor.

Shortly after midnight, after only thirty-four minutes of savage, bloody fighting, the remaining Japanese ships sailed away. They left the destroyers *Marukamo* and *Natsumo* standing by to rescue their sailors struggling in the water. Next morning, while they were still taking survivors aboard, the two destroyers were sunk by dive bombers from Henderson Field. The American destroyer *Duncan* also sank during the day. During the night battle she had pulled in too close in order to fire torpedoes at the Japanese cruisers and was hit by Americans as well as the enemy.

Apart from *Duncan* Scott's losses were light. The seriously damaged *Boise* had to return to Philadelphia for a refit and *Salt Lake City* went to Pearl Harbor for repairs. But the Americans had had their revenge for the first naval battle at Savo where they had fared so badly.

The Tokyo Night Express was interrupted but not stopped. It was, however, useless for the heavy reinforcements which Yamamoto was still determined to land. Forty-eight hours after the Cape Esperance battle American planes sighted more Japanese warships and transports 260 miles away. As a preliminary softening up for the landing of these reinforcements, Yamamoto again sent his two big battleships, *Haruna* and *Kongo*, to slam Henderson Field with their fourteen-inch guns. They sailed unchallenged at night into Sealark Channel. After a plane dropped flares to illuminate the target area, their great guns opened fire. In eighty minutes they fired 918 shells on Henderson Field. The warships reported, 'The airfield is a sea of flames with explosions seen everywhere.'

They did not exaggerate. By the time the shelling ceased, forty-one Americans were dead and most of their aircraft damaged. Relays of Japanese bombers started to raid the field after the shelling ceased. Bombs dropped every few minutes until dawn. When the survivors climbed out of their foxholes, the field was a total wreck. Wrecked planes, torn and burnt clothing and dead men were everywhere. Among the bomb craters they found the jagged noses of shells, fourteen inches in diameter, from the big Japanese guns. The smashed strip could no longer be used by B.17 bombers. Even if they were able to land, Japanese warships and aircraft on guard in Sealark Channel could easily prevent American cargo ships bringing in further supplies of aviation fuel.

While the bombers continued their raids, *Kongo* and *Haruna* shepherded the Japanese transports towards the northern shore. At dawn they landed large reinforcements, including artillery, only a few miles from American troops. American planes attacked them and set fire to three transports, but most of the fresh troops so badly needed to reinforce the 15,000 Japanese already on the island, landed safely. The new men went straight into action with their artillery. At dawn next morning they were shelling the American positions.

It was this determined reinforcement, added to the normal fierce and continual Japanese activity, which gave the Americans the final warning that Yamamoto was determined to hold Guadalcanal. They now realized he did not regard it as a savage but small local defensive engagement, but as a vital major battle. As they began preparing to meet his threat big switches took place in the High Command in the South Pacific. A few days after the battle of Cape Esperance, Admiral William F. (Bull) Halsey Jr, America's best and most experienced carrier commander, was appointed commander of the South-west Pacific Area.

Intelligence reports had already warned Nimitz that the Japanese effort appeared to be 'all-out'. In some ways his plight was worse than before Midway. The carriers *Enterprise* and *Saratoga*, and the battleship *North Carolina*, were still in Pearl Harbor for repairs after their torpedo and bomb damage. Nimitz ordered rush work on *Enterprise* just as he had on *Yorktown* before Midway. Less than a week after the battle of Cape Esperance, she was able to sail out of Pearl Harbor with *South Dakota* and nine destroyers.

Yamamoto was also moving. He sent a staff officer by Tokyo Express destroyer to discuss details of a plan to seize Henderson Field which had been put forward by General Hyakutake, the Japanese commander in charge of Guadalcanal land operations. Yamamoto agreed that Hyakutake should send the Japanese 28th Division, commanded by Lieutenant-General Tadayoshi Sano, to reinforce the Guadalcanal garrison and retake Henderson Field. The only problem was that the division's heavy equipment could not go by Tokyo Express. It would have to force its way through the American ring in transports escorted by battleships.

Yamamoto knew this move must provoke a major battle. To prepare for it he organized two separate task forces. One was to bombard and neutralize Henderson Field. The other task force was to escort the transports from Rabaul to Guadalcanal. As the Japanese reinforcement division began assembling in the harbours between Buin and Rabaul the ships of the Combined Fleet gathered to give them their fullest support.

Admiral Nagumo commanded five carriers, *Zuiho*, *Junyo*, *Hiyo*, *Zuikaku* and *Shokaku*. In addition Vice-Admiral Kondo had four battleships, *Haruna* and *Kongo* which had just been equipped with search radar, and *Kirishima* and *Hiei*, with nine cruisers and twenty-eight destroyers.

The Americans were also assembling their battle fleet. The hastily repaired *Enterprise* with *South Dakota* joined *Hornet* with six cruisers and fourteen destroyers. This two-carrier task force was commanded by Rear-Admiral Thomas G. Kinkaid.

As Yamamoto's fleet sailed, the Japanese pilots below on the mess decks listened to the Hawaiian radio which said, 'Tomorrow is 25 October, Navy Day, and everyone will hear of a big present to the American nation.' They rushed to tell the chief of staff that in their view the Americans were preparing a big attack.

Just after dawn on 26 October an American patrol plane from *Enterprise* found Yamamoto's huge fleet cruising near Santa Cruz Island. At the same time a Japanese plane found *Hornet* 200 miles away. *Zuikaku*, *Shokaku* and *Zuiho* began launching sixty-five planes. Once again the battle was aircraft against ships.

It was nine o'clock and *Enterprise* was hidden under a rain squall but *Hornet* was plainly visible when the Japanese Vals dived out of the sky. One of the Japanese pilots made a spectacular suicide crash and two of his bombs exploded on *Hornet*'s deck. Then torpedo attacks left her listing with her steering gone.

Twenty minutes after the Japanese planes took off, forty-eight planes had left *Hornet* and *Enterprise*. Most of them failed to find the Japanese carriers but attacked Kondo's battleships, concentrating on the cruiser *Chikuma*. She with her sixteen destroyers protecting the task force fired furiously on the American attackers.

Although only fourteen of the American planes found the Japanese carriers they did a lot of damage. They dived on *Junyo*, leaving her slightly damaged. *Zuiho* was more badly damaged and the unlucky *Shokaku* received three bombs, one in her operations room. Her returning planes had to land on her sister carrier, *Zuikaku*.

Both sides then launched a second strike. The Japanese carriers launched forty-four planes and the Americans seventy-three. Sixty miles from the American fleet two air groups passed each other. Zekes tangled with *Enterprise* Wildcats in a short sharp dogfight before they both continued towards their targets.

Hornet's aircraft found *Shokaku* and *Zuikaku* with *Zuiho* still smoking from a previous attack. Three 1,000-lb bombs landed on *Shokaku* and put her out of action for nine months. *Junyo* and *Zuikaku* were unharmed.

The second wave of Japanese planes flew over the crippled *Hornet*, now being towed by the cruiser *Northampton* at three knots. Torpedo planes from *Junyo* went down to sea level and attacked her. Helpless *Hornet* could not avoid the attack, and soon she was blazing like a torch. *Northampton* withdrew, unable to help her further.

In Truk, Yamamoto was following the battle, impatient as a caged tiger. Now that the Americans had committed all their strength this might be his big chance to avenge Midway and destroy their carriers. When he heard that *Hornet* was alone and listing badly he issued hasty orders for Japanese destroyers to race to her. She must not be sunk but towed back to Truk if possible. But when the destroyers reached her she had begun to settle so low in the water that it was obvious she was too far gone. At 1.35 p.m. on 27 October the Japanese destroyer *Arigumo* finished her off with torpedoes.

The fact that he had not been able to tow her in triumph into Tokyo Bay was one of Yamamoto's greatest disappointments. But at last he had got the carrier which had sent Doolittle's bombers over Tokyo—and it was a Japanese destroyer that had sent her to the bottom of the sea.

Enterprise, South Dakota and the light cruiser *San Juan* were also damaged in this battle in which the outnumbered Americans lost twenty planes shot down and fifty-four missing or damaged. After the battle the Japanese ships were all afloat, but three carriers were damaged. The Japanese had also lost a hundred planes. And in spite of this great battle the attempt to land Japanese reinforcements failed.

This was the turning point in naval warfare at Guadalcanal. Yamamoto never used his carriers in close support again but left Admiral Kondo's powerful fleet of battleships and cruisers to co-operate with the army fighting on Guadalcanal.

After the battle of Santa Cruz the battered Japanese carriers sailed back to Yamamoto's headquarters at Truk. They were so badly smashed that after temporary repairs he ordered Nagumo to sail them back to the Inland Sea. The battle was also Nagumo's swan song. He never fought another big carrier battle. The Japanese carriers did not go into action again until the battle of Leyte in 1944. By that time Yamamoto and Nagumo were both dead.

When Yamamoto withdrew Nagumo's fleet there were six American airstrips on Guadalcanal which made carrier operations anywhere near land far too hazardous. It was also now obvious to him that the Japanese army was not winning the battle. They could hold out for a long time but they had little chance of reconquering the island and throwing the Americans into the sea.

Also, the Imperial Navy was at last wearying of these constant battles in which they gained little and took so many losses. They felt strongly that the army was letting them down. One of Yamamoto's senior staff officers, Captain Toshikazu Ohnae, put it like this:

> While the Japanese naval air forces fought desperately in this area the army air forces were idly stationed on the continent and southern districts offering the navy no co-operation and no help. So slow were they to turn their attention to this battle area that it was not until the pattern of defeat on Guadalcanal was so obvious that evacuation problems were already under discussion that a handful of the army air force arrived in the theatre. The principal reason was that the Japanese army could not shake loose from preparations for eventual war on Russia, leaving the navy to bear the responsibility in the Pacific.

Nagumo's departure, three months after the American Marines had first landed, left Halsey's ships in almost undisputed command of the air and sea in the southern Solomons. However, in spite of Captain Ohnae's bitter summing-up, Imperial Headquarters was not going to give up Guadalcanal. At the same time as Yamamoto withdrew his battered carriers the Japanese army began to prepare for a major counter-offensive.

The Tokyo Express still continued to function. In their nightly trips to bring supplies to the Japanese garrison they showed an extraordinary mastery of navigation and evasion. But Yamamoto's admirals were becoming alarmed about the morale of the destroyer crews. They hated these taxi runs, thinking them undignified and lacking in 'face'. So Yamamoto's staff officers proposed to develop a new type of transport destroyer specially for the job which would allow the regular destroyers to return to proper combat duties.

23

Rice over Tokyo Bay

AFTER the battle of Santa Cruz the Americans were as desperate as the Japanese. They too were short of food and ammunition and were taking heavy casualties every day. In the first week of November Halsey flew to Guadalcanal with a vital decision to make. The problem was: Should he continue to fight for Guadalcanal or evacuate it? He felt he could not decide unless he made a careful on-the-spot investigation for himself. Yet he knew there was only one answer. It must be held. For if he did not stop the Japanese there the U.S. Navy would be driven out of the South Pacific for a long time to come.

Halsey promised the Marines all the support he could from the American naval forces. They were inferior to Yamamoto's but battle-experienced and efficient. For the job of holding Guadalcanal Halsey organized them into two groups. One of them, under Admiral Richmond Kelly Turner, was given the job of transporting troops and supplies to the island.

Admiral Norman Scott with a cruiser and four destroyers was to escort three more transports carrying Marines. Admiral Kinkaid's depleted carrier force consisting only of *Enterprise* was to be the long-range protection. Two cruisers and three destroyers, commanded by Rear-Admiral Daniel J. Callaghan, were to be a close escort for the convoys. The American transports arrived safely and anchored off Lunga Point at dawn on 12 November to begin discharging troops and cargo.

The Japanese were also planning to reinforce. From Henderson Field, American planes scouted over the northern waters which Japanese warships and transports must sail to approach Guadalcanal. The Japanese bases were too far away to employ similar air reconnaissance. This gave the Americans the advantage.

At 10.35 a.m. American scout planes reported two Japanese battleships with heavy cruisers and destroyers escorting transports and cargo ships towards Guadalcanal.

The Japanese fleet steaming towards Guadalcanal was led by the battleships *Hiei* and *Kirishima* with a light cruiser and fifteen destroyers. They had orders from Yamamoto to force Sealark Channel and bombard American airstrips on Guadalcanal. Under cover of this heavy bombardment fresh Japanese troops could be landed in safety.

This began the last big Solomons action—an almost continuous three-day running battle from 12 to 15 November—in which battleships participated on both sides.

By evening 90 per cent of the American supplies were unloaded and all cargo ships and transports sailed away. As the American transports withdrew and darkness fell, Admiral Callaghan and Admiral Scott hastily collected all available ships and sailed out against the vastly superior Japanese battleships. It looked like a gallant, forlorn hope as they had only two eight-inch cruisers, one six-inch cruiser, two light cruisers and eight destroyers to fight two great capital ships.

Two factors saved Callaghan's gallant little fleet. One was that the Japanese battleships carried high-explosive ammunition for their fourteen-inch guns ready for the airfield bombardments. This type of ammunition could not penetrate a cruiser's armour. The other factor was that no Japanese carriers were lurking near by because Yamamoto had withdrawn them. Planes could not swoop at dawn to destroy the survivors of a night battle.

Just after one o'clock in the morning on Friday 13 November the cruiser *Helena*'s radar located the Japanese ships 27,000 yards away. Warning was immediately transmitted to Callaghan in his flagship *San Francisco*, whose search radio was inadequate. Callaghan held his fire while American destroyers shot ahead to fire torpedoes. Suddenly the Japanese searchlights switched on, illuminating the American cruisers, and the two big Japanese battleships opened fire on them. One of the first shells hit the bridge of *Atlanta*, killing Admiral Norman Scott. Then Callaghan gave a battle order hardly heard since the days of sail, 'Odd ships commence firing to starboard, even ships to port.' The American column penetrated the Japanese ships and intermingled with them like a battle line of eighteenth-century sailing frigates. What followed was a sea battle as ancient as Salamis and, as it was fought at night, much more confused. Carriers might never have been invented.

Each American ship engaged the Japanese individually. Destroyers dodged and swung round to fire torpedoes while cruisers swerved violently to avoid them. In the darkness, spattered with a greenish light from floating star shells, yellow gun flashes, blinding search-lights and the red glow of burning ships, both sides fired on their own ships.

It was a murderous man-to-man battle in the dark narrow waters, a naval action fought at close quarters like a clash of ancient war galleys. The little destroyer *Laffey* started a duel with the big battle-ship *Hiei*, although it was difficult to make out her shadowy outline in the darkness. At one point she swung right under *Hiei*'s bow but the battleship had no ram. Then great shells smashed into *Laffey* from point-blank range and put her out of action. A torpedo hit her, and swimming survivors were killed when she exploded. A fourteen-inch salvo from *Kirishima* smashed into *San Francisco*, blowing up the bridge and killing Admiral Callaghan and her commanding officer, Captain Cassin Young.

The *San Francisco* continued to fire back at the giant *Hiei* as long as she could bring her main battery to bear. Both *Hiei* and *Kirishima*, with their searchlights switched on, threw shell after shell into the American cruiser from 8,000 yards. They had to keep their search-lights alight as they had no radar. This made the Japanese ships fool-proof targets for the smaller cruisers.

The battle became so fierce and the ships approached so near to each other that they could not depress their big guns low enough to bear. As they loomed up at one another, etched against flames of burning ships, they exchanged machine-gun fire.

The savage, confused fighting in the dark went on for an hour. Two torpedoes hit *Atlanta*, lifting her bodily out of the water. Sheets of flame ran along her decks. Several American destroyers blew up one after another like a series of giant crackers.

Hiei, having sent salvo after salvo crashing back into Callaghan's flagship, suddenly ceased fire. *San Francisco* had done for her, but during the ferocious duel she herself had received fifteen major hits from Japanese guns. She staggered out of the action.

At two o'clock the Japanese warships gave up their attempt to smash through the gallant ring of American vessels. American cruisers had stopped the big Japanese battleships once again from bombarding Henderson Field—but the cost was terrible. Out of thirteen American ships, twelve were either sunk or damaged. The cruisers *Atlanta* and *Junau*, the destroyers *Barton*, *Cushing*, *Laffey* and *Monssen* lay at the bottom of the channel. The heavy cruisers

San Francisco and *Portland* were so badly battered that as soon as it was light they limped back to Cape Esperance.

At first it looked as if the Japanese had got away very lightly with only two destroyers sunk and four damaged. Then just after dawn an American plane found the battleship *Hiei* five miles offshore trying to struggle away. She had been hit no less than eighty-five times in the battle and the only reason she was not already at the bottom was that most of the American shells were duds. She was turning in slow, crazy circles out of control and blazing from stem to stern. Planes from Henderson Field immediately took off to kill her. She was hit by six torpedoes but again they proved mostly duds. That night her crew took to the boats and scuttled her. Her sister ship *Kirishima* escaped.

Although temporarily driven off by the determined gallantry of Callaghan's cruisers, the Japanese were still determined to bring fresh troops into Guadalcanal. Two days after this fierce battle which had killed two American admirals and sunk a big Japanese battleship, eleven transports and cargo ships escorted by twelve destroyers began to approach Guadalcanal. They were carrying 7,700 troops, the main body of General Sano's 38th Division.

Admiral Kinkaid sailed with *Enterprise* towards Guadalcanal to intercept them. Although there were no reports of Japanese carriers he could not believe there were none in the battle area. He flew planes from *Enterprise* to operate temporarily from Henderson Field. This enabled *Enterprise* to steam to safety out of range of any Japanese carrier aircraft.

When *Enterprise*'s planes landed on Henderson Field, they had to be fuelled by hand. The field had still not recovered from the savage bombardment by the Japanese battleships a month before. Even now bombs had to be sweatily and painfully rolled across the muddy patched runway.

It was 8.30 a.m. on 14 November when an American plane 150 miles from Guadalcanal discovered General Sano's 38th Division transports. Their destroyer escort was commanded by one of the toughest and most determined of the Japanese admirals, Raizo Tanaka. *Enterprise*'s planes at once took off from Henderson Field to attack the convoy. The Japanese had no air cover to protect them from the Americans, and seven transports sank before dusk. The four remaining afloat steamed on towards Guadalcanal under cover of darkness.

Another very experienced Japanese admiral, Kondo, was on his way to join the battle. He was sailing back towards Guadalcanal with the battleship *Kirishima*, which had fought the Americans in the night battle forty-eight hours before, and four cruisers to protect the transports. To meet these warships Halsey sent the new battleships *Washington* and *South Dakota* with a destroyer escort, under the command of Rear-Admiral Willis A. Lee.

It was a cloudy night when Admiral Kondo in his 10,000-ton cruiser *Takao* led the way into the Slot followed by her sister cruiser *Atago* and the old battleship *Kirishima*. The sea was calm, and the Japanese and American warships were sailing on a parallel course, neither knowing the other was there. Then *Takao*'s lookouts sighted what they thought were two American cruisers. They were in fact *South Dakota* and *Washington*. It was one minute past midnight when *Washington*'s radar picked up the Japanese ships in the darkness.

Suddenly *Washington* opened fire at 18,000 yards. Japanese destroyers shot ahead while the two Japanese cruisers launched eight torpedoes each. Skimming across the calm sea the firing device in two of them went off too early. They blew up 200 yards away from the Americans. Immediately the Japanese ships switched on their searchlights and the Americans fired off star-shells.

The two Japanese cruisers swerved away after firing their torpedoes but did not open fire with their guns as they were outranged and did not want to give their position away. *Takao*, Kondo's flagship, had a lucky escape when two big shells from an American battleship struck her. One went straight through the bow without bursting, leaving only a small hole. The second hit her in the stern, making a big gap but missing her rudder.

Kirishima's great fourteen-inch guns began to boom but the Americans had her firmly clenched in the radar. Both the American battleships rained shells into her. Within a few minutes she stopped, a blazing shambles, with her steering smashed.

Four columns of smoke shot up near what the Japanese now knew were two American battleships. Kondo thought he had sunk the *South Dakota* but in fact the over-sensitive Japanese torpedoes detonated on a big bow wave as the American battleships tore ahead at full speed.

After eighty minutes it was all over. The Japanese steamed away from one of the few big battleship engagements of the Pacific war.

Only blazing, battered *Kirishima* could not make it. She was so badly damaged that two hours after she was first hit her crew scuttled her in the narrow channel. Next morning both Japanese and American battleships had disappeared from Guadalcanal.

At first Yamamoto was not too displeased at the result of the battle, as he thought Kondo had sunk *South Dakota*, a new battleship, in return for the old *Kirishima*. *South Dakota* had not sunk, but she was in a bad way. She remained afloat but had taken forty-four hits from *Kirishima*'s large-calibre shells and had to return to the United States for a complete refit.

The real importance of the battle, however, was that once again Yamamoto's warships had failed to smash Henderson Field. While this battle was going on, tenacious Admiral Tanaka had put 2,000 troops ashore, mostly from fifteen destroyers laden with reinforcements. At dawn the four surviving Japanese transports were unloading men of the 38th Division in full view of the Americans. They had no chance. The American destroyer *Meade*, the only warship remaining on the scene, leisurely shelled them without any reply. Other guns from shore and sea joined in the shelling, and bombers dived on them. By noon their hulks were sinking and burning in the shallow water surrounded by hundreds of charred, floating corpses.

The Japanese came out much the worse from this mid-November battle. Out of the 7,700 troops of General Sano's 38th Division only 3,000 managed to land on Guadalcanal. Only five tons of supplies landed with them. Another 4,000 men were drowned and 700 were picked up from the sea by Japanese destroyers after the American planes had sunk their transports. Yamamoto also lost two battleships, *Hiei* and *Kirishima*, a heavy cruiser, and three destroyers. Against this the United States lost three cruisers and seven destroyers.

Yamamoto transferred his flag to Japan's latest giant battleship, *Musashi*, to consider the results of the battle. He was not particularly worried about the loss of the two old battleships. They were expendable in this day of the aircraft carrier.

Yet the forty-eight-hour running battle in November was the most decisive of the campaign. It was the last major effort made by the Japanese to recapture Henderson Field by combined sea and ground assaults. By the end of November American forces on Guadalcanal were 39,416 men, but the Japanese were still trying to bring in more reinforcements.

The Americans were now so thick on land and sea that it was

becoming difficult for even the Tokyo Express destroyers to operate. So Yamamoto organized a 'submerged freight service' of thirty-eight submarines stripped of torpedoes. The day after the mid-November battle Yamamoto sent out his orders for this. At least one submarine a day was to make the trip to unload supplies on Guadalcanal after sunset.

All the submarine commanders were bitterly opposed to Yamamoto's supply-landing plan. The crews realized the importance of supplying Guadalcanal but they were dejected at the prospect of the task. They thought it would send their boats to the bottom. They were right.

They only dropped their protests when their admiral, at a conference held on board the submarine flagship at Truk, told them that Imperial Headquarters had ordered that the garrison must be supplied at all costs. The situation at Guadalcanal was now so critical that even surfaced submarines would find it difficult to hand over supplies. It was suggested they should try to eject them from tubes when submerged. Submarine experts at Japan's naval base at Yokusuka tried methods of firing bags of rice from torpedo tubes. None of them was successful. As a result of these experiments rice was scattered all over Tokyo Bay. For three days biscuit tins filled with rice were fired for practice. They mostly broke open. Then a scheme was tried in which rubber containers were released from the deck. The rubber bags burst and the rice became soaked in water and uneatable. It was finally decided to use drums which could be released from the submerged submarine and float to the surface.

Each submarine was so stripped down for supply carrying that she had only one gun and two torpedo tubes left. The rest of her space was packed with provisions. When the first submarines took off, long emotional speeches were made to their crews about the plight of the garrison at Guadalcanal and why such fantastic measures had to be employed.

During the three months from November 1942 until 8 February when Guadalcanal was evacuated, this underwater freight service operated every night. The round trip took four days. Aboard each submarine were supplies which would last 30,000 men for forty-eight hours. But the voyages led to heavy losses, just as the submarine officers gloomily predicted. The operation cost Japan twenty submarines in addition to another four submarines sunk on regular patrol.

The turning point in the submarine war came when all American ships and aircraft were fitted with radar. The only Japanese submarine fitted with radar was one they acquired from the Germans, and that did not reach them until mid-1943, when Guadalcanal was over.

At Guadalcanal American planes could bomb a submarine day or night without waiting to identify it. Any American aircraft coming upon a submarine idly cruising on the surface could assume it was Japanese. On the other hand, if the thirty-eight Japanese submarines in the Solomon Islands had been used offensively instead of as supply runners they might have seriously disrupted the American convoys. There were only three submarines on offensive operations round Guadalcanal, and even then one sank the carrier *Wasp*.

What happened to submarine *I–2* commanded by Lieutenant-Commander Sakamoto on a night supply run to Guadalcanal was typical of the fate of many supply-running underwater craft. After travelling submerged by day, *I–2* came inside the harbour at dusk. At nine o'clock in the evening when she raised her periscope near the beach, she was spotted by a patrolling New Zealand corvette, *Kiwi*, commanded by Lieutenant-Commander G. Bridson. He immediately attacked her with machine-guns and torpedoes. She dived to ninety feet but it was too late. Depth charges exploded right overhead and a terrific shock wave sent the main control switch flying. All the lights went out and it became pitch black inside the submarine. Fumbling in the dark, the crew tried to dive deeper even though they were afraid that if they did she would cave in through heavy water pressure.

The situation became so bad inside the dark, unmanageable submarine that Sakamoto decided to surface and fight it out. As soon as his conning tower rose out of the waves *Kiwi*, accompanied by another New Zealand corvette, *Moa*, commanded by Lieutenant-Commander Peter Phipps, raced towards it. Machine-gun bullets swept the submarine bridge, killing Sakamoto and everyone except the navigator. He raced down the ladder shouting, 'Swords, swords!' As he dashed up on deck, sword in hand, another shell killed the gun crew.

As the submarine began to move erratically to starboard at twelve knots, the navigator peered through the darkness. When *Kiwi* raced alongside he waved his sword and tried to leap aboard her. When she veered away, he was left hanging on the rail in mid-air with one hand on the corvette's rail and one foot on the submarine deck, unable to pull himself aboard. As *Kiwi* pulled away he fell into the sea.

The corvettes switched on searchlights and opened fire again, hitting the submarine repeatedly. With her steering gear completely shattered, she steamed erratically, listing and out of control as three torpedoes narrowly missed her. In spite of her half-wrecked condition, one of the submarine's guns sank an American patrol boat which approached too near. The Japanese submarine crew managed to raise a weak cheer.

As the corvettes came nearer, the desperate Japanese fired at them with rifles. When *Kiwi*'s 4-inch gun became too hot to operate, she rammed the submarine while the Japanese fired at her crew at point-blank range.

The *Moa* continued the battle, but the submarine, which had now been fighting for one and a half hours, was beginning to sink. It was decided to run her aground. Chased by Phipps's corvette, she sank stern first with her bows sticking out of the water. Thirty sailors were drowned by the sudden onrush of water but fifty of her crew managed to scramble ashore pursued by machine-gun bullets from *Moa*.

The only weapons they had left between them were two swords and three rifles. The officers clutched their secret naval code books. They need not have bothered but they did not know that the United States had learned most of their secrets. They were afraid to burn them ashore lest the smoke attract American aircraft, so they tore them into shreds and buried them in the sand.

Then someone remembered that other important code books were still aboard the submarine, having been forgotten in the mad scramble to escape. To prevent them falling into American hands, a junior officer and three men carrying explosives waded into the sea in the darkness and blew up the submarine's protruding bow. The explosions attracted a Japanese destroyer and several submarines, which came inshore and picked up the fifty survivors.

At dawn American aircraft, ordered to complete the destruction of the submarine, were unable to find the sunken wreckage but later U.S. Navy divers recovered a haul of secret documents from the *I-2*.

As long as the Japanese tried to bring in more troops to replace their large casualties, the bitter battle for Guadalcanal still went on. At Tassafaronga on 30 November, seven destroyers of the Tokyo

Express, commanded by the redoubtable Tanaka, tried to land reinforcements. Not only were they carrying ammunition and 5,000 drums of gasoline for their beleaguered garrison, but troops crowded their decks with standing room only, like rush-hour subway trains.

Admiral Carleton H. Wright, with the cruisers *Pensacola, Minneapolis, New Orleans* and *Northampton*, found them. Tanaka directed the battle from the bridge of a destroyer cluttered with soldiers and supplies. In a ferocious night engagement off Tassafaronga, lasting only thirty minutes, Tanaka sent *Northampton* to the bottom and put the other three cruisers out of action. He lost one destroyer and succeeded in putting all his reinforcements ashore.

Northampton was the fifth American heavy cruiser to be lost in Guadalcanal waters. This vicious little night battle off Tassafaronga, however, ended the five months' bloody naval slugging match round the steamy Solomons.

Nimitz and General Walter A. Patch, who had replaced General Vandegrift, still expected the Japanese to make another all-out attempt to retake Guadalcanal. Their view was confirmed in the first week of January 1943, when reports came in from patrol planes that Yamamoto was massing a big fleet at Rabaul and Buin in Bougainville. At the same time Japanese air attacks became heavier.

Nimitz guessed this must mean a major Japanese attack later in January. He ordered everything he could muster to Guadalcanal, including two carriers and seven battleships. In addition to 175 carrier aircraft he had 304 planes flying from the Henderson Field strips. Yet Nimitz was not confident that even this huge fleet and all these planes would be enough. He expected Yamamoto to throw in everything he had in one last mighty crushing blow to dislodge the Americans.

Nimitz was right. Yamamoto's fleet was massing for an attack scheduled for 1 February 1943. However, as the preparations went ahead, the Japanese position became increasingly difficult. General Hyakutake had consistently failed in his attempt to retake Henderson Field from the Americans because the strong additional forces which were sent to help the Guadalcanal garrison had not arrived. Many of them were drowned in the Pacific during the mid-November sea battles.

After that Imperial Headquarters stepped in and decided to change the army command. General Hitoshi Imamura, commanding the 8th

Army in Java, flew to assume overall control. He drew up a plan to land two more divisions to capture the American airfield.

But, as Yamamoto's staff officers bitterly forecast, the army was too late. In January 1943 Imamura had 50,000 men ready at Rabaul when he discovered he could not move them. The American fleet now controlled the area so overwhelmingly that any Japanese transport which put to sea was sunk. A Japanese staff officer declared, 'The superiority and continuous activity of the American air force are responsible for our inability to carry out our plans. They immobilized the Japanese army as if bound hand and foot.'

On the last day of 1943—a little over a year after Pearl Harbor—Imperial Headquarters reluctantly decided to cancel Imamura's big offensive. This meant they faced the bitter truth: it was no longer possible to drive the Americans off Guadalcanal. Yamamoto, who had lost ships every week trying to reinforce this remote Pacific island, had held that opinion for a long time. When the United States had finally gathered enough strength round Guadalcanal to continue the fight indefinitely it was he who persuaded Imperial Headquarters to quit. For if the Japanese army had no hope of retaking Henderson Field he could never use Guadalcanal for a naval base.

On 4 January 1942, Yamamoto ordered Vice-Admiral Jinichi Kusaka, commanding the South-eastern Fleet, to be ready to cover the evacuation of all Japanese troops from Guadalcanal. He also countermanded the plan to build special supply destroyers, as they would no longer be needed.

When General Hyakutake received this order he explained it to his men 'as a change in the disposition of troops for future offensive action'. Imamura sent staff officers by Tokyo Express to the island with details of the army plan for evacuation.

The evacuation of 13,000 Japanese troops from Guadalcanal was one of the great tactical successes of World War Two. It did not begin until two weeks after the plan was given to the garrison. Several things had to be accomplished first. As a deception plan to cover the retreat, 1,000 Japanese reinforcements were put ashore near Cape Esperance. They were the Yano battalion of tough, specially trained rearguard fighters who began intensive attacks against Henderson Field. As they hoped, this led the American command to think it was the start of another major Japanese offensive on Guadalcanal.

One night in the third week of January, Japanese rescue destroyers ran down the Slot to begin the evacuation of Hyakutake's 17th

Japanese Army from Cape Esperance. While the Yano battalion attacked fiercely, each destroyer took 600 men aboard under the cover of darkness. When the destroyers sailed they stood shoulder to shoulder packed into passageways and on deck. When the proximity of American ships halted the destroyers, troops crowded into barges and were picked up at sea away from the coast.

Hospital patients left first, followed by the 38th Division. They were followed by the 17th Army headquarters. During the first week in February the last Japanese troops were put aboard the destroyers. One Japanese soldier did not accompany them. He was Colonel Kiyono Ichiki. As the first Japanese commanding officer to be defeated on land by the Americans he felt it his honourable duty to kill himself.

The new American land commander, General Walter A. Patch, suspected the increased activity of the Tokyo Express meant they were not reinforcing, but taking off the remaining Japanese. No one shared his view. General Hyakutake later admitted that resolute American attacks on the Yano battalion at Cape Esperance might have led to a break-through which would have destroyed his retreating army.

Afterwards the Japanese expressed ironic gratitude for their escape. They said that if the Americans had not moved so gingerly towards the Yano troops, and stopped for so long to consolidate their positions, they would never have got away.

A captured document gave this Japanese estimate of the Americans: 'If he once gains self-confidence he becomes over-bold but if anyone opposes him he becomes radically less aggressive at once. This is seen to be the usual attitude of foreigners.'

At 4.15 p.m. on 7 February 1943, exactly six months after the American marines landed, the last Japanese soldier on Guadalcanal was either evacuated or dead.

During those six months the Americans had fought six major naval battles near the island. In only one of them, Cape Esperance, had they gained any sort of victory. Three were at best inconclusive and the other two were defeats.

Yet in the long run the Americans had won. What was the reason for their victory? Their sailors were no braver and their ships were no better. Captain Toshikazu Ohnae commented: 'The outstanding feature of the Guadalcanal campaign was the employment of radar by the United States, which completely reversed the Japanese navy's traditional superiority in night fighting. It was after the Cape Esperance sea battle on 11 October that the Japanese navy confirmed the use of effective fire-control radar by the United States.'

The battle balance sheet was chilling. The American navy lost two aircraft carriers, *Wasp* and *Hornet*, five heavy cruisers, two light cruisers and fourteen destroyers. Many other ships were badly damaged and put out of action.

Although the Americans had superiority in numbers, gunpower, radar and aircraft, they were consistently out-manœuvred in nearly every naval battle by the Japanese, who scrupulously followed Yamamoto's instruction to conduct a war of attrition. His main aim was to destroy as many American ships as he could. At the end of the battle for Guadalcanal, it could not be said he had failed.

As he had foreseen, it had developed into a savage slugging match. By the time the campaign ended the tonnage of sunken warships lying off the island was much greater than that lost on both sides at Jutland.

Although he had sunk so many American warships, Yamamoto knew he had lost the battle. The naval campaign, which had ended in a draw, had led to the American occupation of Guadalcanal.

The most tangible advantage reaped by the U.S. navy from the Guadalcanal battles arose from the fact that they could quickly replace their losses by their immeasurably greater naval construction and repair programme—while Japan could not. This meant that in the long run Yamamoto had lost much more heavily than Nimitz. He had predicted that after a year or eighteen months the Japanese navy might have shot its bolt. In February 1943 his prediction began to come true.

Midway was a naval disaster. But Japan's first big land defeat of the war was the loss of Guadalcanal. They tried to disguise it by calling it 'advance by turning'. In fact they took it so badly that when the phrase 'strategic retreat' was used by a lecturer at Keio University to describe the Guadalcanal campaign he was warned by the security police never to use such an unfortunate expression again.

Yamamoto rejected any such smooth, disguising phrases. In a letter to a friend he freely acknowledged defeat. After Guadalcanal, in the immaculate brushwork taught to him by his schoolmaster father, he wrote to his old classmate, the C.-in-C. of Japanese submarines, Admiral Mitsumi Shimizu.

In his letter he said: 'Guadalcanal was a very fierce battle. I do not know what to do next. Nor am I happy about facing my officers and men who have fought so hard without fear of death. . . . At this moment I would like to borrow some knowledge from a wise man.'

When Shimizu received this letter Yamamoto was already dead.

24

At 9.35 a.m. Precisely

NEITHER the disaster at Midway nor the shock of the retreat from Guadalcanal shook the confidence of the Imperial Navy or the Japanese people in Yamamoto's leadership. He was still the object of fanatical loyalty. Yet he himself was very much aware that time was running out a little faster than even he had predicted.

After the Guadalcanal withdrawal he also sensed that his men's outlook had changed. The sinkings at Midway and the batterings at Guadalcanal had done a great deal to undermine the feeling of invincibility which had followed Pearl Harbor a year before.

After weeks of conferences analysing details and reasons for the Guadalcanal retreat, Yamamoto planned a series of visits to the Japanese navy's most forward bases in the Pacific. His men were badly in need of a morale builder. Who better than himself? He was still a national hero, almost as much venerated by his sailors as Admiral Togo who had destroyed the Russian fleet.

He decided to go among them personally and with his presence and encouraging speeches change their depression into an unshakeable belief in ultimate victory. With this object in view he planned a series of inspection trips all round the South Pacific. His tour had the required effect. In the steamy tropical bases the appearance of Yamamoto, immaculately dressed in a well-pressed white uniform, seemingly oblivious of the humid heat and the dive-bombing insects, put heart into every officer and sailor. When he spoke to them his theme was: There were many great sea battles yet to be fought and victory or defeat depended entirely upon the conduct of the Japanese navy.

He was particularly anxious to talk to General Hyakutake, commander of the 17th Army which had fought the Guadalcanal battle. On 18 April he planned to fly to Rabaul to see him and then go on to Buin to inspect more front-line naval bases. It was to be a forty-eight-hour visit only. He was to spend the night of 17 April at Rabaul and fly back next day from Buin to his main base at Truk, where his new flagship, Japan's most up-to-date battleship *Musashi*, was anchored.

As he was going into areas which were within range of American planes the programme of his projected tour was top secret. The Japanese were so jumpy about the way American planes kept appearing without warning that they asked him for the first time not to wear his admiral's white uniform. Before he left he changed into khaki drill to make his presence less conspicuous.

He was due to take off from Rabaul at 6 a.m. on 18 April in a Mitsubishi Betty bomber. Accompanying him in a second bomber was his chief of staff, Admiral Matomi Ugaki, and their flight was to be escorted by six Zekes. Code signals were sent out to Japanese forward bases informing them of Admiral Yamamoto's coming visit.

The nearest American radio interception post was in a deep concrete bunker at Dutch Harbor in the Aleutians. High above the fog-bound cliffs climbed seven 300-foot radio masts. At 6.36 a.m. on 17 April a cypher signal from Truk bearing the code sign of Admiral Yamamoto's flagship was picked up at Dutch Harbor and relayed to Washington for decoding. The code breakers studied the groups of figures and compared them with their secret key charts. By eleven o'clock, they had decoded and translated the signal. It was a routine message giving details of Yamamoto's tour. It informed Japanese commanders of the places and times of his visits. It was of no importance. When it was forwarded to Navy Secretary Frank Knox he read it and went out to lunch.

A chance remark over lunch made him wonder. Someone mentioned that in the old days wars used to be settled by duels between opposing commanders. Yamamoto, the leader of the Imperial Navy, was the hated personal foe of every American sailor.

Knox idly began to speculate. As he knew where Yamamoto would be tomorrow at any given time, might it be possible to shoot him down? He was the man behind Pearl Harbor. What a revenge it would be for the 2,000 men killed there, to say nothing of the dead American sailors lying at the bottom of the Pacific after Midway and Guadalcanal. As the lunch progressed, Knox became slightly excited as he mulled over the idea.

Immediately upon his return to his office he sent for General 'Hap' Arnold, Chief of the Army Air Force. Arnold was enthusiastic about the scheme and immediately began to consider how it might be possible. He and Knox pored over maps. The best place to intercept

Yamamoto was as he came into land at Kahili airstrip on Bougainville. It would need a long-range attack. It was nearly 500 miles from
Henderson Field on Guadalcanal to the place where the admiral was
due next day. No P.38 fighter had the range to fly there and return.

But the scheme was taking concrete shape. Arnold sent for Charles
Lindbergh, the lone conqueror of the Atlantic, now an adviser on
long-distance flying, and Frank Meyer from the experimental
department of Lockheeds, the makers of the P.38. Again they
measured maps and discussed fuel tanks and ranges. Both the
experts agreed it was a long shot but possible. But how to fit long-
range tanks to the P.38s? There were none on Guadalcanal.

After two hours' detailed discussion it was decided that Operation
Vengeance, the plan to kill the architect of Pearl Harbor, was on.
At 3.35 p.m. Knox sent two signals. One went to General Kenney,
commander of the South-west Pacific Air Forces, in Australia urgently requesting long-range tanks. Messages began to flash from
Kenney's Australian headquarters to New Guinea and three hours
later four Liberators took off from Milne Bay. They were carrying
eighteen 165-gallon auxiliary tanks and the same number of 310-
gallon tanks that could be jettisoned when empty.

The second signal was sent to Guadalcanal. Japanese bombers
were raiding the strip when it was decoded at 4 p.m. A tropical rainstorm began to beat against the army headquarters huts half hidden
in the palm trees at Tassafaronga as a message went to Henderson
Field to Major John W. Mitchell commanding 339 Squadron. It
ordered him and his two flight commanders, Lieutenants Besby T.
Holmes and Thomas G. Lanphier Jr, to report at once to headquarters.

It was just after five o'clock in the evening when their jeep skidded
up, sending up showers of muddy water against the camouflaged army
huts. Mitchell was handed a telegram, which he read in silence. It said :

Washington Top Secret. Secretary Navy to Fighter Control
Henderson. Admiral Yamamoto accompanied chief of staff and
seven general officers Imperial Navy including surgeon grand
fleet left Truk this morning eight hours for their trip inspection
Bougainville bases stop admiral and party travelling in two Betty
escorted six Zekes stop escort of honour from Kahili probable
stop admiral's itinerary colon arrive Rabaul 16.30 hours where
spend night stop leave dawn for Kahili where time of arrival 09.45

hours stop admiral then to board submarine chaser for inspection naval units under Admiral Tanaka stop.

Squadron 339 P.38 must at all costs reach and destroy Yamamoto and staff morning April eighteen stop auxiliary tanks and consumption data will arrive from Port Moresby evening seventeenth stop intelligence stresses admiral's extreme punctuality stop president attaches extreme importance this operation stop communicate result at once Washington stop Frank Knox Secretary of State for Navy stop ultra-secret document not to be copied or filed stop to be destroyed when carried out stop.

Mitchell nodded. Then he and his two flight commanders sat down to plan the operation over a supper of canned sausages washed down with mugs of fruit juice.

Several problems had to be faced. They planned to attack thirty miles east of Kahili airstrip. But if Yamamoto was as punctual as he was known to be this meant they must be in position ready for the attack at 9.35 a.m. precisely. And what height would he be flying at? This was vitally important if surprise was to be obtained. They reasoned that the two bombers, containing admirals and high-ranking staff officers, would not fly above 10,000 feet; otherwise they would have the annoying necessity of having to use oxygen masks.

Mitchell decided he would lead twelve P.38s at 20,000 feet to give high-level protection to his other fighters flying below him at 11,000 feet whose task would be to intercept Yamamoto's two bombers. Take-off would have to be at 7.20 a.m. This would make certain they arrived near Kahili airstrip exactly two hours and fifteen minutes later.

While they sat round the table strewn with maps, puddles formed on the floor as the rainstorm battered on the roof and thunder rolled round the central mountains of Guadalcanal. At 9 p.m. they heard the heavy roar of the four-engined Liberators bringing the long-range tanks. They made wobbly landings on the short steel-wire strip lit only by flickering lamps. Mud was nearly a foot deep as fitters started to haul the extra tanks out of the bombers. Major Mitchell directed their work as they splashed and staggered across the airfield towards the P.38s, slapping at clouds of mosquitoes dancing in the beams of their electric torches.

It was after dawn before the last of the thirty-six tanks was clamped onto the fighters. Mitchell snatched a few biscuits and some canned meat for breakfast. Then, haggard and unshaven, he led his crews to the eighteen P.38s standing on the strip, their wings and bellies bulging with extra tanks.

At 7.20 a.m. to the minute, the first P.38 rolled clanking over the steel netting of the strip and took off into the blue sky, washed clear by last night's storm. Two fighters had trouble and could not get off but the remaining sixteen circled round the palm-strewn island of Guadalcanal before swinging on course towards Bougainville.

April 17 had been a stormy day of a different kind at Rabaul, where Yamamoto was holding a conference to consider new plans for continuing the war against the Americans. The conference was urgent because, as he said, 'It is two months since our withdrawal and they will be gearing themselves up for a new attack. They will start island-hopping any minute now. We must be prepared to meet them from any direction. We must be ready.'

As the planning conference got down to details, a series of petty recriminations developed between admirals. Each accused the other of commanding men lacking in morale. This was the very situation which worried Yamamoto. It was to prevent it that he had decided to show himself personally to the troops. When he eventually silenced the squabbling officers, he still remained extremely uneasy about their attitude.

That night he sat in the mess playing his favourite game of *go* with his chief planning officer, Captain Yasuji Watanabe, who was flying with him the next day. Suddenly he said, 'You had better stay behind, Watanabe. I am not satisfied with the way things went today. I want you to hold another planning conference tomorrow and settle all the details.'

The last extra tanks were still being fitted onto the P.38s on Henderson Field when at 6 a.m. next morning Admiral Yamamoto took off from Rabaul in his green-striped camouflaged bomber. With him in the plane were his secretary, Commander Ishizaki, Surgeon Rear-Admiral Takata and his air staff officer, Commander Tobana. In a second khaki-coloured bomber was his chief of staff, Admiral Matomi Ugaki, with Paymaster Rear-Admiral Kitamura and communications officer Commander Muroi.

As the two bombers flew over the volcano at the end of the bay and set a south-easterly course towards Bougainville the only break in the clear blue sky was a scurry of high-flying cloud. The two planes flew in tight formation, their wings almost touching, their six escorting

Zekes formed a protective screen around them. Two fighters flew on each side while the remaining two flew above them and a little behind.

When they saw the jungle fringe of Bougainville's western coastline they went down to 2,000 feet as a precaution. The two camouflaged bombers were almost invisible against the green shadowy pattern of the jungle. It was exactly 9.30 a.m. when they began flying over the matted treetops towards Kahili strip, where they were due a quarter of an hour later.

Mitchell's P.38s had flown 410 miles over water, skimming along only thirty feet above the waves. They were right on schedule with their plan to reach the south-west coast of Bougainville at 9.35 a.m. They were just about to climb ready for the attack when one pilot suddenly broke radio silence to say, 'Eleven o'clock!' Mitchell and his pilots saw a V-formation of planes just nearing the coast. They were his prey—two bombers close together with Zekes surrounding them.

When Mitchell immediately began his climb to 20,000 feet Yamamoto's pilots had not yet noticed his P.38s. The four American pilots in the attack group, Thomas G. Lanphier Jr, Rex T. Barber, Besby T. Holmes and Raymond K. Hine, dropped their long-range belly tanks and climbed up to level with the bombers. Then they began to nose down for the attack. When the Japanese pilots saw them for the first time they were only a mile away from Yamamoto's bomber.

Immediately the two bombers streaked towards the safety of the jungle while the Zekes swung upwards to intercept the American fighters. At first no one inside the bombers could make out what had happened. Yamamoto and his officers scanned the sky anxiously as their plane twisted and rocketed down towards the palm trees. As they began to level out at 200 feet, just over the tree-tops, the wind screamed as the Japanese crewmen unlimbered their machine-guns.

It was 9.33 a.m. when the four P.38s dived on the two camouflaged bombers and saw the red rising sun emblem showing clearly on their wings and sides. Lanphier decided the second Betty with the olive-green stripes must be Yamamoto's and dived towards it. At the same time three Zekes also dropped their long-range tanks and made for him.

At first he thought he had lost the bomber, so he turned on the formation of three Zekes screaming towards him. One yellow and green Zeke shuddered when his cannon shells smacked into it. As the plane overturned and shot past him on its back, he suddenly saw the green-striped Betty once again going down fast towards the jungle.

He nosed over at 400 m.p.h. and followed the bomber down. As he levelled out just over the tree-tops, the bomber swung round, turning broadside to his gun sights. He pressed the button of his 22-cm cannon and 13-mm machine-guns and fired a long burst. A thin black plume of smoke came drifting from the bomber's starboard engine and flames began to lick round the cowling. Then came more trails of black smoke and the wing caught fire. The bomber began to lose speed and fly erratically as Lanphier closed in and gave it a second long burst.

The bomber shuddered and lurched down among the tree-tops. The undamaged wing hit a branch and crumpled. Then the blazing plane crashed into the jungle, bounced once and exploded.

Admiral Ugaki in the other bomber saw the scene like this:

When without warning the motors roared and the bomber plunged towards the jungle, levelling off at less than 200 feet, nobody knew what had happened. Then as we pulled out of the dive to fly horizontally above the jungle we saw our escort fighter turning towards the attacking enemy aircraft now identifiable as the big Lockheed Lightnings. The numerically superior enemy force broke through the Zekes and lunged after our two bombers.

For a few minutes I lost sight of Yamamoto's plane but finally located it far to the right. I was horrified to see it flying slowly just above the jungle with bright orange flames rapidly enveloping the wings and fuselage. About four miles away from us the bomber trailed thick black smoke, dropping lower and lower. As our bomber snapped out of its turn I scanned the jungle. The Betty was no longer in sight. Black smoke boiled from the dense jungle into the air.

Just after this, Lieutenant Rex Barber attacked Ugaki's bomber. The Betty pilot tried to swerve out of the way but, with the Zekes on his tail, Barber fired and a piece of the bomber's tail fell off. It turned and plunged low over the jungle into the water. Admirals Ugaki and Kitamura and other officers in the plane were badly hurt but were dragged out of the floating wreckage by Japanese patrol boats.

Lanphier and Barber, having accomplished their mission, hedge-hopped trees and manœuvred desperately to escape the vengeful

Zekes. They kicked rudders, slipped and skidded to evade the hail of tracer from the Zekes screaming on their tails. Both managed to escape but in the ensuing dogfight Lieutenant Ray Hine's plane was hit in the port engine and he plunged into the sea. Three Zekes of Yamamoto's escort were also shot down.

As the Lightnings set course for Guadalcanal great clouds of dust rose up from Kahili airfield where Zekes were swarming up like angry wasps. But the remaining fifteen fighters, all with bullet holes and two with one engine out of action, were already out of range. Least damaged was Lanphier's plane, with only two Zeke machine-gun bullet holes in the horizontal stabilizer.

The news that Yamamoto's plane had been shot down shattered the Japanese. One of the first to hear was Admiral Kakuda, carrier commander in the Aleutians operation. He had just returned to his flagship, the carrier *Hiyo*, after attending the further planning conference that Yamamoto had ordered, when a signal officer handed him a confidential message.

Kakuda, who was noted for his iron self-discipline even among Japanese officers, paled as he read it. He left the bridge at once and locked himself in his cabin for the rest of the day, refusing to speak to anyone. Within a few minutes groups of grief-stricken and disbelieving officers and ratings gathered on the decks of the Japanese warships in Truk to stand to attention while Yamamoto's flag was lowered from the masthead of his flagship, the great battleship *Musashi*.

On the other hand the Americans were naturally jubilant. Halsey at once sent this signal to Henderson Field: CONGRATULATIONS MAJOR MITCHELL AND HIS HUNTERS SOUNDS AS THOUGH ONE OF THE DUCKS IN THEIR BAG WAS A PEACOCK.

The war-time hatred of Yamamoto, who had ranged the Pacific from Pearl Harbor to Guadalcanal to become the greatest menace to the American fleet, bubbled to the surface. When the news was announced at Halsey's conference next morning his officers whooped and applauded. Halsey observed sourly, 'What's good about it? I had hoped to lead that scoundrel up Pennsylvania Avenue in chains with the rest of you kicking him where it would do the most good.'

But was the peacock really dead? The Japanese navy had little hope he could have escaped from his blazing plane but they had to be certain. Captain Watanabe, the officer who had escaped dying with Yamamoto because he had ordered him to stay behind, took off at once to fly to the spot in the jungle where the still-smoking wreck lay among the charred trees. As his plane circled he threw down tennis balls with messages wrapped round them saying, 'Wave your hand-kerchief if you are still alive.' He flew around for several hours. No one waved.

At dusk a corvette with a hundred Japanese sailors aboard sailed up the river from Buin. At 11 p.m. they reached the nearest spot in the jungle to where the wreckage had been seen. They landed and split up into two parties to hack their way through the dense under-growth. Although the wreckage was only two miles from the river bank, the jungle was so thick that they advanced only a yard at a time. By dawn they were only a few hundred yards from the river. Then a plane circled over them with a message to return. Yamamoto's body had been found.

A Japanese army lieutenant called Hamasuna on a routine jungle patrol had been led to the wreck by natives. He found Yamamoto's charred body thrown clear of the aircraft. Apart from him only the body of Admiral Takata could be identified. The rest of the pas-sengers and crew were just burnt-out embers in the blackened plane.

Natives loaded the bodies of Yamamoto, his officers and the bomber crew—eleven in all—onto bamboo stretchers. Led by Lieutenant Hamasuna and his soldiers, they carried them to the river mouth at Buin. A doctor's post mortem revealed that Yamamoto had been shot through the head and shoulder. He must have been dead before the plane hit the jungle.

The corvette took the bodies back to Bougainville. There a guard of sailors took Yamamoto and those who had died with him in a sad ceremonial parade to the top of a near-by mountain.

The admiral's body was placed in a hastily dug, shallow grave at the peak. The other bodies were laid just below him. Bundles of palm leaves and tree branches were piled onto them. Then gasoline was poured on and set alight. Sailors stood at the salute as the flames roared up into the blue Pacific sky. Within half an hour, all that was left of any of them was a little heap of ash.

Captain Watanabe scooped up Yamamoto's ashes, still mixed with burnt palm leaves, and placed them in a little pinewood box. A piece of rugged mountain rock was inscribed with his name and date of death and placed over the makeshift grave where he was cremated. A group of officers planted a peepul tree. Watanabe flew to Truk with the admiral's ashes and, after another memorial ceremony aboard the flagship, he took them in a destroyer to Japan.

In spite of the grief of the Japanese navy and the rejoicing of the U.S. Pacific Fleet, no details of the momentous tragedy were allowed to leak out while the war was on. Lieutenant Lanphier was promoted to the rank of captain, awarded the Navy Cross, and received a personal telegram of congratulation from President Roosevelt.

The news of his exploit was suppressed for two reasons. One was that the Americans were afraid that an announcement about the way they managed to kill Yamamoto would make the Japanese suspect they had broken their code. Later on there was a more dramatic personal reason. Lanphier's brother, Charles, also a flyer, was shot down over Kahili airstrip and became a prisoner in Japanese hands. The American Government feared reprisals against him.

It was not until 21 May, more than a month after his death and after Watanabe had brought his ashes back to Tokyo, that a Japanese broadcast announced, 'Admiral Yamamoto while directing general strategy in the front line in April of this year engaged in combat with the enemy and met gallant death in a war plane.' Then the announcer choked and wept.

Next day the radio reported: 'When His Imperial Majesty received word of the late Admiral Yamamoto on 20 April he elevated him from the post of Commander-in-Chief Combined Fleet to Fleet Admiral. This gracious gesture on the part of His Imperial Majesty failed to rally the condition of Admiral Yamamoto.'

The radio added that a state funeral, the twelfth ever accorded to a Japanese, had been ordered. The only other admiral ever to be given a state funeral was the man Yamamoto admired most, the victor over the Russians, Admiral Heihachiro Togo.

Following the Tokyo radio reports, there was a great deal of speculation in America about the man and his death. The *New York Times* quoting Radio Tokyo commented, 'This indicates he had not been killed outright but died later from his injuries.' The enigma still remained because there had been no major activity in the Pacific during April. Many people thought he might have been killed in a plane crash, others that he had committed hara-kiri.

In Japan, Yamamoto's ashes were split up to give him two great spectacular funerals. There had never been such scenes of national mourning in any country for an admiral since the British lost Nelson at Trafalgar 140 years before.

On a bright June day a year after his greatest defeat at Midway, nearly the whole population of Tokyo turned out for his state funeral.

The Emperor did not attend. He never attends funerals as he is considered to be above life and death. But every other dignitary in Japan gathered in Hibiya Park in the centre of Tokyo near the Imperial Palace to walk in slow procession to Tamabuchi cemetery, where Yamamoto's urn was placed next to Admiral Togo's. Watching unnoticed and unknown in the dense crowds as the funeral procession passed was a weeping geisha named Kikuji.

The second funeral was even more impressive and moving. It began next day in his home town of Nagaoka. His uniform and sword were placed on a plinth with the urn containing the rest of his ashes. For a week 650,000 people, most of them in tears, filed past. Then he was buried next to his father in a little Buddhist temple on the outskirts of the bustling Japanese market town where his father was once a schoolteacher.

The cemetery is not far from the near-by patchwork of ricefields and mulberry bushes grown for silk-worm food. It is the classic Japanese country scene. It was in such places that Yamamoto used to love to roam as a boy. This was where he asked to be buried. His memorial stone cost only seventy-five yen (ten cents or sixpence) because this was also the way he always wanted it. It was also an inch smaller than his father's—again as he wished.

In December 1943, a full-length statue of Yamamoto was put up at the Kasumigaura flying school where he had once been the commanding officer. After the Japanese surrender, General MacArthur ordered all military statues to be destroyed throughout Japan. Naval officers cut Yamamoto's statue in half with a chisel and threw it into the near-by lake. But they made a chart of where it sank. Ten years later a scrap dealer, searching for copper from other statues, dredged up the head and shoulders.

It was bought from him by several of Yamamoto's old friends, including his Japanese biographer and childhood playmate, Eiichi Soramachi, who placed it in a Buddhist temple near by. In 1956 one of Yamamoto's admirals paid the freight charges for it to be taken by train back to Nagaoka, his home town.

Now it stands on a stone pedestal in the middle of a small park in the centre of the town. Local people subscribed 30,000 dollars (£10,000) to lay out this park as his memorial. Next to his statue is a replica of the little wooden house where he was born. Ironically enough, the original was burnt to ashes in August 1945 during one of the last American fire raids.

His other memorial now lies obscure and unnoticed next to Togo's in the Tokyo cemetery. Once a week a middle-aged man stops his car on his way to the office, takes out a silk handkerchief and devotedly polishes the tombstone. He is Yasuji Watanabe, the man who brought Yamamoto's ashes back from the Pacific, now working for an American export firm. He is one of the few people who cares whether the inscription becomes dusty.

For in today's busy booming Japan the Yamamoto legend is largely forgotten. There are many young people who have never heard of the famous admiral venerated by their father's generation. He was the outstanding admiral of his war. There is no question about his brilliant boldness. His judgment on Pearl Harbor was exactly right. It was his only chance to destroy the U.S. Pacific Fleet without becoming involved in the old-fashioned, chessboard strategy of Plan Rainbow Five, as less unorthodox admirals on both sides of the Pacific wished to do. He did not play the game by their rules.

Knowing his country's naval and industrial weaknesses as he did, he calculated correctly that this below-the-belt blow was his only hope of victory. It came off as a result of superb planning and security, luck in meeting no other ships in the lonely North Pacific, and the helpful peacetime euphoria of the American defenders. It was sheer ill-fortune no carriers were in port.

Whether Vice-Admiral Chuichi Nagumo should have made a third strike against the oil storage tanks is a wise-after-the-event academic argument. Aided by incredible American inefficiency, the attack did much better than even the most optimistic Japanese admiral expected.

But Yamamoto suffered from the type of grievous drawback which Napoleon understood. Whenever he was asked to appoint a high-ranking officer he did not inquire about his military experience or talent. He simply asked: 'Is he lucky?' For Napoleon knew only too well that in great battles, where both sides are approximately equal, luck must be on the side of the victor.

In the last analysis, Yamamoto was not lucky. He also had his share of arrogance, which becomes more evident in his countrymen than in those of most nations when they are on a winning streak. That, added to bad luck and bad judgment in keeping Nagumo as his carrier commander, lost him the battle of Midway.

But what if he had won it? It is one of the most awesome ifs in the history of this century. If he had sunk the American carriers—as he should have done with his great battle fleet—the whole story of

World War Two would have been changed. He might easily have taken Hawaii and certainly harried the long, indefensible Pacific coastline of the United States.

The effect on American morale would have been incalculable. Although it would not have led to a negotiated peace as he hoped, it would have had almost as far-reaching consequences. With the Japanese fleet off the west coast and at the gateway of the Panama Canal, Americans would have had little interest in the war in Europe. All their war effort would have been geared against Yamamoto and the Japanese.

There would have been no Normandy landings because Britain could not have undertaken them alone. With the Japanese on the doorstep, American opinion would not have allowed a single G.I. to sail to Europe. If Germany had been beaten it would have been by the Russians almost unaided. This could have meant that the Iron Curtain would now extend to Calais.

All this might easily have happened if Nagumo, Yamamoto's carrier admiral, had made a different decision at 8.30 a.m. on 4 June 1942 in the central Pacific.

As it was, Midway was not only a victory but a coming-of-age for the Americans. This was the first great battle they had fought to defend their country since colonial days. It proved to them that, although they were unprepared and pacifist, in courage and resolution their fighting men and commanders were equal to any in the world. This, added to the great industrial potential of the United States, meant that final victory was only a matter of time.

Yamamoto's memorial is his skilful, daring use of aircraft carriers which opened a new chapter in naval warfare. It also closed almost as soon as it began. Midway was the first and last gigantic carrier battle in the history of the world. Those formidable plane-loaded ships which roamed the vast Pacific a generation ago are as extinct as the painted Polynesian war canoes which also once proudly ranged the same ocean.

Like the last of the China tea clippers,

> They marked our passage as a race of men.
> Earth shall not see such ships again.

Isoroku Yamamoto was their great captain. He lived not just a generation ago but a whole age away from us.

Postscript

As the war progressed, the great ships and the admirals nearly all departed.

Yamamoto was succeeded, as he wished to be, by Admiral Minei-chi Koga. He met the same fate as his predecessor—death in the air.

Nearly a year after Yamamoto's death, on 27 March 1944, he was travelling in a flying boat from Palau to Davao when his plane crashed and he was killed. In the other plane his chief of staff and former Pearl Harbor planner, Vice-Admiral Shigeru Fukudome, escaped, just as Yamamoto's chief of staff, Admiral Matome Ugaki, had in his crash.

In the summer of 1944 Vice-Admiral Chuichi Nagumo, the Pearl Harbor and Midway carrier commander, committed hara-kiri on Saipan. He led his staff into a hut which one of them set on fire and then they all shot themselves. His body was never found.

The submarines continued with their own special brand of bad luck. Lieutenant Matsuo, one of the co-originators of the midget submarine attack, was bitterly disappointed when he was not chosen for the Pearl Harbor operation. He did not have long to wait. He volunteered to take part in the four-midget attack launched against Sydney Harbour on 31 May 1942, as a diversion for Midway. He never returned. The wreckage of his midget was found at the bottom of the harbour in early June.

Six I-class submarines went to Kiel and the U-boat base at Lorient on the French coast. There German technicians made a detailed inspection of them and criticized their hull vibration and excessive use of underwater signalling devices. On hearing of these deficiencies, Hitler presented the Japanese with two German submarines as models. One was sunk by Allied aircraft in the Atlantic while sailing to Japan with a Japanese crew. In July 1943 the second submarine with a German crew arrived in Kure.

Two gigantic submarines—the *I–401* and *I–402*—were specifically designed and built to destroy the Panama Canal entrance. Their original 4,000 tons was increased to 5,000 and deck hangar space for two seaplanes was enlarged to hold three. They were not ready until the last few weeks of the war. They went straight on the scrapheap after the surrender.

The American submarine story was exactly the reverse. In the middle of 1943 the big 32,000-ton carrier *Taiho*, carrying sixty-two planes, came into service. She was the forerunner of the supercarrier nearing completion, called *Shinano* after the river near Yamamoto's home town. On 19 June 1943, a month after *Taiho* was commissioned, one of her pilots, Warrant Officer Sakio Komatsu, saw a torpedo heading for his carrier and crash-dived his plane onto it. It had been fired from the submarine *Albacore*. He killed himself preventing the torpedo hitting the ship. But a second torpedo struck her.

Immediately everything went wrong for *Taiho*. Fuel from a defective tank seeped into the plane lift spaces. Then an electric spark ignited the accumulated fuel and there was a tremendous explosion. Six hours after the torpedo struck her, she heeled to port, turned over and sank 500 miles west of Saipan.

The huge 64,000-ton battleship *Musashi*, sister ship to Yamamoto's Midway flagship *Yamato*, led the attack on the Leyte beachhead. On 24 October 1944, after being hit by ten torpedoes from American planes, she sank. There went with her to the bottom in this battle four carriers and three other battleships.

The fate of the giant 72,000-ton *Shinano* was the most tragic of all. The sister ship to *Yamato* and *Musashi*, she had been converted to the greatest aircraft carrier ever launched, carrying eighty-seven planes. To protect her from the same fate as other Japanese carriers when dive bombers hit them, her flight deck was lined with twelve-inch steel plates on a reinforced concrete base.

The *Shinano* first floated in Tokyo Bay on 11 November 1944. The Japanese navy, having by this time lost most of its carriers, waited eagerly for her.

At 6 p.m. on 28 November she sailed from Yokusuka naval base towards Osaka Bay on the first leg of her maiden voyage. At 3.12 a.m. in the dim moonlight, lookouts made out a torpedo wake 300 feet from her port side. They had hardly time to give a warning before three more tore a gaping hole below her waterline. They were fired by the U.S. submarine *Archerfish*.

Her commander, Captain Toshio Abe, steamed on at twenty knots because he felt sure there was no danger to his unsinkable ship. He did not even consider making for the nearest safe port. He continued to sail for seven hours although gradually the big ship began to list until foothold was impossible and sea water was pouring in.

Captain Abe gave orders to abandon ship but remained on the bridge. Next to him was Ensign Tadashi Yasuda, top graduate of the Naval Academy of 1943, with the ship's flag draped round his shoulders. He had continued calmly to keep a detailed log from the moment of the first torpedo hit.

At 10.55 a.m. on 29 November *Shinano* sank with 500 men aboard her. In eight hours she would have made her port of destination.

She sank because of her captain's faith in her unsinkability. Also no one can give a reasonable explanation why she was moved at night in waters where American submarines were known to be operating. In daylight, a land-based air escort could have kept a lookout for their periscopes.

Shinano never launched a plane. Her sea life lasted exactly seventeen hours.

The last great battleship to go was Yamamoto's old flagship, *Yamato*. She sank six months after her sister ship *Musashi* in one of the final naval battles of the Pacific war. She led the remnants of Yamamoto's once proud fleet towards Okinawa to try and beat off the Americans poised to invade her homeland. A massed American air attack sent her reeling to the bottom.

After that the Japanese radio no longer broadcast its jingoistic jingle:

> Come out,
> Nimitz and MacArthur,
> Then we will send you tumbling to hell.

But the most ignoble fate was reserved for Yamamoto's original flagship *Nagato*, from whose operations room he planned Pearl Harbor. She was a target at the Bikini nuclear bomb tests.

Appendix I—Three Poems

Like so many Japanese, Admiral Yamamoto wrote poems to celebrate great events in his life.

On Pearl Harbor day he wrote:

> *What does the world think?*
> *I do not care*
> *Nor for my life*
> *For I am the sword*
> *Of my Emperor.*

On the first anniversary of Pearl Harbor:

> *The year has gone*
> *And so many friends*
> *The lost, the uncounted,*
> *The dead.*

His last poem, written a few days before he died:

> *I am still the sword*
> *Of my Emperor*
> *I will not be sheathed*
> *Until I die.*

Translated by the author

Appendix II—Bibliography

AHERMAN, Frederick C.—*Combat Command: The American Aircraft Carriers in the Pacific War* (Dutton, New York)

ANDRIEU, d'Albans and EMMANUEL, M. A.—*Death of a Navy: Japanese Naval Action in World War II* (Devin-Adair, New York/ Robert Hale, London)

BLIVEN, Bruce—*From Pearl Harbor to Okinawa* (Random House, New York)

BUCHANAN, A. R.—*Air War: a Mission Completed* (Harper, New York)

BYWATER, Hector C.—*Seapower in the Pacific* (Constable, London)

CAIDIN, Martin, with Masatake Okumiya and Jiro Horikoshi—*Zero: The Story of the Japanese Navy Airforce* (Dutton, New York/Cassell, London)

CANT, Gilbert—*American Navy in World War II* (Hutchinson, London)

CLOSTERMAN, Pierre—*Flames in the Sky* (Chatto & Windus, London)

COPE, Harley and KARIG, Walter—*Battle Submerged: Submarine Fighters of World War II* (Norton, New York)

CRAIGIE, Sir Robert—*Behind the Japanese Mask* (Hutchinson, London)

EDMONDS, Walter D.—*They Fought With What They Had* (Little, Brown, Boston)

FEIS, Herbert—*Road to Pearl Harbor* (Princeton University Press/ Oxford University Press)

FUCHIDA, Mitsuo and OKUMIYA, Masatake—*Midway: The Battle that Doomed Japan* (U.S. Naval Institute/Hutchinson, London)

HALSEY, William F. and BRYAN, J. III—*Admiral Halsey's story* (McGraw-Hill, New York)

HASHIMOTO, Mochitsura—*Sunk* (Holt, New York/Cassell, London)

ITO, Masanori and PINEAU, Roger—*End of the Imperial Japanese Navy* (Norton, New York/Weidenfeld, London)

JOHNSTON, Stanley—*Queen of the Flat Tops—The Story of the U.S.S. Lexington and the Coral Sea Battle* (Dutton, New York/Jarrolds, London)

KARIG, Walter and KELLY, W.—*Battle Report* (Holt, New York)

KASE, Toshikazu—*Journey to the Missouri*; English title—*Eclipse of the Rising Sun* (Yale University Press/Cape, London)

KATO, Masuo—*The Lost War* (Knopf, New York)

KING, Ernest J.—*The United States Navy at War 1941–1945; Official Reports to the Secretary of the Navy* (U.S. Government Printing Office, Washington)

KING, Ernest J. and WHITEHILL, W. M.—*Fleet Admiral King* (Norton, New York/Eyre & Spottiswoode, London)

LORD, Walter—*Day of Infamy* (Holt, New York/Longmans, London)

MILLER, John Jr—*Cartwheel U.S. Army in World War II: Reduction of Rabaul* (Historical Division Department of the Army, Washington) —*Guadalcanal: The First Offensive* (Historical Division Department of the Army, Washington)

MORISON, Samuel Eliot—*The History of United States Naval Operations in World War II* (Little Brown, Boston/Oxford University Press)
 III *The Rising Sun in the Pacific 1931–April '42*
 IV *Coral Sea, Midway and Submarine Actions May–Aug. '42*
 V *The Struggle for Guadalcanal Aug. '42 – Feb. '43*
 VII *Aleutians, Gilberts and Marshalls, June '42 – April '44*

 —*The Two-Ocean War* (Little, Brown, Boston/Oxford University Press)

POTTER, E. B. and NIMITZ, Chester W.—*The Great Sea War* (Prentice-Hall, New Jersey/Harrap, London)

ROSCOÉ, Theodore—*United States Destroyer Operations in World War II* (U.S. Naval Institute)

 —*United States Submarine Operations in World War II* (U.S. Naval Institute)

ROSKILL, S. W.—*The War at Sea 1939–45* (H.M.S.O., London)

SETH, Ronald—*Secret Servants: A History of Japanese Espionage* (Farrar, Strauss, New York/Gollancz, London)

SHERROD, Robert—*History of Marine Corps Aviation in World War II* (Combat Forces Press, Washington)

SHIGEMITSU, Mamoru—*Japan and Her Destiny* (Dutton, New York/Hutchinson, London

SORIMACHI, Eiichi—*Ningen Yamamoto Isoroku* (Kawada, Tokyo)

TOGO, Shigenori—*The Cause of Japan* (Simon and Schuster, New York)

TOLAND, John—*But Not in Shame. The Six Months After Pearl Harbor* (Random House, New York)

TREGASKIS, Richard—*Guadalcanal Diary* (Random House, New York)

WOHLSTETTER, Roberta—*Pearl Harbor: Warning and Decision* (Stanford University Press)

YOUNG, Desmond—*Rutland of Jutland* (Cassell, London)

ZACHARIAS, Ellis M.—*Secret Missions* (Putnam's, New York)

I also consulted many contemporary accounts, ranging from the Magazine *Yank*, with its first-class Pacific War reporting to the *Infantry Journal, Time, Newsweek, Reader's Digest* and the *New York Times*.

Valuable main sources were:

—*Brassey's Naval and Shipping Annual*
—*The United States Naval Institute Proceedings*
—*The Naval Analysis Division of Survey in Washington*

for accounts of interrogation of Japanese prisoners and action reports which include that of Vice-Admiral Chuichi Nagumo on the attack on Pearl Harbor and the defeat at Midway.

—The findings of the Commission set up by the U.S. Congress to investigate and report the facts relating to Pearl Harbor. In particular Senate Document No. 159 (77th Congress, 2nd Session) and Senate Document No. 244 (79th Congress, 2nd Session).

Index

Index

CHINA

Tankan Bay

ALEUTIAN

E ISLANDS

JAPAN

Sea of
Japan

North

Niigata
Kobe Tokyo Nagaoka
Kasumigaura
Yokohama

Tsushima Strait

Inland Sea

Hiroshima

MIDWAY
ISLANDS

OKINAWA

WAKE
ISLAND

MARIANA
ISLANDS

Philippine
Sea

GUAM

CAROLINE

MARSHALL
ISLANDS

YAP

PALAU

TRUK IS.

I S L A N D S

GILBERT
ISLANDS

Biak

NEW
GUINEA

NEW
BRITAIN

BOUGAINVILLE

Amboina

Lae

Kahili

SOLOMON
ISLANDS

ELLICE
ISLANDS

Port
Moresby

Tulagi

SANTA CRUZ

GUADALCANAL

AUSTRALIA

Coral
Sea

NEW HEBRIDES

FIJI ISLANDS